Essential Writing Skills

Linda Wong

Lane Community College

HOUGHTON MIFFLIN COMPANY   Boston   New York

Senior Sponsoring Editor: Mary Jo Southern
Senior Associate Editor: Ellen Darion
Project Editor: Christina Lillios
Production/Design Coordinator: Sarah Ambrose
Senior Manufacturing Coordinator: Priscilla Abreu
Senior Marketing Manager: Nancy Lyman
Editorial Assistants: Lauren Gagliardi, Kate O'Sullivan

Printed in the U.S.A.
Library of Congress Catalog Card Number: 98-72095

ISBN: 0-395-89965-6

123456789-B-02 01 00 99 98

Contents

To the Instructor

Essential Writing Skills is a workbook text designed to integrate the language skills of spelling, basic grammar, and sentence writing. *Essential Writing Skills* serves as a vehicle for accelerating the learning of these key components of written communication. This textbook provides students with the fundamental understanding of the phonetic and structural components of words in the English language. The words studied through spelling are then used to gain a more thorough understanding of how words work in sentences, and how words function as different parts of speech. With the fundamental knowledge of words and their functions, students learn to construct simple, compound, and complex sentences as well as correct the common writing errors of fragments, comma splices, and run-on sentences.

Throughout this workbook text, both the spelling and the grammar skills are highly sequential and intricately woven together. For example, in the chapters that focus on short-vowel spelling skills, long vowels and other vowel patterns are excluded. In chapters that focus on simple sentence patterns, examples using compound or complex sentence patterns are excluded. In addition, new skills are introduced first with ample explanation, then worked with through recognition-level exercises, and finally demonstrated through application. The developmental, highly sequential nature of this text promotes an organized, structured, step-by-step approach to learning and integrating the spelling, grammar, and writing skills.

Essential Writing Skills is designed to accommodate learners at several academic levels. For students or classes focusing on basic spelling skills, the basic word lists in each chapter can be used for the mastery level of instruction. The advanced word lists, which include word expansion through the addition of prefixes and suffixes, may be used on an instructional level designed to heighten awareness and understanding of the complexities of the English language. For students or classes focusing on advanced spelling skills, the basic word lists lay the foundation skills necessary to comprehend the advanced spelling skills. Mastery level may be set on the advanced word lists. The grammar and sentence writing skills are suited for students of all academic levels. For students needing more instructional assistance, the class lessons and the written exercises may be done as in-class assignments with students working alone, with a partner, or in small groups. Throughout the course, students should be encouraged to learn to use and refer to electronic spell checkers with dictionaries and thesauruses, for this technology boosts students' understanding of words, their parts of speech, and their meanings. Each chapter ends with optional writing assignments that include a journal writing exercise or a paragraph writing exercise. Inclusion of both types of writing assignments offers students the opportunity to apply their writing skills to longer writing assignments, and the writing assignments allow instructors to adjust the course requirements and expectations to the varied academic levels found at the post-secondary level.

The instructional goal of this workbook text is to promote more effective written communication skills through the acquisition of spelling, grammar, and sentence writing skills. The ultimate goal of this workbook text, however, is to alter students' attitudes toward the English language and the process of writing. Through the exploration of word elements, word structure, spelling rules and word functions, the goal is for students to become more curious, intrigued, and fascinated by the complexity and intricacies of the English language. Rather than causing frustration with the writing process, the goal is to have students feel challenged, excited, eager to "break the code" or "find the necessary keys" to become more confident and more powerful writers.

Chapter Features

Instructional Boxes

Spelling and grammar definitions and rules are placed inside easy-to-locate sections throughout the chapters. These instructional sections are the starting points for the introduction of new skills to be presented by the instructor in class. They are excellent points in the chapter for students to review at the completion of each chapter or before a test or final exam.

Basic Word Lists

Each chapter has a basic list of fifty spelling words that are linked directly to the phonetic spelling skills introduced in the chapter. The words in the basic word lists are phonetically regular and reinforce the vowel or the consonant patterns of the chapter. Each basic word list includes space for students to practice writing the words and to apply other spelling rules or skills to the new words.

Instructional Pages

Throughout each chapter, ample explanations, activities, and exercises are included to work with the new skills in the classroom. Open discussions, comments, and questions are encouraged throughout these exercises as students explore the elements of the English language. Though some directions specifically recommend that the work be done with a partner or in a small group, most of the activities lend themselves to cooperative learning.

Numbered Exercises

Each chapter has nine numbered exercises that may be used for in-class assignments or as independent homework assignments. With the exception of the exercises that involve original sentence writing, the student text has the answer keys in the appendix. Students should be encouraged to complete the exercise without accessing the answer key, and to use the answer key to correct their work and analyze any problem areas. The exercises that involve original sentence writing should be evaluated by the instructor.

Building Words

Structural spelling (the addition of prefixes, suffixes, and Greek or Latin roots) is included in each chapter under the heading Building Words. Instruction and exercises are included to demonstrate how larger words are built by adding word parts together and applying specific sets of rules. Cumulative review is incorporated by using previous prefixes, suffixes, and roots in expanded word lists for each chapter.

Chapter Study Sheets

The ninth exercise in each chapter encourages students to create study sheets that include all the key terms, definitions, and rules presented in the chapter. These study sheets provide students with a study tool to strengthen "memory." Once the study sheets are completed, students are asked to cover the right-hand column with the explanations and the definitions, and then to recite the definitions or rules out loud without looking. Feedback from reciting instantly shows whether or not a student understands and can verbalize the foundation skills of the chapter. The study sheets can be used to review course material on an ongoing basis and to prepare for tests or exams. The study sheets can also be used in class for drill work with partners or as a class when the study sheets are presented on the overhead projector.

Chapter Review

Each chapter review includes a variety of exercises to evaluate understanding of the chapter content. The review exercises may be done together as a class, in small groups, with a partner, or independently. Students do not have the answer keys to the chapter review questions, so the chapter reviews may be graded if so desired.

Journal Writing Assignment (optional)

Journal writing, also called "free writing," allows students the opportunity to express themselves without getting slowed down by spelling, grammar, or paragraph structure concerns. The goal is to let the ideas flow and get the ideas on paper. Journal writing can be seen as the first step to a rough draft, but in this textbook, the journal writing goes no further. Instructors may want to observe the level of writing in the journals, but comments should be limited to the content that is expressed. (The last writing assignment in Chapter 10 does ask the student to return to one journal assignment to edit and refine it.)

Paragraph Writing Assignment (optional)

Each chapter ends with a paragraph writing assignment that provides students with the opportunity to apply their sentence writing skills to a paragraph. Each paragraph writing assignment provides students with directions or guidelines for developing the style of paragraph assigned. The types of paragraphs include definition (Chapter 1), narrative (Chapter 2), opinion (Chapter 3), explanatory (Chapter 4), expository (Chapter 5), descriptive (Chapter 6), opinion (Chapter 7), explanatory (Chapter 8), process (Chapter 9), and a variety of paragraph styles for Chapter 10.

Instructor's Resource Manual

The Instructor's Resource Manual includes teaching tips, suggestions for expanding classroom activities, answer keys for all instructional activities that are not numbered exercises, and chapter quizzes that can be varied each term and adjusted to the level of students in class. More comprehensive tests are included to be used for Chapters 1–3 (short vowels), Chapters 4–6 (long vowels and other vowel combinations), and Chapters 7–9 (r-controls, vowel diphthongs, and silent consonants). Several formats for a final exam are included that allow instructors to "cut and paste" the skills and skill levels desired for the final exam.

To the Student

Essential Writing Skills is designed to integrate the skills of spelling, basic grammar, and sentence writing in a step-by-step, highly sequential approach that will lead to greater confidence and success with writing skills. Each chapter begins with basic skills that are included to ensure that you have the essential foundation skills upon which you can build and expand your knowledge and understanding of words in the English language. Because there are several skill levels in each chapter, your instructor will guide you and provide you with directions for the activities and exercises that will be required in your course.

Upon completion of this course, you will have strengthened your phonetic, structural, and sight word-spelling skills. You will have a better understanding of the functions of words and how they work in simple, compound, and complex sentences. In addition to the writing skills you will acquire, you will learn to understand and, hopefully, appreciate and enjoy the intricacies and complexity of the English language.

To gain the greatest benefits from this book, you will want to learn to use and take advantage of the special features that have been incorporated in this textbook to assist your learning process.

Spelling Definitions to Know

As with all courses, there are specific terms that must be understood and learned. The beginning of each chapter presents these terms. Whenever you need to clarify a term or be reminded of its meaning or purpose, return to these instructional sections, which always highlight the most important points. These instructional sections should also be used to review for any chapter quizzes or tests.

Instructional Explanations

Throughout the textbook chapters you will find sections that explain new skills and provide you with the opportunity to practice the skills. In most cases, these instructional explanations will be presented and discussed in class. Sometimes you may do the work as a class, and other times you may be asked to do the work alone, with a partner, or in a group.

Spelling Rules to Know

The spelling rules for each chapter must be understood and memorized, for they are the foundation of building larger words. The spelling rules are also highlighted inside instructional boxes. Study the rules and the examples carefully. Spend time learning to say and to write the rules.

Basic Word List—Beginning with the Basics

Each chapter begins with fifty words that have been carefully selected to practice the phonetic spelling skills introduced in the chapter. Space is provided in your book to practice writing each word. Rather then copying the words rapidly, say the words slowly and "stretch the sounds" as you write the words. The goal is to develop a sense of sound-symbol patterns and relationships. In addition, each basic word list includes an additional activity related to the skills of the chapter. All the word list activities should be completed carefully.

Numbered Exercises

Each chapter has nine different numbered exercises that provide you with the opportunity to work with and apply the skills of the chapter. You are encouraged to use an electronic, hand-held spelling checker with a built-in dictionary and thesaurus to look up information and to check the accuracy of your work. Some of the numbered exercises may be done in class; others may be assigned as graded homework. Follow the directions provided by your instructor. Answer keys for many of the numbered exercises can be found in the Appendix. Always complete the exercise first before you check the answer key. The answer key has been included so you can "self-correct" and get immediate feedback as to whether or not you are understanding the skills in the chapter.

Building Words

Each chapter has a section called Building Words that develops your structural spelling skills. Structural spelling involves adding prefixes and suffixes to words and to Greek or Latin roots. In addition, you will learn how to apply specific spelling rules between the words or the roots and the suffixes so that you can spell thousands of words accurately. You will note how rapidly you can expand your spelling skills by learning to use structural spelling techniques.

Grammar Definitions to Know

The second part of each chapter is dedicated to developing your understanding of parts of speech, how words function in sentences, and how words are combined to form simple, compound, and complex sentences. You will want to learn the terminology listed inside the grammar instructional sections, for these terms are the foundation of writing. Read the definitions, explanations, and examples carefully. Study the definitions of these terms until you are able to say and write the definition for each term given.

Chapter Study Sheets

As with most courses, the number of terms (vocabulary words) that must be learned increases drastically as the semester progresses. The chapter study sheets are designed to be used as an ongoing study tool that can be used at the end of the chapter and as a review tool to use throughout the term to "keep your memory fresh." Most study sheets can be completed quite easily by referring to the instructional sections in the chapter. When you complete the study sheets, include the definition of the term, and examples for terms that are foreign to you or difficult for you to learn. Practice with the study sheet by covering up the definitions in the right-hand column; without looking, recite or write the definitions for each term. Pull down the paper that is used to cover up the definitions; check the accuracy of your answers. Continue to drill this way until you can recite or write all the definitions from memory. With practice, you will soon be able to use these terms when you communicate to others.

Chapter Reviews

Each chapter has several pages of review exercises. Your instructor may have you do the review work in class, in small groups, or with partners, or as homework assignments.

Journal Writing and Paragraph Writing

Each chapter closes with two different writing assignments. Follow the directions given by your instructor.

Word Lists

A complete set of chapter word lists is in the Appendix. Anytime you are working on an exercise that requires you to use words from that chapter's word list, it is much quicker to find answers by referring to the word list in the Appendix. This word list can also be used for partner drill. Ask your partner to dictate the chapter words for you to practice spelling out loud or writing. Be sure to study the word list prior to any chapter quiz or test.

Summary Charts

The next-to-the-last section in the Appendix includes several grammar charts for quick reference. Become familiar with these charts and their location. The information is at your fingertips!

Quiz Forms

The last section in the Appendix consists of Quiz Form A and Quiz Form B, which you may be asked to use for chapter quizzes. Do not write on these forms prior to the quiz in class. Your instructor will provide you with more directions if these forms are to be used.

Acknowledgments

Appreciation is extended to the following reviewers who contributed valuable ideas to strengthen the effectiveness of this textbook for college students.

Phyllis Boatman, Southern Arkansas University Tech (AR)

Ellen Burke, Casper College (WY)

Judy Covington, Trident Technical College (SC)

Lulie Felder, Central Carolina Tech (SC)

Jane Gamber, Hutchinson Community College (KS)

Mary Mears, Macon College (GA)

Vivian Naylor, Meridian Community College (MS)

Martha Rogers, Aiken Technical College (SC)

Kathryn Skulley, Denver Technical College (CO)

Linda Tappmeyer, Southwest Baptist University (MO)

L. W.

ONE

Consonants, Consonant Blends, Consonant Digraphs, and Short Vowels

The topics in this chapter include the following:

- Consonants, consonant blends, and consonant digraphs
- An introduction to base words, prefixes, and suffixes
- The five short vowel sounds
- The *Qu* Rule, the *F, L, S, Z* Rule, the *CK* Rule, and the *TCH* Rule
- Three prefixes and seven suffixes used to build words
- Practice in identifying subjects and verbs in simple sentences
- Practice in identifying nouns and pronouns

Spelling Definitions

Consonants:	Consonants are all the letters of the alphabet that are not vowels.
Vowels:	The most common vowels are the letters *a, e, i, o,* and *u*. However, the letter *y* can be a vowel, and the letter *w* can be a vowel when it appears with another vowel.

> ***Examples:*** sky   saw

Therefore, vowels are the letters *a, e, i, o, u,* sometimes *y*, and sometimes *w*.

Consonant Blends:	Consonant blends are two or three consonants whose sounds blend or slide together quickly. You hear each of the letter sounds.

> ***Examples:*** **st**and   **cr**ust

Consonant Digraphs:	Consonant digraphs are two or three consonants together that make a *new* sound.

> ***Examples:*** **sh**ip   **wh**en   ma**tch**   **ch**est   **th**ink   gra**ph**

Base Words:	Base words are original English words without any prefixes or suffixes.

> ***Examples:*** swift   stop   itch   check

Prefixes:	Prefixes are units of meaning that are placed before the base word.

> ***Examples:*** *re* (means "again") as in *rerun*
> *un* (means "not") as in *unzip*

Suffixes:	Suffixes are units of meaning added to the end of base words. Suffixes often change the base word to a different part of speech.

> ***Examples:*** *ing, ed, er, est, y, ful, ly*

Consonant Sounds

Consonants in English are usually not the problem letters for spelling. Most consonants have *one* basic sound, so when you hear a specific sound, you can write the letter that makes that sound. One easy way to review the sound of a consonant is to think of a word that begins with that consonant. At the beginning of the word, you will hear the consonant sound. For the letter *x*, it is best to think of a word that *ends* in *x* so you can hear the *x* sound *(ax, six, fox)*.

Consonants That Have One Sound

Say the sound of each consonant.

b (bat)	d (dog)	f (fan)	h (hat)	j (jet)	k (kit)
l (leg)	m (man)	n (net)	p (pet)	q (quit)	r (run)
t (ten)	v (van)	w (wet)	x (ax)	y (yes)	z (zip)

Consonants That Have Two Sounds

Three consonants have *two* sounds: *c, g,* and *s*. The *c* can have what is called the **hard *c* sound** or the **soft *c* sound**. The *g* can have the **hard *g* sound** or the **soft *g* sound**. The hard *c* and the hard *g* sounds are used most frequently; the soft *c* and *g* sounds are made only when these letters are followed by the vowels *e, i,* or *y*. Notice these vowels in the words below. The most common sound of *s* is the *ss* sound; there are no rules to tell you when it makes the *z* sound.

c (cat)	*c* sounds like *k*	This is called the **hard c.**
c (cent)	*c* sounds like *ss*	This is the **soft c** because *c* is followed by *e*.
c (city)	*c* sounds like *ss*	This is the **soft c** because *c* is followed by *i*.
c (cyst)	*c* sounds like *ss*	This is the **soft c** because *c* is followed by *y*.
g (gun)	Say the sound.	This is called the **hard g.**
g (gem)	*g* sounds like *j*	This is the **soft g** because *g* is followed by *e*.
g (gin)	*g* sounds like *j*	This is the **soft g** because *g* is followed by *i*.
g (gym)	*g* sounds like *j*	This is the **soft g** because *g* is followed by *y*.
s (sun)	Say the sound.	This is the most common *s* sound.
s (lo**s**e)	*s* sounds like *z*	

Consonant Blends

Consonant blends are two or three consonants together whose sounds slide together quickly. You can still hear each of the consonant sounds, but you may need to listen very carefully. Consonant blends can cause some spelling problems because you might leave out one of the consonants when writing the word. As you will see in this chapter's word list, words can begin and end with consonant blends.

Practice saying the sounds of these common consonant blends:

bl	br	cl	cr	dr	fl
fr	gl	gr	pl	pr	sc
scr	sk	sl	sm	sn	sp
spl	spr	squ	st	ft	ld
lf	lk	lp	ct	nd	nt
lt	pt	st			

Consonant Digraphs

Consonant digraphs are two or three consonants that form a *new* sound. The following consonant digraphs can be found at the beginning or at the end of base words: *sh, ch, th,* and *ph.* The consonant digraph *wh* is found only at the beginning of base words. The consonant digraph *tch,* which is used only following a short vowel, is found only on the end of base words.

Say the sounds of these consonant digraphs:

sh   ch   tch   th   wh   ph

Short Vowel Sounds

Even though we have five basic vowels and two letters that can sometimes be vowels, fifty-six different vowel combinations exist in English. *The vowels and the many different combinations they make are the letters that make English spelling difficult.*

The most basic vowels are the **short vowels.** Short vowels can appear in one-syllable words and in multi-syllable words. Here are a few interesting points about short vowels:

1. Words can begin with short vowels.
2. Short vowels are frequently found in the middle of short words and are the only vowel in the word. The vowel is surrounded or protected on each side by consonants.
3. Short vowels are not found at the end of words.
4. A short curved line above the pronunciation of the vowel indicates that the sound is a short vowel sound.

Short Vowels

Listen carefully to the first sound you hear when you say the following words slowly. The first sound is the short vowel sound.

ă	apple	ant	and	am	add
ě	Ed	end	ebb	ever	enter
ĭ	in	it	if	is	igloo
ŏ	on	octopus	off	odd	October
ŭ	up	ugly	uncle	under	umbrella

Sometimes these short vowel sounds can be remembered more easily when you attach them to a picture of an object that begins with the sound. The picture works as a memory clue of the short vowel sound. If a picture memory clue will help you remember the sounds, sketch an object that begins with each of the short vowels.

ă	ě	ĭ	ŏ	ŭ

Short Vowel Practice—Letter Sounds

Practice saying the following short vowel sounds:

ă ě ĭ ŏ ŭ

ŏ ĭ ě ŭ ă

ŭ ŏ ă ĭ ě

Short Vowel Practice in Words

Listen carefully as your teacher pronounces the short vowel sounds. Write the vowel letter that you hear.

1.   4.   7.   10.

2.   5.   8.   11.

3.   6.   9.   12.

Spelling Rules

The *QU* Rule:

The letter *q* must always be followed by a *u.*

quit   **qu**ilt   **qu**ick   **qu**ack

The *F, L, S, Z* Rule:

Use *ff, ll, ss,* or *zz* right after a short vowel.

mi**ll**   we**ll**   sti**ff**   pu**ff**   pa**ss**   mi**ss**   bu**zz**   ja**zz**

Exceptions: Two-letter words: *if, as, is, us*
Three-letter words: *gas, bus*

The *CK* Rule:

Use *ck* (not just a *c* or just a *k*) right after a short vowel.

sti**ck**   ro**ck**   thi**ck**   flo**ck**

The *TCH* Rule:

Use *tch* (not just *ch*) right after a short vowel.

pa**tch**   i**tch**   ske**tch**   swi**tch**

Exceptions: rich   which

Words—Beginning with the Basics

1. Say each of the following base words slowly. "Stretch the word" so you can hear all the sounds. Pay close attention to the consonant blends, the consonant digraphs, and the short vowel sounds.

2. Write each base word by "stretching" the sounds as you say the word. Then analyze the word by writing the consonant blends or consonant digraphs in the correct column. Finally, name the rule, if any, that is used in the spelling of the word. The first one is done for you.

✎ **PRACTICE**

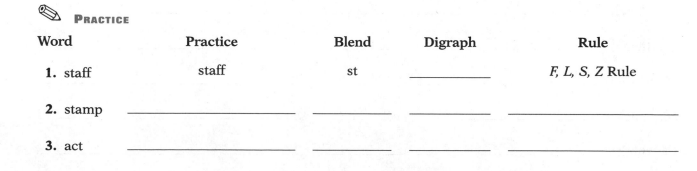

Word	Practice	Blend	Digraph	Rule
1. staff	staff	st	_____	*F, L, S, Z* Rule
2. stamp	_____	_____	_____	_____
3. act	_____	_____	_____	_____

Word	Practice	Blend	Digraph	Rule
4. brass	_____	_____	_____	_____
5. fact	_____	_____	_____	_____
6. ranch	_____	_____	_____	_____
7. patch	_____	_____	_____	_____
8. than	_____	_____	_____	_____
9. clamp	_____	_____	_____	_____
10. craft	_____	_____	_____	_____
11. match	_____	_____	_____	_____
12. graph	_____	_____	_____	_____
13. catch	_____	_____	_____	_____
14. check	_____	_____	_____	_____
15. quest	_____	_____	_____	_____
16. text	_____	_____	_____	_____
17. stress	_____	_____	_____	_____
18. when	_____	_____	_____	_____
19. slept	_____	_____	_____	_____
20. fresh	_____	_____	_____	_____
21. cent	_____	_____	_____	_____
22. stretch	_____	_____	_____	_____
23. sketch	_____	_____	_____	_____
24. then	_____	_____	_____	_____
25. flesh	_____	_____	_____	_____
26. quick	_____	_____	_____	_____
27. think	_____	_____	_____	_____

Word	Practice	Blend	Digraph	Rule
28. switch	_____	_____	_____	_____
29. fill	_____	_____	_____	_____
30. script	_____	_____	_____	_____
31. which	_____	_____	_____	_____
32. thick	_____	_____	_____	_____
33. inch	_____	_____	_____	_____
34. swift	_____	_____	_____	_____
35. strict	_____	_____	_____	_____
36. brisk	_____	_____	_____	_____
37. itch	_____	_____	_____	_____
38. rich	_____	_____	_____	_____
39. cross	_____	_____	_____	_____
40. strong	_____	_____	_____	_____
41. boss	_____	_____	_____	_____
42. lock	_____	_____	_____	_____
43. cloth	_____	_____	_____	_____
44. rust	_____	_____	_____	_____
45. duct	_____	_____	_____	_____
46. brunch	_____	_____	_____	_____
47. buzz	_____	_____	_____	_____
48. trunk	_____	_____	_____	_____
49. dusk	_____	_____	_____	_____
50. fund	_____	_____	_____	_____

✎ **EXERCISE 1.1 Working with Short Vowels, Blends, and Digraphs**

1. Add a **short vowel** to each word below to make a real word. You may be able to use more than one short vowel for some words. Use a dictionary or a spell checker to verify that you are creating a real word.

st_____mp st_____ff cl_____mp b_____ss

p_____tch qu_____ck l_____ck fl_____sh

str_____ng th_____n f_____nd th_____k

2. Use the **CK Rule** to decide when to use k or ck. Use the **TCH Rule** to decide when to use ch to tch. Complete each word below by adding k, ck, ch, or tch. In some cases, more than one word may be possible.

thi_____ sil_____ pa_____ stre_____

brun_____ in_____ i_____ ri_____

ske_____ lo_____ thin_____ ma_____

che_____ trun_____ ca_____ ran_____

3. **Then** and **than** are two words that are frequently confused. Use the definitions below to help you complete the following sentences by adding then or than.
   Then refers to a time sequence. Then basically means "next" or "at that time."
   Than refers to comparisons of two items.

   a. We visited the ranch and _____ got back on the bus.

   b. Write the answers and _____ check your work.

   c. Bill is quicker to plot information on a graph _____ Raymond.

   d. The mutual fund was more profitable _____ the municipal bonds.

   e. The oil baron is richer _____ most people in the world.

   f. The artist sketched the building and _____ began to develop the blueprints.

   g. They knew _____ that the fog was too thick to land.

✎ **EXERCISE 1.2 Sentence Work**

Choose words from this chapter's word list (see pages 5–7) to complete the following sentences.
   Use words with short **a**.

   1. The _____ of the matter is that voters' opinions are more important _____ your personal point of view.

2. The child on the merry-go-round tried to _____ the _____ ring.

3. The county fair _____ made plans for a _____ show.

4. You will need the president's _____ of approval before you include the bar _____ in the final report.

Use words with short e.

1. I advise you to _____ the complete cost before you sign up for the vision _____.

2. Most of the _____ focuses on _____ reduction techniques.

3. They placed the _____ animal _____ in the trap.

4. You will want to _____ the hide and _____ let it dry in the sun.

Use words with short i.

1. I _____ you may want to _____ to another medication.

2. The _____ must be written following _____ writer's guidelines.

3. The river was _____ on that _____ autumn night.

4. The night manager was not sure _____ orders he needed to _____.

Use words with short o.

1. Marcus was not a _____ enough swimmer to _____ the river.

2. My _____ wanted a new _____ for the front door.

3. The _____, rancid odor came from the _____ left in the bucket.

4. The priest placed the _____ on a purple _____.

Use words with short u.

1. The electrician removed the _____ and the debris from the air _____.

2. The bees started to _____ around the patio when we sat down for _____.

3. Information about the trust _____ was found in my uncle's old _____.

4. They volunteered from dawn to _____ to raise money for the special _____.

Write five of your own sentences using words from this chapter. Each sentence must include two *words from the word list on pages 5–7. In your sentences, cir-cle the words that come from the word list.*

1. _____

2. _____

3. _____

4. _____

5. _____

Building Words

The **base words** you have practiced in this chapter are the building blocks or the foundation of larger words. Many words in English are made by adding **prefixes** and **suffixes** to **base words**. For that reason, spelling base words correctly is the first step to spelling longer words correctly. As a review, write the definitions of the following terms:

Base words: _____

Prefixes: _____

Suffixes: _____

New Prefixes: *re-   un-   mis-*

The prefix *re-* means **again** or **back.**
The prefix *un-* means **not** or **reverse.**
The prefix *mis-* means **incorrectly.**

New Suffixes: *-ing   -ed   -er   -est   -y   -ful   -ly*

The suffix *ing* often shows an act or a process.
The suffix *ed* often shows past tense.
The suffix *er* means **a person or a thing that does something,** or means **more.**
The suffix *est* means **the most.**
The suffix *y* describes the quality of something. It sounds like a long *e.* (*ee*)
The suffix *ful* often means **full of.** Remember that only one *l* is used in the suffix.
The suffix *ly* often means **like** or **in the manner or nature of.**

✎ PRACTICE

Word building is done by combining prefixes and suffixes with the base words. In this chapter, no additional spelling rules are needed to combine prefixes and suffixes to the word bases. In the words below, circle the prefixes and the suffixes.

unstretched	mismatched	checkered
strictest	restricted	freshly
refreshing	rusty	recently

✎ **EXERCISE 1.3 Building Words by Adding Prefixes and Suffixes**

The base word is shown in bold print. Add the prefixes and suffixes to the base words. Write the complete word with all the word parts. No spelling changes are needed to build these words. The words are made by simply combining word parts.

1. re +**quest** + ed = _____   re + **quest** + ing = _____

2. un + **stamp** + ed = _____   re + **stamp** + ed = _____

3. **ranch** + er = _____   **ranch** + ing = _____

4. mis + **match** + ed = _____   re + **match** + ing = _____

5. **check** + er + ed = _____   re + **check** + ing = _____

6. **stress** + ful + ly = _____   un + **stress** + ed = _____

7. re + **fresh** + ing = _____   **fresh** + est = _____

8. **quick** + est = _____   **quick** + ly = _____

9. **inch** + ed = _____   **inch** + ing = _____

10. **swift** + ly = _____   **swift** + est = _____

11. **strict** + ly = _____   un + re + **strict** + ed = _____

12. **cross** + ing = _____   un + **cross** + ed = _____

13. un + **lock** + ed = _____   **lock** + er = _____

14. **rust** + ed = _____   **rust** + y = _____

15. re + **fund** + ing = _____   **fund** + ed = _____

Partner Work

Dictate any ten words from the above exercise to your partner for him or her to spell out loud without the use of paper and pencil. If your partner makes a mistake, say the individual word parts and ask your partner to spell each word part separately. Then reverse roles so both partners have the opportunity to dictate and to spell out loud.

✎ **EXERCISE 1.4 Word List Expansion**

All the short-vowel words in the following box have at least one consonant blend and/or consonant digraph. These words are not found in this chapter's original word list. Read each word carefully. Then follow the directions below the box.

plant	strand	blend	drift	squint	risk	frost
help	dress	hunt	dust	spell	pack	stick
stack	brush	crash	shift	wish	stitch	thrash
pluck	duck	thank	trust	sprint	squish	clutch

Prefixes to use: re- un- mis-

Suffixes to use: -ing -ed -er -est -y -ful -ly

Write any six words from the box above. Use one or more prefixes or suffixes to build two additional words that use the word base. An example is done for you.

Word Base	Expanded Word	Expanded Word
frost	frosting	refrosted

✎ EXERCISE 1.5 Sentence Writing

Use the following sentence writing reminders each time you write sentences:
  1. Always begin each sentence with a capital letter.
  2. Always end each sentence with the appropriate ending punctuation
(a period, a question mark, or an exclamation point).
  Write six sentences using any of the words found in Exercise 1.3 on page 12.
Each sentence must include at least two words from page 12. In your sentences,
circle the words that come from this page. Write sentences that are statements
followed by periods. Do not write sentences that require the use of an exclama-
tion point or a question mark.

1. _____

2. _____

3. _____

4. _____

5. _____

6. _____

Use the same directions as above to write six sentences that use words from
page 7. You may use the base words with or without prefixes or suffixes. Re-
member to circle the words used from page 7.

1. _____

2. _____

3. _____

4. _____

5. _____

6. _____

Grammar Definitions

Subject:

The *subject* of a sentence tells *who* or *what* the sentence is about. These are the important points to remember about subjects:

1. Every sentence *must* have a subject.

2. The subject will be a **noun** or a **pronoun**.

3. These are the **pronouns** that can work as subjects:

   I, you, she, he, we, they, it, who

Verb:

The *verb* of a sentence shows the action done by the subject or shows "state of being" by linking the subject to the rest of the sentence. The following are some important points to remember about the verbs:

1. **Action verbs** show the action done by the subject, such as *dance, write, send,* or *swim.*

2. The words *am, is, are, was,* and *were* are examples of common "state of being" verbs that link the subject to the rest of the sentence.

3. Every sentence must have a verb to "go with" the subject.

4. The subjects and the verbs in a sentence work closely together as partners to form the basic structure of the sentence.

Clause:

A *clause* is a group of words that has a subject and a verb. If the *clause* forms a complete thought, it is called an **independent clause.**

Sentence:

A *sentence* is a group of words that has three things:

1. A sentence has a subject.

2. A sentence has a verb.

3. A sentence forms a complete thought.

Simple Sentence:

The *simple sentence* is a sentence with *only one* subject–verb pattern. The following are some important points to remember about simple sentences:

1. A common simple sentence pattern looks like this: S–V. The subject comes first, and the verb follows.

2. Simple sentences do not need to be short sentences. The following sentences have one subject–verb pattern. Each is a simple sentence. In each sentence, the subject is *man* and the verb is *slept.*

   The **man slept.**

   The young **man** with the scruffy dog **slept** by the fire.

   The young **man** inside the waterproof sleeping bag **slept** by the roaring campfire with his scruffy, old dog.

3. Simple sentences are also called **independent clauses.** They can be "independent" and stand by themselves since they have their own subject, have their own verb, and form a complete thought.

Parts of Speech

The term *parts of speech* is used to show how words work or function in sentences. The different parts of speech will be explored throughout this textbook. Before we begin working with nouns, read through the following list to familiarize yourself with the eight parts of speech:

1. nouns
2. pronouns
3. verbs
4. prepositions
5. adjectives
6. adverbs
7. conjunctions
8. interjections

More Grammar Definitions

Noun:

A *noun* is a word that names a *person, place, thing,* or *idea.* The following points may help you understand nouns:

1. Many nouns name objects that you can see. These are called **concrete nouns.** Here are examples of concrete nouns that name a person, place, or thing:

sister	teacher	friend	investigator
school	mall	house	restaurant
car	pencil	ring	camera

2. Some nouns name *ideas,* or things you cannot see. These are called **abstract nouns.** Many students forget that words that tell about ideas, beliefs, values, emotions, and concepts can also be nouns. Here are examples of abstract nouns:

freedom	love	loyalty	friendship
fear	honor	attitude	personality

Pronoun:

A *pronoun* is a word that takes the place of a noun. There are many different kinds of pronouns. The pronouns that we will work with initially are the ones that can work as subjects of sentences:

I, you, he, she, we, they, it, who

Notice what nouns the following pronouns have replaced:

The accountant filed the taxes. **He** did not need to file an extension.

Sara's emotions were genuine. **They** brought tears to our eyes.

Arthur and I are friends. **We** enjoy playing golf together.

The words in Exercise 1.6 are from this chapter's word lists. Some of these words can work as nouns, but some cannot. You can identify the nouns in three different ways:

1. Ask yourself this question: "Does it name a person, place, thing, or idea?"

2. Use your electronic spell checker. Look up the word; you will see "noun" after the word if it can be used as a noun. Sometimes, words can be used as more than one part of speech, so be sure to "scroll" down through all the definitions before deciding if the word can work as a noun. If the word has a suffix, look up the **base word.** Scroll through the definitions. Many times the word with the suffix will follow the definitions, and the part of speech is identified at that point.

3. Try putting the word in one of these test sentences. If the word makes sense in one of these sentences, the word is a noun.

    The _____ is here.

    I have (a/an) _____.

Name _____   Date _____

✎ **EXERCISE 1.6 Identifying Nouns**

Circle all the words that can work as nouns. Remember that words can also work as other parts of speech, but the focus here is to find the words that can work as nouns.

staff	act	brass	fact
match	check	fresh	stretch
quick	think	switch	fill
thick	strict	itch	cloth
buzz	dusk	strand	blend
wish	thrash	clutch	trust
thank	brush	stack	squint

✎ **EXERCISE 1.7 Finding the Noun Subjects**

*Use one line to underline the **subjects** in the following sentences. Remember, the subject in each of these sentences will be a noun. Then use two lines to underline the **action verbs**. Remember, the verbs will be the words that show the action being done by the subject.*

The subject and the verb in each sentence work as partners. To see if you found the partners,

Ask what or who the sentence is about.
Ask what the subject did.
Ask what the action of the sentence is.
Ask who or what did the action.

1. The bossy man yelled at the clerk.

2. The smell of fresh bread filled the air.

3. The elephant's trunk hit the trainer in the back.

4. The glass shattered on the kitchen floor.

5. Sandy's new blender arrived by mail.

6. Excessive stress leads to health problems.

7. The wishing well attracts many visitors.

8. The boxer's fist left a mark on his opponent.

9. The funds provided her with tuition.

10. The cramp in his right leg lasted for an hour.

11. The buzzer sounded at the end of the game.

12. The men squinted in the bright sunlight.

13. The plot lost its appeal in Chapter Three.

14. The stuffing from the turkey stuck to the spoon.

15. The crisp crust crumbled on the fork.

EXERCISE 1.8 Sentence Writing

*Use the following nouns as the **subject** of the sentences. As nouns, these words will be used to tell what the sentence is about. Place the noun (the subject) before the verb. Underline the subject once.*

1. ranch

_____

2. trunk

_____

3. clamp

_____

4. dusk

_____

5. switch

_____

6. act

_____

7. match

_____

8. check

_____

✎ **EXERCISE 1.9 Chapter Study Sheet**

In the right-hand column, write a definition for the term on the left. Practice reciting and learning this definition. Cover up the definition on the right. Recite the definition. Remove the paper to check your answer. Practice until you can define each term accurately.

Consonants

Vowels

Short Vowels

Consonant Blends

Consonant Digraphs

Base Words

Prefixes

Suffixes

QU Rule

F, L, S, Z Rule

CK Rule

TCH Rule

Subject

Verb

Clause

Sentence

Simple Sentence

Independent Clause

Noun

Pronoun

✎ Chapter Review

Match the terms on the left to the definitions on the right.

_____ **1.** consonants

_____ **2.** vowels

_____ **3.** consonant digraphs

_____ **4.** prefixes

_____ **5.** *TCH* Rule

_____ **6.** subject of a sentence

_____ **7.** short vowels

_____ **8.** *F, L, S, Z* Rule

_____ **9.** noun

_____ **10.** pronouns

_____ **11.** consonant blend

_____ **12.** base word

_____ **13.** suffixes

_____ **14.** *QU* Rule

_____ **15.** *CK* Rule

_____ **16.** simple sentence

_____ **17.** verb

_____ **18.** clause

a. units of meaning attached to the front of a base word

b. *a, e, i, o, u*

c. use these letters, not *c* or *k*, right after a short vowel

d. a person, place, thing, or idea

e. use these letters, not *ch*, right after a short vowel

f. two or three consonants that together make a new sound

g. the doubled consonants that are used right after a short vowel

h. who or what the sentence is about

i. all the letters that are not vowels

j. two or more consonants whose sounds slide together quickly but are individually heard

k. a group of words with a subject and a verb

l. *a, e, i, o, u,* sometimes *y,* and sometimes *w*

m. *q* must always be followed with a *u*

n. an original word without any other prefixes or suffixes

o. endings that can be added to base words

p. an independent clause with one subject–verb pattern

q. words that show action or state of being

r. *she, he, they, we, I, you, it*

Read each column of words. Circle the one word spelled incorrectly. Spell it correctly on the line below the column.

quickly	restrikted	itchy	crossing
mispelled	refunded	sketching	rustey
filled	stranded	graff	crashed
thinker	quest	rancher	unstamped

_____ _____ _____ _____

quickest	texts	trunk	fact
checkered	stickey	spelling	wishfull
mismatched	locker	ritchest	buzzed
misstrusted	unlocked	thankful	scripts

_____	_____	_____	_____

Circle the consonant blends in these words.

crispy	acted	silky	briskly
hunted	trusting	script	slept

Circle the consonant digraphs in these words.

flesh	crashing	itching	graph
switch	check	stretch	thickest

*Write **then** or **than** on the blanks to complete each sentence.*

1. Angela knew _____ that the house needed to be cleaned.

2. The sauce was thicker _____ it was supposed to be.

3. The turtle inched its way across the road _____ wandered into the bushes.

4. The driver slowed down for the checkered flag _____ pulled into the pit.

Circle the prefixes and the suffixes. Write the base word on the line.

wishfully _____   shifted _____

misspelling _____   unrestricted _____

refunded _____   requesting _____

swiftly _____   trusty _____

defrosted _____   unpacked _____

Circle the words that can work as nouns.

trust	stack	thank	clutch	which
inch	swift	boss	brass	duct
risk	graph	fact	act	fresh

Underline the subject of the sentence once. Draw two lines under the action verb that is the partner to the subject.

1. The rancher picked from the new crop of mint.

2. The stranded duck hunter risked his life for his friend.

3. Jane's boss squinted in the bright sunlight.

4. The dogcatcher checked the neighborhood for stray dogs.

5. The quest taught him many valuable lessons about life.

6. José's bar graph emphasizes the most important facts of the project.

7. Dusk lasted for an hour.

8. I recently patched the rear tire on his car.

9. My uncle requested money from the trust fund.

10. Her crafts bring extra income to the family.

JOURNAL WRITING ASSIGNMENT

Journal writing is your opportunity to express your ideas freely on paper without worrying about grammar or spelling. With journal writing, you can "brainstorm," or just let your ideas flow freely. Say whatever you want to say without worrying if it is "good," "right," "creative," or "well-structured." The goal is to become more comfortable with the process of writing and expressing your ideas and feelings through your written words.

Topic: What Is Your Writing History?

What are your attitudes about writing? What kinds of writing do you enjoy? Do you like to write letters or poetry or musical verses? What were some of your enjoyable writing experiences? Did you have a favorite teacher who taught writing in a special way or who enjoyed reading your work? What kinds of writing would you like to learn to do better?

PARAGRAPH WRITING ASSIGNMENT

Writing a well-developed paragraph is different in some ways from journal writing. In journal writing, your goal is to write without worrying about spelling, grammar, or structure. Journal writing shows your flow of thought patterns. Some of these same elements also appear in paragraph writing when you begin your first draft.

However, in paragraph writing, you will spend time revising, strengthening, and improving the paragraph after the first draft is written. You will need to proofread to correct any spelling or grammar errors. You may need several revisions before you have a finished paragraph that pleases you.

Topic: A Feeling or an Abstract Concept

Abstract nouns are discussed in this chapter. Many abstract nouns deal with values and feelings. Values and feelings are listed below. You may use one of these or select an original abstract noun to be the topic of your paragraph.

   Values: honesty, creativity, responsibility, wisdom, ambition
   Feelings: love, jealousy, pride, stress, enthusiasm

Follow these steps:

1. Write an opening sentence that shows your feelings or opinion about the topic you selected. For example, if you chose to write about wisdom, this could be a topic sentence: "Wisdom is a gift of knowledge that is acquired through years of experiencing life." If your topic was jealousy, a possible opening sentence could be this: "Jealousy is one emotion that can destroy a relationship."

2. Next, develop your idea by defining what you mean. Add at least four more sentences to provide details, definitions, or examples to explain your opening sentence. Use your spell checker to check the spelling of all the words. Make sure that each sentence has a subject and a verb. Rearrange or revise to refine your paragraph. Your finished paragraph needs to be neatly written or processed on a computer.

TWO

Short Vowels in Multi-Syllable Words

The topics in this chapter include the following:

- Syllables, primary accents, and the schwa
- Roots that can be used to build words
- The C/C Syllable Rule, the /*CLE* Syllable Rule, and the *ES* Rule
- Eight new prefixes, three new suffixes, and six new roots to build words
- Definitions of verbs and simple verb tenses
- Practice in identifying action verbs and linking verbs

Spelling Definitions

Syllable:	A syllable is a unit of spoken language that must have at least one vowel or vowel combination.
Multi-Syllable Word:	A multi-syllable word is a word with two or more syllables. When you say the word slowly, you can tap the rhythm of the word. Each tap or beat in the rhythm is a syllable.

Tap the rhythm of these words to hear the number of syllables:
recreation (4)
syllable (3)
education (4)
probability (5)

Primary Accent:	A primary accent is a written mark that shows which syllable in a multi-syllable word carries more stress or emphasis when the word is spoken. An accent mark is placed at the end of the stressed syllable.

Notice the primary accent in each of these words:

cam'-pus   sim'-ple   con-sent'

Accented Syllable:	An accented syllable is the syllable with the primary accent. This syllable is pronounced with more stress or emphasis.
Schwa:	The schwa is a symbol (ə) used to show that the vowel sound in an unaccented syllable does not make its predicted sound. Instead, a schwa often represents a short *u* (ŭ) sound. If a word has a schwa, the schwa (or slipped vowel sound) will always be in an unaccented syllable.

Notice the schwa in the unaccented syllables. Say each word to hear the schwa sound:

problem (prob'-ləm)   infant (in'-fənt)   object (əb-ject')

Root:	Roots are non-word bases that have meaning but do not become English words until a prefix or a suffix is added. Many roots we use in English come from Greek or Latin. Roots work the same way that word bases work; they are the foundation used to build larger words.

Example of a non-word base: -*ject*
Words built from -*ject: project, reject, object, inject, subject*

Spelling Rules

The C/C Syllable Rule:	In a multi-syllable word, divide the word between the two consonants. Here are a few important points:

1. Divide between the two consonants in the middle of a word. Notice how a vowel often comes before and after the C/C. Examples: trum/pet, traf/fic

2. When you use the C/C Rule, the vowels will usually have a short sound. Examples: pic/nic, ad/dress

3. One exception to the rule is that you *do not separate consonant digraphs.* Example: *kitch-en*

4. When you spell multi-syllable words, spell one syllable at a time to increase spelling accuracy.

The /*CLE* Syllable Rule:

The -*le* syllable usually has one other consonant with it. Here are a few important points to remember:

1. The *le* is seldom in a syllable by itself.

2. You will usually *hear* the other consonant that belongs in the syllable with *le*. Example: *thim-ble*

3. If you *do not hear* another consonant in the *le* syllable, use the consonant that ended the previous syllable.

   Example: brit-tle
   > You do not hear the second *t* but you know that is needed because *le* is seldom in a syllable by itself.

4. The exception to this rule are words with *ck* because the *ck* remains as a unit and is not divided.

   Example: chuck-le (not *chuc-kle*)

The *ES* Rule:

Use the suffix *es* for all words that end in *s, x, z, sh,* or *ch*. Here are a few important points about this rule:

1. This rule helps you learn when to use *es* instead of just *s*.

2. When you add the *es* suffix, you will *hear* it, and you will *hear* that it has made another syllable.

   Example: class + es = classes
   class (1 syllable)   *classes* (2 syllables)

Multi-Syllable Words

1. Say each of the following words slowly. Write the word by syllables on the "Practice" line. Add the primary accent.

2. Place an *X* in the C/C column or the /*CLE* column if the C/C Rule or the /*CLE* Rule was used.

3. Look at the last letter of the word. If the word ends in *s, x, z, sh,* or *ch* and you want an *s* or an *es* suffix, use *es*. Words that end in any other consonants will use just an *s*. In the last column, if a real word could be made by adding an *es* or an *s* suffix, write the word with the suffix.

✎ **PRACTICE**

Word	Practice	C/C	/*CLE*	*Es* or *S* Suffix
1. trumpet	trum'-pet	X		trumpets
2. bandit				
3. rabbit				
4. canyon				

Word	Practice	C/C	/CLE	*Es* or *S* Suffix
5. traffic	_____	_____	_____	_____
6. happen	_____	_____	_____	_____
7. basket	_____	_____	_____	_____
8. chicken	_____	_____	_____	_____
9. campus	_____	_____	_____	_____
10. tennis	_____	_____	_____	_____
11. picnic	_____	_____	_____	_____
12. kidnap	_____	_____	_____	_____
13. infant	_____	_____	_____	_____
14. problem	_____	_____	_____	_____
15. sudden	_____	_____	_____	_____
16. sandwich	_____	_____	_____	_____
17. common	_____	_____	_____	_____
18. address	_____	_____	_____	_____
19. absent	_____	_____	_____	_____
20. insult	_____	_____	_____	_____
21. infect	_____	_____	_____	_____
22. insect	_____	_____	_____	_____
23. contest	_____	_____	_____	_____
24. connect	_____	_____	_____	_____
25. convict	_____	_____	_____	_____
26. consent	_____	_____	_____	_____
27. conquest	_____	_____	_____	_____
28. contact	_____	_____	_____	_____
29. contract	_____	_____	_____	_____
30. object	_____	_____	_____	_____
31. subject	_____	_____	_____	_____

Word	Practice	C/C	/CLE	*Es* or *S* Suffix
32. scramble	_____	_____	_____	_____
33. twinkle	_____	_____	_____	_____
34. brittle	_____	_____	_____	_____
35. sprinkle	_____	_____	_____	_____
36. chuckle	_____	_____	_____	_____
37. straddle	_____	_____	_____	_____
38. saddle	_____	_____	_____	_____
39. sample	_____	_____	_____	_____
40. crumble	_____	_____	_____	_____
41. stumble	_____	_____	_____	_____
42. gentle	_____	_____	_____	_____
43. simple	_____	_____	_____	_____
44. humble	_____	_____	_____	_____
45. meddle	_____	_____	_____	_____
46. middle	_____	_____	_____	_____
47. hassle	_____	_____	_____	_____
48. mangle	_____	_____	_____	_____
49. dribble	_____	_____	_____	_____
50. handle	_____	_____	_____	_____

✎ **Exercise 2.1 Working with Multi-Syllable Words**

1. *The following words have been divided into syllables. Read each syllable carefully. Add the primary accent. Look at the **unaccented syllable.** Write a **schwa** (ə) above the vowel if the vowel sound has changed to a schwa sound. Remember that the schwa usually sounds like a short* u.

can-yon   hap-pen   fran-tic   prob-lem

sud-den   in-fant   com-mon   ab-sent

con-nect   con-sent   con-quest   con-tract

2. *The prefix in- is used in the following words. Notice when you remove the prefix, a non-word base remains. This is called a **root.** Circle the roots in the following words.*

insult   infect   insect

3. *The prefix con- is used in the following words. Notice when you remove the prefix, a base word or a non-word base (a root) remains. Circle the base words or the roots in the following words.*

contest   connect   convict   contact

contract   context   consent   conquest

4. *The **l**CLE **Rule** states that an* le *syllable usually has one more consonant in the syllable. Sometimes, you hear the sound of the consonant with the* le. *Other times, the consonant with the* le *is silent. Write the seven words from this chapter's word list that have the silent consonant with the* le *syllable.*

1. _____

2. _____

3. _____

4. _____

5. _____

6. _____

7. _____

✎ **EXERCISE 2.2 Sentence Work**

Choose from the first twenty-five words on the list on pages 29–30 to complete these sentences.

1. Sammy ordered _____ in a _____ at the drive-through window.

2. The _____ on our community college _____ is a problem.

3. The _____ had a _____ going to sleep.

4. The _____ player's _____ was not on the envelope.

5. The _____ was held on the public _____ courts.

6. Two main roads _____ the _____ to the rest of the valley.

7. _____ viruses _____ the population quickly.

8. When you _____ my integrity, I have a _____ urge to flee.

Choose from words 26–50 on the word list to complete these sentences.

9. Your _____ to the terms of the _____ is required.

10. The _____ of the discussion was _____ bones in women.

11. My neighbor started to _____ when I told her not to _____ in my business.

12. The young rider thought she could _____ the _____ by herself.

13. The quiet, _____ elder looked at me with a _____ in his eye.

14. You can _____ the company to receive a free _____ of the soap.

15. The _____ monument started to _____ during the tremors.

Page 17 listed three strategies to use to determine if a word can work as a noun. Use those strategies to identify the nouns below. Circle the words below that can work as nouns without adding any suffixes.

trumpet	traffic	kidnap	problem
sudden	sandwich	address	convict
twinkle	sprinkle	sample	simple
humble	meddle	hassle	handle

Choose any ten nouns that you circled on page 33. Use these nouns as the subjects of sentences. Place each noun in the beginning part of your sentence. You may make the noun plural by adding s or es if you wish. Do not write sentences that ask questions.

1. _____

2. _____

3. _____

4. _____

5. _____

6. _____

7. _____

8. _____

9. _____

10. _____

Building Words

Base words and **roots** are the building blocks or the foundation of longer words. **Prefixes** and **suffixes** are added to both base words and roots. As a review, write the definitions of the following terms:

Base Words: _____

Roots: _____

Prefixes: _____

Suffixes: _____

New Prefixes: *in-   de-   dis-   con-   ab-   ad-   ob-   sub-*

The prefix *in-* means **in, into, within,** or **not.**
The prefix *de-* means **down, away from,** or **off.**
The prefix *dis-* means **not** or **opposite.**
The prefix *con-* means **with** or **together.**
The prefix *ab-* means **not** or **from.**
The prefix *ad-* means **to, toward,** or **very.**
The prefix *ob-* means **toward** or **against.**
The prefix *sub-* means **under** or **below.**

New Suffixes: *-s   -es   -ion*

The suffixes *-s* and *-es* indicate plural when added to nouns.
The suffix *-ion* means **state or quality, act of,** or **result.**
(The *-ion* suffix is often added to words that end with *t* or *s* to make a *-tion* or a *-sion* syllable. This syllable will sound like *shŭn.*)

New Roots: *ject   fect   vict   tract   dict   tect*

The root *ject* means **to throw.**
The root *fect* means **to make** or **to do.**
The root *vict* means **to conquer.**
The root *tract* means **to pull** or **to draw.**
The root *dict* means **to speak, to say,** or **to tell.**
The root *tect* means **to cover.**

The Suffixes *S* and *ES*

The suffixes *-s* and *-es* are used to make **plural nouns.** These suffixes can also be used on the end of action verbs, as you will see below.

As a review, write the *ES* Rule: _____

_____

✎ **PRACTICE**

Use the **ES Rule** to add an **s** or an **es** to the following words.

stamp _____	act _____	ranch _____	patch _____
graph _____	check _____	stress _____	sketch _____
script _____	switch _____	inch _____	rich _____
boss _____	cloth _____	buzz _____	duct _____
brunch _____	fund _____	strand _____	class _____
dress _____	stick _____	brush _____	crash _____
shift _____	thrash _____	squish _____	clutch _____
campus _____	kidnap _____	sandwich _____	conquest _____
contract _____	address _____	trumpet _____	problem _____

Word building *is done by adding prefixes and suffixes to base words and to roots. The following words have* **roots** *instead of base words. Circle the prefixes and suffixes in the following words. Write the* **root** *on the line.*

infected _____	convicted _____
objecting _____	contracts _____
addiction _____	detected _____
rejection _____	detracted _____
injecting _____	subtracting _____

✏ **EXERCISE 2.3 Building Words by Adding Prefixes and Suffixes**

The **roots** *are shown in bold print. Add the prefixes and suffixes to the roots. Write the complete word with all the word parts on the line. No spelling changes are needed to build these words. The words are made by simply combining the word parts.*

1. in + **fect** + ed = _____   de + **fect** + ion = _____

2. ob + **ject** + ion + s = _____   re + **ject** + ed = _____

3. con + **vict** + ion = _____   con + **vict** + ed = _____

4. dis + **tract** + ion = _____   con + **tract** + ing = _____

5. ad + **dict** + ion = _____   **dict** + ion + s = _____

6. un + de + **tect** + ed = _____   de + **tect** + ing = _____

7. re + in + **ject** = _____   de + **ject** + ed = _____

8. un + in + **fect** + ed = _____   dis + in + **fect** + ing = _____

9. re + **tract** + ion = _____   sub + **tract** + ing = _____

10. sub + **ject** + ed = _____   ob + **ject** + ing = _____

The **base words** *are shown in bold print. Add the prefixes and suffixes to the base words. Write the complete word with all the word parts on the line. No spelling changes are needed to build these words. The words are made by simply combining the word parts.*

11. **sudden** + ly = _____   17. con + **test** + ed = _____

12. un + **common** = _____   18. con + **quest** + s = _____

13. de + **test** + ing = _____   19. re + **cent** + ly = _____

14. in + de + **cent** + ly = _____   20. con + **strict** + ed = _____

15. de + **duct** + ion = _____   21. con + **duct** + ed = _____

16. dis + **trust** + ed = _____   22. de + **frost** + ing = _____

✎ **EXERCISE 2.4 Word List Expansion**

New short-vowel words are listed in the box below. These words can be used as building blocks to which you can add prefixes and suffixes.

miss	tent	sent	band	dent	list
spend	mess	sect	tend	twist	fend
print	vent	rest	test	tact	skill

Prefixes to use: *re- un- mis- in- de- dis- con- ab- ad- ob- sub-*

Suffixes to use: *-ing -ed -er -est -y -ful -ly -s -es -ion*

On the first line below, write a base word from the list above. Then use the prefixes and suffixes to build two new words that use the same base word. Write the words on the lines. Be sure that you create real words. The first one has been done for you.

Base Word	Expanded Word	Expanded Word
band	*disbanding*	*bands*

EXERCISE 2.5 Sentence Writing

Refer to page 37. Choose any eight words from this page. Write one sentence for each word. Remember to begin each sentence with a capital letter and end each sentence with a period. Circle *the word that you used from page 37.*

1. _____

2. _____

3. _____

4. _____

5. _____

6. _____

7. _____

8. _____

Refer to this chapter's word list on pages 29–31. Write eight sentences on the lines below. Each sentence must have two words *from the word lists. You may add* **prefixes** *or* **suffixes** *to the words.* Circle *the words that you used from the word lists.*

1. _____

2. _____

3. _____

4. _____

5. _____

6. _____

7. _____

8. _____

Grammar Definitions

Verbs: Verbs show the action done by the subject, or verbs link the subject to the rest of the sentence. The two main kinds of verbs are action verbs and state of being verbs.

Action Verbs: Action verbs show the action done by the subject.

> *Examples:* run, stumble, write, spell, catch

State-of-Being Verbs: State-of-being verbs show that something exists. The most frequently used state-of-being verbs come from the verb *to be.*

> *Examples:* am, is, are, was, were

Linking Verbs: *Linking verbs* is another term for *state-of-being verbs* because they link the subject to the rest of the sentence. No other verbs are used in the sentence to show action done by the subject. These are "non-action" verbs.

> *Examples* of linking verbs from the "to be" family: *am, is, are, was, were*

There is a second group of words that are also linking verbs because they do not show action. Some of the common linking verbs in this group are *look, sound, smell, taste, feel, appear,* and *seem.*

Simple Verb Tenses: The term *tense* refers to time. The three simple verb tenses are *past, present,* and *future. Past* tells that something has already been or already happened. *Present* refers to *now, at this moment. Future* refers to *a later time.*

> *Examples:* The players dribbled the ball for hours. (past)
> The players dribble the ball for hours. (present)
> The players will dribble the ball for hours. (future)

Simple Past Tense: The simple past tense for action verbs is often made by adding an *-ed* suffix. No other verbs are used with the action verb when simple past tense is used.

> *Example:* dribbled

Simple Present Tense: The simple present tense for action verbs uses one verb.

> *Examples:* I love music.
> You dance well.
> She plays drums.

Simple Present Tense in Third Person: The verb will have an *s* or an *es* suffix when the subject is singular. The verb will have no *s* or *es* suffix when the subject is plural.

> *Examples:* players dribble   player dribbles

Future Tense: The future tense is usually made by adding the verb *will* to the action verb.

> *Examples:* will dribble   will run   will stumble

Linking Verbs

The *To Be* Verbs The most common linking verbs come from the *to be* verb. Notice how the linking verbs below link the subjects to the rest of the sentence and indicate the tense (time) of the sentence. There are no action verbs in these sentences.

1. The <u>canyon</u> *is* ten miles long.   (linking verb = *is;* verb tense = present)
2. The <u>contracts</u> *are* ready for you.   (linking verb = *are;* verb tense = present)
3. <u>I</u> *am* your best friend.   (linking verb = *am;* verb tense = present)
4. The <u>sandwich</u> *was* not fresh.   (linking verb = *was;* verb tense = past)
5. The <u>infants</u> *were* very cute.   (linking verb = *were;* verb tense = past)

Appear and *Seem*

Notice in the following sentences how the verbs *appear* and *seem* do not show any action. They simply state that something exists in a certain way. These verbs are **linking verbs** because they link the subject to the rest of the sentence.

1. The <u>man</u> in the raincoat *appears* to be sick.   (linking verb = appears, verb tense = present)
2. The <u>children</u> *appeared* to be interested in the show.   (linking verb = appeared, verb tense = past)
3. <u>You</u> *seem* to be distracted today.   (linking verb = seem, verb tense = present)
4. The <u>movie</u> *seemed* to be too long.   (linking verb = seemed, verb tense = past)

Look, Sound, Smell, Taste, Feel

This group of verbs can be a little more confusing because sometimes they are **linking verbs** and sometimes they are **action verbs.** If these verbs are simply linking the subject to the rest of the sentence and they are not really the *action* done by the subject, then they are **linking verbs.** If they show the *action* done by the subject, they are **action verbs,** not linking verbs.

1. The <u>girls</u> *looked* at the ships on the horizon.
   (*Looked* is the action done by the subjects. *Looked* is an action verb in past tense.)
2. The <u>bread</u> *looked* stale.
   (Bread cannot look. *Looked* is a linking verb in past tense.)
3. The <u>teller</u> *sounds* the alarm during times of emergency.
   (*Sounds* is the action done by the subject. *Sounds* is an action verb in present tense.)
4. This <u>plan</u> *sounds* like a disaster.
   (The plan is not sounding. *Sounds* is a linking verb in present tense.)
5. <u>I</u> *smelled* the aroma of fresh bread.
   (*Smelled* is the action done by the subject. *Smelled* is an action verb in past tense.)
6. The old <u>car</u> *smells* musty.
   (The car does not have a nose to smell. *Smells* is a linking verb in present tense.)
7. The <u>chef</u> *tasted* the new sauce.
   (*Tasted* is the action done by the subject. *Tasted* is an action verb in past tense.)
8. The <u>beets</u> *tasted* bitter.
   (The beets don't have mouths to taste. *Tasted* is a linking verb in past tense.)
9. <u>Mary</u> always *feels* the fabric in the store.
   (*Feels* is the action done by the subject. *Feels* is an action verb in present tense.)

10. **They** *feel* uncomfortable around her mother.
    (*Feel* is not an action done by the subjects. *Feel* is a linking verb in present tense.)

Action Verbs

Remember that the subject and the verb work as partners. **Action verbs** show what the subject does. To find the verb in a sentence, first identify the subject. Then ask, "What is the subject doing?" The answer to that question will lead you to the action verb.

Additional Ways to Identify if Words Can Work as Verbs

1. **Ask: Is this something I can do?**
   For example, can the word *crumble* be a verb? Is it something you can do? Yes, you can crumble crackers. Therefore, *crumble* can work as a verb.

2. **Ask: Can I add an *-ing* suffix and make a real word?**
   For example, can the word *bottle* be a verb? Is the word *bottling* a real word? Yes, it is, so *bottle* can work as a verb.

3. **Use a dictionary or a spell checker with a dictionary.** Directly following the word entry, you will see a *v*, *vb*, or the word *verb* to indicate the word can work as a verb.

Finding Action Verbs

✎ PRACTICE

Use any one of the techniques above to identify the words below that can work as verbs. Remember, words can work as more than one part of speech. For example, some of the words below can work both as nouns and verbs, depending on how they are used in sentences. For now, circle the words that can work as verbs.

tennis	picnic	kidnap	sudden	sandwich	address
insult	connect	conquest	contact	scramble	brittle
chuckle	sample	straddle	gentle	humble	meddle
hassle	mangle	dribble	handle	miss	band
dent	spend	dress	tact	skill	rest

Present Tense Action Verbs

To use present tense action verbs correctly, the subject must be identified. The following rules are used in present tense when the subject is **not** *I, you,* or *we*. Notice in the chart below that *I* and *we* are called "first person." *You* is called "second person." Everything that is not first or second person is considered "third person." The rules below are for "third person."

1. If the subject is singular (one), the simple present tense verb must have an -*s* or an -*es* suffix:

   The **lawyer** *objects* to the ruling.

   The **chicken** *crosses the road.*

   This **contract** *needs* a signature.

2. If the subject is plural (more than one), the simple present tense verb will *not* have an -*s* or an -*es* suffix. Remember that subjects are nouns or pronouns. Plural nouns are made by using the -*s* or the -*es* suffix. So, if you see an -*s* or an -*es* suffix on the noun that is the subject, or if the subject is a noun word that means plural (such as *men, women, children*), write the simple present tense action verb without an -*s* or an -*es* suffix:

   The **lawyers** *object* to the ruling.

   The **chickens** *cross* the road.

   These **contracts** *need* a signature.

The Verb *Need*

	Singular Form	Plural Form
1st person:	I need water.	We need water
2nd person:	You need water.	You all need water.
3rd person:	Mom need**s** water.	The player**s** need water.
	My plant need**s** water.	Plant**s** need water.

✎ PRACTICE

Read each sentence carefully. Identify the subject by asking, "Who or what is this sentence about?" Notice if the subject is singular or plural. Then circle the correct action verb.

1. Jim's check often (bounces, bounce) at the end of the month.

2. The subjects in her study (requests, request) the right to withhold their names.

3. The subtraction problem (makes, make) no sense to me.

4. The musician frequently (insults, insult) his audiences.

5. Baseball players (squints, squint) in bright sunlight.

6. Our trust fund (grows, grow) each year.

7. Pharmacists at my favorite store (fills, fill) prescriptions quickly.

8. Too many distractions (causes, cause) me to lose my concentration.

9. The company (prints, print) more than a million brochures a year.

10. The contests at work (leads, lead) to increased motivation.

Verb Tenses

When you write, you must pay attention to verb tenses. One common writing error occurs when the writer changes verb tenses within a sentence or within a paragraph. If you are writing a story about something that has already happened, all your verbs must be in the past tense. You must also be consistent if the verbs are in the present tense or the future tense.

EXERCISE 2.6 **Identifying Nouns and Verbs**

Many words can work as nouns or verbs. The following words can be both nouns and verbs depending on how they are pronounced. *Say each of the following words; pay close attention to the* **primary accent.** *Write* **N** *in the blank if the word is a noun. Write* **V** *in the blank if the word is a verb.*

1. con'-vict _____   con-vict' _____

2. ad'-dress _____   ad-dress' _____

3. in'-sult _____   in-sult' _____

4. con'-test _____   con-test' _____

5. con'-tract _____   con-tract' _____

6. ob'-ject _____   ob-ject' _____

7. sub'-ject _____   sub-ject' _____

What pattern do you see when the first syllable is the accented syllable? _____

What pattern do you see when the second syllable is the accented syllable? _____

Read the following sentences. Decide if the word in bold print is working as a noun or as a verb. Write **N** *in the blank if the word is a noun; write* **V** *if it's a verb.*

_____ **1.** They will **convict** her for shoplifting.

_____ **2.** The **convict** served his time and now leads a productive life.

_____ **3.** The scientists **contracted** the virus in the jungle.

_____ **4.** The truckers' **contract** expires at midnight.

_____ **5.** The **subject** of the sentence was difficult to find.

_____ **6.** I would not wish to **subject** anyone to that kind of treatment.

_____ **7.** They will **address** all the envelopes this weekend.

_____ **8.** The stationery had her **address** and phone number printed in gold.

_____ **9.** Too many **objects** were left at the picnic last week.

_____ **10.** The lawyer always **objects** to the judge's attitude.

_____ **11.** The dance **contest** will be held next Saturday.

_____ **12.** The entire family plans to **contest** the will.

_____ **13.** He always tried to **insult** my younger sister.

_____ **14.** The remark was an **insult** to everyone's integrity.

*Many words can work as more than one part of speech. Use the techniques you have learned to tell if the following words can work as **nouns,** as **verbs,** or as both. Write **N** in the blank if the word can be a noun. Write **V** in the blank if the word can be an action verb. Do not add any suffixes to the words because suffixes change words from one part of speech to another. Work only with the given words below.*

picnic _____   consent _____

sandwich _____   twinkle _____

sprinkle _____   chuckle _____

saddle _____   meddle _____

hassle _____   dribble _____

handle _____   miss _____

band _____   dent _____

list _____   tend _____

twist _____   print _____

test _____   skill _____

plant _____   blend _____

stick _____   wish _____

duck _____   thank _____

inch _____   sketch _____

flesh _____   match _____

graph _____   trumpet _____

Sentence Writing

On your own paper, select any ten words *from page 46 that work as nouns or as verbs. Write one sentence that uses the noun form and one sentence that uses the verb form. You can make nouns plural, and you can add the suffixes, -s, -es, or -ed to the verbs. Set your paper up using the following format:*

1. _____ *match* _____

n. The matches were wet and would not light.

v. The fabric for the couch matches the curtain fabric.

EXERCISE 2.7 Finding Subjects and Verbs

Underline the subjects **once** *and the verbs* **twice**. *Remember that the subject must be a noun or a pronoun. The verb may be an action verb or a linking verb.*

1. The taxi driver hassled me for a bigger tip.

2. The twist of lemon landed in the bottom of the glass.

3. The objections by both sides in the lawsuit resulted in a lengthy trial.

4. I defrosted the freezer in the garage.

5. My connection to the Internet is through a local server.

6. Their stress level was far too high.

7. A retraction of the politician's statement appeared in the newspaper.

8. The cowboy at last week's rodeo straddled the bull for three seconds.

9. The construction workers consented to working six days a week.

10. We vented the attic to reduce the heat.

11. The main problem seems to be a lack of sufficient memory.

12. The plant manager conducts a survey of her employees every year.

13. We misspelled ten of the fifty words.

14. The stitching in my dress is faulty.

15. The teenagers inched their way into the restricted zone.

16. You always seem to stick to your goals.

17. The checkered flag fell out of his hand.

18. The section of the highway near milepost nine was the site of the accident.

19. The mechanic twisted the fender back into place.

20. We try to play tennis three times a week.

✏ EXERCISE 2.8   Sentence Writing

Use each verb below in one sentence that is in simple past tense **(P),** *one that is in simple present tense* **(PR),** *and one that is in future tense* **(F).** *These are all action verbs.* Do not use the verbs am, is, are, was, *or* were.

1. object

P _____

PR _____

F _____

2. twist

P _____

PR _____

F _____

3. address

P _____

PR _____

F _____

4. detect

P _____

PR _____

F _____

5. reject

P _____

PR _____

F _____

Use the subject and the verb that are given. Write the sentences in the verb tense that is shown. You may need to add an -s, -es, or -ed suffix to the action verbs. Use simple verb tenses. Do not use the verbs am, is, are, was, *or* were *when you write sentences with action verbs.*

1. subject: *infant*   verb: *rest*   verb tense: present

_____

2. subject: *insect*   verb: *infect*   verb tense: present

_____

3. subject: *brunch*   verb: *cost*   verb tense: present

_____

4. subject: *sandwich*   verb: *appear*   verb tense: present

_____

5. subject: *printer*   verb: *consent*   verb tense: future

_____

6. subject: *boss*   verb: *unlock*   verb tense: past

_____

7. subject: *clamp*   verb: *shift*   verb tense: past

_____

8. subject: *rancher*   verb: fund   verb tense: past

_____

✎ EXERCISE 2.9 **Chapter Study Sheet**

In the right-hand column, write a definition for the term on the left. Practice reciting and learning this definition. Cover up the definition on the right. Recite the definition. Remove the paper to check your answer. Practice until you can define each term accurately.

Syllable

Multi-Syllable Word

Primary Accent

Accented Syllable

Schwa

Roots

C/C Syllable Rule

ICLE **Syllable Rule**

ES **Rule**

Verbs

Action Verbs

Linking Verbs

Three Simple Verb Tenses

Simple Past Tense

Simple Present Tense

Future Tense

Name _____   Date _____

✎ **CHAPTER REVIEW**

Match the item on the left with the definitions on the right. Each definition can be used only once.

_____ **1.** syllable

_____ **2.** *disinfecting*

_____ **3.** primary accent

_____ **4.** accented syllable

_____ **5.** schwa

_____ **6.** roots

_____ **7.** C/C Syllable Rule

_____ **8.** /CLE Syllable Rule

_____ **9.** *ES* Rule

_____ **10.** action verbs

_____ **11.** linking verbs

_____ **12.** three simple verb tenses

_____ **13.** simple past tense

_____ **14.** simple present tense

_____ **15.** future tense

_____ **16.** *look, sound, smell, taste, feel*

a. a syllable that will never have a schwa

b. divide between two consonants in the middle of a multi-syllable word

c. past, present, and future

d. show the action done by the subject

e. a unit of spoken language that must have one vowel or vowel combination

f. usually made by adding an *-ed* suffix

g. a written mark that shows the stressed syllable

h. an example of a four-syllable word

i. needs an *-es* suffix if the subject is singular

j. made by using *will* with the *action verb*

k. non-word bases such as *ject* or *tect*

l. a short *u* sound that some vowels make in unaccented syllables

m. verbs such as *am, is, are, was, were*

n. verbs that can be linking verbs or action verbs

o. usually another consonant is in the *le* syllable

p. use after words that end in *s, x, z, sh,* or *ch*

*Divide the following words into syllables. Add the primary accent. Write **N** in the blank if the word can be a noun. Write **V** in the blank if the word can be a verb.*

kidnap _____   subject _____   campus _____

insult _____   straddle _____   handle _____

inject _____   object _____   trumpet _____

Circle the letter combinations below that can be either prefixes or suffixes.

de   ed   y   ob   fect   es   s

sub   con   dis   in   ion   text   ful

Write the original parts of each word below.

Example: undetected = un + de + tect + ed

1. suddenly = _____

2. detection = _____

3. messy = _____

4. infections = _____

5. addresses = _____

6. recently = _____

Underline the subjects once and the verbs twice.

1. Early detection saves lives.

2. The car manufacturers examined the mangled dummies.

3. Her last boss rejected her request to work on weekends.

4. The last dent in her car happened near the gym.

5. The most common problem appears to be lack of money.

JOURNAL WRITING ASSIGNMENT

Journal writing is your opportunity to express your ideas freely on paper without worrying about grammar or spelling. Let your ideas flow, and say what you want to say. The goal is to become more comfortable with the process of expressing your ideas and feelings through your written words.

Topic: How Attitude Affects Learning

Does your attitude play a role in how easily you learn new things? Think of things in your life that you were able to learn easily. What hobbies or special interests were easy to learn? What subjects in school were easy to learn? Why were they so easy? Did your amount of previous success affect your attitude? Now think of things that were difficult to learn. Why do you think learning these things was harder? Is a person's attitude tied to how easily something can or cannot be learned?

PARAGRAPH WRITING ASSIGNMENT

Let your ideas flow for the first draft of the following paragraph writing assignment. Once you have finished the first draft, edit the draft in the following ways:

1. Check to see that the first sentence is a strong opening sentence that lets the reader know your topic. Revise the sentence if necessary.

2. Check the spelling of all the words.

3. Check to be sure that every sentence begins with a capital letter and ends with closing punctuation.

4. Check that every sentence has a subject and a verb.

5. Check that all the verbs use a consistent verb tense.

Topic: A Valuable Lesson

Write a paragraph that briefly tells about a situation in the past that taught you some kind of valuable lesson. Your opening sentence should name the situation and give the reader a clue about the lesson that was learned. Be specific. Focus on *one event*.

Examples:

Three hours in the Ronald McDonald House taught me the meaning of courage.

The importance of learning CPR finally sank in at the scene of the accident.

On the last hiking trip, I learned the value of trusting my instincts.

THREE

CVC Words (Consonant–Vowel–Consonant)

Spelling Definitions

CVC Words:	CVC words are base words or roots in which the *last three letters* of the word end in *consonant–vowel–consonant.* The vowel in CVC words is usually short.
Vowel Suffix:	A vowel suffix is any suffix that begins with a vowel.

                Examples: *-ing, -ed, -er, -est, -es, -y*

Sounds of the -ed Suffix:

The *-ed* suffix makes three sounds: *ed, d,* and *t.*

Spelling errors are sometimes made if you write only the *d* or the *t* sounds that are heard instead of using the suffix *-ed.*

> hunt**ed**   The *-ed* sounds like *ed.*
>
> ask**ed**   The *-ed* sounds like *t.*
>
> bagg**ed**   The *-ed* sounds like *d.*

Qu Consonant Unit:

The letter *q* must always be followed by a *u.* The *u* makes no sound. The letters *qu* are called a **consonant unit,** meaning that the *qu* will be treated as one consonant.

The word *quit* is considered a CVC word.   qu *i*   t
                                      ↑ ↑ ↑
                                    C V C

CVC One-Syllable Words

Look at the following one-syllable words. *Circle* all the words that are CVC words. To identify CVC words, look at the **last three letters** to determine if they are in the order of **consonant–vowel–consonant.** Remember to count *qu* as a consonant unit.

fit	fist	sit	grab	hit	step	stamp	stop	quiz
bump	quit	win	swim	quiz	boss	bed	blot	shed
flat	strip	plan	drop	spin	chip	chin	slim	drip

CVC Multi-Syllable Words

Multi-syllable words can also be CVC words. To identify multi-syllable CVC words, look at the **last three letters** of the word to determine if they are in the order of **consonant–vowel–consonant.** Circle all the CVC multi-syllable words below.

happen	kidnap	commit	rerun	profit
admit	trample	bracket	unwrap	index
prefer	exit	brittle	canvas	travel
consist	transfer	permit	submit	propel
combat	compass	transit	predict	pretend

The Different Sounds of -ed

✎ **PRACTICE**

Add -ed to each of the following words. Say the word carefully. Circle the sound that -ed makes when you say the complete word.

staff _____	ed d t	act _____	ed d t
patch _____	ed d t	clamp _____	ed d t
match _____	ed d t	graph _____	ed d t
stress _____	ed d t	inch _____	ed d t
itch _____	ed d t	rust _____	ed d t
plant _____	ed d t	strand _____	ed d t
squint _____	ed d t	dress _____	ed d t
dust _____	ed d t	pack _____	ed d t
trust _____	ed d t	convict _____	ed d t
happen _____	ed d t	insult _____	ed d t
contract _____	ed d t	object _____	ed d t

Spelling Rules

First Doubling Rule: Double the last consonant in a one-syllable CVC word before you add a vowel suffix. Do not double if you are adding a suffix that begins with a consonant.

Examples of one-syllable CVC words + vowel suffix:

plan + ing = planning   *run + y = runny*

Examples of one-syllable CVC words + suffix that begins with a consonant:

sad + ly = sadly   *mad + ness = madness*

There are three important parts to this rule. Double the last consonant only when all three conditions occur:

1. You have a one-syllable word.
2. The one-syllable word is a CVC word.
3. The suffix you want to add begins with a vowel.

Exception: Never double the consonant *x*.

Examples: *box + er = boxer*   *box + ing = boxing*

Reminder: count a *qu* combination as one consonant.

Example: *quit + er = quitter*

one-syllable CVC + vowel suffix = Use the First Doubling Rule

Second Doubling Rule: Double the last consonant in a multi-syllable CVC word only when the CVC is the stressed syllable and when you want to add a vowel suffix. In other words, the primary accent must be on the CVC syllable.

>**Examples:** *unwrapping un-wrap'-ing* (doubling)
>*happening hap'-pen-ing* (no doubling)

There are three important parts to this rule. Double the last consonant only when all three conditions occur:

1. You have a multi-syllable CVC word without suffixes.

2. When you say the entire word with the desired suffixes, the CVC syllable at the end of the base word or root has the primary accent or stress.

3. You want to add a vowel suffix.

Words—Beginning with the Basics

1. All of the words in the list below are CVC words with short vowels. Read each word carefully.

2. Write each word with an *-ed* suffix. Put an **X** on the line if an *-ed* suffix cannot be added to the base word to make a real word. Remember to use the First Doubling Rule.

3. Write the sound that the *-ed* makes in each word. Write *ed, d,* or *t.*

4. Add one of the following vowel suffixes to the base word. Use the First Doubling Rule.

    Vowel Suffixes: *-ing, -es, -er, -est, -y*

✎ **PRACTICE**

Word	Base + *ed*	Sound of *ed*	One More Suffix
1. bag			
2. brag			
3. big			
4. box			
5. bug			
6. chip			
7. cram			
8. dim			
9. drag			
10. drip			
11. flag			

Word	Base + *ed*	Sound of *ed*	One More Suffix
12. flat	_____	_____	_____
13. fit	_____	_____	_____
14. fog	_____	_____	_____
15. hit	_____	_____	_____
16. hop	_____	_____	_____
17. hot	_____	_____	_____
18. hum	_____	_____	_____
19. mad	_____	_____	_____
20. map	_____	_____	_____
21. mix	_____	_____	_____
22. net	_____	_____	_____
23. pit	_____	_____	_____
24. plan	_____	_____	_____
25. plug	_____	_____	_____
26. quit	_____	_____	_____
27. quiz	_____	_____	_____
28. rob	_____	_____	_____
29. rot	_____	_____	_____
30. run	_____	_____	_____
31. sad	_____	_____	_____
32. scrap	_____	_____	_____
33. scrub	_____	_____	_____
34. ship	_____	_____	_____
35. shop	_____	_____	_____
36. skim	_____	_____	_____
37. skin	_____	_____	_____
38. slip	_____	_____	_____

Word	Base + *ed*	Sound of *ed*	One More Suffix
39. spit	_____	_____	_____
40. spot	_____	_____	_____
41. stun	_____	_____	_____
42. swim	_____	_____	_____
43. tax	_____	_____	_____
44. tan	_____	_____	_____
45. thin	_____	_____	_____
46. trim	_____	_____	_____
47. trip	_____	_____	_____
48. wax	_____	_____	_____
49. wit	_____	_____	_____
50. whip	_____	_____	_____

EXERCISE 3.1 **Working with CVC Words**

A *"formula" of the First CVC Doubling Rule looks like this:*

	C	
one-syllable CVC	+	vowel suffix

For each of the following words, explain why the last consonant is doubled or why it is not doubled.

Word **Explanation**

mad + ly = madly _____

mad + est = maddest _____

quiz + ing = quizzing _____

soft + er = softer _____

cram + ed = crammed _____

wax + ed = waxed _____

wit + y = witty _____

A *"formula" of the Second CVC Doubling Rule looks like this:*

	C	
multi-syllable CVC	+	vowel suffix

Examples: com/mit′ + ed = committed
e′/xit + ed = exited

For each of the following words, explain why the last consonant is doubled or why it is not doubled.

Word **Explanation**

happen + ed = happened _____

un + be + fit + ing = unbefitting _____

sub + mit + ed = submitted _____

un + tax + able = untaxable _____

✏ **EXERCISE 3.2 Sentence Work**

The following sentences are missing verbs. The verbs needed to complete each sentence are in the word list on pages 58–60. As you complete each sentence, notice that sometimes you need to add suffixes to the verbs for the sentence to be correct. Common verb suffixes that you may need to use are -ing, -s, -es, and -ed.

1. The stranded motorist _____ down the first car for help.

2. Aunt Jeannie _____ the Christmas tree every Christmas Eve.

3. We were _____ in the river and diving from the rocks.

4. Jimmy _____ his tooth last week.

5. The teacher _____ us on the chapter every Friday.

6. The car windows _____ up so badly.

7. The doctor _____ thoroughly before each surgery.

8. The boys were _____ the ball over the fence.

9. The city managers _____ the annual budget in June.

10. The stock market _____ my brother two thousand dollars.

11. The dog _____ the dead mouse into the house.

12. She is _____ the overgrown lettuce.

13. He _____ on his own two feet.

14. That bully _____ to people on a regular basis.

15. I am _____ my job at the end of the month.

16. The restaurant _____ the lights at seven o'clock.

17. Grandma _____ the good old-fashioned tunes.

18. The child was _____ his ears with his fingers.

Return to each sentence and underline the subject once.

Building Words

You have already been introduced to eleven different prefixes, ten suffixes, and six roots. They are shown below. A large number of words can be built by using these combinations. Each time you become familiar with new prefixes, suffixes, or roots, your ability to spell words correctly by using **structural spelling** increases. The new prefixes, suffixes, and roots for this chapter are listed in the box.

PREFIXES: *re-, un-, mis-, in-, de-, dis-, con-, ab-, ad-, ob-, sub-*
SUFFIXES: *-ing, -ed, -er, -est, -y, -ful, -ly, -s, -es, -ion*
ROOTS: *ject, fect, vict, tract, dict, tect*

New Prefixes: *pre- trans- per- pro- com-*

The prefix **pre-** means **before.**
The prefix **trans-** means **across** or **over.**
The prefix **per-** means **through.**
The prefix **pro-** means **for, forward,** or **in place of.**
The prefix **com-** means **together** or **with.**

New Suffixes: *-able -ment -en*

The suffix **-able** means **able to** or **capable of.**
The suffix **-ment** means a **result, state, quality,** or **condition.**
The suffix **-en** means **made of** or **to make.**

New Roots: *fer mit pel stant sist*

The root **fer** means **to carry** or **to bring.**
The root **mit** means **to send.**
The root **pel** means **to drive.**
The root **stant** means **to stand.**
The root **sist** means to cause **to stand** or **to place.**

✎ PRACTICE

Circle the prefixes and the suffixes in the words below. Write the root on the line.

preferring _____   transmitting _____

propelled _____   constantly _____

deferment _____   commitment _____

instantly _____   consisting _____

Add the prefix to each of the base words or roots.

pre-   **trans-**   **per-**

_____ dict   _____ fer   _____ fect

_____ fer   _____ mit   _____ cent

_____ sent   _____ it   _____ mit

_____ tend   _____ act   _____ sist

_____ fix   _____ plant

pro-   **com-**

_____ tect   _____ mit

_____ ject   _____ pel

_____ tract   _____ press

_____ pel   _____ bat

_____ duct   _____ pass

Add the suffix to each of the base words.

-able   **-ment**   **-en**

swim _____   ship _____   flat _____

tax _____   rot _____

spend _____   sad _____

think _____

stretch _____

fund _____

Partner Work

Work with a partner for dictation. The first partner dictates ten words from the lists above for the second partner to spell out loud without the use of paper or pencil. Then reverse the roles so that each partner has the opportunity to spell out loud.

✎ **Exercise 3.3 Building Words Using Word Bases, Roots, Prefixes, and Suffixes**

The base word or the root is shown in bold print. Add the prefixes and the suffixes. Write the complete word with all the word parts on the line. Remember to check the word carefully to see if it needs the First CVC Doubling Rule or the Second CVC Doubling Rule.

1. pro + **tect** + ion = _____

2. per + **miss** + ion = _____

3. **flat** + en + ing = _____

4. pro + **ject** + ion + s = _____

5. pre + **dict** + ion + s = _____

6. re + **sist** + ed = _____

7. per + **mit** + ed = _____

8. trans + **act** + ion = _____

9. com + **pass** + ion = _____

10. pre + **fer** + able = _____

11. un + com + **mit** + ed = _____

12. in + **stant** + ly = _____

13. trans + **miss** + ion = _____

14. com + **bat** + ing = _____

15. un + **tax** + able = _____

16. de + **fer** + ment = _____

17. in + **tent** + ion = _____

18. ad + **mit** + ing = _____

19. un + pro + **tect** + ed = _____

20. un + pre + **sent** + able = _____

21. pro + **ject** + ion = _____

22. **stun** + ing + ly = _____

23. com + **mit** + ment = _____

24. pro + **fit** + ing = _____

25. de + com + **press** + ion = _____

26. com + **pel** + ing = _____

27. con + **stant** + ly = _____

28. de + **struct** + ion = _____

29. per + **sist** + ed = _____

30. dis + **pel** + ing = _____

31. con + **tend** + er + s = _____

32. trans + **mit** + ing = _____

33. un + re + **fund** + able = _____

34. pre + **plan** + ed = _____

35. re + sub + **mit** + ing = _____

36. pre + **sent** + er = _____

37. ad + **miss** + ion = _____

38. sub + **miss** + ion = _____

✎ EXERCISE 3.4 **Word List Expansion**

*Use the prefixes, suffixes, roots, and word bases that are in the box below to
build your own words. Select combinations that were not used on page 64.
Use a dictionary or spell checker with a dictionary when necessary to be sure
that you are creating a real word. Since you will be working with multi-syllable
words, remember to check the word to see if you need to use the Second Doubling Rule.*

Prefixes	Roots	Suffixes	Word Bases
ab-	dict	-able	miss
ad-	fect	-ed	tent
com-	fer	-en	pass
con-	ject	-er	sent
de-	mit	-es	press
dis-	pel	-est	
in-	sist	-ing	
mis-	stant	-ion	
ob-	tect	-ly	
per-	tract	-ment	
pre-	vict	-s	
pro-		-y	
re-			
sub-			
trans-			
un-			

_____   _____   _____

_____   _____   _____

_____   _____   _____

_____   _____   _____

_____   _____   _____

✎ **EXERCISE 3.5 Sentence Writing**

Use the word list on pages 58–60. Write ten sentences, with each sentence using two words from the word list. You may add prefixes and suffixes to the words. Circle the words that you use from the word list.

1. _____

_____

2. _____

_____

3. _____

_____

4. _____

_____

5. _____

_____

6. _____

_____

7. _____

_____

8. _____

_____

9. _____

_____

10. _____

_____

Write eight sentences that use words from page 64. You need to use only one of the words from this page in each sentence.

1. _____

_____

2. _____

_____

3. _____

_____

4. _____

_____

5. _____

_____

6. _____

_____

7. _____

_____

8. _____

_____

Grammar Definitions

Helping Verbs: Helping verbs are verbs that help the main verb. Some of the same verbs that were called *linking verbs* are used, but they are renamed as *helping verbs* when they are attached to a main verb.

> ***Examples:*** Mary is twenty years old. (*is* = linking verb)
> Mary is planning a trip to Oregon. (*is* = helping verb)

These are the common helping verbs:
am, is, are, was, were, will
These are other verbs that can work as helping verbs:
can, may, would, could, should, shall, might, must, has, have, had, does, do, did, be, been, being

Verb Phrase: A verb phrase is one or more helping vers plus a main verb.

> ***Examples:*** The clerk <u>was stamping</u> the envelopes.
> The swimmer <u>may set</u> a world's record.

Important points to remember:

1. The verb phrase begins with a helping verb and ends with the main verb.

2. When you underline verbs, you must underline both the helping verb and the main verb (action verb).

3. Sometimes the verb phrase is split up by another word, such as an adverb in the following examples:

    > Steven <u>was</u> *not* <u>waxing</u> his car.

    > Karen <u>is</u> *never* <u>going</u> to agree to these terms.

4. The main verb often has an *-ing* or an *-ed* suffix.

Verb Infinitive: A verb infinitive is a verb in its original form. The word *to* comes before the verb. An infinitive verb is *never* the action verb of the sentence.

> ***Example:*** My sister wanted *to go* to the movies. (infinitive: *to go*)

Preposition: A preposition is a word that shows a relationship between a noun and some other word in the sentence. The relationship tells how, when, where, why, or to whom something is related.

> ***Examples:*** with incredible speed   in the morning   in my yard

A list of prepositions is given on the next page.

Prepositional Phrase: A prepositional phrase is a group of words that *always* begins with a preposition and ends with a noun or a pronoun. It is marked in a sentence by parentheses.

> ***Examples:*** *on the table   in a last attempt   for me*

The subject and the verb of a sentence will *never* be in a prepositional phrase.

> ***Examples:*** <u>He</u> <u>ran</u> (*to the house*) (*on the corner*) to see the fire.

Working with Prepositions

As a review, write the definition for each of the following:

preposition: _____

prepositional phrase: _____

Prepositions

about	before	except	off	to
above	behind	for	on	toward
according to	below	from	onto	under
across	beneath	in	out of	underneath
after	beside	inside	outside	until
ahead of	between	in spite of	over	unto
against	beyond	into	past	up
along	by	like	since	upon
among	despite	near	through	with
around	down	next	throughout	within
at	during	of	till	without

Reminders

1. When you need to identify the **subject** and the **verb** of a sentence, you can eliminate some of the words in the sentence by first identifying the prepositional phrases. Why? The subject and the verb are *never* inside a prepositional phrase. So, once you have identified the prepositional phrase, you can then examine the remaining words to locate the subject and the verb.

2. Remember that the prepositional phrase *begins with the preposition* and *ends with a noun or a pronoun.*

✎ **Practice**

Mark the prepositional phrases by using parentheses ( ).

1. The couple inside the motor home was looking at the stars from the top of the cliff.
2. The witty professor in the plaid jacket whipped a comic book from his briefcase.
3. During the storm, all of the flags were torn off the flagpoles.
4. My most sincere wishes to you are included in this poem.
5. She placed the flowers with the wilted leaves near the sprinkler next to the fence.

Working with Verb Infinitives

Be careful not to confuse **prepositional phrases** with **verb infinitives.** If you see the word *to* come before a verb, you have a **verb infinitive.** Prepositional phrases will not have verbs. Examples of infinitives are *to brag, to hit, to run, to hop, to shop, to flatten.*

PRACTICE

*In the groups of words below, write **P** for **prepositional phrase** and **VI** for **verb infinitive**.*

_____ to the winners   _____ to receive   _____ to Mom

_____ to drip   _____ to them   _____ to cram

_____ to drop   _____ to the computers   _____ to school

Mark the prepositional phrases with parentheses (   ). Mark the verb infinitives with brackets [   ].

1. The hunters wandered into the nearest town to buy more supplies to last for one more week.
2. Each of the employees uses a time card to record the amount of time spent on lunch.
3. The greatest advertisements for television viewers to watch are shown during the Super Bowl.
4. During the months at sea, the sailor wanted to receive letters from his home in Maine.
5. We planned to drive through the Redwood Forest to avoid the heat in the valley.

For additional practice marking prepositional phrases and verb infinitives, return to Exercise 1.2 (pages 8–9), Exercise 1.7 (pages 18–19), Exercise 2.2 (page 33), Exercise 2.7 (page 47), and Exercise 3.2 (page 62).

Working with Linking Verbs, Action Verbs, and Verb Phrases

As a review, write the definition of each of the following terms:

linking verb: _____

action verb: _____

verb phrase: _____

 PRACTICE

*Assume that all of the following are working as verbs in a sentence. Write **L** for **linking verb**, **A** for **action verb**, **VP** for **verb phrase**, and **VI** for **verb infinitive**.*

_____ is permitting   _____ can persist   _____ preferred

_____ was   _____ seems   _____ may resist

_____ am admitting   _____ were   _____ should project

_____ appears   _____ to protest   _____ thinned

_____ to skin   _____ had been tanning   _____ feels

Working with Gerunds (-*ing* Words)

A word that ends in -*ing* **must have a helping verb with it** for it to work as a verb. Words that end with -*ing* that do not have a helping verb are -*ing* words that often work as **nouns.** These are called **verbals** or **gerunds.** As nouns, they name a **type** of activity, process, or action, but they are *not* verbs. We will see in later chapters that -*ing* words can also work as **adjectives** (words that describe nouns or pronouns).

These -*ing* words are verbs because they have helping verbs right before them:

The children at the summer camp *were swimming* in the lake.

The counselors *were watching* the swimmers closely.

The following -*ing* words are not verbs. They are working as nouns. Notice that the italicized words do not have helpers with them. Instead, the words tell about a kind of activity or process.

The children went *swimming* in the lake.

Watching the children was not an easy task.

Taxing smokers to increase revenues for road construction is going to the voters.

We waited quietly on the beach for the *setting* of the sun.

✎ **EXERCISE 3.6 Identifying Prepositions, Nouns, and Verbs**

*Remember that words can work as more than one part of speech. For each of the words below, write **N** in the blank if the word can work as a **noun,** **V** if the word can work as a **verb,** and **P** if the word can work as a **preposition.** You may have more than one part of speech marked for some words. Do not add any suffixes to the words when you determine the part of speech. You may use a dictionary or a spell checker with a dictionary.*

bag	_____	chip	_____	cram	_____
for	_____	around	_____	hum	_____
map	_____	by	_____	mix	_____
plug	_____	scrap	_____	until	_____
shop	_____	slip	_____	down	_____
quiz	_____	trim	_____	wit	_____
drag	_____	rot	_____	near	_____
transplant	_____	admit	_____	project	_____
compress	_____	between	_____	combat	_____
defer	_____	present	_____	prefix	_____
percent	_____	transfer	_____	perfect	_____

Sentence Writing

Use your own paper for this exercise. Choose any ten words from the group above that can work both as nouns and as verbs. Write one sentence that uses the word as a noun. Write one sentence that uses the word as a verb. In both sentences, add at least one prepositional phrase. Refer to the lists of prepositions on page 70. Use the following format.

Word

1. (noun) _____

2. (verb) _____

✎ **EXERCISE 3.7 Finding Subjects, Verbs, and Prepositions**

*Read the following sentences carefully. Begin by marking all the **prepositional phrases** by using parentheses ( ). Look outside the prepositional phrases to find the subjects and the verbs. Draw one line under the **subjects.** Draw two lines under the **verbs.** Put brackets [ ] around the **verb infinitives.***

1. The shipping and handling fees for the merchandise are unrefundable.

2. Consumer groups want to protect the public from inferior products.

3. The transit station is a perfect location to place flyers about the upcoming concert.

4. This dead transmission was removed from the first car in the third row of the dealership lot.

5. To reach Michael's ranch, you will need to go up the hill, past the barn, and beyond the railroad tracks.

6. Raymond received the teacher's permission to be able to do a joint-research project with Joe.

7. The frisky, little puppy along with two kittens slipped through the side door of the church.

8. Without a doubt, the heart transplant added many years to my father's life.

9. According to the newspaper, the protesters stood outside the construction site for six hours.

10. The salmon swim against the current in an effort to spawn.

11. The lumber under the back porch started to rot and to attract termites.

12. The connection between the two crimes was discovered by a young detective.

13. The company decided to submit the proposal to request more funding for expansion.

14. Melinda keeps her driver's permit inside the glove compartment of her father's car.

15. You can stop looking over your shoulder for Amy.

16. We were told to quit transmitting messages to Australia on our short-wave radio.

17. The district court judge objected to the constant outbursts in her courtroom.

18. At the scene of the crime, the mangled bodies were burned beyond recognition.

✎ **EXERCISE 3.8 Sentence Writing**

Complete each of the following prepositional phrases. Remember that a prepositional phrase never includes the subject or the verb and that it must end with a noun or a pronoun. The pronouns that can be used inside a prepositional phrase are **me, you, her, him, us, them,** *and* **it.**

(about	)	(above	)	(across	)
(among	)	(at	)	(before	)
(beneath	)	(beside	)	(between	)

(by	)	(during	)	(for	)
(from	)	(in	)	(near	)
(of	)	(through	)	(to	)
(under	)	(until	)	(with	)

Select from the following list of action verbs. Write fourteen sentences. Each sentence must use one of the prepositional phrases above and one of the verbs below. Do not use a prepositional phrase or a verb twice. You may add suffixes to the verbs. Follow the sentence writing directions below. Sample sentences can be found in the appendix.

prefer	propel	defer	transmit	commit	consist	predict
present	pretend	transfer	transplant	perfect	permit	persist
project	compress	resist	combat	admit	protect	profit

Note: Three words in the preceding box can be either nouns or verbs. When they are pronounced with the accent on the second syllable, they are **verbs.** *The three words are* present, perfect, *and* project. *If you select these words, remember to use them as the action verbs of the sentence.*

1. Write a sentence in present tense. Use the simple verb, not a verb phrase.

_____

2. Write a sentence in present tense. Use a verb phrase (helping verb + action verb).

_____

3. Write a sentence in future tense.

_____

4. Write a sentence in past tense. Use the simple past tense, not a verb phrase.

_____

5. Write a sentence in present tense that also has an infinitive.

_____

6. Write a sentence in past tense. Use a verb phrase.

_____

7. Write a sentence in future tense.

_____

8. Write a sentence in present tense. Use a simple present tense verb.

_____

9. Write a sentence in past tense. Use a simple past tense verb.

_____

10. Write a sentence in future tense.

_____

11. Write a sentence that uses the helping verb *should*.

_____

12. Write a sentence that uses the helping verb *has*.

_____

13. Write a sentence that uses the helping verb *does*.

_____

14. Write a sentence that uses the helping verb *must*.

_____

✎   **EXERCISE 3.9 Chapter Study Sheet**

In the right-hand column, write a definition for the term on the left. Practice reciting and learning this definition. Cover up the definition on the right. Recite the definition. Remove the paper to check your answers. Practice until you can define each term accurately.

CVC Word

Vowel Suffix

Three Sounds of *-ed*

***Qu* Consonant Unit**

First Doubling Rule

Second Doubling Rule

Helping Verb

Verb Phrase

Verb Infinitive

Preposition

Prepositional Phrase

✏️ **CHAPTER REVIEW**

Match the terms on the left with the definitions on the right.

_____ **1.** CVC word

_____ **2.** vowel suffixes

_____ **3.** sounds of *-ed*

_____ **4.** *qu*

_____ **5.** First Doubling Rule

_____ **6.** Second Doubling Rule

_____ **7.** primary accent

_____ **8.** helping verbs

_____ **9.** verb phrase

_____ **10.** verb infinitive

_____ **11.** preposition

_____ **12.** prepositional phrase

a. *ed, d, t*

b. a consonant and a vowel that are treated as one consonant unit

c. a part of speech that shows relationships between nouns and other words

d. the original verb, without suffixes, that follows the word *to*

e. double the last consonant of a multi-syllable CVC word when the CVC is accented and you add a vowel suffix

f. *-en, -ed, -ing, -er, -est, -y*

g. words such as *has, could, will, may, is, are, was,* and *were* when they are used before the main verb

h. a helping verb plus an action verb

i. the last three letters are in a consonant–vowel–consonant pattern

j. a mark to show which syllable carries a stronger stress when spoken

k. double the last consonant of a one-syllable CVC word when you add a vowel suffix

l. a group of words that begins with a preposition and ends with a noun or a pronoun

Circle all the word parts below that are **roots:**

com   per   mit   fer   pel   stant

sist   pro   tract   dict   fect   ment

Circle all the combinations below that are **prefixes:**

pre   per   pel   ment   ab   dis

de   trans   com   sub   pro   tect

Circle all the combinations below that are **suffixes:**

pel   able   mit   ment   en   ion

y   s   es   ful   ly   de

Look at each pair of words. Circle the word that is spelled correctly.

braging   transmiter   preferable   scrubing

bragging   transmitter   preferrable   scrubbing

transfering   propeled   shipment   sadly

transferring   propelled   shippment   saddly

flatenning   uncomitted   profitable   exited

flattening   uncommitted   profittable   exitted

Add the prefixes and suffixes to the following roots and base words. Write the complete word on the line.

con + fer + ed = _____   un + wrap + ed = _____

dim + ly = _____   chip + er = _____

un + box + ed = _____   flat + est = _____

hum + ing = _____   skim + er = _____

quiz + ed = _____   un + plug + ed = _____

com + pel + ing = _____   un + think + able = _____

Read each sentence carefully. Tell if the word in bold print is working as a **noun,** *a* **verb,** *or a* **preposition.** *Write* **N, V,** *or* **P** *on the line.*

_____ **1.** The fox hid **beneath** the bushes.

_____ **2.** They **perfected** the database system at work.

_____ **3.** The Boy Scouts lost the **compass** somewhere in the woods.

_____ **4.** They will **project** the sales figures for the next year.

_____ **5.** **During** the election, the mayor frequently spoke to the senior citizens.

_____ **6.** You can get **permission** from the Division of Motor Vehicles.

_____ **7.** Carl is **resisting** the move to another city.

_____ **8.** The flower **shop** sells roses at a discount every Friday.

Mark the prepositional phrases with parentheses (   ). Underline the subject once. Underline the verb twice. Put brackets [   ] around verb infinitives.

1. You can type your address on the envelope near the upper-left corner.

2. The quizzes on Friday consist of words to spell and definitions to write.

3. The heavyweight contender will box at Madison Square Garden in New York on Friday night.

4. The artist needed to trim the wax from the top of the candle.

5. All of your transactions will be handled by Marianne at the downtown bank.

6. Protection from the sun is possible by using sunblocks and sunscreens.

7. During the last concert, the school charged an admission fee of ten dollars.

8. She whipped the butter to put on top of the baked potatoes.

JOURNAL WRITING ASSIGNMENT

Topic: Writing on the Job

Computers provide great assistance for writers. Spell checkers eliminate many spelling errors. The use of word processing functions makes revising and editing a much less demanding process. Yet computers do not replace the need to know how to spell accurately, construct grammatically correct sentences, or express ideas clearly in written words. Members of the business community continue to seek employees with strong writing and communication skills.

In your journal, discuss the need for strong writing skills in all kinds of employment. Your discussion might include why you think employers are concerned about the way their employees write, or you might discuss the kinds of problems that could occur when the level of writing is substandard. Give examples of different kinds of jobs in which writing skills are important. When you enter the work force, what kind of writing tasks will you possibly have to perform that will require effective writing?

PARAGRAPH WRITING ASSIGNMENT

Topic: Our Transit System

Write a paragraph that gives your opinion about whether your town or city needs to develop or improve its transit system. The transit system could include a bus, train, or rail system; a freeway system; wider streets; or whatever your town or city needs. Give individual examples, facts, or reasons to support your opinion. When writing an opinion paragraph, choose *one* response (yes or no) and include only details that support that response. Take a stance and state your opinion with conviction.

Your opening sentence should inform the reader about the topic of your paragraph and provide a clue for the reader to know your stance or opinion. Since this is *your* opinion, you will be writing this paragraph from the *first person position*, which means you will use the word *I* instead of *you*, *he*, *she*, or *they*.

Examples:

1. The last time I rode the subway, I became very aware of the need for this city to improve transit services for commuters.

2. I believe our city has one of the finest transit systems in the country.

3. The traffic jams are horrendous, the toxic fumes are alarming, and there is no relief in sight unless city government wakes up and sees the need to create a local transit system.

Let your ideas flow for the first draft. Once you have finished the first draft, edit the draft in the following ways:

1. Check to see that the first sentence is a strong opening sentence that lets the reader know your topic. Revise the sentence if necessary.

2. Check the spelling of all the words.

3. Check to see that every sentence begins with a capital letter and ends with closing punctuation.

4. Check that every sentence has a subject and a verb.

5. Check to see that all the verbs use a consistent verb tense.

FOUR

Long-Vowel Words with Final *E*

The topics in this chapter include the following:

- Introduction to long vowels and long-vowel words that end in a final *e*
- Introduction to soft *c* and soft *g*
- The Final *E* Dropping Rule and the Soft *C* and Soft *G* Rule
- One new prefix, five new suffixes, and eleven new roots to build words
- Introduction to regular and irregular verbs
- Compound subjects and compound verbs
- Four simple sentence patterns

Spelling Definitions

Long Vowels: The long vowels are *a, e, i, o,* and *u*. When these vowels make a long-vowel sound, they "say their alphabet names." A straight line placed above the vowel shows that the vowel sound is long.

> ***Examples:*** ape   (long *a*)   āp¢
> eve   (long *e*)   ēv¢
> ice   (long *i*)   īc¢
> owe   (long *o*)   ōw¢
> use   (long *u*)   ūs¢

Final *E* Words: Final *e* words are any one-syllable or multi-syllable words that end with the letter *e*. If there is another vowel in the same syllable that ends with *e*, the other vowel is usually long. The final *e* is silent. A diagonal line drawn through the *e* shows that it is silent.

> ***Examples:*** trād¢   man-dāt¢   phōn¢   stam-pēd¢

Soft *C*:   The "soft *c*" sound like "ssss." The consonant *c* makes the soft *c* sound when it is followed by an *e, i,* or *y.*

> ***Examples:*** **ci**ty   **ce**nt   **cy**cle   ra**ce**   sli**ce**

Soft *G*:   The "soft *g*" sounds like the *j* sound. The consonant *g* makes the soft *g* sound when it is followed by an *e, i,* or *y.*

> ***Examples:*** **ge**m   **ge**ntle   **gi**n   **gy**m   **gy**psy   ran**ge**   stran**ge**
>
> ***Exceptions:*** **gi**rl   **gi**ft   (The *g* keeps the hard *g* sound.)

Marking Long Vowels and Silent *E*

✎ **PRACTICE**

Say the following words. Draw a straight line above the long vowels and a diagonal line through the silent e.

strange	blaze	brave	chase	haste	late	paste	quake
state	taste	waste	theme	eve	bride	crime	drive
quite	shine	choke	globe	stove	fuse	cute	mute

Making Long-Vowel Final *E* Words

✎ **PRACTICE**

Add any of the long vowels (a, e, i, o, or u) to make a real word. More than one vowel is possible for some of the words.

sh_____ne   w_____ve   l_____ne   br_____ke

gr_____pe   pr_____ze   tr_____be   w_____fe

ch_____se   n_____se   sp_____ke   m_____le

Marking the Vowels in CVC Words and Long-Vowel Final *E* Words

Perhaps two of the largest "vowel families" are the CVC words and the final *e* words. These two patterns are very significant and are the source of many spelling errors. The CVC Doubling Rule and the Final *E* Dropping Rule, which is discussed below, are two of the most important rules to know. The understanding of both rules begins with being able to differentiate between the short-vowel patterns and the long-vowel patterns.

✎ PRACTICE

*On the words below, mark the **short vowels** with a short, curved line. Mark the **long vowels** with a straight line. Draw a diagonal line through the **silent vowels**.*

bit	bite	cod	code	dim	dime
grip	gripe	hop	hope	not	note
rid	ride	shin	shine	spin	spine
can	cane	cop	cope	hat	hate
pan	pane	rob	robe	gap	gape
slid	slide	van	vane	cap	cape
cut	cute	fin	fine	hid	hide
pin	pine	man	mane	slim	slime
mat	mate	past	paste	plan	plane
grim	grime	rip	ripe	strip	stripe
rod	rode	win	wine	whine	

Partner Dictation

Dictate fifteen of the above words to each other to spell out loud.

Spelling Rules

Final *E* Dropping Rule:

When a word ends in *e*, drop the *e* if you are adding a suffix that begins with a vowel (vowel suffix). If you are adding a suffix that begins with a consonant, keep the *e*.

> ***Examples:*** pave + ing = paving
> pave + ment = pavement
> hope + ing = hoping
> hope + ful = hopeful

Soft *C* and Soft *G* Rule:

When a word ends in *ce* or *ge*, drop the *e* only if the suffix you are adding begins with *e*, *i*, or *y*. If the suffix begins with any other letter, you must keep the *e* to maintain the soft *c* or the soft *g* sound.

Examples: change + ing = chan**ging**   (Drop the *e.*)
*change + able = change*able   (Keep the *e.*)
repla**ce** + ing = repla**cing**   (Drop the *e.*)
repla**ce** + ment = repla**cement**   (Keep the *e.*)

✎ PRACTICE

The ending letters of a word are shown below. A suffix is added to this "word." Circle **keep** *if you would keep the final* e *in this situation. Circle* **drop** *if you would drop the* e.

1. _____ e + able	**keep drop**	_____ e + ment **keep drop**
2. _____ e + en	**keep drop**	_____ e + ion **keep drop**
3. _____ e + est	**keep drop**	_____ e + y **keep drop**
4. _____ e + ful	**keep drop**	_____ e + ly **keep drop**
5. _____ ce + ing	**keep drop**	_____ ge + less **keep drop**
6. _____ ce +ous	**keep drop**	_____ ge + ness **keep drop**
7. _____ ce + age	**keep drop**	_____ ge + y **keep drop**

Words—Beginning with the Basics

1. All of the following words are long-vowel words with a final *e*. Read each word carefully. Under the "Word" column, mark the vowels as long or silent.
2. In the second column, write the word with an *-ed* ending. If an *-ed* suffix added to the base word does not form a real word, place an **X** on the line.
3. For all the words in which you could add an *-ed* ending, say the word slowly. Write the sound that the *-ed* makes in the word (*ed, d,* or *t*).
4. In the last column, write the word with an *-ing* suffix. Place an **X** on the line if the base word plus *-ing* does not make a real word.

✎ PRACTICE

Word	Base + *ed*	Sound of *ed*	Base Word + *ing*
1. base	_____	_____	_____
2. baste	_____	_____	_____
3. blaze	_____	_____	_____
4. brake	_____	_____	_____
5. brave	_____	_____	_____
6. chance	_____	_____	_____

Word	Base + *ed*	Sound of *ed*	Base Word + *ing*
7. change	_____	_____	_____
8. face	_____	_____	_____
9. fame	_____	_____	_____
10. flame	_____	_____	_____
11. frame	_____	_____	_____
12. grace	_____	_____	_____
13. grate	_____	_____	_____
14. hate	_____	_____	_____
15. late	_____	_____	_____
16. male	_____	_____	_____
17. paste	_____	_____	_____
18. place	_____	_____	_____
19. quake	_____	_____	_____
20. safe	_____	_____	_____
21. scale	_____	_____	_____
22. shade	_____	_____	_____
23. shake	_____	_____	_____
24. shame	_____	_____	_____
25. state	_____	_____	_____
26. taste	_____	_____	_____
27. trace	_____	_____	_____
28. waste	_____	_____	_____
29. bribe	_____	_____	_____
30. chime	_____	_____	_____
31. drive	_____	_____	_____
32. grime	_____	_____	_____

Word	Base + *ed*	Sound of *ed*	Base Word + *ing*
33. pride	_____	_____	_____
34. quite	_____	_____	_____
35. shine	_____	_____	_____
36. spire	_____	_____	_____
37. spice	_____	_____	_____
38. stripe	_____	_____	_____
39. tribe	_____	_____	_____
40. broke	_____	_____	_____
41. chose	_____	_____	_____
42. home	_____	_____	_____
43. phone	_____	_____	_____
44. spoke	_____	_____	_____
45. zone	_____	_____	_____
46. theme	_____	_____	_____
47. cute	_____	_____	_____
48. fuse	_____	_____	_____
49. mute	_____	_____	_____
50. use	_____	_____	_____

✎ **EXERCISE 4.1 Working with Long-Vowel, Final *E* Words**

As a review, write the following rules that will be used with words in this chapter.

Final *E* Dropping Rule: _____

_____

Soft *C* and Soft *G* Rule: _____

_____

Circle the vowel suffixes in the list of suffixes below. Some of the suffixes are new, and some are from previous chapters.

able	ment	en	s	es	less
ion	ing	ed	er	est	ness
y	ful	ly	age	ous	ual

Use the rules above to combine the following words using the suffixes provided. Review the two rules above before you add the suffixes.

base + ment = _____ baste + ing = _____

brave + ly = _____ change + ing = _____

fame + ous = _____ grace + ful = _____

grate + ful = _____ cute + ness = _____

shame + less = _____ place + ment = _____

tribe + al = _____ state + ly = _____

use + age = _____ broke + en = _____

Confusion between reading and spelling CVC and final e *words occurs because, in many cases, there is only one letter that is different. When you see doubled letters, the vowel is usually short. By analyzing the base word, you can tell if the base word is a CVC word or if it is a short-vowel word that uses the* F, L, S, Z *Rule. If you see one consonant, the vowel will usually be long because the base word is a word that ends in a final* e.

Try reading the following list of words without any mistakes. You will need to shift between short and long vowel sounds.

griped	gripped	diner	dinner
hoping	hopping	shinning	shining
pining	pinning	panned	panes
robed	robbed	gapping	gaping
capped	caped	cuter	cutter

mated	matted	planed	planned
striped	stripped	winning	wining
copping	coping	whiner	winner
filled	filed	scraping	scrapping

Mark the vowels of the base word as long or short. Then read the list without making any errors.

bitten	coded	dimly	biting	ridden
shiny	sliding	vanes	hidden	finely
hiding	manly	slimmer	pasted	slimy
grimness	ripped	grimy	ripen	spiteful
fusses	hatless	spitting	fuses	pasts
cutting	pastes	hoped	piles	pills

Partner Dictation

Each partner dictates any fifteen words from the list for the other partner to spell out loud.

EXERCISE 4.2 Sentence Work

*Use words from the word list on pages 86–88 to complete the following sentences. Above each word that you add, write **N** for **noun** and **V** for **action verb** or **verb infinitive**. If a word is a part of speech other than a noun or a verb, you do not need to mark the part of speech. Put **parentheses** around the **prepositional phrases** and **brackets** around the **verb infinitives**.*

1. The detailer marked the _____ on the side of the car to paint the _____.

2. It is a _____ to _____ leftover restaurant food.

3. This will be my last _____ to _____ to the coast in my truck.

4. There was no _____ of the village after the devastating _____.

5. I could not _____ that _____ in the chicken casserole.

6. The interview will be the mayor's final _____ to _____ his position.

7. Your mother expects you to _____ _____ once a week.

8. The teenager was involved in _____ a _____ attempt to save the child.

9. The _____ of the play was about _____ crimes in America.

10. The bride _____ the silver picture _____ for her gift.

11. The world's best chefs _____ homemade tomato _____ for Italian sauces.

12. The fire fighter poured _____ retardant on the _____ set by careless campers.

13. The new lamp _____ was for the lamp with a yellow _____.

14. Melissa _____ the silence and _____ to her ex-roommate.

15. My grandmother's _____ showed her enormous sense of _____ at my college graduation.

16. You can _____ the rugs outside to remove the grit and _____.

17. The members of the _____ voted to make a _____ in the treaty.

18. With a _____ little smile on her face, the young child said _____ before dinner.

Building Words

The following new prefixes, suffixes, and roots can be used to build many new words. Notice that the new roots use the final *e* pattern: the final *e* is silent, and the other vowel is long. These new word parts can be combined with word parts from previous chapters to build a large number of words.

New Prefix:　*ex-*

The prefix *ex-* means **out**.

New Suffixes:　*-age　-ous　-less　-ness　-ual*

The suffix *-age* means **that which is** or **that which does.**
The suffix *-ous* means **given to** or **marked by.**
The suffix *-less* means **without.**
The suffix *-ness* means **quality** or **state.**
The suffix *-ual* means **describes something.**

New Roots:　*cede　cide　cise　clude　duce　mote　plete　pute
quire　sume　vise*

The root *cede* means **to go** or **to yield.**
The root *cide* means **to cut** or **to kill.**
The root *cise* means **to cut.**
The root *clude* means **to close** or **to shut.**
The root *duce* means **to lead.**
The root *mote* means **to move.**
The root *plete* means **to fill.**
The root *pute* means **to think** or **to reckon.**
The root *quire* means **to ask** or **to seek.**
The root *sume* means **to take.**
The root *vise* means **to see.**

✎　**PRACTICE**

*Circle all the combinations below that are **suffixes**.*

age	able	trans	ous	less	ness
ful	ly	s	de	ab	ual
y	ion	ing	dis	pel	sist

Circle the **prefixes** *and the* **suffixes** *in the following words. Write the* **root** *on the line. Remember, if the original spelling of the root ends with an* e, *you need to add the* e *to the root when you spell the root on the line.*

excluding = _____   remoteness = _____

conceded = _____   deciding = _____

precision = _____   reducing = _____

completeness = _____   computer = _____

requirement = _____   resuming = _____

consumer = _____   revision = _____

precisely = _____   promotion = _____

disputable = _____   receding = _____

Add the following suffixes to the base words. Add an extra consonant if you need to use the CVC doubling rule to double the last consonant. Draw a diagonal line through a final e *if you need to use the Final* E *Dropping Rule before adding the suffix.*

-less	*-ness*	*-ual*	*-age*
face _____	late _____	mute _____	band _____
shame _____	cute _____	fact _____	mess _____
taste _____	dim _____	use _____	use _____
trace _____	flat _____		
home _____	mad _____		
skin _____	sad _____		
spot _____	gentle _____		
thank _____	thick _____		
use _____	swift _____		

Partner Dictation

Work with a partner to take turns dictating any ten of the words used above for your partner to spell without the use of paper or pencil. Reverse roles so that both partners spell ten words.

✏ **EXERCISE 4.3 Building Words Using Word Bases, Roots, Prefixes, and Suffixes**

The base word or the root is shown in bold print. Add the prefixes and the suffixes. Write the complete word with all the word parts on the line. Remember to check the word carefully to see if you need to use the First CVC Doubling Rule, the Second CVC Doubling Rule, the Final E Dropping Rule, or the Soft C and G Rule.

1. in + **fame** + ous = _____

2. pre + **cise** + ly = _____

3. re + **pute** + able = _____

4. un + **use** + ual + ly = _____

5. un + **grate** + ful = _____

6. un + in + **spire** + ed = _____

7. pro + **mote** + ion + s = _____

8. **bribe** + er + y = _____

9. com + **mote** + ion = _____

10. re + **frame** + ing = _____

11. **use** + less + ly = _____

12. re + **quire** + ment = _____

13. **fact** + ual + ly = _____

14. con + **fuse** + ion = _____

15. re + in + **state** + ment = _____

16. con + **spire** + ing = _____

17. **broke** + er + age = _____

18. trans + **late** + ing = _____

19. com + **plete** + ion = _____

20. **shame** + ful + ly = _____

21. un + **trace** + able = _____

22. **grace** + ful + ly = _____

23. **hope** + less + ness = _____

24. per + **spire** + ing = _____

25. re + **place** + able = _____

26. **mute** + ual + ly = _____

27. ex + **clude** + ing = _____

28. in + dis + **pute** + able + y = _____

29. pro + **duce** + er = _____

30. re + pro + **duce** + ing = _____

31. re + **place** + ment = _____

32. **shake** + y = _____

33. trans + **fuse** + ion = _____

34. re + **fuse** + al = _____

35. un + ex + **change** + able = _____

36. pre + dis **pose** + ed = _____

✎ EXERCISE 4.4 **Word List Expansion**

Use the prefixes, suffixes, roots, and word bases that are in the box below to build your own words. Select combinations that were not used on page 93. Use a dictionary or spell checker with a dictionary when necessary to verify that you are creating a real word. Since you will be working with multi-syllable words, remember to check the word to see if you need to use the Second Doubling Rule. Also remember to apply the Final E Dropping Rule and the Soft C and G Rule when necessary.

Prefixes	Roots	Other Bases	Suffixes
com-	cede	nice	-al
con-	cide	pose	-age
de-	cise	grade	-ed
dis-	clude	age	-er
in-	dict	strange	-ion
ex-	duce		-less
mis-	mit		-ly
per-	mote		-ment
pre-	plete		-ness
pro-	pute		-ual
re-	quire		-y
sub-	sist		
trans-	sume		
un-	vise		

_____ _____ _____

_____ _____ _____

_____ _____ _____

_____ _____ _____

_____ _____ _____

✎ EXERCISE 4.5 **Sentence Writing**

Use the base words on pages 86–88 to write five sentences. In each sentence, use two words from the word lists. Circle the words in each sentence that come from the word lists.

1. _____

2. _____

3. _____

4. _____

5. _____

Select any five words from page 93. Use each word in a sentence below. Circle the word.

1. _____

2. _____

3. _____

4. _____

5. _____

Select any seven words from page 94. Use each word in a sentence below. Use a dictionary to check the meaning of any of the words that are unfamiliar to you. In each sentence, circle *the word taken from page 94.*

1. _____

2. _____

3. _____

4. _____

5. _____

6. _____

7. _____

Grammar Definitions

Regular Verbs: Regular verbs are verbs whose past tense is made by adding *-ed*.

> ***Examples:*** We always *chase* the dogs through the woods. (present)
> We *chased* the dogs through the woods yesterday. (past)
> They *skim* the fat off the top of the milk. (present)
> They *skimmed* the fat off the top of the milk. (past)

Irregular Verbs: Irregular verbs are verbs whose past tense is not made by using the *-ed* suffix. The past tenses of irregular verbs are made by changing to a different word or keeping the same word as present tense.

> ***Examples:*** I *choose* to take the bus to work. (present)
> I *chose* to take the bus to work. (past)
> We *cut* firewood every winter. (present)
> We *cut* firewood all day Saturday. (past)

Compound Subjects: Compound subjects are two or more subjects in an independent clause (a simple sentence). The sentence pattern often looks like this: SS–V (Two subjects before the verb).

> ***Examples:*** The <u>buyer</u> and the <u>seller</u> agreed upon a price.
> The <u>cat</u> and the <u>dog</u> chase the squirrels in the park.

Important points about compound subjects are on the next page.

Compound Verbs: Compound verbs are two or more verbs in an independent clause. If the verbs are action verbs, two *different* actions are done by the subject. **A verb phrase** is considered *one action* and, therefore, is *not* considered a compound verb.

> ***Examples:*** The sun <u>is shining</u> today. (not a compound verb)
> The sun <u>shines</u> and <u>brightens</u> up my day. (compound verb)

Simple Sentence Patterns: Four basic simple sentence patterns use combinations of compound subjects and compound verbs. The four patterns are S–V, SS–V, S–VV, and SS–VV.

> ***Examples:*** <u>Mark</u> <u>drives</u> to work.
> <u>Mark</u> and <u>Alice</u> <u>drive</u> to work.
> <u>Mark</u> <u>drives</u> to work and <u>parks</u> near the arcade.
> <u>Mark</u> and <u>Alice</u> <u>drive</u> to work and <u>park</u> in the garage.

Gerunds: Gerunds are *ing* words that work as nouns. Helping verbs do *not* come before gerunds. Gerunds are considered singular nouns.

> ***Examples:*** *Skinning* a chicken takes a lot of time.
> *Driving* to work is more convenient.
> You might consider *phoning* your grandmother.

Regular Verbs

Refer back to the exercises in which you added *-ed* suffixes to base words. All of the words with *-ed* suffixes are examples of regular verbs: The Three Sounds of *-ed* (page 57), Chapter 3 words (pages 58–60), and Chapter 4 words (pages 86–88).

Irregular Verbs

As a review, write the definition of **irregular verbs**:

_____

Anytime that you are unsure of the correct past tense of a verb, you can refer to a dictionary or to a spell checker with a dictionary. After the word entry, look for the abbreviation identifying the word as a verb. This abbreviation may be a *v.* or *vb.* Immediately following the abbreviation for a verb, you will find the past tense. Sometimes only the ending of the word with the *-ed* suffix is given. In some dictionaries, no past tense is given. If no past tense is given, an assumption is made **that you know that means the verb is regular and an *-ed* is needed to make the past tense.** If the verb is an irregular verb, or if a spelling change occurs, the first word immediately following the abbreviation for a verb will be the past tense.

> *Examples:* **insult (in-sult′)** *v.* -sulted
> **bat (băt)** *v.* batted
> **baste (bāst)** *v.* basted

If you are using a spell checker with a dictionary, look up the base word. Scroll to the point where you see *verb.* Immediately after the word *verb,* the past tense is given. Also notice that if you look up the **past tense** of a verb in a spell checker, it automatically gives you the base word. The words in past tense are not defined because they have the same meaning as the present tense verb except that the verb occurs in the past.

✎ PRACTICE

Write the past tense for the following irregular verbs. Use a dictionary or a spell checker with a dictionary if needed.

fit _____   hit _____   quit _____

swim _____   shake _____   drive _____

shine _____   spend _____   stick _____

catch _____   think _____   run _____

✎ **EXERCISE 4.6 Identifying Nouns and Verbs**

*For each of the words below, write **N** in the blank if the word can work as a **noun**. Write **V** in the blank if the word can work as a **verb**. Both N and V may be necessary for some words. Do not add any suffixes to the words when you determine the part of speech. You may use a dictionary or a spell checker with a dictionary to check your answers.*

base _____	baste _____	brake _____
bribe _____	change _____	face _____
fame _____	frame _____	fuse _____
grace _____	grate _____	hate _____
home _____	male _____	phone _____
place _____	pride _____	safe _____
scale _____	shade _____	shake _____
shame _____	shine _____	spice _____
spoke _____	stripe _____	taste _____
theme _____	use _____	waste _____

Sentence Writing

Use your own paper for this exercise. Select any ten words from the above exercise that can be both nouns and verbs. Use the format shown below. Begin by writing the word you selected. Then write one sentence that uses this word as a noun. Write a second sentence that uses the word as a verb. You may add suffixes to the words in your sentences. Underline the subject once and the verb twice. An example has been done for you.

1. base

(n.) The military base is located ten miles outside of town.

(v.) The judge based her opinion on a previous Supreme Court case.

Compound Subjects

When independent clauses (simple sentences) have compound subjects, **the subjects and the verbs must agree** in number. This means that singular subjects must have singular verbs, and plural subjects must have plural verbs.

Important Points About Compound Subjects

1. Compound subjects joined by the word *and* usually require a plural verb. Remember that **a plural verb in present tense means the verb does not have an *-s* or an *-es* suffix.**

   Correct: The *producer* and the *director* **live** in L.A. (*Live* is the plural verb.)

   Incorrect: The *producer* and the *director* **lives** in L.A. (*Lives* is a singular verb.)

2. When compound subjects are joined by the words *either . . . or* or *neither . . . nor*, the verb agrees with the subject closer to the verb. So, if the sentence is in present tense and the subject closer to the verb is singular, the verb will have an *-s* or an *-es*.

   Examples: Either Karen's *aunts* or her *mother has* the book.
   Neither the books nor the *movie tells* the true story.

   If the sentence is in present tense and the subject closer to the verb is plural, the verb will not have an *-s* or an *-es*.

   Examples: Either *Karen* or her *sisters have* the address book.
   Neither the *movie* nor the books *tell* the true story.

✎ **PRACTICE**

Read each sentence carefully. Mark the prepositional phrases. Remember that the subjects and the verbs will never be inside a prepositional phrase. Underline the subjects once. Circle the correct verb that agrees with the subject.

1. The plant manager and the plant supervisor (sends, send) memos to us weekly.

2. Neither the teachers nor the students on campus (wants, want) an increase in quarterly fees.

3. The compass and the dehydrated food packets (is, are) essential for our trip.

4. The scraps of lumber and the leftover shingles (works, work) well for kids' projects.

5. Three ships and one yacht (uses, use) this dock in the summer.

6. One yacht and three ships (uses, use) this dock in the summer.

7. Your gym locker and your hall locker (needs, need) to be cleaned out by Friday.

8. Either the plug or the hose (drips, drip).

9. Either the plugs or the hose (drips, drip).

10. Either the hose or the plugs (drips, drip).

Compound Verbs

When a sentence has compound action verbs, there will be **two separate actions** done by the subject. A sentence can also have two compound linking verbs.

Important Points About Compound Verbs

1. Compound verbs are usually linked together by the word *and*.

   My boss *opened* **and** *unpacked* the shipping crates.
   The swift river *smashed* against the rocks **and** *pounded* the few remaining docks.
   Stress *affects* mental health **and** *leads* to physical problems.

2. Compound verbs must be the same verb tense.

   Correct: The waitress *washed* her hands and *sliced* the onions.

   Incorrect: The waitress *washes* her hands and *sliced* the onions.

3. When a compound verb is in a verb phrase, the second verb may have an **understood helping verb.** In other words, when the second helping verb is the same as the first helping verb, it is not always stated, but it is understood to be a part of the verb phrase.

   Correct full form: The man *was washing* and *was waxing* his car.
   Correct short form: The man *was washing* and *waxing* his car.
   Incorrect: The man *washing* and *waxing* his car.
   (This would be a fragment, an incomplete sentence, because *ing* words working as verbs must have helping verbs before them.)

4. Even though a verb phrase consists of two words (a helping verb and a main verb), it should not be treated as two separate verbs or two separate actions. You will notice that the joining word *and* is not used in a verb phrase. A helpful reminder is that compound verbs frequently are joined by the word *and*.

   Example: The new managers *are requiring* changes. (This is n to a compound verb.)
   The new managers *are requiring* changes **and** *are expecting* rapid results.
   (Two separate actions occur. This is an example of compound verbs.)

✎ **PRACTICE**

Make the prepositional phrases. Underline the subject or subjects once. Underline the verbs twice.

1. The ranch hands went to the barn and fed the horses.

2. The robber admitted his guilt and apologized for the damage.

3. The committee of volunteers folded the newsletters and addressed the envelopes.

4. The map makers and the production workers worked all night and finally finished the project by dawn.

5. The women and their children organized the campaign and raised money for the homeless.

6. After the phone call, the president of the club called the board and scheduled a meeting.

7. Her nephew objected to the terms and requested a hearing in front of a judge.

8. The wind chimes on the patio chimed all night and disturbed the neighbors next door.

9. I will scrub and wax the floor in the kitchen.

10. Her wishes for peace and quiet on Sunday were honored and fulfilled.

Four Simple Sentence Patterns

The four basic simple sentence patterns show the subject–verb patterns of a sentence.

1. An **S–V** pattern means there is one subject and one verb in the independent clause.
2. An **SS–V** pattern shows a compound subject (two separate subjects) and one verb in the independent clause.
3. An **S–VV** pattern shows one subject with a compound verb (two separate verbs).
4. An **SS–VV** pattern shows both a compound subject and a compound verb.

Return to the sentences in the preceding numbered list. In the left margin, identify and write the sentence pattern that was used in the sentence. Write **S–V, SS–V, S–VV,** or **SS–VV.**

✎ EXERCISE 4.7 **Finding Subjects and Verbs**

Mark the prepositional phrases in the following sentences with parentheses. Then underline the subjects once and the verbs twice. Remember that verb infinitives will never be the verbs of the sentence. In the left margin, write the simple sentence pattern that was used (S–V, SS–V, S–VV, or SS–VV).

1. The rescue workers and the Coast Guard dragged the river for the sunken car.

2. Your predictions are bizarre and ridiculous.

3. For your own protection, you need to invest in mutual funds and in municipal bonds.

4. The logs by the riverbed rotted and started to float down the swollen river.

5. The initial plan was to surprise him with a going-away party.

6. Both of the women on the city council voted to support the room tax.

7. The fishermen and the fish plants were profiting from the longer fishing season.

8. The girls spent the day shopping and hanging out in the mall.

9. The swimming hole and the fishing docks are open to the public.

10. The flattest part of the desert heats up and becomes unbearable in the summer.

11. Her driver's permit and her credit card were found and turned in to the camp ranger.

12. The first transaction at the bank was processed within five minutes.

13. The cement was mixed and poured for the patio on Saturday.

14. During the race, the runner skinned her knees and pulled a tendon.

15. The toddler and his older brother threw a fit and tossed the groceries out of the cart.

16. Protecting the wildlife in the forests is the main goal of the non-profit organization.

17. Your commitment and dedication to the cause inspires many other people.

18. The fog rolled in from the ocean and shut down the airport.

19. The prize fighter quit boxing and started an acting career.

20. Running a marathon requires excellent conditioning and months of hard training.

Gerunds

Gerunds are *ing* words that work as nouns, not as verbs. A gerund is easy to identify by looking at the word or words that come before the *ing* word. If there are no helping verbs, the *ing* word is not a verb; it is a noun.

Gerunds are also easy to identify when they are the subject of the sentence. Notice how all the *ing* words in bold print below are the subjects of the sentences and name an activity or a process.

1. **Planning** the trip involved many details and required several hours of research.
2. **Perfecting** the formula took five years of hard work.
3. **Deferring** the payment of tuition can be done by contacting the finance office.
4. **Transplanting** the flower beds should occur during the dormant season.
5. **Quitting** my job was the best decision under the current circumstances.

✎ Practice

*Mark the word in bold print as a noun or a verb. Then mark the prepositional phrases with parentheses. Underline the subject or subjects and the verb or verbs. In the left margin, write the sentence pattern that is used (**S–V, SS–V, S–VV,** or **SS–VV**).*

1. She decided to try **tracing** around the pattern.

2. The mother hen was **protecting** her chicks.

3. The children wanted to go **swimming** in the river.

4. **Saddling** the wild horse was no easy task for the cowboy.

5. My sister was removing old pictures from the albums and **framing** them for her wall.

6. The loggers were **protesting** the new environmental laws.

7. **Humming** that same tune all day long is annoying.

8. **Loving** and nurturing a newborn create a strong bond between mother and child.

9. The amateurs and the professionals practiced **chipping** the balls to the green.

10. The English teacher was **quizzing** the students on the grammar rules.

11. The inspectors are **detecting** several problems with the design of the new house.

12. The subjects and the verbs in the sentences are **causing** you some problems.

✎ **EXERCISE 4.8 Sentence Writing**

On the following lines, add the -ing suffix to the words shown. First, use the ing *word as a gerund (noun) and as the subject of the sentence. Second, use the* ing *word as part of a verb phrase; you will need to add a helping verb. In both sentences, underline the subject once and the verb twice. In the left margin, write which of the four simple sentence patterns was used (**S–V, SS–V, S–VV,** or **SS–VV**). An example is done for you.*

1. run + ing = <u>running</u>
   S–V <u>Running</u> <u>is</u> one excellent way to stay in shape.
   S–V The <u>men</u> <u>were running</u> to catch the last train home.

2. waste + ing = _____

_____

_____

3. permit + ing = _____

_____

_____

4. compel + ing = _____

_____

_____

5. replace + ing = _____

_____

_____

6. exclude + ing = _____

_____

_____

7. scale + ing = _____

_____

_____

8. require + ing = _____

_____

_____

9. refuse + ing = _____

_____

_____

10. translate + ing = _____

_____

_____

Read each set of directions carefully. Write a sentence that follows the directions. You may need to add suffixes in order to fulfill the requirements of the sentence.

1. Use the word *confusion* in an **S–V** sentence in **past tense** without using a verb phrase.

_____

2. Use the word *swim* in **simple past tense** (no verb phrase) in an **SS–V** sentence.

_____

3. Use the word *bribe* as a **gerund** in an **S–V** sentence in **future tense.**

_____

4. Use the word *drive* in an **SS–VV** sentence in **present tense.**

_____

✎   **EXERCISE 4.9 Chapter Study Sheet**

In the right-hand column, write a definition for the term on the left. Practice reciting and learning this definition. Cover up the definition on the right. Recite the definition. Remove the paper to check your answers. Practice until you can define each term accurately.

Long Vowels

Final *E* Words

Soft *C*

Soft *G*

Final *E* Dropping Rule

Soft *C* and Soft *G* Rule

Regular Verbs

Irregular Verbs

Compound Subjects

Compound Verbs

**Four Simple
Sentence Patterns**

Gerunds

✎ **CHAPTER REVIEW**

Match the terms on the left with the definitions on the right. Each definition can be used only once.

_____ **1.** long vowels

_____ **2.** final *e* words

_____ **3.** soft *c*

_____ **4.** soft *g*

_____ **5.** Final *E* Dropping Rule

_____ **6.** Soft *C* and *G* Rule

_____ **7.** regular verbs

_____ **8.** irregular verbs

_____ **9.** compound subjects

_____ **10.** compound verbs

_____ **11.** independent clause

_____ **12.** simple sentence patterns

_____ **13.** gerunds

_____ **14.** exceptions to the soft *g* pattern

a. makes the sound of *ssss* when followed by an *e, i,* or *y*

b. verbs that use *-ed* to make the past tense

c. two or more verbs that agree with the subject(s) in an independent clause

d. verbs that do not use *-ed* for the past tense

e. *a, e, i, o,* and *u*

f. a group of words with a subject and a verb that forms a complete thought

g. the words *girl* and *gift*

h. S–V, SS–V, S–VV, SS–VV

i. any one-syllable or multi-syllable word that ends with an *e*

j. an *ing* word that is a noun, not a verb

k. makes the sound of *j* when followed by an *e, i,* or *y*

l. drop the *e* when you add a vowel suffix

m. two or more subjects in one independent clause

n. drop the *e* when a word ends in *ce* or *ge* only if the suffix you are adding begins with *e, i,* or *y*

Mark the Vowels

*Mark the vowels in the **base words** by using a short, curved line for **short vowels** and a long, straight line for **long vowels.***

finest	planed	matting	shining	notable	griping
spitting	filed	hoped	gripped	grimy	grimly

Add the following suffixes to the base words. Write the complete word on the line.

baste + ing = _____   fame + ous = _____

place + ment = _____   paste + y = _____

shake + y = _____   slice + er = _____

change + ing = _____   age + less = _____

mute + ual = _____   shine + y = _____

spice + y = _____   use + less = _____

Circle the groups of letters that can work as suffixes.

y   able   age   ous   lly   ness

less   ual   es   ex   meant   ment

Circle the prefixes and the suffixes. Write the base or the root of the word on the line.

receding _____   requirement _____

undisputed _____   infamous _____

resuming _____   excluding _____

bribery _____   contractual _____

replaceable _____   exchanging _____

Use each of the following roots to form a real word. Write the word on the line.

clude _____   mote _____

plete _____   pute _____

quire _____   vise _____

*Each of the following sentences is written in present tense. Above each verb, write the **past tense** of that verb. In the left margin, tell the **simple sentence pattern** that is used.*

1. The children swim and dive at the YMCA pool.

2. The housekeeper shakes the rugs and hits them with a broom to remove the dirt.

3. Bob and Mike flatten the shipping crates and store them in the warehouse.

4. The student quits talking and begins writing.

5. They drive to the mountains and camp near a babbling brook.

Mark the prepositional phrases. Underline the subjects once and the verbs twice.

1. Cramming all the homework into three hours was not very wise.

2. The model plane is propelled by a remote control.

3. Compassionate people are saddened by the number of problems in today's world.

4. Committing oneself to another person through marriage is a major decision to make.

5. Profiting from the hardships of others brings guilt feelings to most people.

Write the following kinds of sentences.

1. Write a sentence with compound subjects.

_____

2. Write a sentence with compound verbs.

_____

3. Write an S–V sentence that uses a gerund.

_____

4. Write a sentence that has an SS–VV pattern.

_____

JOURNAL WRITING ASSIGNMENT

Topic: Grading on Writing Skills

Writing across the curriculum is a concept that is practiced on many college and university campuses. The concept basically supports the notion that writing skills are important and should be included in as many courses as possible. This concept does not support the belief that writing skills should be assessed in only English or writing classes.

In your journal, discuss the topic of writing across the curriculum. What would be the advantages of having all teachers in all subjects grade you on your writing skills? What would be the disadvantages? How would you feel if a science or a math instructor reduced your grade for spelling errors or incorrect grammar? What seems fair to you? What classes other than English or writing class require you to write paragraphs, essays, or research papers?

PARAGRAPH WRITING ASSIGNMENT

Topic: My Talent or Skill

Everyone has a talent or a skill in some area of life. Perhaps your talent shows up in specific courses, or perhaps your talent shows up in a hobby or participation in a specific group or organization. Write a first draft of a paragraph that tells about one of your talents or skills. Then edit and revise your paragraph by checking the points that were listed in Chapter 3 on page 82.

Here are a few suggestions to consider when you write your paragraph:

1. Identify your talent or your skill in the first sentence.

2. Tell when you first began developing this skill or talent.

3. Describe the process you went through to improve and refine this talent or skill.

4. Explain how you use your talent or skill at this time in your life.

FIVE

Long-Vowel Words with Vowel Digraphs

The topics in this chapter include the following:

- Long-vowel patterns made with vowel digraphs
- Introduction to homonyms
- The Vowel + *Y* Rule
- The *-able* and *-ible* suffixes
- Introduction to compound sentences, coordinating conjunctions, conjunctive adverbs, and the semicolon
- Introduction to the run-on sentence error and the comma splice error

Spelling Definitions

Vowel Digraphs: Vowel digraphs are long-vowel patterns made when two vowels are together and the first vowel is long (says its alphabet name) and the second vowel is silent.

Long A	Long E	Long I	Long O	Long U
ai (m**ai**n)	**ea** (s**ea**)	**ie** (p**ie**)	**oa** (b**oa**t)	**ue** (h**ue**)
ay (st**ay**)	**ee** (tr**ee**)		**oe** (t**oe**)	
	ey (k**ey**)		**ou** (s**ou**l)	
			ow (thr**ow**)	

Special Notes:

1. The letter *w* works as a vowel in the vowel digraph *ow*. The *o* is long, and the *w* is silent.
2. In addition to being vowel digraphs, the following vowel combinations have one or more additional sounds:

   ea (ĕ) l**ea**ther   **ea (ā)** st**ea**k   **ie (ē)** br**ie**f
   ei (ā) w**ei**gh   **ue (oo)** bl**ue**

   The two other sounds of *ea* will be discussed in this chapter.
   The other sounds of *ie* will be discussed in Chapter 6.
   The *ue* with the *oo* sound will be discussed in Chapter 8.

3. There are no rules to tell when to use the different long-vowel patterns. Instead, sight spelling is often used. Words are memorized and then "visually checked" to see if the word "looks right."

Homonyms: Homonyms are words that sound the same but have different spellings and different meanings.

Examples: mane—main   see—sea   meet—meat

Spelling Rule

Vowel & *Y* Rule: When words end with a vowel + *y*, add the suffixes without making any spelling changes to the word.

Examples: stay + ing = staying   key + ed = keyed

Words—Beginning with the Basics

1. Say the word slowly. Pay attention to the long-vowel sound. Write the word on the practice line.
2. Identify the vowel digraph and write it on the line.

3. Add any suffix to the word. Remember to simply attach the suffix to words that end in **vowel** + *y* without making any spelling changes. Write an **X** if no suffix can be added to the word.

✎ **PRACTICE**

Word	Practice	Vowel Digraph	Add Any Suffix
1. braid	_____	_____	_____
2. brain	_____	_____	_____
3. claim	_____	_____	_____
4. faith	_____	_____	_____
5. paid	_____	_____	_____
6. paint	_____	_____	_____
7. raise	_____	_____	_____
8. sprain	_____	_____	_____
9. lay	_____	_____	_____
10. pay	_____	_____	_____
11. play	_____	_____	_____
12. spray	_____	_____	_____
13. breeze	_____	_____	_____
14. feel	_____	_____	_____
15. freeze	_____	_____	_____
16. greet	_____	_____	_____
17. keep	_____	_____	_____
18. sneeze	_____	_____	_____
19. speech	_____	_____	_____
20. bleach	_____	_____	_____
21. cheap	_____	_____	_____
22. clean	_____	_____	_____
23. deal	_____	_____	_____

Word	Practice	Vowel Digraph	Add Any Suffix
24. each	_____	_____	_____
25. ease	_____	_____	_____
26. grease	_____	_____	_____
27. lease	_____	_____	_____
28. peach	_____	_____	_____
29. please	_____	_____	_____
30. reach	_____	_____	_____
31. scream	_____	_____	_____
32. speak	_____	_____	_____
33. teach	_____	_____	_____
34. alley	_____	_____	_____
35. chimney	_____	_____	_____
36. honey	_____	_____	_____
37. money	_____	_____	_____
38. valley	_____	_____	_____
39. coach	_____	_____	_____
40. hoax	_____	_____	_____
41. oath	_____	_____	_____
42. poultry	_____	_____	_____
43. though	_____	_____	_____
44. soul	_____	_____	_____
45. follow	_____	_____	_____
46. grow	_____	_____	_____
47. owe	_____	_____	_____
48. throw	_____	_____	_____
49. issue	_____	_____	_____
50. rescue	_____	_____	_____

Taking a Closer Look at Specific Words: *Lay* and *Lie*

The words *lay* and *lie* are sometimes confused. *Lay* means to "put," "place," or "prepare." It always has a direct object, which means that a noun will follow the verb. (This is called a **transitive** verb.) The noun is the item that is put, placed, or prepared. *Lay* is an irregular verb. The past tense is *laid*. The *ing* form is *laying*.

> The mother *lays* the infant in the crib for naps. (present tense)
>
> The mother *laid* the infant in the crib for a nap. (past tense)
>
> Our hen *lays* eggs every day. (present tense)
>
> Our hen *laid* only two eggs. (past tense)
>
> The workers *lay* a solid, concrete foundation. (present tense)
>
> The workers *laid* a solid, concrete foundation. (past tense)
>
> The children *were laying* rocks on the railing. (verb phrase)

In each example above, the verb means to "put," "place," or "prepare." The direct objects are *infant, eggs, foundation,* and *rocks.*

Lie means to "recline as to rest" or "be situated or located." *Lie* does not have a direct object. (This is called an **intransitive verb.**) *Lie* is also an irregular verb. The past tense is *lay,* and the *ing* form is spelled *lying.*

> I *lie* down on the sofa every day to watch soap operas. (present tense)
>
> I *lay* down and fell asleep. (past tense)
>
> The campground *lies* between Monterey and San Francisco. (present tense)
>
> The campgrounds originally *lay* between two freeways. (past tense)
>
> The campers *were lying* in the tent to escape the rain. (verb phrase)

✎ PRACTICE

Write lay *or* lie *in the following sentences that are written in present tense. When the subject is singular, you will need to add* -s.

1. Maria always _____ her books on the kitchen table.

2. I always _____ too many logs on the fire.

3. The kittens _____ in the sun to nap.

4. In the afternoons, I _____ in the shade of the oak tree.

5. My grandmother always _____ a beautiful table for Thanksgiving.

6. We _____ boards over the muddy spots in the garden beds.

7. Uncle Ray _____ on the couch every day after work.

8. The baby _____ quietly in his father's arms.

9. The attendant _____ a gentle hand on patients' shoulders to calm them.

10. The crew _____ cable lines only during the weekdays.

11. The dog _____ on the rug next to the back door.

12. The congregation _____ the man to rest in the cemetery.

13. My father _____ down the law for our whole family to follow.

14. _____ your worries aside.

15. The men _____ low and hope they won't be noticed.

16. We often _____ in the field to look at the stars.

*In the left-hand margin, now write the **past tense** for each of the sentences above.*

✎ EXERCISE 5.1 **Working with Vowel Digraphs**

1. The vowel digraphs ea *and* ee *sometimes cause spelling problems. There are no rules to tell when to use* ea *or* ee. *Sometimes it is helpful to write a word with both vowel digraphs to see which word* looks *correct. This makes use of your* **sight spelling** *skills. Of course, if you are not familiar with a specific word, the sight spelling approach will not help. A dictionary or an electronic spell checker can be used to check which vowel digraph is correct.*

In the following words, write ea *or* ee *to make a real word. There are no homonyms in this list, so only one of the options will be correct.*

f_____l   r_____ch   sp_____k   sp_____ch

sn_____ze   bl_____ch   _____se   scr_____m

d_____l   cl_____n   l_____se   br_____ze

2. *As a review, write the* **ES Rule:** _____

_____

Apply the rule to the following words. Add the suffix -s *or* -es *to the following words.*

braid_____   faith_____   spray_____   speech_____

clean_____   peach_____   reach_____   teach_____

alley_____   hoax_____   rescue_____   oath_____

3. *As a review, write the* **Final E Dropping Rule:** _____

_____

Add the following suffix to these words. Write the complete word on the line.

owe + ing = _____   breeze + y = _____

freeze + er = _____   ease + y = _____

issue + ing = _____   ease + ment = _____

*4. Write the **Vowel + Y Rule:** _____*

_____

add the suffixes to the following words. Write the complete word on the line.

pay + ing = _____   *play + ed =* _____

spray + ed = _____   *play + er =* _____

lay + ing = _____   *pay + ment =* _____

chimney + s = _____   *spray + er =* _____

5. The following verbs are **irregular verbs.** Write the past tense of each verb.
   You may use a dictionary or an electronic spell checker with a dictionary.

lay _____   pay _____

feel _____   freeze _____

deal _____   speak _____

grow _____   throw _____

keep _____   teach _____

6. There are nine words in the list on pages 115–116 that are multi-syllable
   words. Write the nine words below.

_____   _____   _____

_____   _____   _____

_____   _____   _____

Working with Homonyms

As a review, write the definition of **homonyms:** _____

_____

Many homonyms exist because two or more vowel patterns make the same sound. Notice the shift in the vowel patterns below.

Long Vowel with Final *E*—Vowel Digraphs

gate—gait	made—maid	male—mail	mane—main
waste—waist	wave—waive	lone—loan	rode—road, rowed
pane—pain	bored—board	sole—soul	pare—pair, pear

Vowel Digraph—Vowel Digraph

praise—prays, preys	flee—flea	heel—heal
peek—peak	beech—beach	beet—beat
deer—dear	week—weak	meet—meat
reel—real		

Other Vowel Combinations

wait—weight	way—weigh	doe—dough
die—dye	coarse—course	break—brake
grate—great	straight—strait	lie—lye

✎ **PRACTICE**

Parts of the following assignment may be assigned to individual partners or groups to complete and then report back to the class.
*The following sentences show **homonyms** in bold print. Look how the word is working in the sentence. Write **N** in the blank if the word is working as a **noun**. Write **V** in the blank if the word is working as a **verb.** If the word is not a noun or a verb, it is working as an **adjective** to describe a noun. Write **A** for **adjective**. In the right-hand column, write an informal definition of any of the word meanings that are unfamiliar to you.*

Part of Speech   **Sentence**   **Informal Definition**

Part 1

_____ **1.**   Please close the **gate.**

_____ **2.**   The horse's **gait** was graceful.

_____ **3.**   She **made** the beds.

_____ **4.**   I worked as a **maid** for a year.

_____ **5.**   The suspect was a **male.**

_____ **6.**   I will **mail** you the information.

_____ **7.**   The **mail** truck needs new tires.

Part of Speech	Sentence	Informal Definition

_____ **8.** The **mail** is placed in my box.

_____ **9.** The lion's **mane** was matted.

_____ **10.** The water **main** broke on Sunday.

Part 2

_____ **11.** Underline the **main** idea.

_____ **12.** They **waste** too much food.

_____ **13.** Toxic **waste** is dangerous.

_____ **14.** The **waste** disposal site is closed.

_____ **15.** Your **waist** is so small.

_____ **16.** The perm will add a **wave** to your hair.

_____ **17.** The **waves** smash against the rocks.

_____ **18.** We always **wave** good-bye at the airport.

_____ **19.** She **waived** her rights to an attorney.

_____ **20.** The **lone** tree stood on the hill.

Part 3

_____ **21.** I took out a **loan** from the bank.

_____ **22.** We **rode** the train to New York.

_____ **23.** The **road** crew was hired.

_____ **24.** I live on a rocky **road.**

_____ **25.** The **road** to success is bumpy.

_____ **26.** The boys **rowed** across the lake.

_____ **27.** I need to replace the window **pane.**

_____ **28.** The runner felt some **pain** in his calf.

_____ **29.** The movie **bored** me.

_____ **30.** The **bored** audience did not applaud.

Part 4

_____ **31.** We **bored** holes through the wood.

_____ **32.** The Johnsons **board** their horse here.

Part of Speech	Sentence	Informal Definition

_____ **33.**   The student pays me for room and **board.**

_____ **34.**   The neighbors all **board** their windows during hurricanes.

_____ **35.**   You can **board** the 6 o'clock plane.

_____ **36.**   He cut the **board** in half.

_____ **37.**   He resigned his position on the school **board.**

_____ **38.**   We ate **sole,** rice, and black beans for dinner.

_____ **39.**   The **sole** survivor gave an interview.

_____ **40.**   The **sole** on my shoe is very worn.

Part 5

_____ **41.**   She is a very kind **soul.**

_____ **42.**   Motown is the largest producer of **soul** music.

_____ **43.**   The priests pray for the **souls** of others.

_____ **44.**   We need to **pare** down our monthly expenses.

_____ **45.**   We **pare** the apples to make apple pies.

_____ **46.**   The dancers were **paired** based on their heights.

_____ **47.**   I lost my favorite **pair** of socks.

_____ **48.**   She loves **pear** jam.

_____ **49.**   The farmer harvested the **pears.**

_____ **50.**   The **pear** tree grew in the backyard.

Part 6

Use a spell checker or a dictionary to identify the parts of speech for each of the following homonyms. To the right of each word, write a concise definition.

_____ **51.**   **praise**

_____ **52.**   **prays**

_____ **53.**   **preys**

_____ **54.**   **flee**

_____ **55.**   **flea**

Part of Speech   **Informal Definition**

_____ 56.   **heel**

_____ 57.   **heal**

_____ 58.   **peek**

_____ 59.   **peak**

_____ 60.   **beech**

Part 7

_____ 61.   **beach**

_____ 62.   **beet**

_____ 63.   **beat**

_____ 64.   **deer**

_____ 65.   **dear**

_____ 66.   **week**

_____ 67.   **weak**

_____ 68.   **meet**

_____ 69.   **meat**

_____ 70.   **reel**

Part 8

The following sentences show **homonyms** in bold print. Look at how the word is working in the sentence. Write **N** in the blank if the word is working as a **noun**. Write **V** in the blank if the word is working as a **verb**. If the word is not a noun or a verb, it is working as an **adjective** to describe a noun. Write **A** for **adjective**. In the right-hand column, write an informal definition of any of the word meanings that are unfamiliar to you.

_____ 71.   The story was a **real** life situation.

_____ 72.   I wanted to be a **real** estate broker.

_____ 73.   We had a very long **wait** in the doctor's office.

_____ 74.   The children **wait** at the corner for the bus.

_____ 75.   There was too much **weight** in the plane.

_____ 76.   My friends know the **way** to the pond.

Part of Speech	Sentence	Informal Definition

_____ **77.**   The postmasters **weigh** each package.

_____ **78.**   We saw the **doe** in the field.

_____ **79.**   Cookie **dough** can be very sweet.

_____ **80.**   I rolled the **die** on the game board.

Part 9

_____ **81.**   Your flowers will **die** without water.

_____ **82.**   A **die** was used to cut the metal pieces.

_____ **83.**   This red **dye** will run.

_____ **84.**   We **dye** T-shirts and then sell them.

_____ **85.**   The **coarse** fabric will not work.

_____ **86.**   The last **course** was dessert.

_____ **87.**   They took a first aid **course**.

_____ **88.**   The lawyer chose a drastic **course** of action.

_____ **89.**   This rope will **break.**

_____ **90.**   The **break** will heal in five weeks.

Part 10

_____ **91.**   You got a lucky **break.**

_____ **92.**   They get a fifteen-minute coffee **break** at ten o'clock.

_____ **93.**   The game was interrupted for a commercial **break.**

_____ **94.**   There was a three-day **break** in cable service.

_____ **95.**   He did not **brake** in time.

_____ **96.**   I need new **brakes.**

_____ **97.**   The chef **grates** the onions first.

_____ **98.**   My watch fell through the **grate.**

_____ **99.**   Acts of deception really **grate** on my nerves.

_____ **100.** My **great** aunt will turn ninety.

Part of Speech   **Sentence**   **Informal Definition**
Part 11

———— **101.**   You have a **great** idea.

———— **102.**   Draw a **straight** line right here.

———— **103.**   I just wanted a **straight** answer from him.

———— **104.**   He won the poker game with a **straight** flush.

———— **105.**   The freighters moved through the **strait** on a daily basis.

———— **106.**   The eviction left the family in desperate **straits.**

———— **107.**   I needed to **lie** down on my own bed.

———— **108.**   The golfer had a poor **lie** on that shot.

———— **109.**   The child did not tell a **lie** to her teacher.

———— **110.**   The writer **lies** about his past.

✎ **EXERCISE 5.2 Sentence Work with Homonyms**

Circle the correct homonym inside the parentheses for each sentence. Refer back to pages 121–126, and use a dictionary or an electronic spell checker with a dictionary if needed.

1. The jockey (road, rode) the prize-winning racehorse to (gait, gate) three.

2. Using tact is one (weigh, way) to avoid making (waives, waves) at the meeting.

3. (Prays, Praise, Preys) is given to teach a dog to (heal, heel).

4. A short (break, brake) will be given between the two (main, mane) keynote speakers.

5. Hundreds of refugees tried to (flea, flee) across the border during the (peek, peak) of the war.

6. The (beat, beet) of the music could be heard all along the (beech, beach).

7. Several sailors (dye, die) each year trying to maneuver through the (straight, strait).

8. The (break, brake) in your fibula will take about ten (weeks, weaks) to (heel, heal).

9. The president of the (bored, board) has reached the (peek, peak) of his career.

10. A (straight, strait) (coarse, course) is the quickest way to your destination.

11. The old movie (real, reel) was a (waist, waste) of my money.

12. The reporter wanted a (peak, peek) at the executive officer's bank (loan, lone) files.

13. The (loan, lone) survivor had lost a (grate, great) deal of (wait, weight).

14. That (great, grate) writer was a (deer, dear) friend of my sister.

15. Our manager decided to (wave, waive) the deposit for room and (bored, board).

16. Your decision to invest in the televised (course, coarse) carried a lot of (wait, weight).

17. On our farm, we never (waist, waste) the nuts from the (beach, beech) trees.

18. The climbers vowed to (meat, meet) on the top of the mountain (peak, peek).

19. Competing in the upcoming track (meet, meat) is one way to (break, brake) the record.

20. The customers had to (wait, weight) an hour for the (mane, main) (coarse, course).

21. Unfortunately, many people (waist, waste) the (heel, heal) of the bread.

22. They (board, bored) a tunnel in an attempt to (flea, flee) from the guards.

23. The aluminum (dye, die) is too (weak, week) and will (break, brake).

24. The tailor (maid, made) the (waist, waste) on the tuxedo too small.

25. The stained-glass window (pain, pane) is very (deer, dear) to me.

26. In the soap opera last (weak, week), Karen loved Brian with all her heart and (sole, soul).

27. Marsha used the dull (paring, pairing) knife to peel the (beats, beets).

28. The (pare, pear, pair) of seagulls landed on the iron (gait, gate).

29. Roberto (weighs, ways) the significance of being the (soul, sole) heir of the estate.

30. The packing plant (waits, weights) for the troller to bring in fresh (soul, sole) and salmon.

31. The (bored, board) ordered all managers to (pair, pare) their budgets by twenty percent.

32. Cindy wants to (brake, break) her unlucky streak by using her new fishing (real, reel).

33. The (course, coarse) of the night changed with one roll of the (die, dye).

34. The new collar causes (flees, fleas) to (die, dye) within a few hours.

35. Willy's (wait, weight) and the size of his (waste, waist) were the source of many jokes.

36. You will need to (wait, weight) for the fifty-pound (waits, weights).

37. The (lone, loan) coyote is (praying, preying) on the farmer's chickens and ruining the garden.

38. The (soul, sole) survivor gave a lot of (prays, praise) to the Coast Guard rescue crew.

*Return to the thirty-eight homonym sentences in Exercise 5.2. Underline the
subjects once and the verbs twice. Place parentheses around prepositional
phrases and brackets around verb infinitives.*

Building Words

> **New Prefixes:** *im-   e-*
>
> The prefix *im-* means **not, in,** or **into.**
> The prefix *e-* means **former, out,** or **away from.**
>
> **New Suffixes:** *-able   -ible*
>
> The suffix *-able* means **able to** or **capable of.** (See Chapter 3.)
> The suffix *-ible* means **able to** or **capable of.**

✎ PRACTICE

Add the new prefixes to each of the following words.

e-	*im-*
_____ late	_____ press
_____ mit	_____ plant
_____ vict	_____ print

Circle the prefixes and suffixes in the following words. Write the base word or the root on the line.

impairment _____   elections _____

ejected _____   resistible _____

impelling _____   permissible _____

emission _____   imperfect _____

admissible _____   incurable _____

The Suffixes *-able* and *-ible*

The suffixes *-able* and *-ible* have the same meanings, the same pronunciations, and the same function. Both suffixes turn words into **adjectives,** words that describe or modify nouns. (Adjectives are discussed in greater detail in the next chapter.) Both suffixes basically mean "able to" or "capable of."

Read the following words. Notice how the suffixes *-able* and *-ible* do not sound the same as the word *able*. Instead, these suffixes sound like *a bull*.

lovable   stretchable   permissible   visible

Guidelines, Not Rules

There are no rules that work consistently to help you determine if a word needs an *-able* or an *-ible* suffix. However, the following **guidelines** provide you with several "patterns" that will help you increase your odds for selecting the correct suffix spelling.

1. The suffix *-able* is most often used on the end of **base words** (full words). Remove the prefixes and suffixes of the word to which you want to add the *-able* or the *-ible* suffix. If the "starting point" (without prefixes and suffixes) is a real word, use *-able*.

   re**print** = re**print**able   **like** = **lik**able   **change** = **change**able

   Note: Remember to use the Final *E* Dropping Rule when the base word ends in *e* or the Soft *C* and *G* Rule when the base word ends in *ce* or *ge*.

   Exceptions: You will encounter some exceptions to the above pattern. For example, *force* is a base word. However, the *-ible* suffix is used: *forcible*. *Sensible* and *combustible* are two additional exceptions.

2. Base words and roots that end in *ss* tend to use the *-ible* suffix.

   ac**cess**ible   trans**miss**ible   ad**miss**ible

3. The suffix *-ible* is most *often* used when the "starting point" is a root (a non-word base). Be sure to analyze the "starting point" by removing the prefixes from the word.

   de**struct** = de**struct**ible   pro**duce** = pro**duc**ible

   Exceptions: You will encounter some exceptions to the above pattern. For example, in the word *predict*, the root is *dict*. In the word *detect*, the root is *tect*. However, both words use the *-able* suffix: *predictable* and *detectable*.

4. One other guideline can be used to help you determine which suffix to use. The *-ion* suffix and the *-ible* suffix have a language connection. If you can add the *-ion* suffix to make a real word, then most of the time you will be able to use the *-ible* suffix.

   Notice how the words that cannot use an *-ion* suffix tend to use the *-able* suffix. Because this a pattern, not a rule, you will find that this pattern does not work consistently. You will encounter exceptions (*sensible, producible*).

Original Word	**Possible with -ion?**	**-ion = ible**	**No -ion = able**
compress	compression	compressible	
exchange	**no**		exchangeable
replace	**no**		replaceable
destruct	destruction	destructible	
transmit	**no**		transmittable

The above guidelines provide you with some strategies for selecting the *-able* or the *-ible* suffix. However, because there are numerous exceptions, you may want to write the word with *both suffixes* and then use your *sight spelling skills* by deciding if one *looks correct* based on familiarity with the word. An electronic spell checker or a dictionary can be consulted for the correct spelling when in doubt. Note that the word with the *-able* or the *-ible* suffix may not be an entry in the dictionary. In such cases, look up the main word without the suffix. After the definitions are given, **word derivatives** (words from that word family but with different suffixes) follow the definitions. Look for the derivative with the *-able* or the *-ible* suffix.

✏️ **PRACTICE**

Add -able *or* -ible *to the following words. Then write the complete word on the line.*

exchange + _____ = _____

retrace + _____ = _____

cure + _____ = _____

replace + _____ = _____

distract + _____ = _____

cape + _____ = _____

prefer + _____ = _____

reduce + _____ = _____

read + _____ = _____

compress + _____ = _____

-ably and -ibly

As a review, write the **Final *E* Dropping Rule:** _____

_____

The suffix -*y* can be added to words that end in the suffix -*able* or -*ible*. The Final *E* Dropping Rule needs to be applied since the suffix -*y* is a vowel suffix. Here are some examples:

vise + ible + y = visibly

possible + y = possibly

note + able + y = notably

horrible + y = horribly

terrible + y = terribly

reason + able + y = reasonably

✎ **EXERCISE 5.3 Building Words Using Word Bases, Roots, Prefixes, and Suffixes**

The base word or the root is shown in bold print. Add the prefixes and the suffixes. Write the complete word with all the word parts on the line. Remember to check the word carefully to see if it needs the First or the Second CVC Doubling Rule, the Final E Dropping Rule, or the Soft C and G Rule before the suffix is added.

1. **faith** + ful + ly = _____
2. **freeze** + er + s = _____
3. **bleach** + er + s = _____
4. dis + **please** + ing = _____
5. un + **teach** + able = _____
6. un + **reason** + able = _____
7. un + **break** + able = _____
8. **sweat** + er + s = _____
9. **weight** + less + ness = _____
10. **grease** + less = _____
11. **breeze** + y = _____
12. un + pre + **pare** + ed = _____
13. im + per + **miss** + ible = _____
14. re + pro + **duce** + ible = _____
15. e + **mit** + ing = _____
16. im + **press** + ion = _____
17. e + **miss** + ion = _____
18. un + pre + **dict** + able = _____
19. **grease** + y = _____
20. un + **speak** + able = _____

21. re + **pay** + ing = _____
22. **speech** + less = _____
23. im + **peach** + ment = _____
24. un + **reach** + able = _____
25. **deaf** + en + ing = _____
26. **threat** + en + ing = _____
27. **breath** + less + ly = _____
28. in + de + **struct** + ible = _____
29. **pay** + able = _____
30. **soul** + ful = _____
31. re + **pair** + ed = _____
32. in + **cure** + able = _____
33. un + **trace** + able = _____
34. ex + **pel** + ing = _____
35. **rescue** + ing = _____
36. im + **pel** + ing = _____
37. im + per + **miss** + ible = _____
38. im + per + **fect** + ion + s = _____
39. un + **ease** + y = _____
40. **sole** + ly = _____

✎ **EXERCISE 5.4 Word List Expansion**

*In addition to the **long e** sound,* ea *can also make the sound of a **short e** or a* **long a**. *A hierarchy of the* ea *sounds looks like this:*

$$ea$$
$$\downarrow \;\downarrow\; \downarrow$$
$$\bar{e} \quad \breve{e} \quad \bar{a}$$

(bēan) (brĕad) (stēak)

Read each of the words below. Circle the sound made by the ea *combination.*

1. beacon	ēa	ĕ	ā	**15.** weather	ēa	ĕ	ā
2. thread	ēa	ĕ	ā	**16.** eager	ēa	ĕ	ā
3. eagle	ēa	ĕ	ā	**17.** steak	ēa	ĕ	ā
4. deaf	ēa	ĕ	ā	**18.** feather	ēa	ĕ	ā
5. deal	ēa	ĕ	ā	**19.** dealt	ēa	ĕ	ā
6. read	ēa	ĕ	ā	**20.** steady	ēa	ĕ	ā
7. leader	ēa	ĕ	ā	**21.** jealous	ēa	ĕ	ā
8. bread	ēa	ĕ	ā	**22.** break	ēa	ĕ	ā
9. great	ēa	ĕ	ā	**23.** spread	ēa	ĕ	ā
10. instead	ēa	ĕ	ā	**24.** breath	ēa	ĕ	ā
11. heavy	ēa	ĕ	ā	**25.** measles	ēa	ĕ	ā
12. reason	ēa	ĕ	ā	**26.** meadow	ēa	ĕ	ā
13. queasy	ēa	ĕ	ā	**27.** ready	ēa	ĕ	ā
14. threat	ēa	ĕ	ā	**28.** sweat	ēa	ĕ	ā

Note: There are no "rules" to tell you when to use ea *to make a long e sound, a short e sound, or a long a sound. For that reason, many of these words are learned as **sight words**.*

Partner Activity

Each partner selects any ten words from the ea *list above. Say the word for your partner to spell out loud without the use of paper or pencil. Then reverse roles so that each partner has the opportunity to spell out loud. Remember, the consonant sounds are predictable; the vowels used are* ea.

✎ EXERCISE 5.5 **Sentence Writing**

Write ten sentences that use the words from the list on pages 115–116. Each sentence must include two words from the word list. Circle the words from the word list that you use.

1. _____

2. _____

3. _____

4. _____

5. _____

6. _____

7. _____

8. _____

9. _____

10. _____

Write a sentence that correctly uses each of the following words as verbs.

lay (present tense) _____

laying _____

laid _____

lie _____

lying _____

lay (past tense) _____

*Write your own sentences using the following homonyms. In the left margin, write **N** if the homonym is working as a **noun** and **V** if the homonym is working as a **verb**.*

1. gait _____

2. brake _____

3. dyes _____

4. bored _____

5. loan _____

6. heal _____

7. peek _____

8. grate _____

9. dough _____

10. beets _____

11. preys _____

12. waste _____

13. pare _____

14. sole _____

15. reel _____

Select any four additional homonyms from page 121. Use them in sentences below.

1. _____

2. _____

3. _____

4. _____

Grammar Definitions

Independent Clause: An independent clause is a group of words that has a subject and a verb, and forms a complete thought. A single independent clause is also called a **simple sentence.**

Compound Sentence: A compound sentence is a sentence that contains two or more independent clauses and no dependent clauses. (Dependent clauses will be discussed in Chapter 8.)

Important points about compound sentences:

1. Each independent clause will have its own subject, verb, and complete thought.

2. Compound sentences consist of two or more simple sentences joined together by one of these three methods:

   a. a comma and a coordinating conjunction between the independent clauses:
   The driver jumped up and down, **and** he screamed for help.

   b. a semicolon between two independent clauses:
   The driver jumped up and down; he screamed for help.

   c. a semicolon and a conjunctive adverb and a comma between the independent clauses:
   The driver jumped up and down; **also,** he screamed for help.

Coordinating Conjunctions: Coordinating conjunctions are words that are used to join words, phrases or clauses. There are seven coordinating conjunctions: *for, and, nor, but, or, yet,* and *so.*

FAN BOYS: FAN BOYS is a mnemonic or memory trick to remember the seven coordinating conjunctions. Each letter of the words represents one of the coordinating conjunctions:

For, And, Nor, But, Or, Yet, So

Semicolon: The semicolon is a punctuation mark used to separate two independent clauses when a coordinating conjunction is not used:

The dancer was distracted. She missed her cue.

The dancer was distracted; she missed her cue.

Conjunctive Adverb: Conjunctive adverbs are words that connect the idea of one independent clause to the idea in a second independent clause.

Conjunctive adverbs assist the reader in seeing the connection between the two simple sentences that are being linked together:

The dancer was distracted; **consequently,** she missed her cue.

The dancer was distracted; **therefore,** she missed her cue.

Using Coordinating Conjunctions (FAN BOYS)

The seven **coordinating conjunctions** join two simple sentences that are equal in ranking. Become familiar with the different meanings of each of the following coordinating conjunctions so that you can use them correctly to link two simple sentences together.

for *For* means "because," the reason or the cause for something. *For* shows a consequence or a result.

and *And* means "in addition to" or "along with." *And* shows inclusion, similarities, or addition.

nor *Nor* means "not" or "the opposite." *Nor* shows an exclusion or a negative direction.

Note: When the coordinating conjunction *nor* is used, the subject and verb pattern in the second independent clause are often inverted. Notice how the S–V pattern is turned around or inverted:
    The hoax was not appreciated, nor <u>was</u> it legal.

but *But* means "except, however," or "just the opposite." *But* shows a contrast, a difference, or a reversed idea.

or *Or* means "an opposite idea." *Or* shows a choice between equal ideas.

yet *Yet* means "however" or "nevertheless." *Yet* shows a contrast between two ideas.

so *So* means "therefore, in order that," or "as a result." *So* shows a cause and effect or a specific condition.

Adding a Coordinating Conjunction

PRACTICE

Write a compound sentence by joining the two independent clauses together with a coordinating conjunction. Remember to use a comma before the coordinating conjunction. *The sentence pattern will look like this:*

| S–V | , *coordinating conjunction* | S–V. |

1. The gas tank was empty. She had to take the next exit.

_____

2. Manuel washed his car in the morning. He vacuumed and polished the inside.

_____

3. The whole week was cold and gloomy. They decided not to go camping.

_____

4. I asked my son to stop at the store. He has a short memory.

_____

5. She feared the worst. Her mother had been very sick.

_____

6. The soles of his feet were blistered. His whole body ached.

_____

7. I remembered to file the claim. I forgot to call the police.

_____

8. The director approved the first draft. She rejected the second draft.

_____

9. You may accept the contract. You may request mediation.

_____

10. Bill was out of town for one week. He was able to complete his report.

_____

In the compound sentences below, underline the subjects once and the verbs twice; circle the coordinating conjunction. Check your work. If you find a coordinating conjunction that joins two simple sentences, you should be able to cover up the coordinating conjunction and see a sentence to the left and a sentence to the right.

1. The golfers intended to play eighteen holes, but the round was cut short due to bad weather.

2. The deafening roar of the crowd for the one-hundredth game excited the crowd and the media, yet the players were able to tune out the noise.

3. The photograph was reproducible, but the cost of colored enlargements was excessive.

4. The jumper did not hesitate to step out of the plane, nor did he have a sense of fear.

5. The fleas seemed to be throughout the house, so we decided to set off a smoke bomb.

6. The imperfections in the garments need to be corrected, or consumers will not purchase our products.

7. His chances to break the world record are excellent, for the track conditions and the athlete's condition are at an all-time best.

8. The sailors saw the beacon of light, and their hearts filled with new hope.

Adding a Semicolon

The second way to make a **compound sentence** is to replace the period between two independent clauses with a **semicolon**. The semicolon should be used only to link two sentences that are closely related in thought. The reader should be able to understand the relationship between the thoughts of the two independent clauses (simple sentences). The sentence pattern will look like this:

S–V $\boxed{;}$ S–V.

Examples: Mark apologized to the woman. He truly was sorry for his comments.

Mark apologized to the woman; he truly was sorry for his comments.

The eagle landed on the highest limb of the tree. The forest seemed enchanted.

(The two thoughts, or subjects, are not closely related. Keep the period.)

✎ PRACTICE

In the following sentences, replace the periods between the two independent clauses if the thoughts of both sentences are closely related.

1. The bleachers are rotted. They are not safe to use for the game.

2. The driver was very rude and unreasonable. People with such tempers should not drive.

3. Sandy's dog was jealous of the new baby. He would bark to make the baby cry.

4. The senator's speech was emotional. People had tears rolling down their cheeks.

5. Three of the students excelled. Their test scores surpassed everyone else's by thirty points.

Use a Semicolon and a Conjunctive Adverb Followed by a Comma

The third way to write a compound sentence is to use a **semicolon with a conjunctive adverb** between the two independent clauses. The conjunctive adverb is followed by a comma. Conjunctive adverbs work as "bridges" to tell the reader the relationship between the two independent clauses. The sentence pattern looks like this:

S–V $\boxed{\text{;conjunctive adverb,}}$ S–V.

The following chart contains common conjunctive adverbs that can be used to join two independent clauses together to make a compound sentence. The conjunctive adverbs have specific meanings, so be sure to select the best conjunctive adverb to show the relationship between the two independent clauses.

Conjunctive
Adverbs

Conjunctive Adverbs That Show Addition	Conjunctive Adverbs That Show Effects or Consequences	Conjunctive Adverbs That Show Sequence or Time
additionally	accordingly	first
also	as a result	second
besides	consequently	third
furthermore	hence	next
in addition	next	finally
indeed	therefore	afterwards
likewise	thus	in conclusion
moreover		in the meantime
		similarly
		subsequently
		then

Conjunctive Adverbs That Show Contrast	Conjunctive Adverbs That Show Example
however	for example
nevertheless	for instance
nonetheless	in fact
on the other hand	
otherwise	
still	
unfortunately	

PRACTICE

Find the conjunctive adverbs in the following sentences. Place a semicolon be-
fore the conjunctive adverb; place a comma after the conjunctive adverb.

1. Seidah wrote a check to cover the late payment then she drove to the landlord's house.

2. The teachers did not have a reasonable contract therefore talks about a strike began.

3. The emission control on his car was missing consequently he was issued a ticket.

4. An eagle's feather is considered to be sacred furthermore only specific dancers are allowed to retrieve dropped feathers.

5. First, we need to establish a budget for our vacation second we need to make campground reservations.

When you use conjunctive adverbs, it is important to select the adverbs that clearly show the relationship between the two independent clauses. In the following chart, the adverbs are in bold print. The general meaning of each adverb is given.

however means *but*	**also** means *in addition*
nevertheless means *however*	**furthermore** means *in addition*
on the other hand means *however*	**moreover** means *in addition*
instead means *as a substitute*	**thus** means *as a result*
meanwhile means *during that time*	**consequently** means *as a result*
subsequently means *following next*	**therefore** means *as a result*
otherwise means *under other conditions*	**then** means *next, after that*
indeed means *in fact*	**finally** means *at last* or *lastly*

Add a conjunctive adverb and the necessary punctuation to the following compound sentences. Mark the prepositional phrases with parentheses. Underline the subjects and the verbs. Remember that you will have a subject and verb in the first independent clause and in the second independent clause.

1. Smitty approved the final budget _____ he wants to review it one more time.

2. We planned to finish writing the report _____ we would go out to dinner.

3. The vase was replaceable _____ you cannot replace the sentimental value.

4. The managers praised the employees _____ they awarded each employee with an unexpected bonus.

5. The class wanted Kimberley to run for the office _____ Kimberley really was not interested in the position.

6. The fifth step involved sanding the last layer of varnish _____ the last step involved buffing the floor to get a high-gloss shine.

7. Half of the class surveyed the morning students _____ the other half of the class surveyed the evening students.

8. I did not pay my cable bill _____ I no longer have cable service.

9. Robert needs to feel and act strong _____ he may be cut from the team.

10. The permit test is done _____ I still need to take the road driving test.

11. The roots of most plants need plenty of water _____ the plant withers and dies.

12. I had to skip dinner _____ I didn't have time to fix breakfast today.

EXERCISE 5.6   Identifying Nouns and Verbs

*Decide if the following words can work as nouns, verbs, or both. Write **N** in the blank for **noun**, **V** for **verb**, or **B** for **both**. You may use an electronic dictionary to check your work.*

braid _____ claim _____ paint _____

raise _____ pay _____ spray _____

freeze _____ greet _____ ease _____

scream _____ teach _____ money _____

coach _____ hoax _____ poultry _____

follow _____ issue _____ rescue _____

waive _____ road _____ beat _____

praise _____ weigh _____ lie _____

emit _____ resist _____ cure _____

sweat _____ breath _____ break _____

reason _____ threat _____ spread _____

Sentence Writing

Complete the following assignment on your own paper. Use the format outlined below.

    Write five words from Exercise 5.6 that can work both as nouns and as verbs:

a. _____   **b.** _____   **c.** _____   **d.** _____   **e.** _____

*For each word above, use the word as a noun in a compound sentence that uses a **coordinating conjunction** (FAN BOYS). Then use the word as a verb in a compound sentence that uses a **semicolon** or a **semicolon with a conjunctive adverb**.*

a. (word)

*1. Use it as a noun in a compound sentence that uses a **coordinating conjunction**.*

*2. Use it as a verb in a compound sentence that uses a **semicolon** (with or without a **conjunctive adverb**).*

✎ **EXERCISE 5.7 Identifying Simple and Compound Sentences**

Mark the prepositional phrases and the verb infinitives. Then draw one line under the subject or subjects and two lines under the verb or verbs. Analyze the subject–verb (S–V) patterns to determine if you have one independent clause (a **simple sentence***) or two independent clauses (a* **compound sentence***). Remember, compound sentences will use one of these three methods to join two simple sentences together: comma and a coordinating conjunction (FAN BOYS), semicolon, semicolon with conjunctive adverb followed by a comma. Write* **S** *if the sentence is a* **simple sentence***. Write* **C** *if the sentence is a* **compound sentence***.*

_____ **1.** The fishing reel was old and rusty.

_____ **2.** The rescue workers worked through the night and finally located the sunken boat.

_____ **3.** The trees were sprayed, for they were infested with insects.

_____ **4.** The brakes were frayed; consequently, the driver lost control on the steep hill.

_____ **5.** Your lease will expire at the end of the month; you will need to negotiate a new contract.

_____ **6.** The evidence was presented by her lawyer, but it was too weak to win the case.

_____ **7.** The chimneys were cleaned and repaired after the tropical storm.

_____ **8.** After a long wait, the singer finally greeted the audience.

_____ **9.** An outbreak of measles spread throughout the young population.

_____ **10.** Ali was solely responsible for the success of the paper; he deserved the recognition.

_____ **11.** The loan application was completed, and an interview with the bank was scheduled.

_____ **12.** We can begin the process now or wait for another week.

Continue to use the same directions. However, for the following sentences, add the missing punctuation. *You will need to use a* **comma** *before a coordinating conjunction, and you will need to use a* **semicolon** *before a conjunctive adverb and a* **comma** *after the conjunctive adverb.*

_____ **1.** The plane landed safely and no one on board or on the ground was injured.

_____ **2.** Mentors taught students techniques for studying for tests as a result the students showed improvements in test scores.

_____ **3.** The windows were boarded up unfortunately the winds ripped off the boards.

_____ **4.** The course taught students to give speeches and to be comfortable in front of an audience.

_____ **5.** The horse's mane was brushed for the judging and his hoofs were polished.

_____ **6.** The food at the diner was greasy but the prices were very reasonable.

———— **7.** The road to success involves hard work and undying commitment.

———— **8.** The child screamed at the top of her lungs for her mother's attention.

———— **9.** Care must be given for proper handling and cooking of chicken.

———— **10.** The peaches are ripe and it is time to pick them and pack them for the stores.

———— **11.** The money from the lottery will be taxed however the final earnings will still be well over eight hundred thousand dollars.

———— **12.** The pair did not want to travel overseas nor did they want to leave their home state.

———— **13.** We strolled through the narrow alleys and cobblestone streets.

———— **14.** Patty's physical impairments do not slow her down in fact few people can keep up with her level of energy.

———— **15.** The nurse felt queasy then she fainted in the operating room.

Two Common Writing Errors to Avoid

1. *Run-on sentence.* If two independent clauses are joined together without using a semicolon, a coordinating conjunction, or a conjunctive adverb and proper punctuation, the result will be a **run-on sentence.** Correct run-on sentences by adding the proper punctuation and a conjunction.

2. *Comma splice.* If a comma is the only punctuation used to join two independent clauses, the result will be a **comma splice.** A comma by itself is too weak and cannot be used to join two sentences; add a coordinating conjunction or change the comma to a semicolon.

✎ **EXERCISE 5.8 Sentence Writing**

*Write a **compound sentence** using each of the following **conjunctions.** Underline your subjects once and your verbs twice. In the margin, write the sentence pattern that you used. The following are examples of possible sentence patterns.*

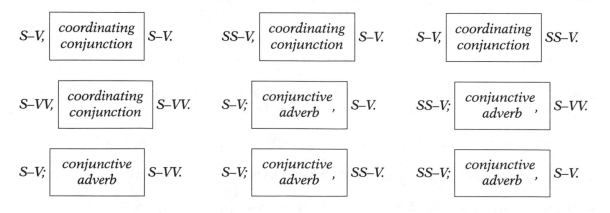

1. coordinating conjunction *and*

_____

2. coordinating conjunction *but*

_____

3. coordinating conjunction *for*

_____

4. coordinating conjunction *yet*

_____

5. coordinating conjunction *so*

_____

6. coordinating conjunction *nor*

_____

7. coordinating conjunction *or*

_____

8. conjunctive adverb *furthermore*

_____

9. conjunctive adverb *therefore*

_____

10. conjunctive adverb *finally*

_____

11. conjunctive adverb *however*

_____

12. conjunctive adverb *in fact*

_____

Carefully read the directions for each sentence below. Write a sentence that includes all of the items given in the directions. You do not *need to write the sentence pattern in the left margin.*

1. Write a **compound sentence** with a **coordinating conjunction.** Use the word *break* as the subject of one of the independent clauses. Write your sentence in **past tense.**

_____

2. Write a **simple SS–V sentence** that has *faith* as one of its subjects.

_____

3. Write a **compound sentence** with the conjunctive adverb *in the meantime.*

_____

4. Write a **compound sentence** that has this pattern: **SS–V; S–V.**

_____

5. Write a **compound sentence** in **present tense** that uses the conjunctive adverb *unfortunately.*

_____

6. Write a **compound sentence** that uses the word *jealous* and uses *and* as the coordinating conjunction.

_____

7. Write a **simple sentence** with an **S–VV** pattern in **present tense.** Use the verb *lay.*

_____

8. Write a **simple sentence** with an **S–VV** pattern that uses the word *dealt* as one of the verbs.

_____

9. Write a **compound sentence** that uses *for* as the coordinating conjunction.

_____

10. Write a **compound sentence** in **past tense** that uses any **conjunctive adverb.**

_____

11. Write a **compound sentence** in **present tense** that uses this sentence pattern: **S–V; S–V.**

_____

12. Write a **compound sentence** in **past tense** that uses the verb *lay.*

_____

13. Write a **simple sentence** that uses the pattern **S–VV** and uses *wave* as one of the verbs.

_____

✎ **EXERCISE 5.9 Chapter Study Sheet**

In the right-hand column, write a definition for the term on the left. Practice reciting and learning this definition. Cover up the definition on the right. Recite the definition. Remove the paper to check your answers. Practice until you can define each term accurately.

Vowel Digraph

Homonyms

Vowel + *Y* Rule

Base Words with *-able*

Coordinating Conjunctions

FAN BOYS

Semicolon

Conjunctive Adverbs

SS Words with *-ible*

Roots with *-ible*

-ion* Words with *-ible

Independent Clause

Compound Sentence

Run-on Sentence

Comma Splice

✎ **CHAPTER REVIEW**

Match the terms on the left with the definitions or word examples on the right.
Each letter may be used only once.

_____ **1.** vowel digraphs

    a. a group of words that has a subject and a verb and forms a complete thought

_____ **2.** homonyms

    b. *and, or, but, nor, for, so, yet*

_____ **3.** Vowel + *Y* Rule

    c. a punctuation mark that replaces a period when two sentences are closely related

_____ **4.** *-able* suffix

    d. a mnemonic for the seven coordinating conjunctions

_____ **5.** *-ible* suffix

    e. two vowels together with the first vowel long and the second vowel silent

_____ **6.** independent clause

    f. a compound sentence that lacks proper punctuation between independent clauses

_____ **7.** compound sentence

    g. incorrect usage of a comma to punctuate

_____ **8.** coordinating conjunctions

    h. usually added to words that end in *ss*, roots, or words that can also have an *ion* suffix.

_____ **9.** FAN BOYS

    i. *therefore, however, for example*

_____ **10.** semicolon

    j. *pain, pane, bored, board, lie, lye*

_____ **11.** conjunctive adverbs

    k. a suffix that is usually added to base words

_____ **12.** run-on sentence

    l. add the suffix to words that end in a vowel plus *y*

_____ **13.** comma splice

    m. a sentence made by joining two simple sentences

Circle the prefixes and the suffixes in the following words. Write the base words
or the roots on the lines.

imprinted _____   retractable _____

incurable _____   impressionable _____

elated _____   impeachment _____

imperfections _____   visibly _____

faithfully _____   owing _____

breakers _____   repairing _____

waiver _____   sweaty _____

Add the suffixes to the following words. Write the complete word on the line.

coarse + ly = _____   oath + s/es = _____

alley + s/es = _____   spray + ed = _____

pray + ing = _____   pay + ment = _____

ease + ment = _____   feather + ing = _____

breath + less = _____   permiss + able/ible = _____

prefer + able/ible = _____   cure + able/ible = _____

grease + less = _____   reduce + able/ible = _____

weak + ness = _____   release + ing = _____

deceive + ing = _____   dispute + able/ible = _____

hoax + s/es = _____   reach + s/es = _____

Read each sentence carefully. Use the context of the sentence to help you select the word inside the parentheses to complete each sentence correctly. Then underline the subjects once and the verbs twice.

1. I want to (lie, lay) in the hammock and (weight, wait) for the sunset.

2. You will need to (lie, lay) new ground rules; then, you may be more comfortable making the (lone, loan).

3. He wanted to be on the (board, bored) and to be the (soul, sole) (mail, male) running for the office.

4. Green (die, dye) was added to the cookie (dough, doe).

5. The jockey (road, rode) the horse to the (mane, main) (gate, gait).

6. The bank robber (maid, made) a (strait, straight) (break, brake) for the back door.

7. The best (coarse, course) of action is to refuse to (lie, lye) as a (weigh, way) to escape the consequences.

8. I have a (great, grate) idea; we can replace the broken (pain, pane) without charging for our labor.

9. The (main, mane) event will be staged on the (beech, beach) at noon next (week, weak).

10. In the ceremony, they (brake, break) the (heal, heel) of the bread into five parts.

11. I will not (waist, waste) my money repairing the (heal, heel) on my shoe; the (souls, soles) are too worn.

12. José (beet, beat) our fastest runner at the track (meet, meat), and now he is on his (way, weigh) to the (peak, peek) performance of his career.

13. I got a (peak, peek) of the snow-covered (peak, peek) during a (break, brake) in the cloud covering.

14. You can (lie, lay) your sorrows aside and give (prays, preys, praise) for your health.

15. The (mane, main) for the plant's (waste, waist) may (brake, break) and cause extensive damage.

16. The committee (paired, pared) down the list of requirements and (waved, waived) the registration fee.

Underline the subjects once and the verbs twice. Add any missing punctuation.
Circle any conjunctions that are used to join two independent clauses. On the
*line, write **S** if the sentence is a **simple sentence**. Write **C** if the sentence is a*
compound sentence.

_____ **1.**   The public employees were on strike so many government offices were closed.

_____ **2.**   The radio was blaring but no one was home at the time.

_____ **3.**   The hikers found shelter in a cave fortunately they were rescued the next day.

_____ **4.**   We walked to the store during our break and bought sandwiches and chips.

_____ **5.**   Fortunately, the check arrived in the mail I was able to pay the rent on time.

_____ **6.**   After the game, we can order a pizza at home or we can go out to dinner.

_____ **7.**   A customer spilled hot coffee on his new suit he was furious.

_____ **8.**   The addition of two temporary employees caused a protest many part-time workers wanted to work more hours.

_____ **9.**   Half of the cars in the funeral procession bore black ribbons to signify the loss of a great community leader.

_____ **10.**   The boxes of junk were moldy and smelly so we loaded them into the pickup and took them to the dump.

_____ **11.**   The officers called for crowd-control assistance for the concert-goers were getting too unruly.

_____ **12.**   The bumper-to-bumper traffic inched through the crowded streets no one was going to arrive at the wedding on time.

Make a compound sentence by finishing each of the following sentences. Use
correct punctuation.

1. I left the keys in the car _____ .

_____

2. Too many items were placed on the agenda _____ .

_____

3. A small beam of light came from the dark, dank basement _____

_____ .

JOURNAL WRITING ASSIGNMENT

Topic: Sentence Combining

Select a newspaper or magazine article that interests you. Read the article carefully. Write ten or more **simple sentences** about the specific facts and details presented in the article. Now explore ways the same information can be presented in **compound sentences** and in **simple sentences with compound subjects or compound verbs.** Within a fifteen-minute period, see how many different ways you can combine the information into new sentences. You can combine ideas in three basic ways:

1. If two sentences use the same verb, you can possibly combine the ideas by writing a **simple sentence with compound subjects.** The patterns would look like this:

   S–V.   S–V. → SS–V.

2. If two sentences have the same subject, you can possibly combine the ideas by writing a **simple sentence with compound verbs.** The patterns would look like this:

   S–V.   S–V. → S–VV.

3. If two sentences are related in thought, you could possibly combine the ideas by writing a **compound sentence that uses a coordinating conjunction, a semicolon, or a conjunctive adverb.** Remember to use the correct punctuation when you use a coordinating conjunction or a conjunctive adverb. The patterns would look like this:

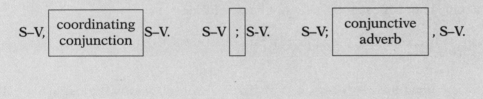

PARAGRAPH WRITING ASSIGNMENT

Topic: An Interesting Magazine Article

Select a newspaper or a magazine article that interests you. Read the article carefully. Write an **explanatory paragraph** that provides the reader with factual information and details about the article you read. Avoid using exact wording or sentences from the article. Instead, combine related pieces of information to write original sentences. The following guidelines will help you write an explanatory paragraph:

1. State the subject of your paragraph in the very first sentence.

2. Assume the role of "reporter" by giving the reader factual information. A well-developed explanatory paragraph includes enough details so that the reader feels well-informed.

3. Be objective. Avoid opinions or personal judgments. Explanatory writing is designed to "explain" or "show" the reader factual information.

4. End the paragraph with a summary or a concluding sentence.

SIX

Additional Long-Vowel Combinations

The topics in this chapter include the following:

- Additional long-vowel combinations
- The Consonant + *Y* Rule, the *Y* to *I* + *ES* Rule, the *F* to *V* + *ES* Rule, the *O* + *ES* Rule, and the *I-E* Rule
- Additional work with homonyms
- One new prefix, three new suffixes, and six new roots to build words
- Introduction of adjectives, adjective-forming suffixes, Adjective Pattern 1, and Adjective Pattern 2
- Additional work with run-on and comma splice errors

Spelling Definitions

Long *A* Combinations: All of the following combinations make a long *a* sound:

    a with a final *e:* name, sale, fame   (Chapter 4)

    ai: main, trait, paid   (Chapter 5)

    ay: stray, pay, play   (Chapter 5)

    ea: steak, great, break   (Chapter 5)

    ey: grey, prey, they   (Chapter 6)

    ei: eight, weight, beige   (Chapter 6)

Long *E* Combinations: All of the following combinations make a long *e* sound:

    e with a final *e:* eve, theme   (Chapter 4)

    ea: eat, dream, bead   (Chapter 5)

    ee: street, free, three   (Chapter 5)

    ey: key, money, chimney   (Chapter 5)

    y: copy, study, ugly   (Chapter 6)

    ei: ceiling, conceit, receive   (Chapter 6)

    ie: belief, chief, niece   (Chapter 6)

Long *I* Combinations: All of the following combinations make a long *i* sound:

    i with a final *e:* ice, rice, drive   (Chapter 4)

    ie: pie, die, lie   (Chapter 5)

    y: try, cry, fly   (Chapter 6)

Long *O* Combinations: All of the following combinations make a long *o* sound:

    o with a final *e:* home, note, lone   (Chapter 4)

    oa: boat, loan, throat   (Chapter 5)

    oe: toe, doe, hoe   (Chapter 5)

    ou: soul, though, poultry   (Chapter 5)

    ow: throw, grow, slow   (Chapter 5)

    words ending with *o*: zero, hero   (Chapter 6)

Long *U* Combinations: All of the following combinations make a long *u* sound:

    u with a final *e:* fuse, mule, mute   (Chapter 4)

    ue: hue, cue   (Chapter 5)

In Chapter 1, we mentioned that "the vowels and the many different combinations they make are the letters that make English spelling difficult." When you look at the combinations above, the truth of this statement becomes apparent. Because of the numerous variations for one sound, many of the words need to be memorized and learned as **sight words.** To become a good speller in English, one really needs to learn to use *four different spelling systems:* (1) **phonetic spelling** to assist sounding out and writing base words, (2) **structural spelling** to learn prefixes and suffixes to add to base words and roots, (3) **homonym spelling** and meanings, and (4) **sight word spelling** to assist with the memorization of words that are exceptions or are a part of a more complex set of rules or patterns. Many of the words in this chapter can be understood through complex **phonetic rules,** but you may find yourself learning them as **sight words.**

✎ **PRACTICE**

Read the words below. Listen to the long vowel sound made by the letter or letters in bold print. Write the long vowel sound on the line after the word.

pr**ey** _____   fl**y** _____   pian**o** _____   ch**ie**f _____

rec**ei**ve _____   h**o**ly _____   fr**ei**ght _____   **ei**ther _____

p**ie**s _____   ob**ey** _____   f**ie**ld _____   potat**o** _____

Spelling Rules

Consonant + *Y* Rule (*Y* to *I* Rule):

When a word ends in a consonant and a *y*, change the *y* to *i* and add the suffix unless the suffix begins with *i*.

vary + ed = varied   vary + ous = various   vary + ing = varying
pity + ed = pitied   pity + ful = pitiful   pity + ing = pitying

Y to I + ES Rule:

When you want to add *s* or *es* to a word that ends in a consonant + *y*, change the *y* to *i* and always use the *es* suffix.

lady + s/es = ladies   copy + s/es = copies

F to V Rule:

When a word ends in *f* or *fe*, change the *f* to *v* when you hear the *vvvv* sound when you say the complete word. If you do not hear the *vvvv* sound, do not change *f* to *v*.

shelf + es = shelves (You hear *vv* when you say the complete word.)

shelf + ing = shelving, (You hear *vv* when you say the complete word.)

belief + s = beliefs (You still hear the *ff* sound in the complete word.)

F to V + ES Rule:

When you want to add an *s* or an *es* suffix to a word in which an *f* was changed to a *v*, always choose the *es* suffix.

shelf + s/es = shelves   half + s/es = halves

O + ES Rule:

When words end in long *o* and you want to add an *s* or *es* suffix, use *es* for most words except musical terms and cylinder shapes. Musical words and cylinder shapes use the *s* suffix.

hero + es = heroes   potato + es = potatoes   tornado + es = tornadoes
piano + s = pianos   tango + s = tangos   solo + s = solos
silo + s = silos   cameo + s = cameos   cello + s = cellos

Exceptions: tattoos, zoos, rodeos, broncos
Both spellings are correct: mangos, mangoes, tuxedos, tuxedoes

The Consonant + Y Rule

You have already learned a rule for words that end in a vowel plus *y*. As a review, write the

Vowel + Y Rule: _____

_____

Now write the **Consonant + Y Rule:** _____

_____

The **Consonant + Y Rule** basically states that you are always going to change the *y* to *i*, with the exception occurring when the suffix already begins with an *i*. This makes sense because you won't find many words in English that have an *ii* combination, and you cannot simply drop the *y* or make it disappear. The most common suffix that begins with *i* is *ing*. As you will notice in the words below, the *ing* is simply added to the base word without altering the base word in any way.

Correct	Incorrect—*ii*	Incorrect—the *y* cannot be "dropped."
studying	studiing	studing
envying	enviing	enving

✎ PRACTICE

Use the Vowel + Y rule and the Consonant + Y Rule to write the following words.

tidy + ing = _____   glory + ous = _____

study + ing = _____   study + ous = _____

valley + s = _____   play + ing = _____

tiny + est = _____   lazy + ness = _____

F to V Rule

To use the *F to V* Rule, you need to say the complete word and *listen* to the word. When you hear the *f* change to a *v* sound, change the *f* to a *v* and add the suffix. If you want to use an *-s* or an *-es* suffix, use the *-es* suffix if the *f* has been changed to a *v*.

✎ PRACTICE

leaf + s/es = _____   wife + s/es = _____

wolf + ing = _____   belief + s/es = _____

puff + s/es = _____   chief + s/es = _____

staff + ing = _____   calf + s/es = _____

Four words that end in *f* can be spelled two ways. These words are pronounced differently in different regions of the country. Which way would you pronounce each word?

> scarf + s/es = *scarfs* or *scarves*
> hoof + s/es = *hoofs* or *hooves*
> roof + s/es = *roofs* or *rooves*
> beef + s/es = *beefs* or *beeves*

ES Rules

There are four different rules for using the *-es* suffix. The *-es* suffix is used to make plural nouns and to make present tense singular verbs. As a review, write the *ES* Rule that you learned in Chapter 2:

_____

_____

The *Y* to *I* + *ES* Rule says to always use the *-es* suffix for words in which the *y* has changed to *i:*

> baby + s/es = babies   study + s/es = studies

The *F* to *V* + *ES* Rule says to always use the *-es* suffix for words in which the *f* was changed to *v:*

> shelf + s/es = shelves   wolf + s/es = wolves

The *O* + *ES* Rule says to use *-es* with words that end with long *o* except for words that are musical terms or cylinder shapes:

> potato + s/es = potatoes   solo + s/es = solos
> volcano + s/es = volcanoes   buffalo + s/es = buffaloes
> soprano + s/es = sopranos   mosquito + s/es = mosquitoes

✎ PRACTICE

Use the four es rules to add the correct suffix to these words. Next to each word, write the rule that was used.

peach + s/es = _____   Rule: _____

loaf + s/es = _____   Rule: _____

banjo + s/es = _____   Rule: _____

tomato + s/es = _____   Rule: _____

body + s/es = _____   Rule: _____

wish + s/es = _____   Rule: _____

elf + s/es = _____   Rule: _____

Spelling Rules (continued)

I-E **Rule:**

Use *i* before *e* when you hear a long *e*, except after *c*.

i before *e* when you hear a long *e:*

achieve	belief	chief	believe	brief
field	grief	relieve	grieve	niece
piece	priest	relief	shield	relieve
siege	shriek	thief	wield	yield

Exceptions: friend, view, patient, patience, sieve

CEI: Use *i* before *e* except after *c* (which means to use *ei* after *c*).

conceit	conceive	deceit	deceive
receive	receipt	perceive	ceiling

Exceptions: ancient   species   conscience glacier

proficient   efficient   deficient

(Notice that in all of these words the *c* makes a *sh* sound.)

EI: Use *i* before *e* when you hear a long *e* (which means to use *ei* if you hear a vowel sound that is not a long *e*).

beige	eight	freight	neighbor	reign
reins	sleigh	their	veil	vein
weigh	weight	feign	height	foreign

Exceptions: either, neither, weird, seize, leisure, protein, caffeine

Note: The *I-E* Rule applies to words in which the *i* and the *e* are in the same syllable. The following words do not use the *I-E* Rule because the vowels occur in separate syllables:

anxi-ety   de-ity   sci-ence   transi-ent

✎ **PRACTICE**

Later in the chapter you will have more opportunities to work with the I-E *Rule.*
For now, complete each word below by writing ei *or* ie.

p_____ce   p_____r   pr_____st   th_____r

w_____ght   bel_____f   glac_____r   ch_____f

dec_____t   l_____sure   n_____ther   rec_____pt

Words—Beginning with the Basics

1. Carefully read each word. Pay attention to the long-vowel combination that is used.
2. Write the word on the first practice line.
3. One of the vowels or vowel combinations used in each word is written on the short line. Write the long-vowel **sound** that is heard ($\bar{a}$, $\bar{e}$, $\bar{\imath}$, $\bar{o}$, $\bar{u}$).
4. Practice writing the word one more time.

✎ **PRACTICE**

Word	Practice	Makes What Sound:	Practice
1. beauty	_____	$y =$ _____	_____
2. body	_____	$y =$ _____	_____
3. copy	_____	$y =$ _____	_____
4. crazy	_____	$y =$ _____	_____
5. duty	_____	$y =$ _____	_____
6. envy	_____	$y =$ _____	_____
7. glory	_____	$y =$ _____	_____
8. holy	_____	$y =$ _____	_____
9. lady	_____	$y =$ _____	_____
10. lazy	_____	$y =$ _____	_____
11. many	_____	$y =$ _____	_____
12. pity	_____	$y =$ _____	_____
13. study	_____	$y =$ _____	_____
14. tidy	_____	$y =$ _____	_____
15. tiny	_____	$y =$ _____	_____
16. trophy	_____	$y =$ _____	_____
17. ugly	_____	$y =$ _____	_____
18. grey	_____	$ey =$ _____	_____
19. they	_____	$ey =$ _____	_____
20. cry	_____	$y =$ _____	_____

Word	Practice	Makes What Sound:	Practice
21. dry	_____	*y* = _____	_____
22. fry	_____	*y* = _____	_____
23. try	_____	*y* = _____	_____
24. echo	_____	*o* = _____	_____
25. hero	_____	*o* = _____	_____
26. piano	_____	*o* = _____	_____
27. potato	_____	*o* = _____	_____
28. radio	_____	*o* = _____	_____
29. stereo	_____	*o* = _____	_____
30. tomato	_____	*o* = _____	_____
31. veto	_____	*o* = _____	_____
32. achieve	_____	*ie* = _____	_____
33. ancient	_____	*ie* = _____	_____
34. belief	_____	*ie* = _____	_____
35. brief	_____	*ie* = _____	_____
36. ceiling	_____	*ei* = _____	_____
37. chief	_____	*ie* = _____	_____
38. either	_____	*ei* = _____	_____
39. friend	_____	*ie* = _____	_____
40. grief	_____	*ie* = _____	_____
41. leisure	_____	*ei* = _____	_____
42. niece	_____	*ie* = _____	_____
43. neighbor	_____	*ei* = _____	_____
44. piece	_____	*ie* = _____	_____
45. relief	_____	*ie* = _____	_____
46. seize	_____	*ei* = _____	_____
47. shield	_____	*ie* = _____	_____

Word	Practice	Makes What Sound:	Practice
48. their	_____	*ei* = _____	_____
49. thief	_____	*ie* = _____	_____
50. yield	_____	*ie* = _____	_____

Looking at Specific Words

1. Some roots belong to closely related word families. In the words below, one pattern is used for the **noun** form, and a closely related pattern is used for the **verb** form. Study and be sure that you know both forms even though the verb forms are not on the basic word list.

Nouns	Verbs
belief	believe
grief	grieve
relief	relieve

2. Mnemonics (memory tricks) can be used to help you remember the words that tend to cause you problems. Here are two mnemonics for words found in this chapter's word list:

   piece *Piece* has a homonym, *peace*. *Piece* refers to parts or portions of something, such as a piece of pie. Notice how it begins with the word *pie*.

   their The word starts with the word *the*. This word uses the *I* before *E* Rule, but many students misspell this word. Simply remember that it begins with *the*.

✎ **EXERCISE 6.1 Working with Additional Long Vowels**

Refer to the word list on pages 159–161 to complete the following work.

1. Write the one-syllable words in which *y* sounds like a long *i*.

_____   _____   _____   _____

2. Write any six words in which the *y* sounds like a long *e*.

_____   _____   _____

_____   _____   _____

3. Write the three words that end in long *o* that refer to music. Add the *-s* plural ending.

_____   _____   _____

4. Write the other five words that end in long *o*. Add the *-es* plural ending.

_____   _____

_____   _____

5. Some words in English may have more than one correct spelling or more than one correct pronunciation. The following words have two correct forms:

grey—gray *Both spellings are correct to describe this color. Which is your preferred way to spell this color?*

neither—either *Depending on the region of the country,* neither *may be pronounced with a long* e *or with a long* i. Either *may be pronounced with a long* e *or with a long* i. *Which is your preferred way to pronounce these words?*

fly + er = flyer *or* **flier** *Both spellings mean "an aviator" or "an advertising circular."*

dry + er = dryer *or* **drier** *Both spellings are correct, but each word has a different meaning. Therefore, the words are homonyms.* Dryer *is a noun that refers to the appliance used to dry, such as a clothes dryer.* Drier *is an adjective that means "more dry," such as "drier air."*

6. As a review, write the definition of **homonyms:** _____

_____

The following words in Chapter 6 have homonyms: piece *and* their.

piece   n.   *a part of a whole*
          v.   *to join into a whole*

peace   n.   *a state of calm and quiet; the absence of war or turmoil*

Write piece *or* peace *to complete each of the following sentences.*

a. I would love to have a _____ of your apple pie.

b. The _____ lasted for three months.

c. The _____ treaty between the nations was signed at the United Nations.

d. The quilters _____ together the fabric squares.

e. We will need to _____ together the details and then make a decision.

f. My grandparents were finally able to enjoy _____ in their retired years.

their: pro.   *a possessive form of the pronoun* they *which can work as an adjective to describe a noun:* Sparky is their dog.

theirs: pro.   *a possessive form of the pronoun* they *that shows ownership:* Sparky is theirs.

there: adv.   *at or in that place or location:* We went there for dinner.

        adv.   *at a point of action or time:* Increase the tempo right there.

        adv.   *used as a "sentence starter" and often followed with a linking verb and then the subject:* There **were** three **players** on the field.

there's: contraction: *a shortened form of* there is *or* there has: There's snow on the hills. There's been controversy over the firing.

they're: contraction: *a shortened form of* they are: They're taking a trip to Europe.

Write their, there, *or* they're *to complete each sentence.*

a. It took us five hours to drive _____ from our home.

b. It took us five hours to drive _____ motor home over the mountains.

c. _____ twins.

d. _____ seems to be a major problem with this billing.

e. _____ are three solos in the performance.

f. She wanted _____ approval to get married.

g. The renters wanted _____ refunds immediately.

h. Begin to sing the soprano part right _____ in the chorus.

Write there's *or* theirs *to complete each sentence.*

a. The final decision is all _____.

b. _____ been a leak in the story.

c. The barking dog is _____.

d. _____ a very slight chance to win the lottery.

7. As a review, write the **Consonant + Y Rule:** _____

_____

Write the *Y* to *I* + *ES* Rule: _____

_____

Apply these rules to the following words. Write the complete words on the lines.

beauty + ful = _____   body + ly = _____

copy + er = _____   copy + ing = _____

copy + s/es = _____   duty + s/es = _____

envy + ous = _____   glory + ous = _____

holy + est = _____   lazy + ness = _____

study + s/es = _____   study + ing = _____

pity + s/es = _____   trophy + s/es = _____

ugly + ness = _____   cry + ed = _____

fry + ing = _____   try + ing = _____

8. *Read each situation below. Write* ie *or* ei. *You may refer back to the rules on page 158.*

Use _____ when you hear a long *e,* except after *c.*

Use _____ if you do not hear a long *e.*

Use _____ if the vowel sound you hear is *a.*

Use _____ right after the letter *c.*

Use _____ right after the letter *c* when the letter *c* sounds like *sh.*

Use _____ when you hear both vowels and when each vowel is in a separate syllable.

Write ei *or* ie *to complete the following words.*

v_____l   r_____gn   ach_____ve   conc_____t

rec_____ve   gr_____f   anc_____nt   w_____ght

sc_____nce   p_____ce   s_____ge   sh_____ld

n_____ghbor   anx_____ty   pr_____st   br_____f

The following words are the **exceptions** *to the rules. Write* ie *or* ei.

fr_____nd   v_____w   pat_____nt   pat_____nce

spec_____s   effic_____nt   w_____rd   l_____sure

prot_____n   caff_____ne   n_____ther   consc_____nce

EXERCISE 6.2 Sentence Work

Circle the word inside the parentheses that will complete each sentence correctly.

1. (They're, There, Their) (believe, belief) honors all men and all living creatures.

2. The family members (grieve, grief) the loss of (their, they're, there) last grandparent.

3. Some (relieve, relief) in the turmoil will come with the new (peace, piece) agreements.

4. It's hard to (believe, belief), but they finally fixed the (drier, dryer) at the lumber mill.

5. The union leaders will (relieve, relief) him of his duties; however, (there, they're, their) not revoking his membership.

6. (They're, Their, There) were signs of anger and (grieve, grief) on the faces of the homeless.

7. (They're, Their, There) trying to (piece, peace) together the complicated jigsaw puzzle.

8. (They're, Their, There) clothes are (dryer, drier), for they finally repaired the (drier, dryer).

9. Our product is good, but (there's theirs) is more effective to (relieve, relief) back pains.

10. (There's, Theirs) a crack in the kitchen ceiling, so we accepted (there, their, they're) offer of a lower sale price.

Return to the above sentences. Mark the prepositional phrases and the verb infinitives. Underline the subjects once and the verbs twice. In the left-hand margin, write **S** *if the sentence is a* **simple sentence**. *Write* **C** *if the sentence is a* **compound sentence**.

Circle the words below that can work as **verbs.**

copy	duty	envy	many	pity	study
tidy	cry	dry	fry	try	echo
piano	radio	veto	achieve	belief	believe
grief	leisure	relief	seize	shield	yield

Use the verbs from the list above in the following sentences. Follow the directions carefully. Do not use a verb from the above list more than once.

1. Write a sentence that uses the verb in a **present tense verb phrase.**

_____

2. Write a **compound sentence** with a **coordinating conjunction.** Use the verb in **past tense.**

_____

3. Use the verb *fry* in simple present tense in a simple sentence that has a **singular subject.**

_____

4. Use one of the verbs in an **SS–VV** sentence pattern. You may use any verb tense.

_____

5. Write a **compound sentence** with a **conjunctive adverb.** Use the verb from the above list in the **second independent clause.**

_____

6. Write **one independent clause** that uses the verb in **future tense.**

_____

7. Use two of the verbs in an **S–VV** sentence in **present tense.**

_____

8. Add *-ing* to one of the verbs to make a **gerund.** Use the gerund as the **subject** of a simple sentence.

_____

Write a sentence that uses the following homonyms.

1. dryer

_____

2. drier

_____

3. peace *(noun)*

_____

4. piece *(noun)*

_____

5. piece *(verb)*

_____

6. their

_____

7. theirs

_____

8. there

_____

9. they're

_____

10. there's

_____

Building Words

As a review, the following list shows all prefixes, suffixes, and roots that have been introduced in previous chapters.

Prefixes		Suffixes		Roots	
re	un	ing	ed	ject	fect
mis	in	er	est	vict	tract
de	dis	y	ful	dict	tect
con	ab	ly	s	fer	mit
ad	ob	es	ion	pel	stant
sub	pre	able	ible	sist	cede
trans	per	ment	en	cide	cise
pro	com	age	ous	clude	duce
ex	im	less	ness	mote	plete
e		ual		pute	quire
				sume	vise

New Prefixes: *se-*

The prefix *se-* means **away, aside,** or **apart from.**

New Suffixes: *-ate   -ive   -ure*

The suffix *-ate* means **to do.**
The suffix *-ive* means **belonging to** or **tending to.**
The suffix *-ure* means **result of** or **state of.**

New Roots: *ceive   cept   gress   fess   lect   tain*

The root *ceive* means **to** or **to seize.**
The root *cept* means **to take.**
The root *gress* means **to go** or **to walk.**
The root *fess* means **to admit.**
The root *lect* means **to read** or **to choose.**
The root *tain* means **to hold.**

✎ PRACTICE

Count the "word parts" in each word below. Each prefix counts as one word part. Each base or root counts as one word part. Each suffix counts as one word part. On the line, write the number of word parts used to build each word.

progressively _____   confessing _____   playfulness _____

unintentionally _____   unobtainable _____   tenure _____

elections _____   objectively _____   greeters _____

resistible _____   preconceived _____   increasingly _____

dictation _____   impressive _____   inspirational _____

plantations _____   elation _____   faithfully _____

retainers _____   maintaining _____   unfriendly _____

Add the following suffixes to these words. Pronounce the words carefully. Pay attention to possible shifts in pronunciation or accents after the suffixes have been added. If a word ends in e *and the* e *needs to be dropped before adding the suffix, cross off the* e.

-ate	*-ive*	*-ure*
dict_____	progress_____	text_____
inspire_____ion	act_____	please_____
compute_____ion	restrict_____	compose_____
repute_____ion	attract_____	press_____
compassion_____	protect_____	script_____

Circle the prefixes and the suffixes. Write the root on the line.

progress _____   deceiving _____

confessed _____   lecture _____

obtained _____   contained _____

obtainable _____   dictating _____

progressive _____   receptions _____

conceptually _____   congressional _____

conception _____   elective _____

receiver _____   pertaining _____

Name _____ Date _____

✎ **EXERCISE 6.3 Building Words Using Word Bases, Roots, Prefixes, and Suffixes**

The base word or the root is shown in bold print. Add the prefixes and the suffixes. Write the complete word with all the word parts on the line. Apply spelling rules as needed before suffixes are added.

1. dis + **please** + ure = _____

2. ob + **ject** + ive + ly = _____

3. un + **please** + ing = _____

4. **act** + ive + ly = _____

5. pro + **duct** + ive + ly = _____

6. con + **tain** + ment = _____

7. per + **cept** + ual = _____

8. de + **ceive** + ing = _____

9. trans + **gress** + ion = _____

10. se + **lect** + ion = _____

11. se + **duce** + ed = _____

12. re + **fry** + ed = _____

13. **anxiety** + es = _____

14. **seize** + ure + s = _____

15. **veto** + ing = _____

16. im + **patient** + ly = _____

17. **glory** + ous + ly = _____

18. **friend** + ly + ness = _____

19. con + **ceive** + ing = _____

20. pro + **tect** + ive = _____

21. im + **press** + ive = _____

22. pro + **gress** + ive + ly = _____

23. con + **duce** + ive = _____

24. **pass** + ion + ate + ly = _____

25. pre + con + **cept** + ion + s = _____

26. re + **ceive** + er = _____

27. con + **ceive** + able = _____

28. se + **clude** + ed = _____

29. se + **quest** + er + ed = _____

30. un + **yield** + ing = _____

31. un + **believe** + able = _____

32. re + **cept** + ion = _____

33. **leisure** + ly = _____

34. **copy** + able = _____

35. pro + **cede** + ure + s = _____

36. se + **pare** + ate + ion = _____

Partner Dictation

Work with a partner. One person dictates the left column for his or her partner to spell. Then reverse roles. The second person dictates the right column.

✎ **EXERCISE 6.4 Word List Expansion**

The following words that end in long o *are not on the basic word list. Add* -s *or* -es *to each word to form its plural. Circle all the words that are musical terms or refer to cylinders. The plurals of these words will be made by adding the suffix* -s.

zero _____   buffalo _____   mosquito _____   banjo _____

solo _____   cello _____   volcano _____   alto _____

soprano _____   cameo _____   cargo _____   silo _____

echo _____   piano _____   mango _____   tuxedo _____

Most of the following words are not on this chapter's word list. Write the **plural form** *of each word on the line. Remember to* say *the word in the plural form; then decide if the* f *needs to be changed to a* v. *Add the plural suffix* -s *or* -es. *You may use an electronic spell checker or a dictionary to complete your answers.*

life _____   leaf _____   safe _____

proof _____   thief _____   calf _____

elf _____   chef _____   chief _____

roof _____   wolf _____   hoof _____

shelf _____   self _____   clef _____

loaf _____   beef _____   half _____

knife _____   gulf _____   brief _____

belief _____   surf _____   golf _____

wife _____   dwarf _____   reef _____

spoof _____   scarf _____   wharf _____

Partner Dictation

Work with a partner. Select any fifteen words from the list above. Dictate the word in its singular form. Ask your partner to spell the singular word and then the plural word. Reverse roles so that each partner has the opportunity to give the words and to spell the words.

Without looking back at any other word lists, "build" twenty different words using the prefixes, suffixes, and roots below. Try to have three or more word parts in each word, and try to use a variety of prefixes, suffixes, and roots.

Prefixes		Roots		Suffixes	
re	un	ject	fect	ing	ed
mis	in	vict	tract	er	est
de	dis	dict	tect	y	ful
con	ab	fer	mit	ly	s
ad	ob	pel	stant	es	ion
sub	pre	sist	cede	able	ible
trans	per	cide	cise	ment	en
pro	com	clude	duce	age	ous
ex	im	mote	plete	less	ness
e	se	pute	quire	ual	ate
		sume	vise	ive	ure
		ceive	cept		
		gress	fess		
		lect	tain		

_____   _____

_____   _____

_____   _____

_____   _____

_____   _____

_____   _____

_____   _____

_____   _____

_____   _____

_____   _____

✎ EXERCISE 6.5 Sentence Writing

Use words from the list on pages 158–161. Write six sentences that have two or more words from the list. Underline the subjects once and the verbs twice. Mark the prepositional phrases.

1. _____

2. _____

3. _____

4. _____

5. _____

6. _____

Choose any of the ei *or* ie *words found on page 158. Use at least one of the* ei *or* ie *words in a **compound sentence**.*

1. _____

2. _____

3. _____

4. _____

5. _____

6. _____

Grammar Definitions

Adjectives:

Adjectives are words that describe or modify nouns or pronouns. Adjectives tell *which one, what kind of, how many,* or *what color.* Adjectives modify or change your understanding of the noun by providing more detail or a stronger image.

> **Examples:** this car   tiny baby   ugly dog
> beautiful child   eighty cats   grey skies

Notes:

1. When you have more than one adjective for a noun, a comma is usually placed between the two *descriptive* adjectives. The comma is needed whenever the word *and* could be placed between the two adjectives:

beautiful and *gentle* child = *beautiful, gentle* child

ugly and *vicious* dog = *ugly, vicious* dog

this beautiful child (no comma)

eighty stray cats (no comma)

2. Pronouns can take on the function of adjectives when they are placed before a noun they describe.

my friend	*this* story
our computer	*that* book
his father	*those* boys
her phone	*these* facts
your notes	*some* people
their house	*any* computer
its box	*many* customers

Adjective-Forming Suffixes:

The following suffixes from previous chapters usually form words that work as adjectives. More adjective-forming suffixes will be presented later in this chapter and in later chapters.

-able	lovable, curable, reachable
-er (when it means "more")	faster, quicker, bigger
-est	fastest, quickest, biggest
-ful	beautiful, restful, useful
-ible	sensible, permissible, accessible
-ive	attractive, progressive, passive
-less	lifeless, penniless, homeless
-ly (also an adverb-forming suffix)	friendly, weekly
-ous	glorious, studious, dangerous
-y	rusty, bossy, foggy

Adjective Pattern 1:

Adjective Pattern 1 occurs when the adjective is right before the noun. This is the most common location of adjectives in English.

His jealous friends envied *his strong, muscular* body.

The *famous* hero rode in the *red* convertible.

Adjective Pattern 2:	Adjective Pattern 2 occurs when the adjective follows a linking verb. The adjective always describes the subject of the sentence. This is called a **predicate adjective.**

The results were *predictable* and *upsetting*.

The stuntman was *crazy* to try to jump through the fire.

Predicate Adjective:	A predicate adjective is an adjective that follows a linking verb. A predicate adjective modifies or describes the subject of the sentence.

The sunset is *beautiful*.   The pyramids are *ancient*.

Run-on Sentence:	A run-on sentence is a writing error that occurs when two independent clauses run together without the correct conjunctions and/or punctuation. To correct run-on sentences, do one of the following:

1. Use a period to form two separate sentences.

2. Use a comma and a coordinating conjunction to form a compound sentence.

3. Use a semicolon between the two independent clauses if the clauses are closely related in thought.

4. Use a semicolon and a conjunctive adverb followed by a comma to join the two independent clauses and show their relationship.

Comma Splice:	A comma splice occurs when a comma is used to join two independent clauses. A comma by itself is a form of punctuation that is too weak. To correct run-on sentences, do one of the following.

1. Use a period to form two separate sentences.

2. Add a coordinating conjunction to form a compound sentence.

3. Replace the comma with a semicolon if the clauses are closely related in thought.

4. Replace the comma with a semicolon and a conjunctive adverb followed by a comma to join the two independent clauses and show their relationship.

Descriptive Adjectives

✎ **PRACTICE**

*The following words are adjectives. After each adjective, write a **noun** that the adjective could describe or modify.*

thin _____   swift _____

rich _____   strong _____

traffic _____   chicken _____

problem _____   gentle _____

simple _____   humble _____

middle _____   big _____

dim _____   flat _____

hot _____   mad _____

sad _____   tan _____

brave _____   safe _____

cute _____   cheap _____

clean _____   brief _____

beauty _____   crazy _____

holy _____   lazy _____

tidy _____   tiny _____

dry _____   radio _____

1. *Work with a partner to write ten sentences that use the above adjectives and nouns. Use Adjective Pattern 1 for all your sentences. Your sentences may be shared with the rest of the class.*

2. *Now return to each of your ten sentences. Add one more adjective so that you have two adjectives modifying the same noun. Remember to use a comma between the adjectives if it is needed.*

Predicate Adjectives

Predicate adjectives come after linking verbs. Look at the **linking verbs** in the list below. You may refer back to pages 40–42.

Linking Verbs				
am	is	likes	seems	are
was	looks	were	feels	appears
	sounds	smells		taste

✎ **PRACTICE**

*In the following sentences, the subject has been given. The **linking verb** is shown in* italic. *Write a **predicate adjective** for each sentence. Be sure that the word you write describes the subject of the sentence.*

1. I *am* _____.

2. The chefs *are* _____.

3. The copies of the documents *were* _____.

4. The dog *looks* _____.

5. The potato *is* _____.

6. The bread *smells* _____.

7. The moment *feels* _____.

8. The tape *sounds* _____.

9. The meat *tastes* _____.

10. The children *seem* _____.

11. The crackers *become* _____.

12. The photograph *appears* _____.

Sentences 2–12 have subjects that are nouns. Use Adjective Pattern 1 to add an adjective before each noun subject.

Adjective-Forming Suffixes

Adjective-Forming Suffixes				
-able	-er	-est	-ful	-ible
-ive	-less	-ly	-ous	-y

✎ **PRACTICE**

Turn the following words into adjectives by using one of the adjective-forming suffixes in the box above. Write the adjective on the line.

Noun	Adj. Suffix		Adjective
copy +	_____	=	_____
envy +	_____	=	_____

friend + _____ = _____

peace + _____ = _____

deceit + _____ = _____

act + _____ = _____

pleasure + _____ = _____

object + _____ = _____

safe + _____ = _____

beauty + _____ = _____

faith + _____ = _____

stress + _____ = _____

itch + _____ = _____

rust + _____ = _____

flat + _____ = _____

combat + _____ = _____

To the right of each word above, write a short, simple sentence that uses the adjective in an Adjective Pattern 1 or Adjective Pattern 2.

Run-on Sentences and Comma Splices

✎ **PRACTICE**

Some of the sentences below are correct. Some of the sentences have either the run-on sentence error or the comma splice error. **Work with a partner** *to analyze each sentence.*

Write **S** *if the sentence is a simple sentence without any errors.*

Write **C** *if the sentence is a compound sentence without any errors.*

Write **RO** *if the sentence is a run-on sentence. Use any method to correct the sentence.*

Write **CS** *if the sentence has a comma splice error. Use any method to correct the sentence.*

_____ **1.** The prominent local family donated to the trust fund, they wanted to help the family in distress.

_____ **2.** Melissa gathered up the newspapers and recycled them by the curb.

———— 3. The arrangement was perfect we both saved on the rent.

———— 4. You can use this restroom, or you can use the one near the main office.

———— 5. The paramedics arrived at the scene of the accident, they were too late to save the driver.

———— 6. Billy's energetic puppy scratches at the door and whines to come in.

———— 7. Her youngest daughter went to the kitchen and made peanut butter sandwiches for the picnic.

———— 8. Everyone in the house looked for my lost keys no one was able to locate them.

———— 9. I prefer to plant my own tomatoes, they are not loaded with color-enhancing chemicals or tainted with pesticides.

———— 10. The jet skidded to a stop smoke started to pour out of one engine.

———— 11. We picked the cherries from the tree and pitted them for canning.

———— 12. Carl studied ten hours for his geology test, for he needed to pass the class to graduate.

———— 13. Unemployment figures remain low, yet I have so many unemployed friends.

———— 14. All of my friends listen to New Age music I find it too strange to enjoy.

———— 15. The tornadoes were expected to touch down near the border and move through three towns.

———— 16. The high winds destroyed roofs and uprooted trees.

———— 17. The computer expert rushed into the room he had heard about the computer virus.

———— 18. At last the rain had stopped, but by then the rivers were swollen past flood stage.

———— 19. One of our most favorite ways to relax is to sit in the back yard and listen to music.

———— 20. The celebration lasted for hours none of the neighbors complained.

———— 21. The flight attendant took our beverage orders I was too nervous to drink anything.

———— 22. The chairperson of the board called an emergency meeting for all shareholders.

———— 23. The show is filmed daily before a live audience.

———— 24. The heroes received plaques and a lot of praise from the community at large.

———— 25. After sleeping in the mountain air, I had trouble returning to the smog and noise of the city.

———— 26. Both of the women want to be attorneys, their commitment to studying is questionable.

———— 27. Junk mail, newspapers, and most other kinds of correspondence can be recycled.

_____ **28.**   The killer whale has been in captivity for three years however he will be released next October.

_____ **29.**   Mark released the ball and hoped for the best the championship was at stake.

_____ **30.**   Today's comic strips show little humor, they usually are used for political or social statements.

_____ **31.**   The ancient ruins are being destroyed by tourists, yet little is being done to monitor the thousands of visitors to the sites.

_____ **32.**   His face turned red, yet he refused to admit his mistake.

_____ **33.**   Vicki's boss listened to her story however she still lost a day's pay.

_____ **34.**   You may pay the entire bill now you may break it into three installments.

_____ **35.**   I wrote an answer to the complaint and filed a copy for future reference.

✎ **EXERCISE 6.6 Identifying Nouns, Verbs, and Adjectives**

*Decide if the words below can work as **nouns, verbs,** or **adjectives.** Write **N, V,** or **A** on the line. Do not add suffixes to the words. Remember that a word can be more than one part of speech. You may refer to a dictionary or an electronic spell checker to confirm your answers.*

beauty _____	crazy _____	holy _____
lazy _____	tidy _____	trophy _____
ugly _____	grey _____	cry _____
potato _____	tomato _____	ancient _____
brief _____	chief _____	piece _____
seize _____	shriek _____	wield _____
view _____	conscience _____	beige _____
eight _____	freight _____	feign _____
reign _____	protein _____	vein _____

Choose any five nouns from the above list. Use each noun as the subject of a compound sentence.

1. _____

2. _____

3. _____

4. _____

5. _____

Choose any five verbs from the above list. Write simple sentences that have one verb, one prepositional phrase, and two adjectives. Each sentence should use one of the five verbs.

1. _____

2. _____

3. _____

4. _____

5. _____

Choose five adjectives from the above list. Use each adjective in a sentence. Use Adjective Pattern 1. (The adjective needs to come before a noun.)

1. _____

2. _____

3. _____

4. _____

5. _____

Choose five different adjectives from the above list. Use each adjective in a sentence. Use Adjective Pattern 2. (The adjective needs to come after a linking verb.)

1. _____

2. _____

3. _____

4. _____

5. _____

✎ EXERCISE 6.7 **Finding Adjectives in Sentences**

*Write **N** above all the nouns in the following sentences. **Circle** all the adjectives in the following sentences. If the adjective comes before a noun, write **1** to show that Adjective Pattern 1 is used. If the adjective comes after a linking verb and describes the subject of the sentence, write **2** to show that Adjective Pattern 2 is used.*

1. This body cream costs twelve dollars per jar.

2. The relief pitcher stepped onto the muddy field, and the hometown crowd cheered loudly.

3. Our new, little kitten is playful and mischievous.

4. After a leisurely walk, the retired couple sat down on the park bench and reminisced.

5. My youngest nephew is loud, conceited, and rude.

6. The piano bar features local artists and superb, inexpensive food.

7. The best radio station in our little town went off the air at midnight.

8. Betty is my study partner; she is intelligent and enthusiastic.

9. The lighted trophy case held football trophies and twelve game balls.

10. Your computations were correct; you received a high score on the physics exam.

11. The active ingredients are listed on the blue part of the label.

12. The recluse lives in a beautiful log-cabin home in the remote area of the northern region.

13. Our new stereo system is beautiful.

14. Mrs. Jacobson is the friendliest teacher and the best teacher in our entire school.

15. Uncle Ben was active, sharp, and healthy; his life was productive and rewarding.

16. The jars of pickled beets were placed inside a pressure cooker.

17. The main speaker at the fund-raising event was inspirational and dedicated.

18. A stale loaf of wheat bread lay on the kitchen counter for three weeks.

✎ EXERCISE 6.8 Sentence Writing

Prepositional phrases and adjectives are used for sentence expansion. Both prepositional phrases and adjectives provide the reader with additional details and provide the writer with methods for creating a stronger, clearer image or expression of information. Expand the following simple sentences by adding at least one prepositional phrase and two or more adjectives. Refer back to page 70 for a list of prepositions that begin prepositional phrases.

1. The ship headed out to sea.

_____

2. The echo was heard.

_____

3. That child is my niece.

_____

4. The musician played the piano.

_____

5. Our neighbor cried.

_____

6. The dryer is new.

_____

7. The patient waited.

_____

8. The view was spectacular.

_____

9. The women were confessing.

_____

Use the following adjectives to write detailed sentences. First, use the word in
Adjective Pattern 1; *then use the word in* **Adjective Pattern 2.**

faithful

1. _____

2. _____

protective

1. _____

2. _____

active

1. _____

2. _____

separate

1. _____

2. _____

beautiful

1. _____

2. _____

friendly

1. _____

2. _____

perceptive

1. _____

2. _____

The suffixes -er *and* -est *are adjective-forming suffixes. The suffix* -er *means "more," and the suffix* -est *means the "most." Add the suffixes to the following words.*

Adjective	+ *er*	+ *est*	Adjective	+ *er*	+ *est*
crazy	_____	_____	lazy	_____	_____
tiny	_____	_____	ugly	_____	_____
thick	_____	_____	quick	_____	_____
thin	_____	_____	foggy	_____	_____
bossy	_____	_____	gentle	_____	_____
big	_____	_____	flat	_____	_____
hot	_____	_____	mad	_____	_____
tan	_____	_____	brave	_____	_____
late	_____	_____	safe	_____	_____
cute	_____	_____	cheap	_____	_____
clean	_____	_____	great	_____	_____

*The adjective with the -er suffix is called a **comparative adjective** because it compares two things. (Bob is cuter than Richard.) The adjective with the -est suffix is called a **superlative adjective** because it is the "most" among three or more things. (Bob is the cutest boy in the fifth-grade class.)*

    *Choose an adjective from the list above. Use the **basic adjective** in sentence one. In sentence two, use the **comparative** form. In sentence three, use the **superlative** form. Continue the process with new adjectives.*

1. _____

2. _____

3. _____

1. _____

2. _____

3. _____

1. _____

2. _____

3. _____

1. _____

2. _____

3. _____

1. _____

2. _____

3. _____

1. _____

2. _____

3. _____

1. _____

2. _____

3. _____

✎ EXERCISE 6.9 **Chapter Study Sheet**

In the right-hand column, write a definition for the term on the left. Practice reciting and learning this definition. Cover up the definition on the right. Recite the definition. Remove the paper to check your answers. Practice until you can define each term accurately.

Long *A* Combinations

Long *E* Combinations

Long *I* Combinations

Long *O* Combinations

Long *U* Combinations

Consonant + *Y* Rule

***F* to *V* Rule**

F to V + ES Rule

O + ES Rule

I-E Rule

Adjective

Adjective Pattern 1

Adjective Pattern 2

Adjective-Forming Suffixes

Predicate Adjective

Run-on Sentence

Comma Splice

Comparative Adjective

Superlative Adjective

Name _____   Date _____

✐ **CHAPTER REVIEW**

Match the terms on the left with the definitions or the example words on the right.

_____ 1.   words that show long *a* combinations

a. *beam, tree, key, duty, belief, conceit, theme*

_____ 2.   words that show long *e* combinations

b. also called the *Y* to *I* Rule

_____ 3.   words that show long *i* combinations

c. use *-es,* not *-s,* on words in which the *y* is changed to *i*

_____ 4.   words that show long *o* combinations

d. *fuse, cue*

_____ 5.   words that show long *u* combinations

e. use the suffix *-es,* not *s,* when you change an *f* to a *v*

_____ 6.   homonyms

f. *mail, stray, great, they, eight, came*

_____ 7.   Consonant + *Y* Rule

g. The wolves ate, they devoured the meat.

_____ 8.   *Y* to *I* + *ES* Rule

h. use *i* before *e* when you hear a long *e* except after *c*

_____ 9.   *F* to *V* Rule

i. adjectives found in Pattern 2

_____ 10.   *F* to *V* + *ES* Rule

j. *ride, die, fry*

_____ 11.   *O* + *ES* Rule

k. words that describe or modify nouns

_____ 12.   *I-E* Rule

l. the adjective comes after a linking verb

_____ 13.   adjectives

m. the adjective is placed before the noun

_____ 14.   Adjective Pattern 1

n. change *f* to *v* when you hear a *v* sound when you say the complete word

_____ 15.   Adjective Pattern 2

o. use *-es,* not *-s,* in words that end with *o* except musical terms or cylinder shapes.

_____ 16.   predicate adjectives

p. *their, they're, there, peace, piece*

_____ 17.   run-on sentence

q. *home, gloat, hoe, soul, mow, zero*

_____ 18.   comma splice

r. The wolves ate they devoured the meat.

Write the vowel sound you hear in the following words.

beige _____   **sie**ge _____   per**cei**ve_____   **they** _____

chief_____   de**cei**t _____   **cei**ling _____   **brie**f _____

weigh_____   h**eigh**t _____   spec**ie**s _____   n**ie**ce _____

Write the **I-E** *Rule:* _____

_____

Circle all the words below that follow the I-E *Rule. Do not circle the exceptions.*

freight   conceit   receive   conscience   priest

chief   relieve   piece   yield   sleigh

weird   ceiling   protein   weigh   field

Add the suffixes to the following words. Write the complete word on the line.

chief + s/es = _____   solo + s/es = _____

yield + s/es = _____   thief + s/es = _____

hero + s/es = _____   shclf + s/cs = _____

half + s/es = _____   pity + s/es = _____

receive + ing = _____   study + ous = _____

pity + ing = _____   obey + ing = _____

envy + ous = _____   crazy + er = _____

tiny + est = _____   cry + ed = _____

achieve + ment = _____   neighbor + ly = _____

seize + ure + s = _____   piece + ing = _____

Circle the correct homonym inside the parentheses.

1. The (piece, peace) of lumber was purchased at (there, their, they're) west lot.

2. (There, Their, They're) simply is not enough effort towards world (piece, peace).

3. (There, Their, They're) going to get relief for (they're, there, their) pitcher.

4. (There's, Theirs) the most expensive commercial (dryer, drier) on the market.

5. I know that (their, there, they're) are two shovels, but that one is definitely (there's, theirs).

6. (There, Their, They're) was one (piece, peace) of chocolate cake left for you.

Circle the prefixes and the suffixes. Write the root on the line.

obtaining _____   elective _____

selection _____   containers _____

confession _____   deceiving _____

receptive _____   transgression _____

Circle all the roots.

fess	ment	mit	tect	sist	sub

trans	tain	cept	ceive	com	dict

plete	duce	gress	age	ual	lect

Circle the suffixes that often work as a adjective-forming suffixes.

-able	-ment	-er	-ure	-est	-es	-s

-ful	-ible	-ion	-ive	-less	-ous	-y

Use any three suffixes above to form an adjective. Use each adjective in a sentence.

1. _____

2. _____

3. _____

In the following sentences, mark the prepositional phrases with parentheses. Underline the subjects once and the verbs twice. Circle the adjectives. Draw an arrow from each adjective to the noun that it modifies.

1. The grey smoke settled in the valley; many allergy sufferers reacted to the smoke.

2. The brief encounter occurred outside of the old restaurant near the shipping docks.

3. Our science teacher was efficient and thorough; the lab was organized and well-stocked.

4. There are four duties for each priest to perform.

5. His achievements won him famous trophies and honors.

6. Her patience is remarkable and makes her an excellent elementary teacher.

7. These potato cakes are delicious; unfortunately, they have a thousand calories.

8. Ancient beliefs of the Amazon tribe have been passed down from one generation to another.

9. The permit was unobtainable; therefore, the annual gathering was discontinued.

10. All of my leisure time has been spent cleaning up the vegetable gardens and the flower beds.

Read each of the following sentences carefully. Add any missing punctuation, or correct any run-on sentences or comma splices. If there are no errors, do not change the sentence in any way.

1. Grief struck the village ten dead sheep were discovered in the field.

2. Our staff assistant was trying to copy the documents but the copy machine kept jamming.

3. After her seizure, a brain scan was given for the doctors feared the tumor had enlarged.

4. A huge sense of relief swept over me finally, I could see the silver lining.

5. The texture was too scratchy so the designer used a different fabric.

6. After a long separation, the pair reunited and made plans to renew their vows.

7. Sequestered juries often feel very secluded from the rest of the world, many jurors cannot deal with the isolation.

8. The sunsets in Hawaii are unbelievable I have never seen such painted skies.

Read the following directions carefully. Write sentences that show all the directions.

1. Write a sentence with **two adjectives** that come before a noun in a **compound sentence.**

_____

2. Write a sentence that begins with the word *their,* has at least one **prepositional phrase,** and has **one adjective** in the **Adjective 2 Pattern.**

_____

3. Use *stereo* as one subject of a **compound sentence** that uses a **conjunctive adverb.**

_____

4. Write a **simple sentence** that has a **superlative adjective.**

_____

5. Write a **simple sentence** that uses the contraction *they're.*

_____

6. Write a **compound sentence** that uses the word *piece* as a **verb** in one of the independent clauses.

_____

7. Write a **simple sentence** that has **two adjectives** that describe the same noun and that has **two prepositional phrases.**

_____

8. Write a **simple sentence** that uses **two predicate adjectives.**

_____

JOURNAL WRITING ASSIGNMENT

Topic: My Positive Traits and Characteristics

Now it is time to focus on all your positive traits and characteristics. Set a timer for ten minutes. Write continuously for ten minutes. In this exercise you will be using many adjectives because you are asked to describe yourself. Rather than one continuous list of adjectives, expand some of the ideas with supporting details.

　　For example, you may start off like this: *I am a sensitive person. I pay attention to other people and care about their feelings. I am also good-natured. I laugh a lot and have a great sense of humor. . . .*

PARAGRAPH WRITING ASSIGNMENT

Topic: A Special Place

A well-written **descriptive paragraph** has the power to create a detailed picture in readers' minds. Descriptive paragraphs, through the effective use of adjectives, evoke feelings and emotions in the reader that are similar to the feelings and the emotions the writer has towards the topic. A careful selection of words that touch the reader's senses—especially sounds, sights, and smells—is essential.

　　Think of a special place the evokes a very specific feeling or emotion in you. This place may be a special room, a river bank, a mountain top, or a sandy stretch of beach. Your goal is to describe this place and all its intricate details to the point that the reader can see the place in his or her mind and can feel the feelings you experience when you visit this place. A few common feelings appropriate for a descriptive paragraph are feelings of immense tranquillity, unity, excitement, or gratitude. Of course, all descriptive paragraphs do not need to focus on positive emotions; unpleasant feelings such as gloom, fear, or despair can also be used in descriptive paragraphs.

　　Make a list of special places and the feelings you experience when you are in each place. Then select one as the topic of your descriptive paragraph. Follow these guidelines to develop the first draft of your paragraph:

1. Name the place and state the feeling in your opening sentence.

2. Give detailed descriptions of objects in that location. Use words related to your senses.

3. If you find yourself using adjectives that are too common or are nondescript, use a thesaurus to locate adjectives that are more precise and evoke the emotional response desired.

4. Limit your choice of adjectives to ones that relate specifically to the images and the feelings you are developing. For example, if you are describing the sense of unity with nature that you feel at your favorite fishing hole, avoid describing rowdy rafters who occasionally float down the river.

5. Read your paragraph to a friend or a classmate. Ask him or her to describe the place to you. Pay attention to images and details that you feel are missing to create an even stronger image.

6. End your paragraph with a closing sentence that summarizes your feelings and connection to this special place.

SEVEN

R-Controlled Vowels

The topics in this chapter include the following:

- *R*-controlled vowels
- The *OR* Suffix Rule
- Additional work with homonyms
- One new prefix, seven new suffixes, and five new roots to build words
- Introduction to sentence combining

Spelling Definitions

R-Controlled Vowels:

R-controlled vowels are the vowels *a, e, i, o,* and *u* followed by the consonant *r.* The five *r*-controlled vowels (also called *r*-controls) are *ar, er, ir, or,* and *ur.*

Er, ir, and *ur* make the same sound as heard in these words:

> *er:* her, nerve, term, verb
> *ir:* first, bird, stir, dirt
> *ur:* fur, church, nurse, turn

Ar has two sounds:

Ar as in *car, hard,* and *star* is the most common *ar* sound.

Ar that sounds like *er* is the second sound:

doll**ar** or coll**ar**

Exceptions to the *ar* sounds: tow**ard**, emb**ar**ass, sc**ar**ce, m**ar**ry, c**ar**ry

Or has two sounds:

Or as in *for, north,* and *storm* is the most common *or* sound.

Or that sounds like *er* is the second sound:

> col**or**   mot**or**   w**or**k   w**or**ld   w**or**ry   rum**or**
> doct**or**   arm**or**   parl**or**   mem**or**y   hum**or**

Some important notes about *r*-controls:

1. There are no rules to tell you when to use *er, ir,* or *ur.* The correct spellings are often learned through sight spelling.

2. There are no rules to tell you when to use *ar* or *or* for the *er* sound. Since these second sounds can be considered "exceptions" to the most common sound of *ar* and *er,* these words need to be learned as sight words.

✎ PRACTICE

Many of the er, ir, *and* ur *words will be learned as sight words. Write* **er, ir,** *or* **ur** *to complete the following words. If you are not sure, write all three combinations, and then use your* **sight spelling skills** *to see which one looks correct. If there is more than one correct spelling, the two different spellings will indicate that the words are* homonyms.

s_____ve	c_____cle	sk_____t	ch_____ch
f_____n	m_____ge	b_____n	h_____d
wat_____	_____n	b_____p	st_____
b_____st	th_____d	b_____th	n_____se
f_____	h_____l	b_____ch	g_____l
t_____n	sp_____	aft_____	b_____d
ch_____p	bl_____	sp_____t	n_____ve

p_____ch	s_____f	st_____n	l_____ch
p_____ge	squ_____t	f_____l	v_____b
d_____t	bl_____t	und_____	sm_____k
f_____st	squ_____m	p_____ple	sl_____
p_____se	l_____k	ev_____y	ex_____t
sl_____p	fl_____t	sh_____t	h_____b
squ_____t	sw_____l	th_____st	t_____m
h_____t	ent_____	v_____se	ev_____

Work with a partner for partner dictation. Give each other any fifteen words from the list above to spell out loud without using paper and pencil.

The following words use the **first and most common** *sounds of* ar *or* or. *Write* **ar** *or* **or** *to complete the following words. In some cases below, both* ar *and* or *will make real words.*

_____m	_____t	c_____k	m_____e
c_____n	b_____n	d_____m	f_____k
f_____m	f_____th	n_____m	g_____ge
c_____	c_____t	c_____d	c_____p
ch_____	ch_____t	n_____th	d_____k
d_____t	ch_____ge	f_____	f_____ce
sc_____e	h_____d	h_____k	sc_____ch
h_____m	h_____p	h_____sh	j_____
sc_____n	l_____ch	l_____d	sh_____e
l_____k	m_____	sh_____t	sp_____se
m_____ch	b_____	sn_____t	m_____k
s_____t	sp_____t	st_____k	m_____sh
p_____ch	st_____m	sw_____d	sw_____n
t_____ch	t_____n	t_____	y_____d
p_____k	p_____t	sc_____	sc_____f
sh_____k	sm_____t	sn_____l	sp_____

sp_____k   st_____   st_____ch   st_____t

d_____k   st_____ve   th_____n   sh_____p

*Work with a partner for partner dictation. Give each other any fifteen words
from the list above to spell out loud without using paper and pencil.*

Spelling Rules

OR Suffix Rule: Both *er* and *or* can be used as suffixes that mean "one who does" or "a thing
that does." If a real word can be made by using an *-ion* suffix, then use the *-or*
suffix. If adding an *-ion* does not make a real word, then use the *-er* suffix.

act: act + ion = action   Therefore, spell *actor* with *or.*

predict: predict + ion = prediction   Therefore, spell *predictor* with *or.*

consume: consume + ion = doesn't exist.   Therefore, spell *consumer* with *er.*

paint: paint + ion = doesn't exist.   Therefore, spell *painter* with *er.*

Exceptions: surviv**or**,   tail**or**,   monit**or**,   scuplt**or**,   govern**or**,

counsel**or**,   desert**er**,   promot**er**,   survey**or**

 **PRACTICE**

In the following list of words, decide if there is an **-ion form** *for the word; circle*
yes *or* **no.** *Then circle the correct spelling of the word with an -er or an -or*
suffix.

Word	-ion Form		Correct
instruct	yes	no	instructer, instructor
compose	yes	no	composer, composor
play	yes	no	player, playor
post	yes	no	poster, postor
supervise	yes	no	superviser, supervisor
transmit	yes	no	transmitter, transmittor
edit	yes	no	editer, editor
build	yes	no	builder, buildor
educate	yes	no	educater, educator
contract	yes	no	contracter, contractor
dictate	yes	no	dictater, dictator

Words—Multi-Syllable Words with *R*-Controls

1. Read each word carefully. Draw a line to divide each word into syllables.
2. Write the word on the practice line.
3. If an *-ing* suffix can be added to make a real word, write the word on the
   line. Write an **X** if no word can be made with the *-ing* suffix.
4. Add any other suffix to the word to make a real word. You may use suffixes
   already presented as well as other suffixes you know that have not yet been
   presented.

✎ **PRACTICE**

Word	Practice	With -*ing*	With Any Suffix
1. article	_____	_____	_____
2. bargain	_____	_____	_____
3. carpet	_____	_____	_____
4. harvest	_____	_____	_____
5. marble	_____	_____	_____
6. market	_____	_____	_____
7. marvel	_____	_____	_____
8. spa**rk**le	_____	_____	_____
9. sta**rt**le	_____	_____	_____
10. target	_____	_____	_____
11. summ**ary**	_____	_____	_____
12. sal**ary**	_____	_____	_____
13. ha**rass**	_____	_____	_____
14. burg**lar**	_____	_____	_____
15. calend**ar**	_____	_____	_____
16. gramm**ar**	_____	_____	_____
17. doll**ar**	_____	_____	_____
18. alt**er**	_____	_____	_____
19. ang**er**	_____	_____	_____
20. av**er**age	_____	_____	_____
21. canc**er**	_____	_____	_____
22. cent**er**	_____	_____	_____
23. des**er**t	_____	_____	_____
24. dess**er**t	_____	_____	_____
25. eag**er**	_____	_____	_____
26. gen**er**al	_____	_____	_____

Word	Practice	With -ing	With Any Suffix
27. govern	_____	_____	_____
28. master	_____	_____	_____
29. mercy	_____	_____	_____
30. merge	_____	_____	_____
31. modern	_____	_____	_____
32. mystery	_____	_____	_____
33. person	_____	_____	_____
34. thunder	_____	_____	_____
35. whisper	_____	_____	_____
36. wonder	_____	_____	_____
37. circus	_____	_____	_____
38. virtue	_____	_____	_____
39. border	_____	_____	_____
40. forest	_____	_____	_____
41. gorge	_____	_____	_____
42. morning	_____	_____	_____
43. normal	_____	_____	_____
44. tornado	_____	_____	_____
45. burden	_____	_____	_____
46. furnish	_____	_____	_____
47. hurry	_____	_____	_____
48. pursue	_____	_____	_____
49. surgery	_____	_____	_____
50. surprise	_____	_____	_____

Looking at Specific Words

The words *desert* and *dessert* are often confused. Have you ever received an invitation for a reception with "desert"? Confusion can be avoided by learning the following definitions and a memory trick.

desert: *n.*   (des′-ert) a dry, arid, barren region
            adj. (des′-ert) describing something that is related to a dry, arid, barren region
            v. (de-sert′) to abandon

dessert: *n.*   (des-sert′) a sweet food or food served at the end of a meal
            To remember that *dessert* has *ss,* use this mnemonic (memory trick):
            Dessert is So Sweet (SS).

✎ **PRACTICE**

Write desert *or* dessert *to complete the following sentences.*

1. The chocolate cheesecake was ordered for _____.

2. Many men do not _____ their families during crises.

3. The _____ plates were chilled.

4. The camels moved slowly across the _____.

5. The _____ heat made traveling difficult.

Name _____ Date _____

✎ **Exercise 7.1 Working with *R*-Controls**

1. As a review, write the **Second CVC Doubling Rule:** _____

_____

Write any ten two-syllable CVC words found in the word list on pages 201–202. Then circle any of the CVC words in your list that have the CVC syllable accented when you say the word with the -ing suffix. These will be the words in which the last consonant will be doubled.

_____ _____ _____ _____ _____

_____ _____ _____ _____ _____

2. As a review, write the **-LE** *Syllable Rule:* _____

_____

Write the four words from the list on pages 201–202 that end with an -le syllable.

_____ _____ _____ _____

3. Write the six words from the list in which the ar *sounds like* er.

_____ _____ _____

_____ _____ _____

4. Write the eleven words from the Spelling Definitions on page 198 in which the or *sounds like* er.

_____ _____ _____

_____ _____ _____

_____ _____ _____

_____ _____

5. Refer back to the Spelling Definitions on page 198. Write the five words that are exceptions to the two sounds of **ar.** *In these words,* **ar** *does not sound like* ar, *nor does it sound like* er.

_____ _____ _____

_____ _____

6. As a review, write the **Consonant + Y Rule** *(also known as the "Y to I Rule"):*

_____

Write the six words from the word list on pages 201–202 that end in a consonant and a y. *Then add the* -s *or the* -es *suffix and write the complete word on the line.*

_____ + s/es = _____

_____ + s/es = _____

_____ + s/es = _____

_____ + s/es = _____

_____ + s/es = _____

_____ + s/es = _____

7. *In addition to the words written in number 6 above, there are three more words in the word list on pages 201–202 that will use the* -es *suffix instead of the* -s *suffix. Write those three words with the* -es *suffix on the lines below.*

_____   _____   _____

8. *Nine words in the word list have a soft* c *or a soft* g *combination. Find those nine words and write them on the lines below.*

_____   _____   _____

_____   _____   _____

_____   _____   _____

Homonyms with *R*-Controls

✎ PRACTICE

Parts of the following assignment may be assigned to individual partners or groups to complete and then report back to the class.

　　The following sentences show **homonyms** *in bold print. Look at how the word is working in the sentence. Write* **N** *in the blank if the word is working as a* **noun.** *Write* **V** *if the word is working as a* **verb.** *Write* **A** *if the word is working as an* **adjective.** *In the third column, write an informal definition of any of the word meanings that are unfamiliar to you.*

Part of Speech	Sentence	Informal Definition
_____	**1.** The actress wore a fake **fur** coat.	
_____	**2.** The **fur** was hanging in the closet.	
_____	**3.** They cut down the **fir** tree.	
_____	**4. Fir** was used to make the dresser.	
_____	**5.** Her husband's ashes will remain in the **urn.**	
_____	**6.** The kitchen committee is looking for a coffee **urn.**	
_____	**7.** Both children always **earn** their summer camp money.	
_____	**8.** Students usually **earn** their degrees within five years.	
_____	**9.** The **birth** of a child is a special event.	
_____	**10.** The **birth** of civilization is believed to be in Africa.	
_____	**11.** My child's **birth** certificate is locked in the safe.	
_____	**12.** The ocean liner is in **berth** fifty-two.	
_____	**13.** I do not want to sleep on the top **berth.**	
_____	**14.** The **flower** withered away.	
_____	**15.** I prefer to use wheat **flour** in the bread.	
_____	**16.** You will need to **flour** the board for the dough.	
_____	**17.** The chef rolled the mixture into **flour** tortillas.	
_____	**18.** The flight attendant's **collar** was frayed.	
_____	**19.** The FBI **collared** the couple near the docks.	
_____	**20.** The tenth **caller** won the trip to Orlando.	

Part of Speech	Sentence	Informal Definition

_____ **21.** Let's have coffee in the **morning.**

_____ **22.** Jamaal is not a **morning** person.

_____ **23.** The town was **mourning** the loss of its doctor.

_____ **24.** The tailors **alter** trousers for five dollars.

_____ **25.** The sisters **alter** their plans every hour.

_____ **26.** Candles burned on the **altar.**

_____ **27.** Keith was an **altar** boy for three years.

_____ **28.** Lee planned to **minor** in music.

_____ **29.** You cannot come in; you are a **minor.**

_____ **30.** The **minor** disturbance lasted a few short minutes.

_____ **31.** My **minor** is sociology.

_____ **32.** My uncle was a coal **miner** all his life.

_____ **33.** The gym has five **stationary** bikes.

_____ **34.** The weather front is **stationary.**

_____ **35.** All her letters are written on fine **stationery.**

_____ **36.** The **stationery** store stocks all your writing needs.

_____ **37.** The ranchers **herd** the livestock in the evenings.

_____ **38.** A **herd** of buffalo roamed the plains.

_____ **39.** Everyone in town **heard** the rumor.

Name _____   Date _____

✎ **EXERCISE 7.2 Sentence Work**

Circle the correct homonym to complete each sentence.

1. Many people cut Douglas (fur, fir) at Christmas time.

2. The animal's (fur, fir) was smooth and soft.

3. Metal (earns, urns) are used to store ashes.

4. You will need to (urn, earn) your keep by doing chores.

5. The couple awaited the (berth, birth) of their first child.

6. The (birth, berth) on the submarine is narrow and uncomfortable.

7. The caterer placed a delicate (flower, flour) on the top of the cake.

8. My neighbor's son is allergic to white (flower, flour).

9. The flea (collar, caller) irritated the dog's neck.

10. The family is in (morning, mourning) for a full year.

11. The (mourning, morning) sun poured in through the stained-glass windows.

12. After kneeling at the (alter, altar), the solemn man asked for forgiveness.

13. The architects can (altar, alter) the blueprints to make a larger master bedroom.

14. He was a (miner, minor) in possession, so he must appear in court.

15. The (stationery, stationary) comes with paper and matching envelopes.

16. The third hurricane of the season is (stationery, stationary) over the Bahamas.

17. Everyone in the park (herd, heard) the young child scream.

18. The (heard, herd) of wild elephants stampeded through the tropical jungle.

In the above sentences, underline the subjects once and the verbs twice. Mark the prepositional phrases by using parentheses. Circle all the adjectives.

Use words 1–25 on page 201 to complete the following sentences. You will need to add an -ing suffix to the words for the sentences to be grammatically correct.

1. The soldier was charged with _____ his troop.

2. The investigators are _____ their focus on an arsonist.

3. The investments are _____ a fourteen percent return.

4. The union will be _____ for better benefits.

5. The _____ will be laid on Friday.

6. _____ female students will not be tolerated.

7. Our _____ efforts paid off with higher profits.

8. The farmers will be _____ their crops in August.

9. The _____ waters were captured in the photograph.

10. The research findings were _____.

Use words 26–50 on page 202 to complete the following sentences. You will need to add an -ing suffix to the words for the sentences to be grammatically correct.

1. _____ the rules of spelling is a difficult task.

2. The two largest companies will be _____ in January.

3. Alicia was asked to stop _____ to her friend in class.

4. This whole situation is _____ on the absurd.

5. We were _____ to catch the last train home.

6. Thomas is always _____ new dreams.

7. We are _____ her with a baby shower.

8. The royal family will be _____ the palace with antiques.

9. The _____ unit will vote on the proposal by the end of the week.

10. I was _____ about the wisdom of his decision to retire.

Building Words

New Prefix: *oc-*

The prefix *oc-* means **toward** or **against.**

New Suffixes: *-or -ance -ant -ence -ent -ist -ic*

The suffix *-or* means **a person who does** or **a thing that does.**
The suffix *-ance* means **an action, a quality, or a condition.**
The suffix *-ant* means **to perform or cause an action.**
The suffix *-ence* means **an action, a quality, or a condition.**
The suffix *-ent* means **to perform or cause an action.**
The suffix *-ist* means **a person who.**
The suffix *-ic* describes.

New Roots: *vert   verse   tort   cur   port*

The root *vert* means **to turn.**
The root *verse* means **to turn.**
The root *tort* means **to turn.**
The root *cur* means **to run or to move on course.**
The root *port* means **to carry.**

The Suffixes *-ance,* *-ant,* *-ence,* and *-ent*

The suffixes *-ance* and *-ence* are **noun-forming suffixes;** they often sound the same. There are no rules to learn to know which suffix spelling is needed. Words ending with these suffixes need to be learned as sight words or need to be looked up in a dictionary or a spell checker.

The suffixes *-ant* and *-ent* can be **adjective-forming suffixes.** If the noun form ends in *-ance,* the adjective form ends in *-ant.* If the noun form ends in *-ence,* the adjective form ends in *-ent.* If you know the adjective form of a word, then you will automatically know the correct suffix to use for the noun form.

✎ **PRACTICE**

*In the following words, complete the words by adding the **noun suffixes** and the **adjective suffixes.** Remember, -ance and -ant are related, and -ence and -ent are related. Use the Second CVC Doubling Rule and the Drop the Final E Rule when needed.*

Noun (Add -ance or -ence.)	Adjective (Add -ant or -ent.)	Noun (Add -ance or -ence.)	Adjective (Add -ant or -ent.)
toler _____	toler _____	perman _____	perman _____
import _____	import _____	observe _____	observe _____
persist _____	persist _____	concur _____	concur _____
confide _____	confide _____	compet _____	compet _____

depend _____ depend _____ differ _____ differ _____

excel _____ excel _____ exist _____ exist _____

intellig _____ intellig _____ reside _____ reside _____

The Suffixes *-est* and *-ist*

Spelling errors can be avoided between *-est* and *-ist* by applying the definitions of the suffixes. Remember that *-est* forms superlative adjectives; *-est* means "the most." The suffix *-ist* is a noun-forming suffix that means only "a person who."

✎ PRACTICE

Add -ist *or* -est *to the following words.*

art _____ dirty _____ perfection _____ dark _____

short _____ smart _____ novel _____ humor _____

harsh _____ motor _____ race _____ alarm _____

pure _____ *or* pure _____ expression _____ stormy _____

Add the prefix or the suffix shown at the top of each column. Apply any spelling rules that are needed before the suffix is added. Remember to use the **OR Rule** *for the words in the* -or *column.*

oc-	*-or*	*-ic*
_____cur	predict_____	hero_____
_____curring	sect _____	artist _____
_____currence	operate _____	base _____
_____casion	dictate _____	realist _____
_____clude	eject _____	class _____
_____cult	defect _____	muse _____

Read the following words carefully. Count and write the number of word parts on the line. Write the base word or the root on the second line. The first one is done for you.

Number	Base Word or Root	Number	Base Word or Root
clearances ___3___	___clear___	grievances _____	_____
conferences _____	_____	pleasantly _____	_____
insistence _____	_____	preference _____	_____
subversive _____	_____	adversary _____	_____

Number	Base Word or Root	Number	Base Word or Root
averted _____	_____	marriages _____	_____
expressionist _____	_____	referencing _____	_____

Circle all the prefixes below.

re	y	ad	oc	age	ous
pro	im	ual	tain	se	es

Circle all the suffixes below.

er	or	ject	ant	ly	ence
vert	per	ness	ure	ual	ive
ist	ic	ful	full	ment	s

Circle all the roots below.

trans	mote	vise	tort	cur	port
cide	verse	stant	ible	com	vert
tect	tract	tiss	fer	mit	gress

✎ EXERCISE 7.3 **Building Words Using Word Bases, Roots, Prefixes, and Suffixes**

The base word or the root is shown in bold print. Add the prefixes and suffixes. Write the complete word with all the word parts on the line. Remember to check for any rules needed to add the suffixes.

1. dis + **tort** + ion + ist = _____

2. re + **vert** + ed = _____

3. con + **fer** + ence + ing = _____

4. **marry** + age = _____

5. re + **fer** + ance/ence = _____

6. trans + **port** + ate + ion = _____

7. de + **port** + ment = _____

8. dis + **tort** + ed = _____

9. **port** + able/ible = _____

10. **blur** + y = _____

11. **starve** + ate + ion = _____

12. **market** + ing = _____

13. **salary** + ed = _____

14. **cancer** + ous = _____

15. **mystery** + ous + ly = _____

16. re + **forest** + ate + ion = _____

17. **tornado** + s/es = _____

18. **surgery** + s/es = _____

19. **scarce** + ly = _____

20. re + **verse** + able/ible = _____

21. in + de + **pend** + ant/ent = _____

22. **tort** + ure + ous = _____

23. oc + **cur** + ance/ence = _____

24. please + ant/ent + ly = _____

25. sup + **port** + ive = _____

26. oc + **cur** + ing = _____

27. ex + **port** + s/es = _____

28. in + **form** + al + ly = _____

29. nerve + ous + ness = _____

30. dark + en + ing = _____

31. summary + s/es = _____

32. alter + ate + ion = _____

33. govern + ment = _____

34. virtue + ous = _____

35. wonder + ful = _____

36. pursue + ing = _____

37. worry + ing = _____

38. per + **sist** + ant/ent = _____

EXERCISE 7.4 **Word List Expansion**

Each time new prefixes, suffixes, and roots are added to the lists in this text-book, the number of words that can be constructed increases rapidly. Without looking back at any words in previous exercises, construct words that have at least three word parts from the parts given below. The roots are from Chapters 6 and 7. The prefixes and the suffixes are from all the chapters.

Prefixes		Roots		Suffixes	
ab	ob	ceive	port	able	ing
ad	oc	cept	tain	age	ion
com	per	cur	tort	ance	ist
con	pre	gress	verse	ant	ive
de	pro	fess	vert	ate	less
dis	re	lect		ed	ly
e	se			en	ment
ex	sub			ence	ness
im	trans			ent	or
in	un			er	ous
mis				es	s
				est	ual
				ful	ure
				ible	y
				ic	

_____ *convertible* _____   _____   _____

_____   _____   _____

_____   _____   _____

_____   _____   _____

_____   _____   _____

_____   _____   _____

_____   _____   _____

_____   _____   _____

_____   _____   _____

_____   _____   _____

✎ **EXERCISE 7.5 Sentence Writing**

Return to the list of ar *and* or *words on pages 201–202. Write eight **compound sentences.** Each sentence must have **two** words from the* ar *and* or *word list.*

1. _____

2. _____

3. _____

4. _____

5. _____

6. _____

7. _____

8. _____

Return to the list of er, ir, *and* ur *words on pages 201–202. Write eight sentences that each use **two** words from the list. In each sentence, have at least one **prepositional phrase** and one **adjective.**

1. _____

2. _____

3. _____

4. _____

5. _____

6. _____

7. _____

8. _____

Write a sentence that uses the following homonyms.

1. minor

_____

2. stationary

_____

3. altar

_____

4. berth

_____

5. caller

_____

All the words below can work as **adjectives.** *Select three words to use in sentences that use Adjective Pattern 1. Choose three more words to use in sentences that use Adjective Pattern 2.*

| third | average | former | parched | sharp | virtuous | hard | charred | sparse |
| marble | deserted | eager | modern | normal | mysterious | general | dark | smart |

1. _____

2. _____

3. _____

4. _____

5. _____

6. _____

Grammar Definitions

Sentence Combining: Sentence combining involves joining the thoughts and the information of two or more sentences into one new sentence. If all or most of the sentences used in a paragraph or an essay are short, simple sentences, the writing style is often seen as uninteresting. Sentence combining can add a higher level of interest and sophistication to paragraphs and essays. *Note:* Additional sentence combining techniques will be presented in Chapters 8 and 10.

Three methods of sentence combining:

1. Combine the subjects into one sentence if the subjects share the same predicate or verb. The result is a sentence with ***compound subjects.***

   Mary is a very tolerant person. **Marcus is** a very tolerant person.

   Combined: **Mary and Marcus are** very tolerant people.

   My **teacher heard** the rumor. Several **students heard** the rumor.

   Combined: My **teacher and** several **students heard** the rumor.

2. Combine the verbs into one sentence if the verbs have the same subject. The result is a sentence with **compound verbs.**

   The heroic **miner scaled** the wall. **He climbed** out of the mine safely.

   Combined: The heroic **miner scaled** the wall and **climbed** out of the mine safely.

   Jesse plays the trumpet. **He composes** music.

   Combined: **Jesse plays** the trumpet and **composes** music.

   Note: Remember that **pronouns** replace or rename nouns. If the subject of the second sentence is a pronoun, check to see if it renames the subject of the first sentence—for example, *he* replaces *Jesse.*

3. Use one of the methods for creating a **compound** sentence. Join the two sentences by using a coordinating conjunction, a semicolon, or a semicolon with a conjunctive adverb. Note the differences in meaning that occur with the following conjunctions.

   Lynn's life changed. Her partner moved out.

   Combined: Lynn's life changed, **for** her partner moved out.

   Lynn's life changed, **so** her partner moved out.

   Lynn's life changed; her partner moved out.

   Lynn's life changed; **as a result,** her partner moved out.

   Lynn's life changed; **unfortunately,** her partner moved out.

   Lynn's partner moved out; **consequently,** her life changed.

Sentence Combining

✎ **PRACTICE**

*Sentence combining provides you, the writer, with options. Ideas can always be expressed in more than one way. As the writer, your objective is to select the method that best expresses your ideas in an interesting way. Choose any method of sentence combining to combine the following sentences into **one** sentence. Then select a second method of combining the sentences into **one** sentence. Be sure to use correct punctuation when you make compound sentences. Place a star next to the sentence that you prefer.*

Example: *The tractor runs well.   The body is rusty.*

Combined: a. *The tractor runs well, but the body is rusty.*
                 b. *The tractor runs well; however, the body is rusty.*

1. The salary at the mill is above average. Many people apply for job openings.

a. _____

b. _____

2. The minor was nervous. He was worried. He was going to take his permit test.

a. _____

b. _____

3. The governor vetoed the bill. She asked the subcommittee to draft a new bill.

a. _____

b. _____

4. The tailor measured the inseam. The tailor measured the waist.

a. _____

b. _____

5. The chef charred the steaks. The chef stirred the broth. He tossed the salad.

a. _____

b. _____

Name _____   Date _____

✎ **EXERCISE 7.6 Identifying Nouns, Verbs, and Adjectives**

The following suffixes tend *to be noun-forming suffixes, verb-forming suffixes, or adjective-forming suffixes. However, remember that words can often be used in a variety of ways, so it is still necessary to consider the different ways that the words can work in sentences when you try to identify the part of speech. For example, -ed is often a verb-forming suffix; however, words with -ed could also work as adjectives:* I unintentionally charred *(verb)* the steaks on the grill. The charred *(adjective)* steaks were still delicious.

Noun-Forming Suffixes	**Verb-Forming Suffixes**	**Adjective-Forming Suffixes**
age (storage)	*s, es* (runs, boxes)	*able, ible* (lovable, responsible)
er (teacher, sprayer)	*ing* (burning)	*er* (shorter)
or (conductor)	*ed* (stirred)	*est* (shortest)
ist (artist)	*en* (lighten)	*ful* (hopeful)
ment (payment)	*ate* (compensate)	*ive* (massive)
ness (happiness)		*less* (homeless)
ion (transportation)		*ly* (lovely)
ure (pleasure)		*ous* (glorious)
ance (insurance)		*ual* (gradual)
ence (independence)		*y* (blurry)
		ant (resistant)
		ent (independent)

*In the following list of words, write **N** in the blank if the word can work as a noun. Write **V** if the word can work as a verb. Write **A** if the word can work as an adjective. In some cases, the suffixes may provide some clues. More than one answer may be needed for some of the words. You may use a dictionary or an electronic spell checker to confirm your answers.*

independent _____	humorist _____	modern _____
wonder _____	mysterious _____	mystery _____
occur _____	sector _____	department _____
sparse _____	stormy _____	harmful _____
exert _____	squirming _____	darkness _____
starving _____	editor _____	marble _____
calendar _____	furnished _____	basic _____
supportive _____	repellent _____	reference _____

Choose any five nouns from page 218. Use one noun per sentence. Use the noun as the subject of a compound sentence.

1. _____

2. _____

3. _____

4. _____

5. _____

Choose any three verbs from page 218. Use one verb per sentence. Write simple sentences that have one verb, one prepositional phrase, and two adjectives.

1. _____

2. _____

3. _____

Choose three adjectives from page 218. Use each adjective in a sentence. Use Adjective Pattern 1. (The adjective needs to come before a noun.)

1. _____

2. _____

3. _____

Choose three more adjectives from page 218. Use each adjective in a sentence. Use Adjective Pattern 2. (The adjective needs to come after a linking verb.)

1. _____

2. _____

3. _____

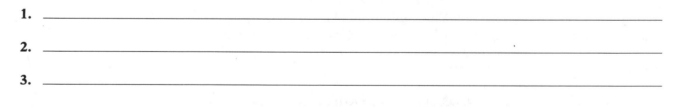

EXERCISE 7.7 Finding Subjects, Verbs, Prepositional Phrases, Verb Infinitives, and Adjectives

Mark the prepositional phrases with parentheses and the verb infinitives with brackets. Underline the subject or subjects once and the verb or verbs twice. Circle all the adjectives.

1. The well-known promoter of boxing champions met the press and expressed his opinion.

2. The morning seemed normal, but then strange events started to happen at the mansion.

3. There were three transmitters damaged by the tornado; consequently, the community had no electricity.

4. You were smart to swerve and were lucky to miss hitting the deer in the road.

5. The surprised motorist was angered by the careless littering by the driver in front of him.

6. The novelist is a perfectionist; her work is recognized throughout the literary circles.

7. Lisa's parents were supportive of her decision to marry; however, Jimmy's parents objected to the decision.

8. My brother is exploring opportunities in the import and export business.

9. The transportation department announced a change in collecting road fees.

10. The stationery is wonderful; I will use it for my thank-you notes.

11. All of the residents gave the manager an excellent recommendation.

12. The differences in our opinions resulted in many disagreements; we are no longer friends.

13. I was the innocent target of his anger, but I refused to quit or to pursue other avenues.

14. The composer and the sculptor promoted the cultural event and received praise for their work.

15. The surf pounded the shores of Miami Beach; all swimmers were asked to leave the water.

16. The top berth broke; there were no extra berths on the train.

17. The reporter expressed the importance of independence and freedom for his country.

18. Observance of the Martin Luther King holiday occurs in most state and government offices.

Mark the prepositional phrases with parentheses and the verb infinitives with brackets. Underline the subject or subjects once and the verb or verbs twice. Circle all the adjectives. Correct any comma splice or run-on sentences by adding missing words and/or punctuation.

1. The existence of UFOs is debated however I believe in their existence.

2. The harshest winter on record for flooding occurred during the year of 1996.

3. The governor whispered to his assistant and scribbled a short message on the note pad.

4. One swimmer could not escape the swirling waters of the rapid river.

5. He is a master of deception his performances sell out in every city.

6. The golfers and the gallery left the course to seek shelter from the lightning storm.

7. One predictor of the college success is regular attendance in classes.

   8. Food was scarce, starvation and disease were killing entire populations.

   9. Marble tiles were laid in the hallways plush carpeting was laid in every room.

   10. Fortunately, the wind in the gorge died down motor homes still could not get through the canyon.

   11. The summary disclosed the importance of the merger of the two largest companies.

   12. Security clearances were given for us to attend the press conference at the Capitol.

   13. You will need to use wheat flour white flour does not work in this recipe.

   14. All references must be typed in alphabetical order, handwritten work will not be accepted.

   15. In a spurt of creativity, the artist altered his painting by using an airbrush technique.

   16. Many grievances were filed the miners protested the working conditions.

   17. The cancer center was awarded a private grant to research cancer in children.

   18. She is wonderful, she never wastes time worrying about little things in life.

   19. The editor of the newspaper displayed our poster on his wall it became a conversation piece.

   20. Upon my supervisor's insistence, I applied for the job and was hired.

EXERCISE 7.8 Sentence Writing

A noun is given for each section below. First, write two sentences that express your ideas about this topic. Then use any method to combine the two sentences into one sentence. You can add, delete, or alter words for the sentence to be correct. An example is given below.

persistence

1. Persistence is needed in many areas of life.

2. Persistence is essential for job hunting.

Combined: *Persistence is needed in many areas of life; for example, persistence is essential for job hunting.*

confidence

   1. _____

   2. _____

Combined: _____

intelligence

1. _____

2. _____

Combined: _____

marriage

1. _____

2. _____

Combined: _____

confidence

1. _____

2. _____

Combined: _____

harassment

1. _____

2. _____

Combined: _____

humor

1. _____

2. _____

Combined: _____

sports

1. _____

2. _____

Combined: _____

marketing

1. _____

2. _____

Combined: _____

music

1. _____

2. _____

Combined: _____

The following sentences are too basic and lack sufficient details. Expand each sentence by using any combination of the following methods:

   1. Add another subject or verb (compound subjects and/or compound verbs).

   2. Add prepositional phrases.

   3. Add descriptive adjectives.

   4. Add another independent clause to make a compound sentence.

1. The barn burned.

_____

2. He is average.

_____

3. The lanes merge.

_____

4. He was sworn in.

_____

5. There is a shark.

_____

6. The dictator died.

_____

7. We ordered dessert.

_____

8. She is competent.

_____

9. Surgery is scheduled.

_____

✎   **EXERCISE 7.9 Chapter Study Sheet**

In the right-hand column, write a definition for the term on the left. Practice reciting and learning this definition. Cover up the definition on the right. Recite the definition. Remove the paper to check your answers. Practice until you can define each term accurately.

R-Controlled Vowels

Two Sounds of AR

Exceptions to the Two AR Sounds

Two Sounds of OR

ER, IR, UR

OR Suffix Rule

Exceptions to the OR Suffix Rule

**Noun-Forming
Suffixes**

**Verb-Forming
Suffixes**

**Adjective-Forming
Suffixes**

**Methods of Sentence
Combining**

**Methods for Sentence
Expansion**

Name _____ Date _____

✎ CHAPTER REVIEW

Match the terms or the sample words on the left with the definitions on the right.

_____ **1.** *r*-controlled vowels

_____ **2.** word with the most common *ar* sound

_____ **3.** word with the second *ar* sound

_____ **4.** three *r*-controls that often sound the same

_____ **5.** *OR* Suffix Rule

_____ **6.** common exceptions to the *OR* Rule

_____ **7.** *desert*

_____ **8.** *dessert*

_____ **9.** *fur*

_____ **10.** *fir*

_____ **11.** *minor*

_____ **12.** *miner*

_____ **13.** *stationery*

_____ **14.** *stationary*

_____ **15.** *ence, ance*

_____ **16.** *ent, ant*

a. *er, ir, ur*

b. the outer hair of an animal

c. a person underage; something of little importance

d. can mean "to abandon"

e. paper, envelopes, writing paper

f. *ar, er, ir, or, ur*

g. fixed, not moving

h. starred

i. an evergreen

j. humor

k. use *or* if a real word can also be made by an *ion* suffix

l. adjective-forming suffixes

m. *survivor, tailor, governor, counselor, promoter, surveyor, monitor*

n. eaten after a meal and is often "so sweet"

o. the suffix on this word means "a person who"

p. noun-forming suffixes

Write ar, er, ir, or, or ur to complete the following words.

n_____vous   n_____sing   ch_____ches   doll_____s

v_____bs   st_____ring   f_____st   b_____sting

hum_____ous   m_____ging   wat_____ing   sw_____ving

p_____ches   squ_____med   c_____rying   d_____kest

sp_____sely   sp_____kling   t_____ches   h_____mful

ev_____y   sh_____test   sk_____ted   t_____ring mast_____ed   t_____geting   gen_____al   h_____ass

ang_____   eag_____ly   occ_____red   v_____tue

Write the **OR** *Suffix Rule:* _____

_____

Write **er** *or* **or** *to complete the following words.*

doct_____s   tail_____   supervis_____   mot_____   monit_____

promot_____   edit_____   operat_____   surf_____   herd_____

farm_____   surviv_____   govern_____   survey_____   confess_____

contract_____   quitt_____   predict_____   protect_____   desert_____

project_____   shipp_____   produc_____   distract_____   perceiv_____

Write **est** *or* **ist** *to complete the following words.*

humor_____   sharp_____   furri_____   art_____

hard_____   perfection_____   dark_____   smart_____

pure_____   motor_____   alarm_____   terror_____

Write **ant, ance, ent,** *or* **ence** *to complete each word. If there are two possible answers, you need to write only one of the two answers.*

excell_____   insist_____   prefer_____   repell_____

refer_____   import_____   intellig_____   compet_____

accept_____   resist_____   toler_____   confer_____

appear_____   depend_____   clear_____   exist_____

endur_____   guid_____   persist_____   occurr_____

The following suffixes are **noun-forming suffixes.** *Write any noun with this suffix; then use the word as a noun in a sentence. An example is done for you.*

ist   word: ___*artist*___   *The artist drove to the coast for the opening of the art gallery.*

1. er   word: _____   _____

2. or   word: _____   _____

3. ment   word: _____   _____

4. ness   word: _____   _____

*The following suffixes are **adjective-forming suffixes.** Write any adjective with this suffix; then use the word as an adjective in a sentence. An example is done for you.*

ive   word: *attractive*   *The attractive model has an excellent contract.*

1. ful   word: _____   _____

2. est   word: _____   _____

3. able   word: _____   _____

4. y   word: _____   _____

5. ive   word: _____   _____

Circle the prefixes and the suffixes. On the line, write the number of word parts.

hurtful _____   recurring _____   vertical _____

conversations _____ receptive _____   portable _____

transportation _____ professionally _____ elected _____

pertaining _____   converted _____   importance _____

torturing _____   reports _____   educationally _____

government _____   nervously _____   floured _____

Add the prefixes and the suffixes to the base words or the roots. Write the complete word on the line.

marry + age + s = _____   worry + ing = _____

pursue + ing = _____   con + tort + ion + ist = _____

re + fer + ence + ing = _____ con + verse + ion = _____

trans + port + ate + ion = _____   un + real + ist + ic = _____

ex + cel + ance/ence = _____   re + side + ant/ent = _____

pro + fess + er/or = _____   re + sist + er/or = _____

surgery + s/es = _____   hurry + s/es = _____

harass + ment = _____   collar + ed = _____

average + ing = _____   mercy + ful = _____

sharp + en + er = _____   re + verse + able/ible = _____

marvel + ous = _____   dark + en + ed = _____

sparkle + er + s/es = _____   con + cur + ent = _____

ex + tort + ion + ist = _____   main + tain + ing = _____

Write the kinds of sentences described. Use the homonym that is given.

1. SS–V. Use the word *fur.*

_____

2. S–V; conjunctive adverb, S–V. Use the word *mourning* as a verb.

_____

3. S–VV. Use the word *collar* as a verb.

_____

4. S–V in a compound sentence with a coordinating conjunction. Use the word *alter.*

_____

5. S–V in future tense. Use the word *minor* as a verb.

_____

6. S–V in present tense. Use the word *stationary* as an adjective.

_____

Combine each pair of sentences into one sentence.

1. My favorite representative studied the petition. He decided to support it.

_____

2. I finished my last test on Wednesday. I felt a great sense of relief.

_____

3. The alarm sounded. The alarm was a fire alarm. Volunteer fire fighters hurried to the station.

_____

4. I was impatient. I was tired of waiting in the office. I wanted to cancel the appointment.

_____

JOURNAL WRITING ASSIGNMENT

Topic: I'm Proud to Be Me

Many times people have difficulty naming fifteen or twenty great traits or characteristics about themselves, yet they can name that many positive traits about their friends or family members. Perhaps a sense of modesty holds people back from proudly telling about their good qualities. However, that won't be the case in this journal entry! Set a timer or note the starting time; write continuously for fifteen minutes telling about your good traits. So that your journal entry isn't one continuous list, briefly explain each trait. For example, you could say, "I am fair. I never try to cheat anyone or take advantage of anyone. I am patient. I don't lose my temper often; I work patiently with young children."

If you need a few ideas to get started, look at the "starter list" below of different traits; use any of the traits that you feel are true for yourself. Once you get started, then continue the process with more of your own ideas.

enthusiastic	motivated	goal-oriented	honest	curious	sincere
optimistic	confident	flexible	competent	skilled	productive
efficient	brave	organized	fun	friendly	creative
joyful	humorous	kind	sensitive	forgiving	thoughtful
smart	attentive	supportive	responsible	dedicated	generous

PARAGRAPH WRITING ASSIGNMENT

Topic: Heroes

Many people have "heroes," people whom they admire or respect. Who is your hero? Why is this person your hero? What qualities does he or she have? If you don't have a "hero," you may want to explore this topic from another perspective. Why do you think people have, want, or need heroes? Is heroism of value, or would we be better off not admiring or putting people on pedestals? Explore the notion of heroes from any one point of view.

Use the following suggestions as you develop your paragraph about heroes:

1. Use the word *hero* in your opening sentence. Include your main idea, opinion, or perspective on the topic of having a hero.

2. Since this paragraph is obviously an opinion, avoid using terms such as *I think* or *I feel*, since these weaken the impact of your opening sentence. Speak from a point of strong conviction and assertiveness.

3. Develop your paragraph with at least four more sentences that explain your thinking.

4. Include specific details, descriptions, or examples.

5. Avoid sentences that begin with *There is* or *There are*, since these are weak sentence starters. Instead, place the noun subject first in the sentence and then follow it with an action-oriented verb whenever possible.

6. End your paragraph with a summary or concluding sentence.

7. Proofread your work. Check for correct spelling, punctuation, and sentence combining.

EIGHT

Vowel Diphthongs

The topics in this chapter include the following:

- Vowel diphthong combinations
- Review of previous spelling rules
- Additional work with homonyms
- Three new prefixes, five new suffixes, and four new roots to build words
- Introduction to confusable words
- Introduction of the dependent clause, complex sentences, and subordinate conjunctions

Spelling Definitions

Vowel Diphthongs	Vowel diphthongs are two vowels together in the same syllable that make a new sound.

        Examples: **ca**u**se, d**aw**n, f**eu**d, c**oo**l, t**oo**k, j**oi**n, b**oy**, t**ou**ch, gl**ue**

oo	The vowel diphthong *oo* has two sounds. You can hear these sounds when you pronounce the following words. The diacritical markings that will be seen in a dictionary are shown below.

        too (o͞o)   **boo**k (o͝o)

oi, oy	The vowel diphthongs *oi* and *oy* sound the same. You can hear these sounds when you pronounce the following words.

        joi**n**   **b**oy

au, aw	The vowel diphthongs *au* and *aw* sound the same. You can hear these sounds when you pronounce the following words. They sound like a short *o* (ŏ).

        sau**ce**   **s**aw

eu, ew	The vowel diphthongs *eu* and *ew* sound the same. They sound like a long *u* (ū). You can hear these sounds when you pronounce the following words.

        feu**d**   **f**ew

ue	The vowel diphthong *ue* sounds like *oo*. You can hear the sound when you pronounce the following words. (Remember that *ue* can also be a vowel digraph in which the *u* is long and the *e* is silent: *hue, cue, rescue*.)

        true   **s**ue   **d**ue

ou	The *ou* vowel diphthong is the most complicated, for it has eight different sound combinations. You can hear the sounds when you pronounce the following words.

        tou**ch, d**ou**ble, c**ou**sin**   (ŭ)

        fou**ght, s**ou**ght, br**ou**ght**   (ŏ)

        hou**se, p**ou**nd s**ou**th**   (ŏw)

        cou**rt, f**ou**r, g**ou**rd**   (or)

        cou**rage**   (er)

        sou**l, th**ou**gh, b**ou**lder**   (ō)

        cou**ld, sh**ou**ld, w**ou**ld**   (o͝o)

        grou**p, s**ou**p, y**ou**th**   (o͞o)

Note: There are no rules to indicate which vowel diphthong to use when you are spelling words. Therefore, many of these words will be learned as *sight words.*

Rhyming Word Families

✎ **PRACTICE**

Add the vowel diphthong given at the top of each list. Read the words created. One sight word spelling technique to use to spell a new word involves thinking of a rhyming word. The rhyming word may give you spelling clues for the word you want to spell. As you have seen in previous chapters, however, words can rhyme but not be a "member of the same word family." For example, loan *and* bone *rhyme, but the spelling of one is not related to the spelling of the other. Thus, rhyming is one sight word technique that can be tried, but it will not be accurate every time.*

aw	**aw**	**aw**	**ew**
cr_____	br_____n	_____l	bl_____
cl_____	d_____n	b_____l	br_____
dr_____	dr_____n	br_____l	ch_____
fl_____	f_____n	cr_____l	cr_____
j_____	l_____n	dr_____l	d_____
l_____	p_____n	scr_____l	dr_____
p_____	pr_____n	sh_____l	f_____
r_____	sp_____n	spr_____l	fl_____
s_____	y_____n	**oo**	gr_____
squ_____	**oy**	b_____k	kn_____
str_____	b_____	br_____k	n_____
oi	c_____	c_____k	sl_____
_____l	j_____	h_____k	st_____
b_____l	pl_____	l_____k	str_____
br_____l	t_____	n_____k	thr_____
c_____l		sh_____k	y_____
f_____l		t_____k	
s_____l			
sp_____l			
t_____l			

ou

b_____nd

f_____nd

gr_____nd

h_____nd

p_____nd

r_____nd

s_____nd

w_____nd

oi

c_____n

j_____n

gr_____n

l_____n

ou

_____t

p_____t

r_____te

sc_____t

sh_____t

sn_____t

spr_____t

st_____t

tr_____t

oo

b_____m

bl_____m

br_____m

d_____m

gl_____m

gr_____m

r_____m

ou

b_____ght

br_____ght

f_____ght

_____ght

s_____ght

th_____ght

oo

l_____n

m_____n

n_____n

sp_____n

oo

c_____l

dr_____l

f_____l

p_____l

sch_____l

sp_____l

st_____l

ue

bl_____

d_____

fl_____

gl_____

s_____

tr_____

ou

c_____ch

cr_____ch

gr_____ch

p_____ch

Partner Work

Select any twenty words from the rhyming word family lists above to dictate to your partner. Your partner may write the words in his or her book. Then have your partner dictate twenty different words for you to write below. Together, check the accuracy of the answers.

1. _____   3. _____

2. _____   4. _____

5. _____   13. _____

6. _____   14. _____

7. _____   15. _____

8. _____   16. _____

9. _____   17. _____

10. _____   18. _____

11. _____   19. _____

12. _____   20. _____

Add **oo** or **oi** to complete the following words.

b_____st   v_____ce   p_____dle   n_____dle

ch_____ce   f_____st   h_____st   m_____se

mushr_____m   pr_____f   m_____st   p_____se

b_____t   gr_____ve   v_____d   g_____se

n_____se   s_____the   p_____nt   dr_____p

b_____th   r_____st   tr_____p   t_____th

Add **au** or **aw** to complete the following words.

s_____ce   g_____k   h_____l   f_____lt

fr_____d   v_____lt   h_____k   squ_____k

fl_____nt   l_____nch   _____ning   c_____se

_____e   cl_____se   p_____se   _____ful

g_____ze   g_____k   s_____   h_____nt

Add **ou.** Circle the sound made by **ou** *when you say the word.*

t_____ch   ŭ   ō   ōw   or   ŏ   oo   c_____rt   ŭ   ō   ōw   or   ŏ   oo

f_____r   ŭ   ō   ōw   or   ŏ   oo   s_____ght   ŭ   ō   ōw   or   ŏ   oo

gr_____p   ŭ   ō   ōw   or   ŏ   oo   sh_____ld   ŭ   ō   ōw   or   ŏ   oo

s_____p   ŭ   ō   ōw   or   ŏ   oo   y_____th   ŭ   ō   ōw   or   ŏ   oo

c_____nt   ŭ   ō   ōw   or   ŏ   oo   tr_____ble   ŭ   ō   ōw   or   ŏ   oo

c_____ple	ŭ ŏ ŏw or ō oo	br_____ght	ŭ ŏ ŏw or ō oo
f_____ght	ŭ ŏ ŏw or ō oo	ab_____t	ŭ ŏ ŏw or ō oo
b_____nce	ŭ ŏ ŏw or ō oo	f_____nd	ŭ ŏ ŏw or ō oo
cl_____d	ŭ ŏ ŏw or ō oo	t_____r	ŭ ŏ ŏw or ō oo
sp_____se	ŭ ŏ ŏw or ō oo	dr_____ght	ŭ ŏ ŏw or ō oo
c_____gh	ŭ ŏ ŏw or ō oo	m_____th	ŭ ŏ ŏw or ō oo
l_____nge	ŭ ŏ ŏw or ō oo	m_____nt	ŭ ŏ ŏw or ō oo
n_____n	ŭ ŏ ŏw or ō oo	sc_____r	ŭ ŏ ŏw or ō oo
s_____nd	ŭ ŏ ŏw or ō oo	s_____th	ŭ ŏ ŏw or ō oo
h_____se	ŭ ŏ ŏw or ō oo	gr_____p	ŭ ŏ ŏw or ō oo
c_____ld	ŭ ŏ ŏw or ō oo	th_____ght	ŭ ŏ ŏw or ō oo

Partner Work

Select any twenty words from page 235 and this page to dictate to your partner. Your partner may write the words in his or her book. Then have your partner dictate twenty different words for you to write below. Together, check the accuracy of the answers.

1. _____   11. _____

2. _____   12. _____

3. _____   13. _____

4. _____   14. _____

5. _____   15. _____

6. _____   16. _____

7. _____   17. _____

8. _____   18. _____

9. _____   19. _____

10. _____   20. _____

Spelling Rules: Review

No additional spelling rules will be presented in this textbook. All the major spelling rules that you need to know to add suffixes to base words or word roots have already been presented. Your spelling accuracy will show strong improvements if you know and apply these rules consistently to your writing.

Chapter 1	**Chapter 2**	**Chapter 3**
The *QU* Rule	C/C Syllable Rule	First CVC Doubling Rule
The *F, L, S, Z* Rule	C/*LE* Syllable Rule	Second CVC Doubling Rule
The *CK* Rule	*ES* Rule (*S, X,*	
The *TCH* Rule	*Z, SH, CH*)	

Chapter 4	**Chapter 5**	**Chapter 6**
Final *E* Dropping Rule	Vowel + *Y* Rule	Consonant + *Y* Rule (*Y* to *I* Rule)
Soft *C* and Soft *G* Rule	*Able/Ible* Guidelines	*Y* to *I* + *ES* Rule
		F to *V* Rule
		F to *V* + *ES* Rule
Chapter 7		*O* + *ES* Rule
OR Suffix Rule		*IE* Rule

✎ PRACTICE

Look at the following words. Decide which rule or rules from the list above are used in each word below. Write the name of the rule on the line. Write X if no rule is used.

squawk _____   pew-ter _____

poo-dle _____   launch + es _____

noise + y _____   voice + less _____

joy + ous _____   country + es _____

cloud + y + ncss _____   hoof + s/es _____

vouch + er _____   audit + or _____

shoulder + ing _____   sub + due + ing _____

cur-few _____   courage + ous _____

annoy + ing _____   proof + s _____

Words with Vowel Diphthongs

1. Say each word slowly. Practice writing the word twice.
2. Write the vowel diphthong and the sound that it makes. The first three are done as examples. (For *oo*, you do not need to mark o͞o or o͝o.)

✎ **PRACTICE**

Word	Practice	Practice	Diphthong and Sound
1. tycoon			*oo = oo*
2. author			*au = ō*
3. trouser			*ou = ōw*
4. tabloid			*oi = oi*
5. raccoon			
6. source			
7. avenue			
8. turmoil			
9. poison			
10. construe			
11. astronaut			
12. curfew			
13. ounce			
14. doubt			
15. trauma			
16. boycott			
17. nephew			
18. autumn			
19. souvenir			
20. courage			
21. vowel			
22. typhoon			
23. because			
24. audience			
25. laundry			
26. revenue			

Word	Practice	Practice	Diphthong and Sound
27. caution			
28. exhaust			
29. audit			
30. faucet			
31. turquoise			
32. routine			
33. assault			
34. daughter			
35. thousand			
36. enough			
37. sewer			
38. news			
39. annoy			
40. maneuver			
41. could			
42. count			
43. country			
44. authentic			
45. auditorium			
46. nourish			
47. sirloin			
48. destroy			
49. cartoon			
50. cousin			

Many of the words on pages 238–239 will be easier to learn if you spell them by syllables. Say each of the following words slowly. Let your voice help you decide where to divide the words into syllables. Note that vowel diphthongs must remain together in the same syllable. Use a diagonal line to show where to divide the following words. Remember that every syllable must have a vowel.

tycoon	author	trouser	tabloid
raccoon	turmoil	avenue	curfew
poison	construe	trauma	astronaut
boycott	nephew	autumn	souvenir
typhoon	vowel	because	audience
laundry	revenue	caution	assault
audit	faucet	turquoise	thousand
maneuver	country	authentic	auditorium
cartoon	sirloin	cousin	nourish

✎ EXERCISE 8.1 **Working with Words with Vowel Diphthongs**

Refer to the word list on pages 238–239 for all of the following directions.

1. Find the six words that are **one-syllable** words. Write the words below.

_____   _____   _____

_____   _____   _____

2. Find the four words that have **silent consonants.** Write the words below.

_____   _____   _____   _____

3. Write the eleven words that have *r*-controls. Do not use the word *souvenir,* which has an irregular *ir* sound, and do not use the *ou* words *source, courage,* or *nourish.*

_____   _____   _____

_____   _____   _____

_____   _____   _____

_____

4. Write the five words that have **soft *c*** or **soft *g*.**

_____   _____   _____

_____   _____

5. The letters *ph* are consonant digraphs. They make the sound *fff.* Find the two words that have the *ph* **consonant digraph.**

_____   _____

6. Although the word *news* looks like a plural noun, it is treated as a singular noun. Select the present tense singular verb in the following sentences.

a. The news (is, are) reported at six o'clock.

b. The news on television (cover, covers) local and national news.

c. Our local news (show, shows) community events.

✎ EXERCISE 8.2 **Sentence Work**

Use words 1–25 from the list on page 238 to complete the following sentences.

1. The _____ loved hearing the _____ describe his space walk.

2. There was too much _____ in the house for the child to concentrate.

3. It took great _____ to publicly confront that powerful _____ about his overseas business operations.

4. The _____s often exaggerate and _____ details about the lives of famous people.

5. The _____ of the _____'s facts for her book were not disclosed.

6. I _____ that the teenagers will pay attention to the eleven o'clock _____.

7. _____ often occur in the Pacific Ocean during the _____ months.

8. Right after my _____'s accident, he was rushed to the _____ unit in Cleveland.

9. The _____ was a keychain with a picture of a _____ in a natural setting.

10. Hundreds of people marched along the main _____ to support the _____ of grapes and other farm products.

Use words 26–50 to complete the following sentences.

1. The IRS will _____ your business and will check the sources of all your _____.

2. You need to call the plumber; you are about to _____ my kitchen _____.

3. The silver and _____ jewelry was exported out of the _____.

4. A _____ label was attached to the _____ pipe on my car.

5. The county authorities told all home owners that they _____ hook up to the new _____ system by the end of the year.

6. My _____ always seems to _____ his way out of difficult situations.

7. The _____ on the motorist was reported on the evening _____.

8. My _____ has had _____; she finally quit her job.

9. The performance of _____ Mexican folk dance was held in the new _____.

10. More than one _____ _____ steaks were served at the rodeo.

All of the following words have vowel diphthongs. Read the words carefully; use a dictionary to check the meanings of any words that are unfamiliar to you. All these words can work as adjectives to describe or modify nouns or pronouns.

shrewd	lewd	cruel	south	four	young	double
rough	tough	loud	proud	smooth	loose	good
moist	loyal	awful	scrawny	feudal	royal	neutral
plausible	authentic	yew	true	few	round	new

Choose fifteen adjectives from the list above. For sentences 1–10, write sentences that use one or more of the adjectives in Adjective Pattern 1.

1. _____

2. _____

3. _____

4. _____

5. _____

6. _____

7. _____

8. _____

9. _____

10. _____

For sentences 11–15, write sentences that use one or more of the adjectives in Adjective Pattern 2.

11. _____

12. _____

13. _____

14. _____

15. _____

*At the end of each sentence you will see a verb inside parentheses. Each verb is an irregular verb. Complete each sentence by writing the **past tense** of the verb. You may refer to a dictionary to check the spelling of the past tense if necessary.*

1. Mary _____ the arrow into the center of the target. (shoot)

2. We _____ next to the auditorium door. (stand)

3. They _____ us how to use computers in the fourth grade. (teach)

4. All of the people on the commercial charter _____ fish. (catch)

5. I _____ that movie on Saturday. (see)

6. I _____ all the string for the kite onto this spool. (wind)

7. The whistles _____ exactly at noon. (blow)

8. Heather and Kenneth always _____ the correct answers. (know)

9. The knights in shining armor _____ the dragons. (slay)

10. Both pitchers _____ curve balls late in the game. (throw)

11. They _____ the Civil War on these grounds. (fight)

12. Everyone _____ a potluck dish. (bring)

13. The women _____ access to the locker room. (seek)

14. The students _____ the required computer software. (buy)

Homonyms

✎ **PRACTICE**

Match the homonyms on the left to their definitions on the right. Each letter will be used only once.

_____ 1. troop a. offensive; wet and stormy; unfair; to break the rules in a game

_____ 2. troupe b. the past tense of the verb *blow*

_____ 3. fowl c. a group of stage performers

_____ 4. foul d. animal feet; handles rudely; strikes with a foot

_____ 5. forth e. sharp nails of an animal; scratches; digs

_____ 6. fourth f. past tense of the verb *know*

_____ 7. blue g. cavalry; soldiers; a collection of people

_____ 8. blew h. not old or familiar

_____ 9. haul i. after three and before five; one of four equal parts

_____ 10. hall j. sixty minutes

_____ 11. clause k. a bird or a chicken

_____ 12. claws l. a corridor; a large building; a lobby; a large room or an auditorium

_____ 13. pause m. forward

_____ 14. paws n. past tense of the verb *teach*

_____ 15. new o. a color; melancholy; sad

_____ 16. knew p. a small child

_____ 17. our q. brief interruption; to stop briefly

_____ 18. hour r. possessive form of the pronoun *we*

_____ 19. wood s. to draw, pull, transport, carry; amount carried or distance transported

_____ 20. would t. separate part of a document; a group of words with a subject and a predicate

_____ 21. taught u. a helping verb that shows willingness

_____ 22. tot v. product that comes from trees; lumber

Read the definitions of the following homonyms. Then write the correct homonyms on the lines to complete the sentences.

to, too, two

to: a preposition that means "in the direction of," "at," "on," or "near" (*to the station, to school*) part of a verb to make a verb an infinitive (*to write, to carry, to drive, to run*)

too: an adverb that means "excessively" (*too hot, too young, too expensive*)
an adverb that means "in addition" or "also" (*I, too, want to go. I want to go, too.*)

two: a noun, a pronoun, or an adjective that means "one more than one" (*two shoes, two dollars*)

1. I wanted _____ write a letter _____ my mother, but there were _____ many other things _____ do.

2. The mare was _____ tired _____ leave her stall.

3. The _____ girls want _____ go _____ the mall with you, _____.

4. It was _____ o'clock in the morning; it was _____ late for the _____ hungry teenagers _____ order a pizza.

5. There was way _____ much food for _____ people _____ eat.

dew, due, do

dew: a noun that means "moisture that condenses at night"

due: an adjective that means "owed," "appropriate," or "expected"
a noun that means "something that is appropriate"

do: a verb that means "to work to accomplish," "to behave," "to prepare," or "to fix up"

1. The ground was covered with _____.

2. _____ you cover your tomato plants to protect them from the _____?

3. The library book is _____.

4. I was _____ a tax refund; I planned to _____ many things with the money.

5. You can _____ that later in the week, but it is _____ no later than Monday.

flu, flew, flue

flu: a noun that means "a minor virus or ailment"

flew: a past tense verb for the verb *fly*, which can mean "to float," "soar," or "flee"

flue: a noun that means "a smoke, air, gas, or steam duct in a chimney or a boiler"
a noun that means "a type of fishing net"

1. The dirty _____ was the source of the fire.

2. The family packed up their belongings and _____ the coop.

3. Five students had the _____ and could not attend classes.

4. The bird _____ out the opened window.

5. The _____ was hoisted onto the fishing vessel.

through, threw

through: a preposition that means "into one side and out the other side," "by the way of," "among," "between," or "all around" an adjective that means "finished," "done," or "completed"

threw: a past tense of the verb *throw*, which can mean "propelled through the air," "caused to fall," put suddenly into a certain condition," or "moved quickly"

1. The player on first base _____ the ball _____ the picture window.

2. My nephew _____ a temper tantrum in the grocery store.

3. We drove _____ the tunnel on the way to the coast.

4. I am _____ with the term paper.

5. My family _____ a surprise party for my birthday.

four, fore, for

four: a noun, a pronoun, or an adjective that means "one more than three"

fore: an adverb that means "in or toward the front"
an adjective that means "being or coming before in time, place, or order"; "at or toward the bow of a ship"
a noun that means "front"
an interjection used in golf to warn other players of a ball heading their way

for: a preposition that is used to show purpose, in the direction of, or intended for a coordinating conjunction that means "because"

1. _____ now, friendship is in the _____; everything else can wait.

2. I bought _____ red roses _____ my sweetheart.

3. She was a nightmare on the course; she had to yell "_____" _____ times on the first three holes.

4. _____ the sake of your _____ children, seriously consider the job.

5. Move to the _____ of the boat, _____ too much weight is in the back.

Spell the other homonyms for each of the words below.

troupe _____   fowl _____

forth _____   blue _____

hall _____   claws _____

paws _____   new _____

hour _____   wood _____

tot _____   threw _____

flew _____ _____   for _____ _____

two _____ _____   do _____ _____

Use all the homonyms shown above. Write the homonyms under their parts of speech. Some words may need to be written in more than one column.

Noun	Pronoun	Verb	Adjective	Preposition	Adverb

Building Words

> **New Prefixes:**   *a-   en-   be-*
>
> The prefix *a-* means ***in, on, not,*** or ***without.***
> The prefix *en-* means ***in.***
> The prefix *be-* means ***to do, to make, about,*** or ***around.***
>
>
> **New Suffixes:**   *-ship   -hood   -ite   -ism   -ize*
>
> The suffix *-ship* means ***state or quality of something.***
> The suffix *-hood* means ***state or quality of something.***
> The suffix *-ite* means ***formed, showing, or marked by something.***
> The suffix *-ism* means ***state or quality of something.***
> The suffix *-ize* means ***to cause to be, become, or make into.***
>
>
> **New Roots:**   *nate   pense   turb   soci*
>
> The root *nate* means ***to be born.***
> The root *pense* means ***to hang*** or ***to weigh.***
> The root *turb* means ***to agitate, disturb,*** or ***confuse.***
> The root *soci* means ***sharing.***

✎ PRACTICE

The following new prefixes can be added to words from this chapter as well as words from previous chapters. Use the prefix shown at the top of each column. Look up the meanings of any unfamiliar words. Write the part or parts of speech inside the parentheses. Use N for noun, V for verb, Adj for adjective, Prep for preposition, and Adv for adverb. (Adverbs will be covered in Chapter 9.)

a-	en-	be-
_____bout ( )	_____act ( )	_____come ( )
_____cross ( )	_____rich ( )	_____cause ( )
_____drift ( )	_____trust ( )	_____fit ( )
_____bound ( )	_____tail ( )	_____fore ( )
_____cute ( )	_____list ( )	_____friend ( )
_____way ( )	_____case ( )	_____have ( )
_____wait ( )	_____lighten ( )	_____tray ( )
_____board ( )	_____gulf ( )	_____low ( )
_____trophy ( )	_____force ( )	_____little ( )
_____do ( )	_____large ( )	_____rate ( )

Assimilation

Assimilation is the process in language in which one word part is modified to resemble the next or the adjacent word part. The prefix *a-* undergoes assimilation when placed next to word bases or roots that begin with *c, d, f, g, n, p, r, s,* and *t*. Therefore, the prefix *a-* becomes *ac-, ad-, af-, ag-, an-, ap-, ar-, as-,* and *at-*. The assimilation of the prefix *a-* can be seen in the following words:

ac-count	ac-cord	ad-dict	ad-dress
af-fect	af-ford	ag-gress	ag-gravate
an-nounce	an-noy	ap-ply	ap-point
ar-range	ar-ray	as-set	as-sist
at-tire	at-tract		

New Suffixes

✎ **PRACTICE**

The following new suffixes can be added to words from this chapter as well as words from previous chapters. Use the suffix shown at the top of each column. Apply any spelling rules that are needed to spell the new word correctly. Look up the meanings of any unfamiliar words. Note that the -ite suffix is often combined with the -y suffix. Some examples are given below.

-ship	*-hood*	*-ite*	*-ism*	*-ize*
friend_____	neighbor_____	graph_____	social_____	social_____
court_____	brother_____	social_____	national_____	national_____
relation_____	sister_____	compose_____	capital_____	capital_____
receiver_____	lively_____	define_____	race_____	civil_____
dealer_____	woman_____		real_____	real_____
member_____	man_____	***-ity (ite + y)***	critic_____	critic_____
fellow_____	likely_____	sane_____	tour_____	formal_____
partner_____	parent_____	real_____	hero_____	natural_____
town_____		grave_____	terror_____	actual_____
				verbal_____

As a review, write the definition of each of the following parts of speech:

Noun: _____

Verb: _____

Adjective: _____

In Chapter 7, page 218 listed noun-forming, verb-forming, and adjective-forming suffixes. Look at the words that were created on page 250 with the suffixes -ship, -hood, -ite, -ity, -ism, and -ize. Decide which suffixes are noun-forming, which are verb-forming, and which are adjective-forming. Use this information to complete the following sentences.

1. The suffix *-ship* is often a(n) _____-forming suffix.

2. The suffix *-hood* is often a(n) _____-forming suffix.

3. The suffix *-ite* or *-ity* is often a(n) _____-forming suffix.

4. The suffix *-ism* is often a(n) _____-forming suffix.

5. The suffix *-ize* is often a(n) _____-forming suffix.

Combine the information above with the information given on page 218 to complete a summary chart of noun-forming, verb-forming, and adjective-forming suffixes.

Summary Chart

Noun-Forming Suffixes	Verb-Forming Suffixes	Adjective-Forming Suffixes

✎ **EXERCISE 8.3 Building Words Using Word Bases, Roots, Prefixes, and Suffixes**

Combine all the following word parts. Apply any spelling rules needed to add the suffixes to the roots or the base words.

1. feud + al + ism = _____

2. sane + ite + ate + ion = _____

3. at + tend + ance = _____

4. ap + ply + ic + ate + ion = _____

5. be + witch + ing = _____

6. pro + duct + ive + ite + y = _____

7. man + er + ism + s/es = _____

8. con + cept + ual + ize = _____

9. friend + ship + s/es = _____

10. en + force + ing = _____

11. form + al + ize + ate + ion = _____

12. author + ite + y + s/es = _____

13. act + ive + ite + y + s/es = _____

14. dis + turb + ance = _____

15. in + nate + ly = _____

16. nate + ion + al + ite + y = _____

17. un + soci + able = _____

18. in + dis + pense + able = _____

19. ac + count + ant = _____

20. as + sist + ant = _____

21. be + rate + ing = _____

22. nate + ure + al + ize = _____

23. ap + ply + ing = _____

24. im + pose + ite + ion = _____

25. pro + pense + ite + y = _____

26. in + fine + ite + y = _____

27. be + long + ing = _____

28. re + in + force + ment + s = _____

29. pro + fess + ion + al + ism = _____

30. author + ize + ate + ion = _____

31. form + al + ite + y + s/es = _____

32. scarce + ite + y = _____

33. per + turb + ed = _____

34. nate + ure + al + ly = _____

35. soci + al + ize + ing = _____

36. com + pense + ate + ion = _____

37. pense + ion + s/es = _____

38. en + rage + ed = _____

✎   EXERCISE 8.4 **Word List Expansion**

Some words have two vowels together, but the vowels are not vowel digraphs or vowel diphthongs because the vowels are in two separate syllables. Study the following words, in which the vowels that are together exist in separate syllables.

diary (di-ar-y)	piano (pi-a-no)	mania (ma-ni-a)	medium (me-di-um)
giant (gi-ant)	stadium (sta-di-um)	violin (vi-o-lin)	period (pe-ri-od)
idea (i-de-a)	area (a-re-a)	linear (li-ne-ar)	pancreas (pan-cre-as)
quiet (qui-et)	science (sci-ence)	genius (gen-ius)	criterion (cri-ter-i-on)
theory (the-o-ry)	lenient (len-i-ent)	suicide (su-i-cide)	fuel (fu-el)

Partner Work

Each partner dictates ten of the above words for the other partner to write on paper.

Nate, Pense, Turb, and *Soci*

✎   **PRACTICE**

The following words have the new roots for this chapter. Study each word carefully. Write the number of word parts found in each word.

Nate	*Pense*	*Turb*	*Soci*
national _____	compensation _____	disturbing _____	socialization _____
nationality _____	compensatory _____	disturbances _____	social _____
nationalities _____	expensive _____	perturbed _____	socialite _____
native _____	indispensable _____	disturbingly _____	socially _____
nativity _____	pension _____	disturbed _____	socialism _____
natural _____	dispense _____	perturbing _____	socialistic _____
naturalist _____	pensive _____	undisturbed _____	sociable _____
naturally _____	inexpensively _____	disturber _____	unsociable _____
nature _____	dispenser _____	disturbs _____	socializing _____
innately _____	suspension _____	perturbations _____	socials _____

Confusables

Confusables are words that are frequently confused because they differ by one or two letters. Read the following information carefully. Pay attention to the letters in bold print because they are often the point of confusion.

ch**oo**se	verb	*Choose* means "to select or decide." All the letter sounds follow phonetic patterns.
ch**o**se	verb	*Chose* is the past tense of *choose.* All the letter sounds follow phonetic patterns.
ch**oi**ce	noun	*Choice* means "the selection" or "the decision." All the letter sounds follow phonetic patterns.
through	preposition	*Through* means "into at one side and out the other," "by the way of," or "among, between, or around." The word begins with a consonant digraph plus an *r*. The *ough* sounds like *oo*.
	adjective	*Through* also works as an adjective meaning "finished" or "done with."
though	conjunctive adverb	*Though* means "however" or "despite the fact." The word begins with a consonant digraph. The *ough* sounds like a long *o*.

thorough	adjective	*Thorough* means "omitting or overlooking nothing," or "complete." The word begins with a consonant digraph and than an *r*-controlled vowel that sounds like *er.* The *ough* sounds like a long *o.*
thought	verb	*Thought* is the past tense of *think.* The word begins with a consonant digraph and ends with the *t* sound. The *ough* sounds like a short *o.*
loose	adjective	*Loose* means "slack," "not fixed or not tight," or "not exact." All the letters follow phonetic patterns.
lose	verb	*Lose* means "to no longer have or possess," "to be deprived of," "to waste," "to be defeated in," or "to fail to keep." The word looks like a "final *e*" word, but the vowel is not long. Instead, it sounds like *oo.* The *s* uses the second sound of the consonant *s;* it sounds like a *z.*
loss	noun	*Loss* refers to a thing that is lost, gone, no longer in existence or in your possession. It can also refer to the feeling of no longer having something, or it can mean the failure to win. All the letters follow phonetic patterns. The vowel is short. *Ss* is used because of the *F, L, S, Z* Rule.
lost	adjective	*Lost* means "not used," "not won," or "not claimed," or "unable to find the way."
	verb	*Lost* as a verb is the past tense of *lose.*

✎ **PRACTICE**

Choose from the underlined words at the top of each group of sentences. Write the word to correctly complete each sentence.

choose, chose, choice

1. The Scouts _____ a campsite and proceeded to put up their tents.

2. I want to _____ a career goal this term.

3. You will have a _____ between morning or afternoon classes.

4. Please _____ your friends carefully.

5. You made a very wise _____.

6. She _____ to ignore the blinking lights.

through, though, thorough, thought

1. _____ cleaning of the utensils prevents contamination.

2. We went _____ all the directions for the financial aid forms.

3. I really _____ about our discussion.

4. _____ Pedro was not feeling well, he still went to work.

5. A _____ investigation will be conducted.

6. I should be _____ with the assignment in an hour.

loose, lose, loss, lost

1. I often seem to _____ my car keys.

2. I felt a tremendous _____ when he died.

3. The dogs were _____ in the neighborhood.

4. Kenneth _____ the vision in his right eye.

5. These trousers are too _____ .

6. Many people tend to _____ their way coming to my house.

✎ **EXERCISE 8.5 Sentence Writing**

Use the following homonyms in sentences. Refer to pages 245–247 if necessary.

1. troop _____

2. troupe _____

3. fowl _____

4. foul _____

5. forth _____

6. fourth _____

7. blue _____

8. blew _____

9. haul _____

10. hall _____

11. clause _____

12. claws _____

13. pause _____

14. paws _____

15. new _____

16. knew _____

17. our _____

18. hour _____

19. wood _____

20. would _____

21. taught _____

22. tot _____

23. to _____

24. too _____

25. two _____

26. dew _____

27. due _____

28. do _____

29. flu _____

30. flew _____

31. flue _____

32. through _____

33. threw _____

34. four _____

35. fore _____

36. for _____

Now write one sentence for each of the following "confusables."

1. choose _____

2. chose _____

3. choice _____

4. through _____

5. though _____

6. thorough _____

7. thought _____

8. loose _____

9. lose _____

10. loss _____

11. lost _____

As a review, write the seven **coordinating conjunctions:**

_____   _____   _____   _____   _____

_____   _____

Use any of the homonyms or confusable words from above to write four different compound sentences. Underline the subjects once and the verbs twice. You may use the homonyms or the confusables anywhere in the sentence.

1. _____

2. _____

3. _____

4. _____

Grammar Definitions

Dependent Clause

A dependent clause is a group of words with a subject and a verb, but it is not capable of standing by itself as a sentence because it does not form a complete thought. Dependent clauses are attached to one or more independent clauses to form a complete sentence.

> ***Examples:*** Because it <u>rained</u> all day
> When the <u>ground</u> <u>shook</u>
> If <u>you</u> <u>do</u> a thorough job cleaning

Complex Sentence

A complex sentence is a sentence that has a *dependent clause* and an *independent clause*. The dependent clause may occur first in the sentence, or it may occur after the independent clause. Both clauses have subjects and verbs.

dependent clause + *independent clause:*

Because it rained all day, *we canceled* the picnic at the beach.

independent clause + **dependent clause:**

Everyone started to scream **when the ground shook.**

Subordinate Conjunctions (Spoilers)

Subordinate conjunctions are sometimes nicknamed "spoilers" because they spoil a subject–verb pattern from being an independent clause (or complete sentence). The use of subordinate conjunctions is one common way to make complex sentences.

Important Points About Punctuating a Complex Sentence:

1. If a sentence begins with a "spoiler" and has a subject and a verb, the complex sentence begins with a dependent clause.

2. If a sentence begins with a dependent clause, *use a comma after the dependent clause.*

   Since it rained yesterday, I do not need to water the lawn today.

   Unless you change the order, your bill will be ninety-six dollars.

3. If a sentence begins with an independent clause that is followed by a spoiler in a dependent clause, there is no punctuation between the clauses.

   I called the hospital **when I heard about the accident.**

   I took the practice test **before I took the midterm exam.**

4. The dependent clause can usually be moved to the beginning or the end of the sentence.

   Whether you go or not, I plan to attend the poetry reading.

   I plan to attend the poetry reading **whether you go or not.**

The following words may work as subordinate conjunctions (spoilers). These words are important; you will need to be very familiar with these words so that you can identify them quickly in sentences and use them correctly in your writing. Subordinate conjunctions show the relationship between the dependent and the independent clause. The general relationship is shown at the top of each list.

Subordinate Conjunctions (Spoilers)	Time	Cause/Condition	Comparison/Contrast	Place
	after	as	although	where
	as soon as	because	as if	wherever
	before	if	as though	
	once	even if	provided that	
	until	even though	though	
	when	since		
	whenever	so that		
	while	unless		
	whereas	what		
		whatever		
		whether		

The following are all dependent clauses. They all begin with subordinate conjunctions (spoilers). If the following clauses are intended as sentences, the result will be a **fragment error.** *A fragment is part of a sentence. To correct this type of fragment error, you can:*

1. Remove the subordinate conjunction and make a simple sentence.
2. Join the dependent clause to an independent clause to make a complex sentence.

✎ PRACTICE

Use the following dependent clauses to make complex sentences. Remember to add the comma after the dependent clause.

1. When the author contacted his publisher _____

_____.

2. After I filed my tax return _____

_____.

3. Unless you have a better solution _____

_____.

4. If the awning costs three hundred dollars _____

_____.

✎ EXERCISE 8.6 **Identifying Dependent Clauses**

Find and circle all the subordinate conjunctions (spoilers) in the following sentences. Add a comma at the end of the dependent clause if the dependent clause begins the sentence.

1. I cannot remember when I filed the request for a hearing.

2. Because Lynn is going on vacation I volunteered to water her house plants.

3. Since the order was turned in on time the books will be here for the first day of class.

4. You cannot get a final grade until you finish your research project.

5. Although Billy is old enough to drive he has no interest in getting his license.

6. As soon as I receive the refund I will apply it to this bill.

7. I do not know where you put your briefcase.

8. I drink a cup of tea every day before I shower and dress.

9. If you boil the shrimp too long it will be tough and lose its flavor.

10. While you were out of the office three reporters came to see you.

11. Though the boycott lasted only one day the effects at the gas station were obvious.

12. The library book will be due on Monday unless you ask us for an extension.

13. The cartoonist is well-paid because her work is the best in the industry.

14. My children will be furious unless I bring them each a souvenir.

15. I was totally exhausted after I did eight loads of laundry.

16. Whether the astronaut leaves the spaceship or not the mission is already a success.

17. Since I have the flu I have no interest in cooking meals for anyone.

18. Although the trauma center has an excellent reputation it still finds itself involved in lawsuits.

19. Once I spent the whole day at the county fair I had no desire to return again.

20. The cat's claws were removed because the cat was ruining too many pieces of furniture.

Return to the sentences above. Mark all the subjects and all the verbs.

✎ EXERCISE 8.7 **Finding Subjects and Verbs in Simple, Compound, and Complex Sentences**

*Read each sentence carefully. Draw a box around any **coordinating conjunctions, conjunctive adverbs,** or **subordinate conjunctions.** Analyze the sentence to determine if the sentence is a* simple sentence, *a* compound sentence, *or a* complex sentence. *Remember that a simple sentence will be one independent clause. A compound sentence will have two independent clauses joined together. A complex sentence will have an independent clause and a dependent clause.*

*Write **S** for simple sentence, **C** for compound sentence, and **CX** for complex sentence. Underline the subjects once and the verbs twice. Remember that both dependent clauses and independent clauses have subjects and verbs.*

The first three sentences have been done for you as examples.

S   1.   There <u>was</u> so much <u>turmoil</u> during the discount sale.

C   2.   Four <u>raccoons</u> <u>entered</u> our campground; unfortunately they <u>ate</u> all our food.

CX   3.   <u>I</u> <u>will buy</u> the lounge chair this week since the <u>voucher</u> <u>expires</u> in seven days.

_____   4.   The financial planner decided to sell the stock because it was dropping in value.

_____   5.   The dessert is loaded with calories, for it consists of four kinds of chocolate.

_____   6.   The sirloin was tough and burned, but the boys ate it anyway.

_____   7.   The revenue from this project will reduce the amount of company debt.

_____   8.   The country singers were fantastic, but the opening comedy act was disappointing.

_____   9.   Although autumn is beautiful with all the colored leaves, my favorite season is spring.

_____ 10.   Not many people wanted to live there, for the sewage plant really stank.

_____ 11.   Not many people wanted to live there because the sewage plant really stank.

_____ 12.   The cook took the spoons off the hooks and washed them thoroughly.

_____ 13.   The dew covered the ground and felt cool on our bare feet.

_____ 14.   The mail route goes around the lake; however, many days the roads are closed.

_____ 15.   Mom brought the tourists to our house when the storm closed the airport.

*Write **S** for simple sentence, **C** for compound sentence, and **CX** for complex sentence. Underline the subjects once and the verbs twice. Add any missing punctuation.*

_____ 16.   The price of the computer is $2,000 however you can get a student discount.

_____ 17.   The proof may exist but I have not yet seen it.

_____ 18.   If your spouse is interested you can sign up for these dance lessons.

_____ 19.   Wherever Arthur goes she always follows.

_____ 20.   The school launched a new fund-raising drive because the band needed uniforms.

_____ **21.** When the parade is in progress the avenues will be closed.

_____ **22.** Rusty was a loyal dog and I was his proud owner.

_____ **23.** Although curfew is at midnight many teenagers are still out on the streets.

_____ **24.** Throughout the neighborhood, flags were flying and flapping in the wind.

_____ **25.** The true stories will not be found in the tabloids.

_____ **26.** An ounce of gold was taken from the river when we panned for gold.

_____ **27.** When Herman was in the Army maneuvers in Panama lasted two weeks.

_____ **28.** The instructor taught us the rules as a result we all passed the test.

_____ **29.** A thousand young fans stomped their feet and yelled throughout the entire concert.

_____ **30.** Since Halloween is on Tuesday most Halloween parties will be held on Saturday.

_____ **31.** The investors were elated for the stock market was at an all-time high.

_____ **32.** Mushrooms in salads taste good and are good for you.

_____ **33.** When the tot bounced the basketball his parents grabbed the video camera.

_____ **34.** Raw tuna was served however I refrained from trying it.

_____ **35.** Until the torch is lit the Olympics have not officially started.

Exercise 8.8 Sentence Writing

Write a complex sentence that uses the following subordinate conjunction to be-gin the dependent clause. You may place the dependent clause before or after the independent clause. Use correct punctuation.

1. when _____

2. until _____

3. because _____

4. although _____

5. since _____

6. while _____

7. if _____

8. whether _____

A complex sentence pattern with a specific subordinate conjunction is shown below. Create a sentence that matches this pattern. You may add verb infinitives, prepositional phrases, and/or adjectives to each pattern.

1.

After S–V,	S–V.

_____

2.

S–V	because S–V.

_____

3.

S–V	before S–V.

_____

4.

Though S–V,	S–V.

_____

Two simple sentences are given below. Combine the sentences first by making a **compound sentence***; then combine the sentences by making a* **complex sentence***. You may rearrange or add words if needed so that the sentence makes sense. An example with several possibilities is done for you.*

> *The witness asked for the sheriff. Deputy Williams answered the call.*
> C: *The witness asked for the sheriff, but Deputy Williams answered the call.*
> C: *The witness asked for the sheriff; however, Deputy Williams answered the call.*
> CX: *Even though the witness asked for the sheriff, Deputy Williams answered the call.*
> CX: *When the witness asked for the sheriff, Deputy Williams answered the call.*
> CX: *Deputy Williams answered the call even though the witness asked for the sheriff.*

1. No one could hear the performer. The young people in the audience were screaming loudly.

C: _____

_____

CX: _____

_____

2. A brook usually flows through my property. Now it is dried up.

C: _____

_____

CX: _____

_____

3. Take time to soothe the baby. She will fall asleep.

C: _____

_____

CX: _____

_____

4. The hawk soared through the sky. The hawk perched on the treetop.

C: _____

_____

CX: _____

_____

The following words are from this chapter. Use each word in a sentence that follows the directions given. Use the dictionary to check the meaning of any unfamiliar words.

1. Use the word **flaw** as the subject of an independent clause in a complex sentence.

_____

2. Use the verb **sought** in the dependent clause of a complex sentence.

_____

3. Use the adjective **neutral** in a complex sentence that uses the subordinate conjunction **if.**

_____

4. Use the adjective **authentic** in the dependent clause of a complex sentence.

_____

5. Use the noun **flue** in a complex sentence that uses the subordinate conjunction **when.**

_____

6. Use the word **engulfed** in a complex sentence.

---

7. Use the verb **criticize** in the independent clause of a complex sentence.

✎   EXERCISE 8.9 **Chapter Study Sheet**

In the right-hand column, write a definition for the term on the left. Practice reciting and learning this definition. Cover up the definition on the right. Recite the definition. Remove the paper to check your answers. Practice until you can define each term accurately.

Vowel Diphthongs

Assimilation

Confusables

Dependent Clause

Complex Sentence

Subordinate Conjunctions

Spoilers

Fragment

✎ CHAPTER REVIEW

Match the terms on the left with the definitions or the words on the right.

_____ **1.** vowel diphthongs

a. *feud, few*

_____ **2.** words with *oo* sounds

b. *ou*

_____ **3.** words in which the vowel diphthongs sound like short *o*

c. *ac, ad, af, ag, an, ap, ar, as, at*

_____ **4.** words with vowel diphthongs that make a long *u* sound

d. *too, books, due, true, could, soup*

_____ **5.** a vowel diphthong with eight sounds

e. words such as *choose, chose, choice* or *though, thorough, through,* and *thought*

_____ **6.** assimilation

f. a sentence with a dependent clause and an independent clause

_____ **7.** variations of the prefix *a-*

g. *saw, sauce, sought*

_____ **8.** confusables

h. words that make a clause be dependent

_____ **9.** dependent clause

i. only a part of a sentence

_____ **10.** complex sentence

j. *oo, oi, oy, au, aw, eu, ew, ue, ou*

_____ **11.** examples of "spoilers"

k. *because, if, when, since, before*

_____ **12.** subordinate conjunctions

l. the process in which one word part is modified to resemble the next word part

_____ **13.** fragment

m. a group of words with a subject and a verb that can be joined to an independent clause

Short Answers

1. Explain when a comma is needed between clauses in a *complex sentence.*

2. A dependent clause by itself is a *fragment.* Explain the two ways to correct this kind of error.

*Write **au, aw,** or **ew** to complete each word.*

str_____   _____thority   br_____l   gr_____

br_____   br_____n   h_____nt   squ_____k

thr_____   fl_____   scr_____l   fl_____nt

*Write **ou** or **oo** to complete each word.*

h_____nd   n_____se   r_____st   b_____nce

dr_____l   r_____te   tr_____t   sn_____t

bl_____m   gr_____m   gr_____ch   m_____se

Circle all the roots in the list below.

ance   pel   pense   soci   verse   less

cur   trans   turb   nate   ize   ship

Circle each prefix and suffix. Write the root or the base word on the line.

regrouped _____   foolishly _____   likelihood _____

resourceful _____   poisonous _____   socialite _____

assistant _____   betrayal _____   appointments _____

cloudiness _____   naturalize _____   disturbing _____

inactive _____   berating _____   imposition _____

propensity _____   professional _____   innately _____

choosing _____   scarcity _____   feudalism _____

sanitation _____   application _____   heroism _____

friendships _____   verbalize _____   conceptualize _____

Read each sentence carefully. Circle the word inside the parentheses that best completes the sentence.

1. (Through, Though, Thought) the dance (troop, troupe) was small, it was very professional.

2. The violin strings were (to, too, two) (lose, loss, loose), so the music did not sound right.

3. (Hour, Our) friendship has lasted (thorough, through, though) many years of problems.

4. You will be (through, thought, threw) with the report when you tie up all the (lose, lost, loose) ends and include all the charts.

5. The (claws, clause) in the contract required us to (hall, haul) away all the waste materials.

6. I (due, do, dew) (two, too, to) many things on the weekend, so I can't find time to relax.

7. We (knew, new) that the (hour, our) would come (too, to, two) soon.

8. A very (fowl, foul) smell came (threw, thorough, through) the air ducts.

9. My sister (tot, taught) in the (forth, fourth) grade (for, fore, four) (for, fore, four) years.

10. The (lose, loss, lost, loose) of the cabin was (do, dew, due) to a fire in the (flu, flew, flue).

11. The (hall, haul) was (to, too, two) smoky, so many people left the party.

12. The (paws, pause) in the performance was (fore, four, for) a very specific reason.

13. (Thorough, Though, Thought) the (chose, choose, choice) was made (to, too, two) travel (thorough, though, through) town, (to, too, two) members took the scenic route.

14. I (new, knew) that the company (would, wood) (haul, hall) the (would, wood) for us.

15. The pioneers went (fourth, forth) (too, to, two) find coastal lands to settle.

16. (Ours, Hours) is (to, too, two) (knew, new) to evaluate objectively.

17. The pigeon (flu, flue, flew) right (thorough, through, though) the house and out the door.

18. I feel (to, too, two) weak from the (flue, flu, flew) (to, too, two) talk (to, too, two) them.

19. She taught the (to, two, too) tots not (to, two, too) kiss strangers.

20. The library book is (due, dew, do) by (to, two, too) on Monday.

Write N if the word is a noun, V if the word is a verb, and A if the word is an adjective. Use the suffixes to help you identify the part of speech.

friendships _____   formalize _____   likelihood _____   disturbs _____

socialite _____   brotherhood _____   squawk _____   professionalism _____

naturalize _____   oily _____   snout _____   feudalism _____

yawned _____   heroism _____   acute _____   purity _____

traumatic _____   relationship _____   moist _____   raw _____

Combine the following word parts. Write the complete word on the line.

re + in + force + ment + s = _____   en + act + ment = _____

in + ex + pense + ive + ly = _____   nate + ure = _____

com + pose + ite + s = _____   country + s/es = _____

sub + due + ing = _____   audit + er/or = _____

re + source + ful + ness = _____   loose + ly = _____

ag + grave + ate + ion = _____   a + cute + ly = _____

un + be + come + ing = _____   sane + ite + y = _____

nate + ion + al + ite + y + s = _____   scarce + ly = _____

ap + ply+ ic + ate + ion = _____   chose + en = _____

in + dis + pense + able = _____   oil + y + ness = _____

Circle all the words and terms that can work as subordinate conjunctions in complex sentences.

but	however	where	since	until	when
for	while	therefore	even if	although	though
after	before	during	once	yet	so
if	whether	nor	thus	because	then

Place a box around all the subordinate conjunctions. Underline the subjects once and the verbs twice. Add any missing punctuation.

1. Wherever Michael went his fans appeared and asked for his autograph.

2. My parents set up a trust fund so that their children and grandchildren could attend college.

3. The coach taught his players to bounce back even if they lost an important tournament.

4. As soon as the toy hit the shelves customers rushed to the store and depleted the stock.

5. The pawnshop held my guitar for two weeks before the shop manager sold it.

6. When the grass starts to grow my allergies are triggered.

7. The grooves in the pottery were made before the pottery was placed in the kiln.

8. If the drought does not end soon the farmers will lose all of their crops.

9. The bride cried in disbelief when the groom failed to show up for the wedding.

10. The poodle stood completely still while the judges scored the competition.

11. The governor did not accept our petition because we lacked sufficient, valid signatures.

12. After everyone left the party we found a fifty-dollar bill between the cushions of the couch.

13. As soon as you pay your cable television bill service will be restored.

14. Though only four students were able to recite the complete poem most students had memorized the first three stanzas.

15. Our neighborhood was quiet until the family with all the dogs moved in.

16. The children behave well when we go out to dinner at fancy restaurants.

17. Wherever the typhoon hit it left a path of destruction and turmoil.

18. Before the formal campaign began the cartoonist made political statements about each candidate through his drawings.

19. Only the immediate family members know where Karen and Gene plan to live.

20. The church members meet for fellowship each Sunday after the service ends.

Draw a box around any coordinating conjunctions, conjunctive adverbs, or subordinating conjunctions. Draw one line under the subjects and two lines under the verbs. Analyze each sentence carefully. Write **S** *if the sentence is a simple sentence. Write* **C** *if the sentence is a compound sentence, and write* **CX** *if the sentence is a complex sentence.*

_____   1.   Many people cannot afford to buy a home because the down payment is too much.

_____   2.   When the dealership was charged with fraud, many consumers boycotted the business and took their money elsewhere.

_____ **3.** As soon as I saw the sign in the window, I went in and completed an application for employment.

_____ **4.** The computer came with factory-installed software; however, no back-up disks were included in the package.

_____ **5.** After the shower, we returned to the golf course to play the last nine holes.

_____ **6.** As soon as the composite drawing is completed, the news channels will air it.

_____ **7.** When the whistle blew, the crew threw down their hats and headed home.

_____ **8.** We were so worried about our daughter because she was driving the truck through the mountain passes during one of our worst winter storms.

_____ **9.** After that lewd gesture was made, the store clerk filed a complaint.

_____ **10.** My nephew is too young to know better, for he is only two years old.

_____ **11.** You are hired provided that you can pass the drug test.

_____ **12.** Before she realized it, the friendship turned into a courtship.

_____ **13.** Each of the boys enlisted in the military to learn new skills and to travel.

_____ **14.** Arrangements can be made for you to fly to Memphis if you are interested in interviewing for the position.

_____ **15.** The poisonous gases started to leak from the pipes; fortunately, the neighborhood was evacuated quickly.

_____ **16.** The young child could not tell us where he had left his tricycle.

JOURNAL WRITING ASSIGNMENT

Topic: My Five-Year Plan

What is your "five-year plan"? What goals have you set for yourself for the next five years? What changes do you foresee happening in the remainder of this year? What are your plans for next year and then the year after? Describe where you would like to be, what you would like to be doing, and what you hope your life will be like in five years. In your freewriting, brainstorm and discuss the route you would like to see your life take during the next five years.

PARAGRAPH WRITING ASSIGNMENT

Topic: My Favorite Kind of Music

This explanatory paragraph should give at least four reasons that you prefer a specific kind of music. As you write your first draft, use the following suggestions:

1. Begin your paragraph by clearly stating the kind of music that is your favorite.

2. Use **ordinals,** words such as *first, second,* etc., to transition from one reason to another.

3. Add interesting details or examples to develop each reason.

4. Remember that short ideas can be expanded by adding descriptive adjectives and prepositional phrases.

5. Include a variety of sentence patterns so that you have some simple, compound, and complex sentences in your paragraph.

6. End your paragraph with a summary sentence.

7. Check the spelling and the grammar in your sentences.

NINE

Silent Consonants

- Silent consonants in words
- Additional work with homonyms
- Five new prefixes, two new suffixes, and three new roots to build words
- Introduction of adverbs

Spelling Definitions

Silent Consonants   Silent consonants are simply consonants that are not pronounced. When many of the words with silent consonants were originally introduced into the English language, the consonants were pronounced. Over time, the pronunciations were altered, and the sounds were dropped from the words. All of the following consonants are silent in some words: *b, g, gh, h, k, l, n, p, s, w,* and *t.*

Examples: com**b**, si**g**n, thou**gh**, **h**onest, **k**nife, cal**f**,
colum**n**, **p**sychology, i**s**land, **w**rite, lis**t**en

The following words have appeared in previous chapters. Read each word carefully. Circle *the consonant or consonants that are silent in each word.*

foreign	knew	autumn	science
receipt	brought	freight	straight
would	doubt	sleigh	exhaust
calf	herb	sought	know
knife	weigh	half	though

The following words have not appeared in previous chapters and are not included in this chapter's word list. Read each word carefully. Circle *the consonant or consonants that are silent in each word.*

Wednesday	yacht	mnemonic	handkerchief
gourmet	filet	raspberry	benign
malign	scissors	solemn	hymn
ghetto	ghastly	ghost	ballet
hasten	heirloom	wrench	stalk
succumb	bomb	knoll	rhetoric

knapsack   thumb   yolk   sigh

aisle   psalm   champagne   wreath

Words—Beginning with the Basics

1. Say the word slowly. Notice the silent consonant or consonants.
2. Write the word once on the practice line.
3. Write the silent consonant or consonants on the line.
4. Add any suffix to the word. Write the expanded word on the last line. Write **X** if no suffix can be added to the word to make a real word. You may refer to your dictionary when necessary.

✎ **PRACTICE**

Word	Practice	Silent	Add Any Suffix
1. answer			
2. campaign			
3. castle			
4. climb			
5. column			
6. comb			
7. condemn			
8. corps			
9. debt			
10. exhibit			
11. fasten			
12. gnarl			
13. gnaw			
14. heir			
15. honest			
16. honor			
17. hour			

Word	Practice	Silent	Add Any Suffix
18. hustle			
19. knead			
20. kneel			
21. knight			
22. knit			
23. knot			
24. knuckle			
25. light			
26. limb			
27. listen			
28. mortgage			
29. muscle			
30. often			
31. plumber			
32. reign			
33. rhyme			
34. rhythm			
35. rough			
36. rustle			
37. salmon			
38. scene			
39. sign			
40. sight			
41. subtle			
42. walk			
43. wrap			

Word	Practice	Silent	Add Any Suffix
44. wrestle	_____	_____	_____
45. wring	_____	_____	_____
46. wrinkle	_____	_____	_____
47. write	_____	_____	_____
48. written	_____	_____	_____
49. wrong	_____	_____	_____
50. wrought	_____	_____	_____

Rhyming Words with Silent Consonants

✎ **PRACTICE**

1. The words *knight, light,* and *sight* have silent *gh* consonants. Many other words belong to the same word family as these words. Add *ight* to the following letters.

r_____   t_____   br_____   sl_____

fr_____   m_____   n_____   bl_____

f_____   fl_____   pl_____   wr_____

2. The word *walk* has a silent consonant *l.* The following words come from the same rhyming word family. Add *alk* to the following letters.

t_____   st_____   ch_____   b_____

3. The word *thought* has the silent *gh* consonants. Add *ought* to the following letters.

b_____   s_____   br_____   f_____

✎ **EXERCISE 9.1 Working with Silent Consonants**

1. Write the seven words from this chapter's word list that end in *-le*.

_____ _____ _____ _____

_____ _____ _____

2. As a review, write the */CLE* **Syllable Rule:** _____

_____

The */CLE* Syllable Rule should state what *usually* happens when a word ends in *-le*. One exception to this rule occurs when a word has a *ck* before the *-le*. The *ck* combination cannot be divided. Therefore, in a word such as *crackle,* the *ck* stays with the first syllable. In this case, the *-le* is a syllable by itself: *crack-le.*

Return to the words above that end in -le. Divide each word into syllables.

3. As a review, write the **First CVC Doubling Rule** for one-syllable words: _____

_____

Write the three words from this chapter's word list that are **one-syllable CVC words:**

_____ _____ _____

4. As a review, write the **Second CVC Doubling Rule** for multi-syllable words: _____

_____

Write the nine words from this chapter's word list that are **multi-syllable CVC words.**

_____ _____ _____

_____ _____ _____

_____ _____ _____

5. Use the first and second CVC doubling rules to add the following suffixes to the words. Write the complete word on the line.

honor + able = _____   answer + ing = _____

exhibit + er/or = _____   fasten + er/or = _____

knit + ed = _____   knot + s/es = _____

plumber + s/es = _____   wrap + able/ible = _____

6. In each word below, one letter is in bold print. Say the word carefully. On the line, write the vowel with a short diacritical mark above it if the vowel makes a short sound. If the letter in bold makes a long vowel sound, write the vowel sound heard; add the long vowel marking above the vowel. If the vowel is not long and is not short, write a schwa (ə).

castle _____   climb _____   comb _____   condemn _____

debt _____   fasten _____   hustle _____   knead _____

knight _____   knot _____   limb _____   reign _____

rhyme _____   rhythm _____   rustle _____   salmon _____

scene _____   sign _____   sight _____   subtle _____

wrap _____   wrinkle _____   write _____   written _____

7. As a review, write the five different **r-controls:** _____   _____   _____   _____   _____

Write the six words from this chapter's word list that have *r*-controls. (Do not include the words *hour* or *heir*, which do not have true *r*-controls.)

_____

_____

_____

_____

_____

_____

Homonyms

The words in bold print are from this chapter's basic word list. Homonyms for the words are then shown. Notice the spelling changes and the different phonetic elements and "word families" that are used to make the homonyms.

corps—core	**hour**—our	**heir**—air
knead—need	**knight**—night	**knot**—not
reign—rain, rein	**scene**—seen	**sight**—site, cite
wrap—rap	**wring**—ring	**write**—right, wright
writes—rights, rites	**wrought**—rot	

✎ PRACTICE

Partner or Group Work

Parts of the following assignment may be assigned to individual partners or groups to complete and then report back to the class.

*The following sentences show **homonyms** in bold print. Look how the word is working in the sentence. On the left, write **N** if the word is working as a **noun.** Write **V** if the word is working as a **verb.** Write **A** if the word is working as an **adjective.** In the right-hand column, write an informal definition of any of the word meanings that are unfamiliar to you.*

Part of Speech   **Sentence**   **Informal Definition**

Part 1

_____ 1.   The **Corps** of Engineers manages the reservoir.

_____ 2.   Samuel joined the Marine **Corps** in August.

_____ 3.   You will need to **core** the apples first.

_____ 4.   The **core** of the earth is molten rock.

_____ 5.   He won't quit until he gets to the **core** of the problem.

_____ 6.   I waited until the last **hour** to file the forms.

_____ 7.   This is the **hour** of truth.

_____ 8.   You are invited to **our** house for dinner.

_____ 9.   The oldest son is the **heir** to the estate.

_____ 10. The senator has a sophisticated **air.**

Part 2

_____ 11. I want to **air** out this room.

_____ 12. Smog filled the **air.**

_____ 13. Millions of people prefer to travel by **air.**

Part of Speech	Sentence	Informal Definition

—————— **14.**   The attendant turned on the **air** pump.

—————— **15.**   Grandma loves to **knead** the bread dough.

—————— **16.**   Her first **need** is to find a place to live this term.

—————— **17.**   You will **need** extra travel money.

—————— **18.**   The family is in **need** of food and clothing.

—————— **19.**   She longed for a **knight** in shining armor.

—————— **20.**   He was **knighted** by King Arthur.

Part 3

—————— **21.**   Everyone in my house is a **night** owl.

—————— **22.**   Russ called Maria late last **night.**

—————— **23.**   The sailor showed me how to tie several **knots.**

—————— **24.**   The saw bent when it hit the **knot** in the wood.

—————— **25.**   My son likes to **knot** my shoelaces together.

—————— **26.**   Nautical miles are measured in **knots.**

—————— **27.**   The king **reigned** over the kingdom for twenty years.

—————— **28.**   The Magna Carta was signed during King John's **reign.**

—————— **29.**   The sudden **rain** and lightning ended the golf game.

—————— **30.**   The meteorologist said it will be **raining** this weekend.

Part 4

—————— **31.**   One **rein** fell from the rider's hands.

—————— **32.**   She keeps tight **reins** on her young son.

—————— **33.**   The police arrived at the **scene** of the accident.

—————— **34.**   Kim made quite a **scene** in front of the theater.

—————— **35.**   The fifth **scene** was the most dramatic.

—————— **36.**   The **scene** from the mountain top was breathtaking.

—————— **37.**   I had **seen** the movie on television.

—————— **38.**   The **sight** on the gun was scratched.

Part of Speech	Sentence	Informal Definition

_____ **39.** The valley at dawn was a beautiful **sight.**

_____ **40.** We **sighted** the whales offshore.

Part 5

_____ **41.** The camp **site** was rustic.

_____ **42.** Many businesses now have web **sites.**

_____ **43.** The officers **cite** people for speeding.

_____ **44.** You must **cite** the source of your information.

_____ **45.** He was **cited** with a medal of honor.

_____ **46.** She placed the **wrap** around her shoulders.

_____ **47.** The clerks will **wrap** your gifts for you.

_____ **48.** There was an unexpected **rap** on the window.

_____ **49.** The trainer **raps** the tiger's paws to teach it tricks.

_____ **50.** The guys often sit around and **rap** about sports.

Part 6

_____ **51.** **Rap** on the door when you are ready to leave.

_____ **52.** **Rap** music is heard on many radio stations.

_____ **53.** The innocent man took the **rap** for the crime.

_____ **54.** Drivers always **wring** their necks to see accidents.

_____ **55.** She **wrings** her hands whenever she is nervous.

_____ **56.** She gave the clothes a **wring** before hanging them on the line.

_____ **57.** **Wring** the water out of the mop.

_____ **58.** The keys are on a large, metal **ring.**

_____ **59.** The **ring** of car thieves must be stopped.

_____ **60.** The farmers **ring** the noses of pigs.

Part 7

_____ **61.** My ears started to **ring.**

_____ **62.** The circus **ring** was full of activity.

Part of Speech	Sentence	Informal Definition
_____ **63.**	The performer rode through the **ring** of fire.	
_____ **64.**	Bobby **rings** the horseshoe around the pole every time.	
_____ **65.**	He wants to **write** screenplays for television.	
_____ **66.**	I like to **write** with a fountain pen.	
_____ **67.**	The **right** answer appeared on the screen.	
_____ **68.**	You have a **right** to be upset.	
_____ **69.**	It is not **right** to cheat on your exams.	
_____ **70.**	You can **right** the situation by confessing.	

Part 8

_____ **71.**	They **righted** the canoe after capsizing.	
_____ **72.**	My uncle works as a mill**wright.**	
_____ **73.**	The man's **rights** were definitely violated.	
_____ **74.**	The priest performed the last **rites.**	
_____ **75.**	The **rites** are celebrated on a child's twelfth birthday.	
_____ **76.**	**Wrought** iron will be used to make the fence.	
_____ **77.**	The food started to **rot** in the sun.	
_____ **78.**	Dry **rot** was found under the front steps.	
_____ **79.**	Leaves **rot** after they fall from the trees.	
_____ **80.**	The leftovers **rot** to make compost.	

✏️ **EXERCISE 9.2** **Sentence Work with Homonyms**

Circle the correct homonym inside the parentheses for each sentence.

1. The (heir, air) to the throne (rains, reins, reigns) over the kingdom until death.

2. James joined the (core, corps) because he felt it was (write, right) for him.

3. The (sighting, citing) of the UFO was (knot, not) confirmed.

4. The (sights, cites, sites) for the new office buildings are (write, right) next to the freeway.

5. The builders like to use (rot, wrought) iron because it does not (wrought, rot) like wood.

6. The words in the (rap, wrap) have a familiar (wring, ring) to them.

7. The (scene, seen) was not a (site, cite, sight) I ever wish to see again.

8. She had (scene, seen) the napkin (wring, rings) earlier in the day.

9. The (night, knight) was loyal for the length of the king's (rein, reign, rain).

10. It was (reining, raining, reigning) at the launch (cite, sight, site).

11. You will (need, knead) to take all the (corps, core) curriculum to graduate from high school.

12. A check (needs, kneads) to be written for the (sight, site, cite) license to build the office complex.

13. I (sited, cited, sighted) the deer and suddenly got a (not, knot) in my stomach.

14. The (rights, rites) of marriage involve exchanging wedding (wrings, rings).

15. The bells at (our, hour) church (wring, ring) every day on every (our, hour).

16. My ears did (not, knot) (wring, ring) when the shelf fell on my head.

17. The (night's, knight's) armor is (not, knot) for sale (write, right) now.

18. The (rights, rites, writes) were performed at the (site, sight, cite) of the drowning.

19. All the gifts were (rapped, wrapped) and left by (hour, our) front door.

20. We will (wring, ring) in the new year with our annual (rights, rites).

Building Words

New Prefixes: *col- for- inter- intro- sur-*

The prefix *col-* means **together.**
The prefix *for-* means **away, off,** or **apart.**
The prefix *inter-* means **between** or **among.**
The prefix *intro-* means **within.**
The prefix *sur-* means **over, beyond,** or **above.**

New Suffixes: *-ial   -ish*

The suffix *-ial* means **of, concerning,** or **pertaining to.**
The suffix *-ish* means **like** or **resembling.**

New Roots: *mote   mune   spect*

The root *mote* means **to move.**
The root *mune* means **to make common** or **to change.**
The root *spect* means **to look.**

✎ PRACTICE

Add the following prefixes to the base words and roots shown below.

col-   *for-*   *inter-*

_____lect   _____get   _____act

_____late   _____give   _____net

_____lapse   _____mat   _____change

_____lide   _____bid   _____cept

intro-   *sur-*

_____duce   _____face

_____spect   _____charge

_____vert   _____mise

_____duction   _____real

Add the following suffixes to the base words or roots below. Apply any necessary spelling rules before attaching the suffix.

-ial	*-ish*
part_____	tickle_____
face_____	self_____
race_____	fool_____
cord_____	baby_____

Add the roots to the following prefixes.

mote	*mune*	*spect*
pro_____	com_____	intro_____
de_____	im_____	re_____
e_____		in_____
re_____		pro_____

*Circle all the **prefixes** in the list below.*

ab	intro	be	mit	cur	sur
inter	for	com	col	per	ous

*Circle all the **suffixes** in the list below.*

ist	ite	fer	ish	est	ial
al	tort	sur	ize	ite	ism

*Circle all the **roots** in the list below.*

inter	for	tort	spect	psych	pense
mune	mote	soci	ance	hood	nate

✎ **EXERCISE 9.3 Building Words**

*The **base words** or **roots** are shown in bold. Combine the prefixes and the suffixes to the base words or roots. Write the complete word on the line. Apply any necessary spelling rules.*

1. in + **debt** + ed + ness = _____
2. **fast** + en + ing = _____
3. dis + **honor** + able = _____
4. sur + **real** + ist = _____
5. **rhyme** + ing = _____
6. **scene** + ic = _____
7. **sign** + al + ing = _____
8. **wrestle** + ing = _____
9. im + **mune** + ize + ate + ion = _____
10. in + sur + **mount** + able = _____
11. sur + **round** + ing = _____
12. inter + **ject** + ion = _____
13. inter + **nate** + ion + al = _____
14. im + **part** + ial + ite + y = _____
15. inter + **face** + ing = _____
16. com + **mune** + ic + able = _____
17. inter + **change** + able = _____
18. **fine** + ance + ial + ly = _____
19. de + **sign** + ate + ion = _____
20. con + **sign** + ment = _____

21. **exhibit** + ion + ist = _____
22. **honest** + ly = _____
23. inter + **act** + ive = _____
24. **listen** + er = _____
25. **rough** + est = _____
26. **sign** + ate + ure = _____
27. **fool** + ish + ly = _____
28. **wrong** + ful + ly = _____
29. sur + **plus** + s/es = _____
30. ex + **cite** + ment = _____
31. intro + **spect** + ion = _____
32. inter + **cept** + ion + s = _____
33. inter + **race** + ial = _____
34. inter + **mit** + ent = _____
35. sur + **pass** + ing = _____
36. com + **mune** + ic + ate + ion = _____
37. inter + **sect** + ion + s = _____
38. **column** + ist = _____
39. ob + **scene** + ite + y = _____
40. com + **mune** + ite + y + es = _____

✎ **EXERCISE 9.4 Word List Expansion**

*The **base words** or **roots** are in bold. The base words, roots, prefixes, and suffixes are in a scrambled order below. Rearrange the word parts to spell a real word. Write the word on the line. Apply any spelling rules as needed.*

1. de ing **sign** re = _____
2. s **sign** ment as = _____
3. ate s ion **sign** re = _____
4. s **sign** de er = _____

5. re ment as **sign** = _____

6. al **mote** pro ion = _____

7. ing **mote** pro = _____

8. **mote** com ion = _____

9. er pro **mote** s = _____

10. ly re **mote** = _____

11. **mote** e al ion ly = _____

12. s **mote** ive = _____

13. **mote** ed de = _____

14. **mune** im y ite es = _____

15. ist Com **mune** = _____

16. al **mune** com = _____

17. **spect** pro or = _____

18. **spect** ly ful re = _____

19. s **spect** or in = _____

20. **spect** dis ful re = _____

EXERCISE 9.5 Sentence Writing

*Select any twenty words from the list on pages 281–283. Use each word in a sentence. In the left margin, identify the part of speech for the word based on how the word was used in the sentence. Write **N** for noun, **V** for verb, and **A** for adjective.*

1. _____

2. _____

3. _____

4. _____

5. _____

6. _____

7. _____

8. _____

9. _____

10. _____

11. _____

12. _____

13. _____

14. _____

15. _____

16. _____

17. _____

18. _____

19. _____

20. _____

*Write the past tense for each of the following verbs. Then use any ten verbs in ten different **complex sentences**.*

Present	Past	Present	Past
answer	_____	campaign	_____
climb	_____	condemn	_____
exhibit	_____	fasten	_____
gnarl	_____	gnaw	_____
honor	_____	hustle	_____
kneel	_____	knit	_____
mortgage	_____	rhyme	_____
rough	_____	wrinkle	_____
wrap	_____	wring	_____
wrestle	_____	write	_____

1. _____

2. _____

3. _____

4. _____

5. _____

6. _____

7. _____

8. _____

9. _____

10. _____

Grammar Definitions

Adverbs

Adverbs tell *when, where, how,* and *to what extent* something happens.

> *Examples:* The inspector will file the report **later.** (when)
> The commuter flight ends **here.** (where)
> Answer the question **carefully.** (how)
> The knot is **too** tight. (to what extent)

Important points about adverbs:

1. Adverbs are words that describe or modify **action** verbs. These adverbs often end in *-ly.* They can be placed right before or after the action verb, or in other locations in the sentence.

   The heir **quickly** signed the papers.

   The student answered **honestly.**

   The audience laughed **loudly.**

   The bus **frequently** stops in front of my house.

   The interviewer listened to my responses **intently.**

2. Adverbs are also words that describe adjectives. These adverbs are usually placed right before the adjective.

   The traveler was **extremely** tired.

   The children were **very** respectful to their elders.

   The woman's suit was **slightly** wrinkled.

   Our keynote speaker was **too** talkative.

   Angela is the **most** intelligent person in class.

   The plot in the movie was **so** complex.

3. Adverbs are also words that describe other adverbs. These adverbs are usually placed right before the adverbs.

   The banker acted **quite** foolishly.

   Their actions were **not** racially motivated.

   The nurse spoke **very** softly to the sick man.

   This is the **most** beautifully balanced exhibit at the convention.

   The computer-generated report was **more** professionally done.

4. Words that tell **when** are adverbs. These are adverbs that tell **when.**

yesterday	today	tomorrow	now
soon	later	then	early
late	sometimes	seldom	never

5. Though many adverbs end in *-ly,* the following words need to be learned as adverbs. They can describe other adjectives or adverbs.

almost	already	also	back	better	down
even	ever	far	here	home	how
least	less	more	most	much	not
often	quite	rather	really	so	still
there	too	very	up		

✏️ **PRACTICE**

Change the words in bold print to adverbs by adding the -ly suffix. Then draw an arrow to the action verb, the adjective, or the adverb that the adverb in bold print modifies. An example is done for you.

Example: *I cleaned the kitchen cupboards **thorough**ly.*

 1. My youngest sister is **extreme**_____ responsible about doing her homework.

 2. You are **definite**_____ late for your appointment.

 3. The train was traveling **exceeding**_____ fast right before the accident.

 4. The stage was **bright**_____ lit for the final performance.

 5. I was **honest**_____ concerned about your decision to travel alone.

 6. The technician passed the cloth **light**_____ across the computer screen.

 7. You are **cordial**_____ invited to the wedding reception.

 8. She is **emotional**_____ stable at this time.

 9. The professor **careful**_____ assigned the final grades.

 10. The new law was **quick**_____ enforced.

Each of the following sentences contains at least one adverb that does not have an -ly suffix. Locate and circle the adverbs in the following sentences.

 1. Tomorrow is too soon to begin packing my suitcases.

 2. The lecture was quite interesting, but now I need to get to work on the summary.

 3. The carpet cleaners usually arrive late, but yesterday they came early.

 4. Even though the project is almost completed, I still feel very stressed.

 5. It is much too early to tell if the treatment was effective.

 6. The fans never seem to understand the catcher's hand signals.

 7. The budget will most likely pass sometime today or tomorrow.

 8. Your dog is quite friendly most of the time.

 9. The package was not here when I arrived.

 10. The Bahamas are usually cool this time of year, but during our trip, the weather was too hot.

Adjective and Adverb Confusion

Sometimes adjectives and adverbs are confused because they both modify other words. To decide if a word is working as an adjective or as an adverb, identify the word that it modifies. Then use these reminders:

1. If the word it modifies is a **noun,** the modifier is an **adjective.**

   Example: The **daily** paper arrives before six o'clock in the morning.

   (*Daily* modifies *paper. Paper* is a noun. *Daily* is an adjective.)

2. If the word comes after a linking verb and refers to the subject, the word is an **adjective** in the Adjective Pattern 2 position.

   Example: The food at the new restaurant was **good.**

   (*Good* modifies *food,* which is the subject of the sentence. It comes after a linking verb. *Good* is an adjective.)

   The patient feels **well** today.

   (*Well* is a predicate adjective related to the patient feeling healthy.)

3. If the word modifies an **action verb, an adjective,** or another **adverb,** it is an **adverb.** One example is given below, but many other examples are given on page 296.

   Example: Suzanne dives and swims **well.**

   (*Well* modifies the action verbs *dives* and *swims.* Because an action verb is used, an adverb is needed. *Well* is an adverb. The word *good* is an adjective. It is not correct to say: "Suzanne dives and swims good.")

✎ **PRACTICE**

*Read the following sentences. Write **ADJ.** on the line if the word in bold print is working as an adjective. Write **ADV.** if the word in bold print is working as an adverb. Remember to look at the word that is modified to help you distinguish between adjectives and adverbs.*

_____ **1.** She is **friendlier** when she is not under so much stress.

_____ **2.** You can be **so** stubborn.

_____ **3.** Michael is much **better** at fixing cars and repairing appliances.

_____ **4.** We bought the **daily** paper.

_____ **5.** The jeweler **carefully** polishes his finished pieces.

_____ **6.** The mail is **more** regular during the off-season.

_____ **7.** The invitation stated to wear **casual** dress.

_____ **8.** The bus was **late.**

_____ **9.** We arrived home **late** on Saturday night.

_____ **10.**   The cruise was **too** expensive.

_____ **11.**   The runners were **definitely** ready for the race.

_____ **12.**   I felt **better** after I drank the tea.

_____ **13.**   We went to bed **early** because we had a seven o'clock meeting.

_____ **14.**   He is the **kindest** man in the world.

_____ **15.**   Vanessa is **much** prettier with long hair.

Good and *Well*

> *Good* and *well* are frequently used incorrectly. *Good* works as an adjective to describe nouns. It can be found in the Adjective Pattern 1 position or the Adjective Pattern 2 position (after a linking verb). *Well* can also be an adjective when it refers to a state of health or well-being. For *well* to work as an adjective, it must modify or define a noun. *Well* more often works as an adverb to modify an action verb.

PRACTICE

Complete the following sentences by circling good *or* well.

1. The raspberry jam is very (good, well).

2. She dances the samba very (good, well).

3. I am feeling very (good, well).

4. She works (good, well) with other people.

5. You need to brush your teeth (good, well) after every meal.

6. Joseph looks (good, well) in that suit.

7. We could not see (good, well) through the muddy window.

8. Kathy did (good, well) with her presentation today.

9. Your reasons for leaving are (good, well).

10. This banana pudding tastes (good, well).

11. Recognition is given to employees who do their work (good, well).

12. Speaking (good, well) in front of audiences requires practice.

13. The twins play together (good, well).

14. Her great grandmother is not doing (good, well).

15. Cindy always feels (good, well) after she completes her daily run.

✎ **EXERCISE 9.6 Identifying Parts of Speech**

*Decide if the following words can work as nouns, verbs, adjectives, or adverbs. Do not add or delete suffixes to the words. Write **N** in the blank for **nouns, V** for **verbs, A** for **adjectives,** and **ADV** for **adverbs**. Remember that some words can be more than one part of speech.*

_____ answer	_____ blight
_____ campaign	_____ combing
_____ flight	_____ soon
_____ gnarl	_____ gnawing
_____ honorable	_____ hourly
_____ lightness	_____ limber
_____ reign	_____ rhythm
_____ salmon	_____ scenic
_____ signal	_____ least
_____ wring	_____ wrong
_____ cite	_____ sight
_____ babyish	_____ collide
_____ communal	_____ cordial
_____ design	_____ emotionally
_____ fastening	_____ forgiveness
_____ inspector	_____ quite
_____ very	_____ now
_____ introvert	_____ remotely
_____ selfishly	_____ wrongfully
_____ surcharge	_____ signature
_____ seldom	_____ partially

_____respect   _____never

_____tomorrow   _____subtle

_____rightfully   _____foolish

Look at the word in bold print. Write **N, V, A,** *or* **ADV** *to show how the word is working in the sentence.*

_____ 1.   Her problems seem **insurmountable.**

_____ 2.   The honorable judge will enter the room **soon.**

_____ 3.   My parents had a **slight** change of plans.

_____ 4.   The **columnist** received recognition for his honest work.

_____ 5.   The hustler was **condemned** by the jury.

_____ 6.   The inspector found a lot of **rot** underneath the floorboards.

_____ 7.   The castle was built much **later** in the century.

_____ 8.   A lot of **commotion** occurred when the stock cars collided.

_____ 9.   Jackson was **very** determined to join the Job Corps program.

_____ 10.   I was **cited** for ignoring the stop sign.

_____ 11.   My friend **always** forgets to bring her identification.

_____ 12.   This is a **financially** sound business plan.

_____ 13.   **There** were five interceptions in Monday night's game.

_____ 14.   **Rhyming** is something that young children enjoy doing.

_____ 15.   There **never** are enough surpluses to meet the needs.

✎ **EXERCISE 9.7 Finding Adverbs**

The following technique can be used to identify adverbs in sentences.

1. Underline the **subjects** once and the **verbs** twice.
2. Mark the **prepositional phrases** using parentheses and the **verb infinitives** using brackets.
3. Locate the **nouns** in the sentence. Write **N** above the nouns.
4. Examine the remaining words to see if they are working as **adjectives** to describe the nouns. **Circle** the adjectives.

5. Look at the remaining words. Usually, what "is left" are the **adverbs.** Examine these remaining words. Do they tell *when, where, how,* or *to what extent? Do they modify an action verb, an adjective, or another adverb?* Do they end in *-ly?* Do they come from the list of words that are adverbs that do not have an *-ly* suffix? Write **ADV** above the adverbs.

Use the technique described above to identify the subjects and the verbs and to label the parts of speech of each word in the following sentences. A sample sentence has been done for you.

                    ADV   *ADV*   *N*

Example: <u>We</u> <u>walked</u> briskly [to get] out (of the (horrendous) rain).

1. Our summer vacation to Europe was thoroughly enjoyed by the entire family.

2. The landing site is most frequently visited by tourists during the summer months.

3. Communication skills can be extremely difficult for introverted individuals to develop.

4. The directions said to turn right at the intersection and then to go three blocks.

5. All of the salmon runs are recorded annually and examined extensively by conservationists.

6. There was quite an increase in the mortgage payment for our new home.

7. All passengers are required to fasten their seat belts properly.

8. The screaming child was clearly not interested in listening to her mother.

9. All complaints will be handled much more promptly under this new system.

10. My youngest sister is the most jealous person in our family.

***Fragments** are incomplete sentences. To form a complete sentence, you must add a missing subject, a missing verb, and/or a complete thought. Change the following fragments to sentences. Check your sentences for proper punctuation.*

1. Tightly wrapping the box for shipping

_____

2. The columnist for the local newspaper

_____

3. Before you start the interactive video program

_____

4. Forbidding the use of computer lab time for personal use

_____

5. After a long commute on the freeway

_____

6. Because all of my assignments are late

_____

7. Brought the campaign to a halt

_____

8. The prospector with a dream and a box of mining maps

_____

9. Wrestling the purse snatcher to the ground

_____

10. When the fire fighter climbed onto the roof

_____

*Most of the following sentences have **comma splice errors** or **run-on sentence errors**. In the blank, write **CS** for **comma splice** or **RO** for **run-on sentence**. Then add or delete punctuation to correct each sentence. You may add words if they are needed to correct the sentence. If the sentence is **correct**, write **0** (for zero errors).*

_____   **1.**   The salmon bake was held at the park yesterday the sponsors were very pleased with the turnout.

_____   **2.**   The data entry operator started to format the document right before the power outage she lost all her work.

_____   **3.**   During the reign of King Emanual, many reforms were made in Brazil.

_____   **4.**   One of the longest reigns in England's history was that of King Henry III, he ruled for fifty years.

_____   **5.**   The steel beams collapsed suddenly during the construction work at the airport.

_____   **6.**   The bubble gum knotted in Lindy's hair, consequently, she had to cut her hair short.

_____   **7.**   The gnarled traffic in New York City angered many of the commuters.

_____ **8.** The cat went out on the limb and could not get down on his own.

_____ **9.** The grower complained that blight had ruined his plants when he was on vacation.

_____ **10.** The new law is written on the books, announced on television, and printed in the newspapers.

_____ **11.** She fought back they were not going to collect for the lost compact discs.

_____ **12.** Her signature was not on the citation it was not even dated properly.

_____ **13.** The mortgage payment on the duplex is due tomorrow and needs to be paid.

_____ **14.** The hikers sought shelter in a deserted cabin in a remote section of the forest.

_____ **15.** Because all the children were immunized, none of them ever got the measles.

_____ **16.** The clothes were left on consignment for three weeks, all of the clothes were sold.

_____ **17.** Introductions were made I don't remember a single name.

_____ **18.** The millwright worked extremely long hours and never took vacation time.

EXERCISE 9.9 Chapter Study Sheet

In the right-hand column, write a definition for the term on the left. Practice reciting and learning this definition. Cover up the definition on the right. Recite the definition. Remove the paper to check your answers. Practice until you can define each term accurately.

Silent Consonants

Adverbs

The Four Questions That Adverbs Answer

Examples of Adverbs That Tell *When*

Examples of Adverbs That Do Not End in *-ly*

Fragment

Comma Splice

Run-on Sentence

Name _____   Date _____

✎ **CHAPTER REVIEW**

Match the terms on the left with the definitions or the examples on the right.
There will be some extra answers that will not be used.

_____ **1.**   words with a silent *g*

_____ **2.**   words with a silent *l*

_____ **3.**   words with a silent *k*

_____ **4.**   words correctly divided into syllables

_____ **5.**   words that use the First CVC Doubling Rule

_____ **6.**   homonyms

_____ **7.**   a prefix that means "within"

_____ **8.**   irregular verbs

_____ **9.**   adverbs

_____ **10.** a common adverb-forming suffix

_____ **11.** adverbs that tell *when*

_____ **12.** a homonym that means "location"

a. *knitted, wrappers, knotting*

b. *intro-*

c. *kneel, write, wring*

d. *wrink/le, knuck/le, lis/ten*

e. words that modify action verbs, adjectives, or other adverbs

f. *knife, knead, know*

g. *soon, today, tomorrow, never*

h. *fastening, honoring, wrapped*

i. *site*

j. *foreign, sign, gnaw*

k. *col-*

l. *cas/tle, knuc/kle, wres/tle*

m. *seen, scene*

n. *calf, yolk, half*

o. *-ly*

p. *already, too, not*

Silent Consonants

Read each word carefully. Circle all the silent consonants.

freight	scissors	sigh	thumb
debt	climb	column	gnarl
plumber	mortgage	rustle	salmon
muscle	wrong	write	wring

Add the missing consonants from the following words.

ans___er   campai___n   colum___   condem___

de___t   ___naw   hus___le   rei___n

rus___le   su___tle   ___rinkle   ___rong

Word Parts

Circle the prefixes and suffixes. Write the word bases or the roots on the line.

communal _____   demotions _____

dishonorable _____   impartiality _____

foolishness _____   inspections _____

respectfully _____   miscommunications _____

mighty _____   ritual _____

wrongfully _____   interfacing _____

resignations _____   surmising _____

signatures _____   resurfaced _____

Homonyms

Use the following words in the kind of sentences stated in the directions.

1. Use *rites* in a **compound sentence** that has at least one **adverb.**

_____

2. Use *heir* as the **subject** of an **independent clause.**

_____

3. Use *knead* as a **past tense verb** in a simple **S-VV** sentence.

_____

4. Use *wring* as the verb in a **dependent clause** in a **complex** sentence.

_____

5. Use *write* in a sentence that has at least two **adjectives.**

_____

6. Use *core* in an **SS-V** sentence in any verb tense.

_____

7. Use *rights* in a **complex sentence.**

_____

8. Use *reign* as the **subject** of a sentence that also has at least one adjective and one adverb.

_____

9. Use the adverb *well* in a sentence that has an action verb.

_____

10. Use the adjective *good* in a sentence that has a linking verb.

_____

Sentence Expansion

*The following sentences lack interest and details. In each sentence, add at least one **adjective,** one **prepositional phrase,** and one **adverb.** An example is done for you.*

Example: *The attendant resigned.*

           ADJ   *ADV*

      *The **flight** attendant **suddenly** resigned (from her job).*

1. The sign hung above the door.

_____

2. The exhibit ended.

_____

3. She gave me a facial.

_____

4. The woman knitted sweaters.

_____

5. That was subtle.

_____

6. They condemned her.

_____

7. The student collates papers.

_____

8. The words rhyme.

_____

9. The fight started.

_____

10. The plumber arrived.

_____

Adverbs

Complete the following sentence.

Adverbs are words that modify _____, _____, or

other _____.

Circle the words below that can work as adverbs.

sometimes	very	wrap	brightly	chalky
honestly	bright	too	quite	rather
lightly	often	rightfully	limb	there
better	babyish	unseemingly	impartially	heir
intermittently	cordially	rhythm	less	almost
fastener	already	wrongfully	exhibited	here

Write ten different sentences that use any ten of the adverbs from the list on page 311. Circle the adverbs in each sentence.

1. _____

2. _____

3. _____

4. _____

5. _____

6. _____

7. _____

8. _____

9. _____

10. _____

JOURNAL WRITING ASSIGNMENT

Topic: Characteristics of Successful Students

As you head toward the end of the term, undoubtedly you have learned much about attitudes, habits, study skills, and academic skills that lead to success in college courses. For fifteen minutes or more, write about these different qualities, habits, skills, or attitudes. These may be attributes you have learned to acquire or attributes you have seen in others that you wish to develop in yourself. Be creative and cover as many different aspects of college success as possible.

PARAGRAPH WRITING ASSIGNMENT

Topic: How to . . .

Writing clear, concise directions for completing a process or a task requires careful attention to details and an understanding of the individual steps involved. Brainstorm lists of processes or tasks that you are familiar enough with to teach them to someone else. These processes or tasks may be something you learned in a lab class, such as a science or a computer lab, or they may involve something you learned on a job. They may also involve some type of home repair, or they may involve the steps needed for a specific hobby or special interest. *Avoid writing recipes or providing steps for something familiar to most people, such as brushing your teeth or washing a car.*

List some possibilities here:

Use the following guidelines to write your **process paragraph:**

1. Make a list of the individual steps involved in the process.

2. Write a strong opening sentence that names the process or task and identifies the number of steps involved.

   Examples: Colorful, fragrant flowers can be dried in four easy steps.
   Five basic steps can be used to train even the most unruly dog.

3. Write a sentence that introduces the first step. Use the ordinal word *first.* Then add one or more sentences that give additional details. These sentences may provide the reader with background information, cautionary notes, or more detailed directions on how to complete the step.

4. Continue using the above format for each of the steps. Assume that your reader does not know the process. Include sufficient details to "walk" the reader through each step.

5. Close the paragraph with a concluding or a summary sentence stating the final result that will be obtained by following the steps.

TEN

Frequently Misspelled and Frequently Confused Words

The topics in this chapter include the following:

- Frequently misspelled words
- Additional work with confusable words, homonyms, and sentence combining
- Introduction of prefixes with meanings that relate to numbers or quantities
- Additional work with new roots to build words
- Introduction of appositives, relative pronouns, and relative pronoun clauses
- Additional work with sentence combining

Spelling Definitions

Frequently Misspelled Words

Many words are misspelled because they are pronounced incorrectly, do not follow common English phonetic or word patterns, or contain schwas. Many times the frequently misspelled words must be learned as sight words and learned through rote memory by practicing the words frequently.

> ***Examples:*** Correct spelling: government
> Common error: goverment
> Correct spelling: mischievous
> Common error: mischievious
> Correct spelling: optimist
> Common error: optomist

Frequently Confused Words

Frequently confused words (**confusables**) are similar in spelling or similar in pronunciation. Because they *do not sound the same*, they are not homonyms. Frequently confused words need to be studied and learned as vocabulary words. Understanding the meaning and the usage of each word is essential.

> ***Examples:*** advise—advice   elude—allude

Homonyms

Homonyms are words that sound the same but have different spellings and different meanings. As with frequently confused words, homonyms need to be studied and learned as vocabulary words. Attention must be given to meanings and correct usage.

> ***Example:*** compliment—complement

Read the following words carefully. The letters in bold print have the **schwa** sound.

alcohol	category	dilemma
mathematics	optimistic	privilege

Read the following words carefully. The letters in bold print show the point of common errors due to mispronunciation.

athlete	disastrous	entrance	environment
February	government	laboratory	mischievous
prescription	restaurant	sophomore	mathematics

Read the following words carefully. The letters in bold print are the combinations that sometimes cause spelling problems.

acknowledgment	alphabet	amateur
anxious	bureaucracy	conscientious
fatigue	guarantee	maintenance
miscellaneous	prejudice	questionnaire
schedule	surprise	syllable
technique	vacuum	

1. Carefully read each of the following words. Focus your attention on the different vowel and consonant units in the word and on the individual syllables.
2. Practice writing each word two times. Say each syllable as you practice writing the complete word.

✎ **PRACTICE**

Word	By Syllables	Practice	Practice
1. acknowledge	ac-knowl-edge	_____	_____
2. advise	ad-vise	_____	_____
3. affect	af-fect	_____	_____
4. alcohol	al-co-hol	_____	_____
5. alphabet	al-pha-bet	_____	_____
6. amateur	am-a-teur	_____	_____
7. anxious	anx-ious	_____	_____
8. argument	ar-gu-ment	_____	_____
9. athlete	ath-lete	_____	_____
10. bureaucracy	bu-reau-cra-cy	_____	_____
11. category	cat-e-go-ry	_____	_____
12. chocolate	choc-o-late	_____	_____
13. compliment	com-pli-ment	_____	_____
14. conscientious	con-sci-en-tious	_____	_____
15. counsel	coun-sel	_____	_____
16. dilemma	di-lem-ma	_____	_____
17. disastrous	di-sas-trous	_____	_____
18. education	ed-u-ca-tion	_____	_____
19. elicit	e-lic-it	_____	_____
20. elude	e-lude	_____	_____
21. emigrate	em-i-grate	_____	_____
22. entrance	en-trance	_____	_____
23. environment	en-vi-ron-ment	_____	_____
24. except	ex-cept	_____	_____
25. fatigue	fa-tigue	_____	_____
26. February	Feb-ru-ar-y	_____	_____

Word	By Syllables	Practice	Practice
27. government	gov-ern-ment	_____	_____
28. guarantee	guar-an-tee	_____	_____
29. judgment	judg-ment	_____	_____
30. laboratory	lab-o-ra-to-ry	_____	_____
31. maintenance	main-te-nance	_____	_____
32. mathematics	math-e-mat-ics	_____	_____
33. miscellaneous	mis-cel-la-ne-ous	_____	_____
34. mischievous	mis-chie-vous	_____	_____
35. moral	mor-al	_____	_____
36. optimistic	op-ti-mis-tic	_____	_____
37. personnel	per-son-nel	_____	_____
38. prejudice	prej-u-dice	_____	_____
39. prescription	pre-scrip-tion	_____	_____
40. presence	pres-ence	_____	_____
41. principal	prin-ci-pal	_____	_____
42. privilege	priv-i-lege	_____	_____
43. questionnaire	ques-tion-naire	_____	_____
44. restaurant	res-tau-rant	_____	_____
45. schedule	sched-ule	_____	_____
46. sophomore	soph-o-more	_____	_____
47. surprise	sur-prise	_____	_____
48. syllable	syl-la-ble	_____	_____
49. technique	tech-nique	_____	_____
50. vacuum	vac-u-um	_____	_____

✎ **Exercise 10.1 Working with Frequently Misspelled or Confused Words**

Use the words from this chapter's word list (pages 317–318) to complete the following.

1. Write any six words that are **two-syllable** words.

_____ _____ _____

_____ _____ _____

2. Write any six words that are **three-syllable** words.

_____ _____ _____

_____ _____ _____

3. Write any six words that are **four-syllable** words.

_____ _____ _____

_____ _____ _____

4. Write any two words that are **five-syllable** words.

_____ _____

5. Look carefully at the pairs of words below. Circle the correct spelling of each word.

emmigrate—emigrate guarantee—guarrantee February—Febuary

tecknique—technique disasterous—disastrous dilemma—dilemna

maintanance—maintenance sophomore—sophmore restraunt—restaurant

enterance—entrance catagory—category amatuer—amateur

6. The following words can be broken into word parts to show the prefixes, base words or roots, and suffixes. Show the individual word parts. Note that word parts are not the same as syllables. An example has been done for you.

affect = af + fect

a. advise = _____ + _____

b. compliment = _____ + _____ + _____

c. education = _____ + _____ + _____ + _____

d. elude = _____ + _____

e. except = _____ + _____

f. government = _____ + _____

g. prescription = _____ + _____ + _____

7. Write the five words from the word list that have the *-ous* suffix.

_____ _____ _____

_____ _____

8. Write the four words from the word list that have the *-ment* suffix.

_____ _____

_____ _____

9. Write the two words from the word list that have the *-ion* suffix.

_____ _____

10. Write any eight words that have a soft *c* or a soft *g*.

_____ _____ _____ _____

_____ _____ _____ _____

Homonyms

The words below in bold are in this chapter's basic word list. Homonyms for the words are then shown. Notice the spelling changes and the different phonetic elements and "word families" that are used to make the homonyms.

compliment—complement   **counsel**—council

presence—presents, present's   **principal**—principle

PRACTICE

Partner or Group Work

Parts of the following assignment may be assigned to individual partners or groups to complete and then report back to the class.

The following sentences show **homonyms** *in bold print. Read each sentence carefully to determine how the word is working in the sentence. On the left margin, write* **N** *if the word is working as a* **noun.** *Write* **V** *if the word is working as a* **verb.** *Write* **A** *if the word is working as an* **adjective.** *Beside or beneath the sentence, write an informal definition of any of the word meanings that are unfamiliar to you.*

Part 1

_____ 1. Some people have difficulty accepting **compliments.**

_____ 2. The sergeant received a **compliment** from his commander.

_____ 3. My high school coach frequently **compliments** his players on their effort.

_____ 4. Your wisdom is a **complement** to your beauty.

_____ 5. The **complement** in this geometry problem will result in a ninety-degree angle.

_____ 6. Dry white wines **complement** many fish entrées.

_____ 7. The word is the **complement** to the subject.

_____ 8. Academic advisors **counsel** hundreds of students.

_____ 9. The rookie lawyer sought **counsel** from his supervisor.

_____ 10. The therapist **counsels** couples in problem resolution.

Part 2

_____ 11. I often seek **counsel** from my friends.

_____ 12. The tycoon hired **counsel** to defend him.

_____ 13. Marcos was appointed to the city **council.**

_____ 14. The **council** will meet to discuss the proposal.

_____ **15.** A **council** decision is needed by Friday.

_____ **16.** The mayor's **presence** was appreciated.

_____ **17.** Everyone felt honored by your **presence.**

_____ **18.** Your **presence** is required at the banquet.

_____ **19.** The **presents** were placed under the tree.

_____ **20.** The mother-to-be received many baby **presents.**

Part 3

_____ **21.** The wrapped **presents** were shipped yesterday.

_____ **22.** The **present's** contents are a mystery.

_____ **23.** The **principal** called the students to her office.

_____ **24.** The **principal** industry is logging.

_____ **25.** The interest and the **principal** are paid monthly.

_____ **26.** José received the **principal** part in the play.

_____ **27.** She considers herself to be a person of high **principles.**

_____ **28.** My **principles** often dictate my actions.

_____ **29.** The country is based on the **principle** of democracy.

_____ **30.** The **Principle** of Indemnity allows insurance payments for replacement costs only.

More About Homonyms

compliment— complement

1. An easy mnemonic (memory trick) to use for these homonyms is to remember this saying: "**I** give compl**I**ments." The homonym that means flattering remarks, praise, or recognition is something **I** like to do. It has the letter **I** (not **E**) in it. The word "complement" refers to something that completes or makes a whole.

2. Both *compliment* and *complement* can have an *-ary* suffix. In both cases, the words relate back to the original meanings. "Complimentary" also means "free," or "without a charge."

   I received a very *complimentary* note from my manager.

   The bottle of wine was *complimentary*.

   Complementary efforts will be needed by each pair of workers.

counsel—council

1. The word *counsel* always relates to giving advice. The word *council* relates to a group or a body of individuals.

2. Both *counsel* and *council* can have an *-or* suffix. Both words also have two correct spellings; however, the first spelling is more frequently used. Each

word is related back to the original meaning of giving advice or being a part of a group or body of individuals.

counselor (or counsellor)   councilor (or councillor)

3. One mnemonic to use is to think of someone on a **ci**ty coun**ci**l. Both words have a **ci.**

presence— presents—present's

1. The word *presence* is always a noun referring to appearance or participation. The word *presents* is a plural noun meaning "gifts."

2. The word *present's* is a possessive form of the singular noun *present*. *Present's* works as an adjective to describe something that belongs to or is related to a present.

The *present's* wrapping was torn.

The *present's* contents were unknown.

3. The word *presents* as a noun is divided and accented this way: pres'-ents. The word *presents* can be pronounced differently to become a verb: pre-sents'. (In previous chapters, other words were discussed that shift from nouns to verbs by shifting the accent.)

We will present our idea to the class on Wednesday.

principal—principle

1. The word *principal*, meaning the head of a school, is often remembered by this mnemonic: "The princi**pal** is your **pal**." However, *principal* has several other meanings as well. It can mean "the primary" or "most important," or it can be a financial term stating the amount of money before interest is applied.

2. The word *princi**ple*** always refers to some type of rule. Both words end in **le.**

Name _____   Date _____

✎ **EXERCISE 10.2 Sentence Work with Homonyms**

Circle the correct homonym to complete each sentence.

 1. The student body (counsel, council) meets each Tuesday.

 2. The (counselor, councilor) can help you plan your schedule of classes.

 3. I cannot (counsel, council) you on legal issues.

 4. The (principal, principle) factor must first be identified.

 5. I received a (complimentary, complementary) gift with my new subscription.

 6. The newly hired receptionist felt intimidated by the (presents, presence) of the president.

 7. All of her (presence, presents) were stacked on the reception table.

 8. I only wanted to pay you a (compliment, complement).

 9. The (principal, principle) on the loan is two thousand dollars.

10. The interest is calculated on the (principal, principle.)

11. As a matter of (principal, principle), I will not attend the award ceremony.

12. Your (presents, presence) is expected at the annual stockholders' meeting.

13. His meticulous ways (compliment, complement) your sloppy habits.

14. I sought (counsel, council) for my legal situation.

15. The (counselor, councilor) will resign his position on the city (council, counsel).

16. My son blushed when I paid him a (compliment, complement) in front of his friends.

17. The (presence, presents, present's) size led us to believe the gift was a ring.

18. The angle plus its (compliment, complement) give the sum of ninety degrees.

19. His (principal, principle) motive was to get hired for the position.

20. All of the (counselors, councilors) and the (principal, principle) plan to discuss the situation.

Building Words

The following prefixes are number-related. Knowing the definitions of these prefixes helps you understand and begin to define the meanings of many words.

New Prefixes: *bi-   hepta-   hexa-   mono-   multi-   oct-   penta-   poly-   quadr-   sept-   sex-   tetra-   tri-   uni-*

The prefix *bi-* means **two.**
The prefix *hepta-* means **seven.**
The prefix *hexa-* means **six.**
The prefix *mono-* means **one.**
The prefix *multi-* means **many.**
The prefix *oct-* (also *octa-* or *octo-*) means **eight.**
The prefix *penta-* means **five.**
The prefix *poly-* means **many.**
The prefix *quadr-* (also *quad-* or *quart-*) means **four.**
The prefix *sept-* (also *sep-*) means **seven.**
The prefix *sex-* (also *sext-*) means **six.**
The prefix *tetra-* means **four.**
The prefix *tri-* means **three.**
The prefix *uni-* means **one.**

✎ PRACTICE

Add the prefix shown at the top of each list. Read the words you create and their definitions.

One = *mono-*

_____gamy   *one* marriage partner

_____gram   *one* letter (or set of initials)

_____logue   *one* speaker

_____plane   *one* pair of wings

_____pod   *one* foot

_____rail   *one* rail for a train

_____tone   *one* tone of voice

One = *uni-*

_____corn   *one* horn (a fictitious animal)

_____from   *one* form

_____fy   to make *one*

_____lateral   *one* side

_____sex   *one* sex (no gender distinctions)

_____son   *one* sound

_____ty   the state or condition of being *one*

_____verse   *one* world

two = *bi-*

_____weekly   once every *two* weeks

_____monthly   once every *two* months

_____cycle   *two* "circles" (wheels)

_____focals   *two* focuses for better vision

_____lateral   *two* sides

_____lingual   *two* "tongues" (languages)

_____nomial   *two* names or terms

_____partisan   *two* (political) parties

_____plane   *two* wings

_____pod   *two* legs

_____polar   *two* poles

_____sect   *two* parts

_____racial   *two* races

three = *tri-*

_____ad   a group of *three* numbers or people

_____angle   *three* angles

_____archy   *three* rulers (government)

_____cycle   *three* circles (wheels)

_____lateral   *three* sides

_____logy   *three* literary works related to the same theme

_____mester   *three* months

_____nomial   *three* names or terms

_____ple	consisting of *three* parts
_____plex	*three* parts (as in a housing unit)
_____plicate	*three* parts
_____pod	*three* legs

four = *quadr-, quad-, quart-*

_____angle	*four* angles (a rectangle)
_____uple	*four*-fold or *four* parts
_____uplet	one of *four* offspring born in a single birth
_____et	*four* singers or *four* voices

four = *tetra-*

_____gon	*four*-sided polygon (a quadrilateral)
_____pod	*four* feet or legs

five = *penta-*

_____gon	*five* sides (for example, the Pentagon—the U.S. Department of Defense)
_____thlon	*five* contests or athletic events

six = *hexa-*

_____gon	*six* sides
_____gram	*six*-pointed star
_____pod	*six* legs or feet

six = *sex-, sext-*

_____ant	navigational instrument based on *six* parts of a circle
_____uplet	one of *six* offspring born in a single birth.

seven = *hepta-*

_____gon	*seven* sides
_____hedron	a polyhedron with *seven* sides

seven = *sept-, sep-*

_____et	*seven* voices or singers
_____uple	consisting of *seven* or multiplied by *seven*
_____ember	was once the *seventh* month in a calendar year

eight = *oct-, octa-, octo-*

_____gon	*eight* sides
_____ve	the interval of *eight* degrees between tones on a musical scale
_____et	*eight* singers
_____pod	*eight* legs or feet
_____pus	*eight* feet
_____uple	*eight* parts or copies
_____ober	was once the *eighth* month in a calendar year

many = *multi-*

_____ethnic	*many* or a variety of ethnic groups
_____media	several or *many* forms of media or communication
_____ped	*many* feet or legs
_____ple	consisting of several or *many* parts or forms
_____ply	to increase several or *many* times
_____tude	*many* in number

many = *poly-*

_____andry	having *more than one* husband at the same time
_____chrome	having *many* colors at one time
_____gamist	a person who has *more than one* spouse
_____gamy	having *more than one* husband or wife at the same time
_____glot	a person who speaks, reads, or writes in *several* languages
_____gon	a geometric figure with three *or more* sides
_____graph	a written record that records *many* body responses
_____gyny	having *more than one* wife at the same time
_____nomial	*more than two* names or terms

Roots

Learning the meanings of the following roots can also help you understand and define many words. Many of the roots are probably already familiar to you. However, as you will notice with the words below the box, words can be formed by combining roots. You will see many examples of *root + root = an English word*.

New Roots: *anthro aqua astro audi biblio bio chrono gene
geo graph gram hydro meter morph naut path
philos phobia photo psych ology ologist seismo
sophos tele therma*

The root *anthro* (also *anthropo*) means **man.**
The root *aqua* means **water.**
The root *astro* means **stars.**
The root *audi* means **to hear.**
The root *biblio* means **books.**
The root *bio* means **life.**
The root *chrono* (also *chronos*) means **time.**
The root *gene* (also *gen, genea*) means **birth.**
The root *geo* means **earth.**
The root *graph* (also *graphy*) means **to write** or **written record of.**
The root *gram* means **letter.**
The root *hydro* means **water.**
The root *meter* means **to measure.**
The root *morph* (or *morphe*) means **form** or **shape.**
The root *naut* means **ships** or **navigator.**
The root *path* (or *pathos, pathy*) means **feeling** or **suffering.**
The root *philos* (or phile) means **liking** or **loving.**
The root *phobia* means **fear** or **dislike.**
The root *photo* means **light.**
The root *psych* (or *psyche*) means **mind** or **spirit.**
The root *ology* means **the study of.**
The root *ologist* means **one who studies.**
The root *seismo* means **earthquake.**
The root *sophos* (or *sopho*) means **wise.**
The root *tele* means **far.**
The root *therma* means **heat.**

✎ **PRACTICE**

Use the meanings of the roots above to write a meaning for the following words.

1. *anthropologist* means _____

2. *aquanaut* means _____

3. *astrology* means _____

4. *audiometer* means _____

5. *bibliography* means _____

6. *biography* means _____

7. *chronological* means _____

8. *genealogy* means _____

9. *geography* means _____

10. *graphology* means _____

11. *telegram* means _____

12. *hydroelectric* means _____

13. *thermometer* means _____

14. *morphograph* means _____

15. *astronaut* means _____

16. *pathology* means _____

17. *philosopher* means _____

18. *hydrophobia* means _____

19. *photograph* means _____

20. *psychologist* means _____

21. *geologist* means _____

22. *seismograph* means _____

23. *sophomore* means _____

24. *telecommunication* means _____

25. *thermotherapy* means _____

ology and *ologist*

✎ **PRACTICE**

Complete the following sentences. Name the subject or discipline that is studied and the word for the person who does this kind of study. The meanings for the roots are given on page 329. You may use a dictionary if necessary. On the second line, add the ogist *suffix to all the words except one. One word will require an* -er *suffix.*

Example: *Biology is the study of* _____life_____ *that is done by a* _____biologist._____

1. Anthropology is the study of _____ that is done by an _____.

2. Astrology is the study of _____ that is done by an _____.

3. Audiology is the study of _____ that is done by an _____.

4. Chronology is the study of _____ that is done by a _____.

5. Genealogy is the study of _____ that is done by a _____.

6. Geology is the study of _____ that is done by a _____.

7. Graphology is the study of _____ that is done by a _____.

8. Hydrology is the study of _____ that is done by a _____.

9. Methodology is the study of _____ that is done by a _____.

10. Morphology is the study of _____ that is done by a _____.

11. Mythology is the study of _____ that is done by a _____.

12. Pathology is the study of _____ that is done by a _____.

13. Philosophy is the study of _____ that is done by a _____.

14. Psychology is the study of _____ that is done by a _____.

15. Sociology is the study of _____ that is done by a _____.

16. Seismology is the study of _____ that is done by a _____.

17. Volcanology is the study of _____ that is done by a _____.

Partner Practice

Each partner selects any ten words from above to dictate for his or her partner to spell. Exchange roles so both partners have the opportunity to dictate and to spell.

✎ **EXERCISE 10.3 Building Words**

*The base words or the roots are shown in bold print. Combine the word parts
and write the complete word on the line. Apply any necessary spelling rules.*

1. ac + **know** + **ledge** + ment = _____

2. af + **fect** + ion + ate = _____

3. **amateur** + ish = _____

4. **athlete** + ic + al + ly = _____

5. e + **duce** + ate + ion + al + ly = _____

6. **judgment** + al = _____

7. **vacuum** + ing = _____

8. uni + **form** + ite + y = _____

9. uni + **verse** + al + ly = _____

10. tri + **logy** + s/es = _____

11. astro + **logic** + al = _____

12. chrono + **logic** + al + ly = _____

13. geo + **graph** + ic = _____

14. tele + **vise** + ion = _____

15. **philo** + **soph** + ic + al = _____

16. **phil** + **anthrop** + ist = _____

17. **tele** + com + **mune** + ic + ate + ion = _____

18. geo + **therm** + al = _____

19. con + **gene** + ial = _____

20. com + **ply** + ment + s = _____

21. ad + **vise** + or/er = _____

22. **alphabet** + ic + al + ly = _____

23. **argument** + ate + ive = _____

24. **category** + s/es = _____

25. **govern** + ment + al = _____

26. **labor** + ate + or + y + s/es = _____

27. **principal** + ite + y = _____

28. **unify** + ing = _____

29. bi + **cycle** + ist = _____

30. **multiple** + ic + ate + ion = _____

31. bio + **graph** + ic + al = _____

32. **psych** + ic + s/es = _____

33. **graph** + ic + s/es = _____

34. tele + **phone** + ing = _____

35. hydro + **plane** + ing = _____

36. geo + **logic** + al = _____

37. sym + **path** + ize + ing = _____

38. **biblio** + **phile** = _____

39. ef + **fect** + ive + ly = _____

40. im + **moral** + ite + y = _____

EXERCISE 10.4 Word List Expansion

The following words are also "the study of" a specific discipline or field. Use your background knowledge or the help of a dictionary to write the meaning of the new root that is in bold print. On the second line, complete the sentence by writing the term used for the person who studies this discipline or field; most (but not all) of the "people" words will use the ologist *ending.*

1. **Theo**logy is the study of _____ that is done by a _____.

2. **Astro**logy is the study of _____ that is done by an _____.

3. **Meteor**ology is the study of _____ that is done by a _____.

4. **Eco**logy is the study of _____ that is done by an _____.

5. **Physi**ology is the study of _____ that is done by a _____.

6. **Micro**biology is the study of _____ that is done by a _____.

7. **Para**psychology is the study of _____ that is done by a _____.

8. **Crimin**ology is the study of _____ that is done by a _____.

9. **Zoo**logy is the study of _____ that is done by a _____.

10. **Gynec**ology is the study of _____ that is done by a _____.

11. **Archae**ology is the study of _____ that is done by an _____.

12. **Geront**ology is the study of _____ that is done by a _____.

13. **Dermat**ology is the study of _____ that is done by a _____.

Use your background knowledge or the help of a dictionary to write the meaning of the words in bold print. Begin by identifying the word parts. Then do a "memory search" to see if you can associate the roots with information you already know. Write "your" informal definition.

1. **helio**centric means: _____

2. **corpor**al means: _____

3. poly**gamy** means: _____

Use your knowledge of word parts to complete the following sentences. You may use a dictionary if necessary.

1. The prefix *a-* means "not or without." *Path* means "feelings." Therefore, *apathy* means:

_____

2. The prefix *sym-* means "with" or "together." *Path* means "feelings." Therefore, *sympathy* means:

_____

3. The prefix *em-* means "in." *Path* means "feelings." Therefore, *empathy* means:

_____

4. A _____graph is a piece of equipment that records *many* different body responses, such as heartbeat, blood pressure, and rate of respiration. This equipment is also called a lie detector.

5. A _____graph is a written record of *images of light.*

6. A _____graph is a written record of *earthquakes.*

7. A _____graph is a written record from *far away.*

8. Would you want to practice philanthropy, or is it something you would want to avoid? Use your knowledge of meanings of roots to write your own definition for the word *philanthropy:*

_____

Now consult a dictionary. Write the dictionary definition here: _____

_____

A person who practices *philanthropy* is called a _____.

Confusables: Frequently Confused Words

Confusables are words that are frequently confused because of similarities in either spelling or pronunciation. The *meanings* of the words need to be learned in order to use the words correctly in writing. In the list below, the words from this chapter are in bold print.

advise—advice	**affect**—effect	**conscientious**—conscience,
counsel—consul, console	**elicit**—illicit	conscious
emigrate—immigrate	**except**—accept	**elude**—allude
personnel—personal		**moral**—morale

advise, advice

advise	verb	To give advice or counsel to
advice	noun	A recommendation for a course of action or options to take

✎ PRACTICE

Write advise *or* advice *to complete the following sentences.*

1. The amateur athlete enjoys giving free _____ to young athletes.

2. A new counselor will _____ me about my scheduling options.

3. The financial advisor's _____ is not a guarantee of profits.

4. The instructors _____ all students to wear goggles in the laboratory.

5. I was surprised by the sound _____ given to me by my grandfather.

affect, effect

affect	verb	To influence or to pretend (transitive verb that will have an object)
effect	noun	A result, an influence
	verb	To accomplish, to produce, or to bring about

✎ PRACTICE

Write affect *or* effect *to complete the following sentences.*

1. The mediators hope to _____ a settlement between the two parties.

2. Extreme heat and humidity _____ my blood pressure.

3. Crude jokes _____ me.

4. The undercooked meat had a bad _____ on my digestive system.

5. Air and water pollutants _____ the quality of our environment.

6. The new welfare reform laws will _____ many Americans.

conscientious,	*conscientious*	adjective	Honest, hard-working, done with a conscience
conscience,	*conscience*	noun	An awareness of right and wrong, sense of rightness
conscious	*conscious*	adjective	Aware, awake, mentally alert, intentional

✎ **PRACTICE**

Write conscientious, conscience, or conscious to complete the following sentences.

1. A person's ——————————— can create feelings of guilt.

2. I was very ——————————— of the impact of my decision.

3. ——————————— students devote the necessary time to learning course content.

4. The victim was ——————————— when she arrived at the emergency room.

5. Let your ——————————— guide you.

6. She made a ——————————— choice about attending school full-time.

counsel, consul,	*counsel*	verb	To give advice
console	*consul*	noun	A person assigned to a government position in a foreign country
	con' sole	noun	A cabinet or part that has controls or a control panel
	con sole'	verb	To soothe someone's grief, to provide comfort and understanding

✎ **PRACTICE**

Write counsel, counsul, or console to complete the following sentences.

1. The warranty on the ——————————— has expired.

2. The immigrants sought ——————————— from the sponsoring church organization.

3. The family members gathered to ——————————— the grieving mother.

4. Her new job as an American ——————————— will be challenging.

5. Lights started blinking and alarms started sounding on the pilot's ———————————.

6. The lawyer asked for time to ——————————— his client.

| **elicit, illicit** | *elicit* | verb | To draw forth, to bring out, to encourage a response, to evoke |
| | *illicit* | adjective | Not lawful, illegal, improper |

✎ PRACTICE

Write elicit *or* illicit *to complete the following sentences.*

1. The FBI hoped to _____ information from the prisoner.

2. The community will not tolerate _____ behavior in its neighborhoods.

3. You will _____ a response from him every time you mention taxes.

4. The list of laws and legal consequences are designed to reduce _____ acts.

5. The counseling techniques _____ honest communication among teenagers.

| **elude, allude** | *elude* | verb | To evade or to avoid, to escape notice of |
| | *allude* | verb | To refer indirectly to |

✎ PRACTICE

Write elude *or* allude *to complete the following sentences.*

1. Anniversary dates of family members always _____ me.

2. Many students' reports _____ to specific studies but do not clearly identify the studies or the research findings.

3. The couple tried to _____ the police officers.

4. Many times it is not possible to _____ the consequences of your actions.

5. The government documents _____ to misappropriation of funds.

| **emigrate, immigrate** | *emigrate* | verb | (emigrate to) To leave one's own country to settle elsewhere. The noun form is *emigrant*. |
| | *immigrate* | verb | (immigrate from) To come or arrive into a country to live. The noun form is *immigrant*. |

✎ PRACTICE

Write emigrate to, emigrant, immigrate from, *or* immigrant *to complete the following sentences.*

1. Each year, thousands of foreigners long to _____ the United States.

2. Many workers _____ Vietnam to the United States and Canada.

3. The _____ enrolled in classes to improve his English language skills.

4. The _____ waited impatiently for permission to leave her country.

5. My cousins from Africa will _____ the United States in February.

except, accept	*except*	preposition	Excluding or but
		conjunction	But (subordinate conjunction)
		verb	To omit, exclude, or make an exception of
	accept	verb	To receive willingly, agree to, approve of

✎ PRACTICE

Write except *or* accept *to complete the following sentences.*

1. Everyone in his family went to the school play _____ his elderly grandmother.

2. Sometimes it is best not to _____ the first offer too quickly.

3. When Sandy moved, she took everything _____ her sofa.

4. If you _____ his apology, it will be a sign of forgiveness.

5. Some people find that it is difficult to _____ compliments.

moral, morale	*moral*	adjective	Relating to the principles of right and wrong, conforming to a standard of right behavior
		noun	The point of a story, a lesson
	morale	noun	An emotional attitude, spirit, or outlook

✎ PRACTICE

Write moral *or* morale *to complete the following sentences.*

1. Many fairy tales involve a _____ .

2. When almost every student failed the test, the _____ in class was low.

3. The church guides individuals to lead a _____ life.

4. The theme of the movie was based on one man's _____ dilemma.

5. _____ was high when the striking employees won a new contract.

personnel, personal	*personnel*	noun	A body of people employed in an organization or business
		adjective	Describing something related or belonging to a body of people
	personal	adjective	Relating to or affecting a specific person, private in nature

✎ PRACTICE

Write personnel *or* personal *to complete the following sentences.*

1. _____ ads for friendship and romance are placed in most newspapers.

2. I need to spend more time writing _____ letters.

3. The morale problems in the company's _____ office are escalating.

4. The turnover in _____ at the manufacturing plant is minimal.

5. The reason for my fatigue is _____.

EXERCISE 10.5 Sentence Writing

*Read each of the word sentences carefully. The frequently confused word (confusable) is in bold print. Write **N** if the word is working as a noun. Write **V** if the word is working as a verb. Write **A** if the word is working as an adjective and **ADV** if the word is working as an adverb.*

_____ 1. The new student was **counseled** into a grammar review class.

_____ 2. Signing up for extra insurance is a **personal** decision.

_____ 3. I am not trying to **elude** you; I just don't have time to visit right now.

_____ 4. Our moral fiber is linked to our **conscience.**

_____ 5. You can get some professional **advice** about changing your diet.

_____ 6. My family tree shows the family members who **immigrated** from South America almost one hundred years ago.

_____ 7. What you eat can definitely **affect** your strength and endurance.

_____ 8. The Japanese **consul** resides at this address.

_____ 9. You **alluded** that you knew what caused the fire.

_____ 10. The new **personnel** forms will be available on Wednesday.

_____ 11. You are a joy to be around when your **morale** is high.

_____ 12. You can make a **conscious** effort to become a better listener.

_____ 13. The **console** television will be on sale in February.

_____ 14. Please **accept** this small gift as a token of my appreciation.

_____ 15. The **effects** of massive radiation are now well-researched.

_____ 16. The good news is that the child is **conscious.**

_____ 17. Please **accept** my deepest sympathy.

_____ 18. The judgment involved a stiff fine for **illicit** drug activities.

Use the following phrases in sentences that provide the reader with details. To make your sentences interesting and informative, include a variety of adjectives, adverbs, and prepositional phrases.

1. advise you

_____

2. gives good advice

_____

3. will affect us

_____

4. visual effects

_____

5. conscientious objector

_____

6. your conscience

_____

7. was conscious

_____

8. consoled me

_____

9. elude the officer

_____

10. can elicit

_____

11. moral of the story

_____

12. personal business

_____

13. allude to the truth

_____

14. emigrate from

_____

15. immigrate to

_____

16. except me

_____

17. accept the money

_____

Grammar Definitions

Appositive   An appositive is a group of words that renames or adds details about the noun
                          that precedes it. The appositive is set off by commas.

> *Example:* Mr. Davis, **my advisor,** helped me plan a schedule of classes.
> (The appositive is *my advisor.* This is shorter than using two
> simple sentences: *Mr. Davis is my advisor. Mr. Davis helped me
> plan a schedule of classes.*)

Important information to know about appositives:

1. The appositive must come immediately after the noun.

2. Appositives provide writers with a technique to combine information into
   one sentence and to clarify by adding more details.

3. Appositives can be used in simple, compound, and complex sentences.

Appositives

✎ PRACTICE

*Combine the following sentences by using appositives. Begin by identifying the
nouns that are common to both sentences. Then take the information from one
sentence (usually the second sentence) and insert the information as an appositive in the first sentence. The information in bold print can be converted to an
appositive.*

1. My cousin moved to Canada. My cousin was **a conscientious objector.**

_____

2. The campaign manager predicted a win. He was **an optimistic person.**

_____

3. Fatigue has several health consequences. Fatigue is **a common stress indicator.**

_____

4. Carlos has a promising future. Carlos is **an amateur athlete.**

_____

5. Sam's Restaurant accepts reservations after eight o'clock. Sam's is **the best barbeque restaurant in
town.**

_____

More Grammar Definitions

Relative Pronoun

That, which, who, whom, whose, when, or *where* can be relative pronouns that refer to a specific noun or pronoun in the sentence. (*When* and *where* have already been discussed as subordinate conjunctions, or "spoilers.")

> ***Examples:*** Mr. Davis, **who is my advisor,** helped me plan a schedule of classes.
>
> The bus **that I take to school each day** arrives at 8:30 A.M.
>
> The personnel director, **whose name I have forgotten,** called me today.

Important information to know about relative pronouns:

1. The relative pronouns *who* and *whom* are used to refer only to people. Only *who* works as the subject of a clause.

2. The relative pronoun *whose* can refer to people or to objects.

3. The relative pronoun *that* refers to objects; *which* can refer to objects or to people.

4. The relative pronoun *when* refers to time.

5. The relative pronoun *where* refers to a location or a place.

Relative Pronoun Clause

A relative pronoun clause is a group of words that begins with a relative pronoun and has a subject and a verb. The relative pronoun may be the subject, or it may precede the subject of the clause.

> ***Examples:*** The beverage, **which is complimentary,** can be any drink of your choice.
>
> The hot chocolate **which the *man ordered*** will be served in a minute.

Important information about punctuating relative pronoun clauses:

1. A relative pronoun clause that begins with *that* does not use commas.

2. A relative pronoun clause that begins with *which, who, whom,* or *whose* is set off by commas when the information is not essential to identify or understand the subject. This is called a *nonessential* or *nonrestrictive* clause. (This topic is discussed later in the chapter.)

3. A relative pronoun clause that begins with *which, who, whom,* or *whose* is not set off by commas when the information is essential to identify or understand the subject. This is called an *essential* or a *restrictive clause.* (This topic is discussed later in the chapter.)

Dependent Clause

Dependent clauses are groups of words with subjects and verbs that do not form a complete thought (or a complete sentence) by themselves.

Important information to know about dependent clauses:

1. Dependent clauses must be attached to an independent clause.

2. Dependent clauses by themselves are **fragments.**

3. Dependent clauses may begin with a "spoiler" (subordinate conjunction) or with a relative pronoun.

Relative Pronoun Clauses

✎ **PRACTICE**

Draw a box around the relative pronoun clauses in the following sentences. Then underline the subject in the clause once and the verb twice.

Example: *Lynne has a new boyfriend* ⎡*who is a professional football player.*⎤

1. Here is the money that I borrowed from you yesterday.

2. My company hired Julio Santos, whom my boss met last year in Portland.

3. He told a story that had no moral.

4. The point guard is one of the players who really enjoys the pressure.

5. The customer who demanded to see the manager was very confrontational.

6. The peaches that were dipped in hot water can now be peeled.

7. I paid the travel expenses, which were minimal, out of my own pocket.

8. The police identified the person whose fingerprints were on the windowpane.

9. My brother, who finally bought a car, won't let anyone else drive it.

10. The argument, which lasted an hour, damaged our friendship for good.

Restrictive (Essential) and Nonrestrictive (Nonessential) Clauses

Sometimes it is difficult to determine if a relative pronoun clause with *who, which, whose,* or *whom* should be set off with commas. The following steps can help you determine whether or not to set the clause off with commas.

1. Identify the noun that is being modified or described by the clause. The noun will come right before the clause.

2. If the noun is specific enough, the relative pronoun clause is "extra" information. The relative pronoun clause is **nonrestrictive (nonessential).** Commas are used to show that the information is "extra" and can be omitted without affecting the meaning of the sentence.

   Robert, **who is my neighbor,** plans to sell his house.

   (Robert is specific. The reader is not left to wonder who will sell a house.)

   My math teacher, **who earned a degree from Yale,** is patient with students.

   (The word *my* indicates a specific teacher. The teacher is distinguished from all the other math teachers in the school. The relative pronoun clause is "extra.")

3. If the subject or the noun is vague or nonspecific, then the relative pronoun clause is essential information to clarify the meaning of the sentence.

   The girls **who qualified for the state tournament** are leaving on Saturday.

   (*Girls* is vague. What girls are being referred to here? The girls are specified by the relative pronoun clause. The relative pronoun clause is essential, so it is not set off by commas.)

✎ PRACTICE

The relative pronoun clause is in bold print in the following sentences. Decide if the relative pronoun clause is restrictive (essential) or nonrestrictive (nonessential). Add commas before and after the relative pronoun clauses that are nonrestrictive.

1. The students **who attended the conference** learned about the valuable, new research findings.

2. Their favorite baby sitter **whom they trust completely** spends weekends with their children.

3. The cemetery **which is on the north side of town** dates back to the early 1900s.

4. Mrs. Esther Sanders **who is our current president** was once the president of a large corporation.

5. Missy **whom I know loves old movies** goes to the movies every weekend.

6. We wanted to recommend Ms. Thompson **who is already experienced in marketing.**

7. The computer network system **which was purchased last year** is extremely easy to operate.

8. This is the software program **which came with the computer system.**

9. The program director **who wrote the initial grant** is very competent and efficient.

10. Local businesses are seeking graduates **whose communication skills are strong.**

Sentence Combining Using Relative Pronoun Clauses

Converting part of a sentence into a relative pronoun clause and attaching that clause to a separate sentence is one way to combine sentences for more concise writing. In order to combine the sentences, each sentence must have the same common noun. The relative pronoun clause is then placed next to the noun in the first sentence. Notice how this works in the two examples below.

1. The **bus** cannot be repaired. The **bus** was severely damaged in the accident.

   delete   convert to a relative pronoun clause

The bus **that was severely damaged in the accident** cannot be repaired.

2. The insurance agent brought me a **new policy.**
   The **new policy** covers earthquake damages.

   delete   *convert*

   The insurance agent brought me a new policy **that covers earthquake damages.**

✏️ **PRACTICE**

Combine the following simple sentences into one complex sentence by using a relative pronoun clause. The nouns that are common to both sentences are in bold print.

1. The **woman** holds two jobs. The **woman** has three children.

   _____

2. My **parents** were immigrants. My **parents** came from Poland.

   _____

3. The narrow mountain trails led to the **valley floor.** The **valley floor** was rich with flora.

   _____

4. A **sophomore** won the essay contest. The **sophomore** just transferred to our school.

   _____

Who and Whom

Who is a subject pronoun. If the relative pronoun clause does not have a subject, use *who*. *Who* becomes the subject of the clause. If the relative pronoun clause already has a subject, use *whom* to combine the clauses.

Examples: The children, *whom I think are adorable,* will perform in the center of the mall.
   The children *who want to attend the play* will get free tickets.

✏️ **PRACTICE**

Add who *or* whom *to the following sentences.*

1. The president of the college has a son _____ is a president of a different college.

2. Dr. Martinez, _____ I know from my surgery, is highly recommended.

3. I know _____ is coming to your bachelor party.

4. The city councilor, _____ everyone trusts completely, will be re-elected this year.

5. We do not know _____ ran over the street signs.

✎ **EXERCISE 10.6 Working with Relative Pronoun Clauses**

Place a box around the relative pronoun clauses. Within the relative pronoun clause, underline the subject once and the verb twice. Remember that the relative pronoun may function as the subject. Then, in the independent clause, underline the subject once and the verb twice.

1. The compliment was paid to Joe by the young lady whose office was next to his.

2. All the vehicles that have bad brakes were removed from service.

3. The young boy who has already been in several plays will play the leading role of Romeo.

4. The vase that you broke was a valuable antique.

5. The chief mechanic who was trained in Germany is capable of repairing any foreign model.

6. The famous writer who lives in San Francisco has ten books on the best-seller list.

7. Joan, who is my very best friend, writes to me at least once a week.

8. The tiger, which is the team's mascot, leads the cheers at the games.

9. Guitars that are not played very often lose their pitch and need to be retuned.

10. The octopus, which usually has eight legs, lost one leg during an underwater battle.

11. Stephen King is one author whom many people admire.

12. We parked the car in the lot which is close to the campus bookstore.

13. I wonder whose name will appear on the top of the list.

14. We can meet at the park where there is a rose garden.

15. Mr. Chee, who is my landlord, lives in the penthouse.

16. All of the new buildings have windows which cannot be opened.

17. People who are optimistic tend to have happier lives.

18. The knowledge that you learn in school often helps you later in life.

19. The answer that was given in class was incorrect.

20. It was very apparent that he wanted the job.

Complete each sentence below by filling in an appropriate relative pronoun. Add any missing punctuation before or after the relative pronoun clauses.

1. Without thinking, I blurted out the only answer _____ popped in my mind.

2. Bureaucracy _____ can be an endless stream of red tape is complex.

3. The laboratory assistant _____ advice is usually wise told me to study chapters two and three for the test on Thursday.

4. The famous blues singer _____ died last year will live on forever in our hearts.

5. The third fire fighter _____ was conscious told us the sequence of events.

6. The privilege _____ you earned can also be revoked.

7. The moral dilemma _____ she faced caused her to lose sleep at night.

8. The high jumper's technique _____ has been tried by other athletes is his trademark.

9. The contestant chose the last category on the board _____ was "famous cars."

10. The effects of the medication _____ is new on the market have been well-researched.

11. We finally met the real estate lady _____ I had talked to on the phone.

12. San Diego _____ the cruise ship docked offers tourists many sights to see.

13. The city council thanked the woman _____ had volunteered fifty hours of work.

14. The man _____ eluded the police for a week was finally apprehended.

15. The manager wants to discuss the issue _____ is affecting employee morale.

16. I finally got a prescription _____ works on my allergy problems.

17. Your private tutor _____ I believe is very good also works with Marcy.

18. Uniforms are worn to work by all the employees _____ deal with customers.

19. These bifocals _____ cost ninety dollars give me headaches.

20. Mathematics is a course _____ requires many hours of homework.

EXERCISE 10.7 **Working with Dependent Clauses**

As a review, write the definition of a **complex sentence:** _____

_____

*The following are complex sentences. The dependent clause begins with either a
subordinate conjunction (a spoiler) or a relative pronoun. Draw a box around
the dependent clause in each sentence. Add any missing punctuation. On the
line, write the subordinate conjunction or the relative pronoun.*

_____ **1.** All of the chocolate cakes that you ordered are on the kitchen counter.

_____ **2.** The Hawaiian alphabet which has only thirteen letters uses the five English vowels.

_____ **3.** Armed guards were stationed where they could see the entrance to the bank.

_____ **4.**   Though everyone was to sing in unison Bobby never found the right rhythm.

_____ **5.**   My mother who is an excellent tennis player is now learning to play golf.

_____ **6.**   Your conscience can guide you if you take time to listen to your inner voice.

_____ **7.**   The student who was to receive the award was very anxious.

_____ **8.**   When the monorail begins operating on Monday more parking spaces may be available in the downtown area.

_____ **9.**   The keynote speaker will be a psychologist whose research on delayed memories is being widely debated.

_____ **10.**   You can see the beauty of the resort when the photographs are developed.

_____ **11.**   The Greek philosopher whom I chose to research is Aristotle.

_____ **12.**   Aristotle was the pupil of Plato who was originally named Aristocles.

_____ **13.**   Meteorologists can predict when meteor showers will appear in our hemisphere.

_____ **14.**   Gerontology which is the study of aging has become big business in our society.

_____ **15.**   As the baby boomers age the need for more health care services and retirement options increases.

*The following dependent clauses are **fragments**. Correct these fragment errors by adding the dependent clause to an independent clause to form a complex sentence.*

Examples: *Because you are so judgmental*
*You do not have many friends **because you are so judgmental.***
***Because you are so judgmental,** you do not have many friends.*

Who are dedicated to exploring space
*The astronauts **who are dedicated to exploring space** risk their lives on missions.*
*The featured article is about the astronauts **who are dedicated to exploring space.***

1. who is very congenial

_____

_____

2. when the geologists saw the seismograph

_____

_____

3. whom I find very attractive

_____

_____

4. that sociology often compares cultural values

_____

_____

5. which is the study of the origin and history of people, their deities, and their heroes

_____

_____

6. who is a famous explorer in history

_____

_____

7. because the principality has grown so large

_____

_____

8. which involves vacuuming all the rooms

_____

_____

9. that the criminologist must pay attention to fine details

_____

_____

10. that the polygraph results are inadmissible in court

_____

_____

11. which affects all Americans

_____

_____

12. whose principal source of income is Social Security

_____

_____

Sentence Combining

Effective writers are able to use a variety of sentence patterns to create a style of writing that captivates the interest of the reader. Writing that consists mainly of simple sentences with single subjects and single verbs often seems "choppy" and underdeveloped. Writing that consists mainly of compound sentences joined together with coordinating conjunctions such as *and* or *but* becomes monotonous. Ineffective use of sentence patterns and sentence combining also leads to unnecessary wordiness.

The following sentence-combining techniques have been introduced throughout this textbook. When you are writing, experiment with different sentence-combining combinations until you find the combination that best expresses your idea in a powerful way. You may find other combinations or techniques that are not listed below. Remember that writing is a process that often begins with a draft that is then rewritten, reworded, and revised several times.

Sentence-Combining Options

1. When two sentences have the same verbs, combine the sentences into one sentence by using **compound subjects.**

2. When two sentences have the same subjects, combine the sentences into one sentence by using **compound verbs.**

3. Use **coordinating conjunctions** to join two simple sentences. The coordinating conjunctions are *for, and, nor, but, or, yet,* and *so.*

4. Use a **semicolon** to join two closely related sentences together.

5. Use a **semicolon and a conjunctive adverb** to join two closely related sentences together and to emphasize their relationship. Common conjunctive adverbs are *however, therefore, consequently, then, thus,* and *as a result.*

6. Use a **subordinate conjunction** when one idea is subordinate to the other. The subordinate conjunction (also called a *spoiler*) forms a dependent clause. The dependent clause may come before or after the independent clause. Common subordinate conjunctions are *because, since, if, when, though, before,* and *after.*

7. Use a **relative pronoun** to form a relative pronoun clause when the same noun is used in each sentence that you want to combine. The common relative pronouns are *that, which, who, whom, whose, where,* and *when.*

8. Use an **appositive,** which is a phrase made by deleting a noun in the second sentence that already appears in the first sentence. The appositive must be placed right after the noun that is common to both sentences. An appositive is sometimes a relative pronoun clause that has been shortened; the relative pronoun has been omitted. For some appositives, additional words need to be added for clarity.
   Relative Pronoun: Raymond, **who has been my neighbor for ten years,** is retiring.
   Appositive: Raymond, **my neighbor for ten years,** is retiring.

The following example shows you the results of using a variety of combining techniques:

The morale was low. It was affecting the quality of work.

Technique 1: The same verbs are not used in these sentences, so this technique won't work.

Technique 2: The morale was low and was affecting the quality of work.

Technique 3: The morale was low, and it was affecting the quality of work.

Technique 4: The morale was low; it was affecting the quality of work.

Technique 5: The morale was low; consequently, it was affecting the quality of work.

Technique 6: Since morale was low, the quality of work was affected. The quality of work was affected because morale was low. When morale was low, the quality of work was affected.

Technique 7: The morale, which was low, affected the quality of work.

Technique 8: Morale, low in most departments, affected the quality of work.

Other: Low morale affected the quality of work.

PRACTICE

Partner Work

Use the techniques above to combine the following two sentences. You can work below or write your sentences on your own paper.

Television desensitizes people. Television breeds apathy.

Technique 1: _____

Technique 2: _____

Technique 3: _____

Technique 4: _____

Technique 5: _____

Technique 6: _____

Technique 7: _____

Technique 8: _____

Other: _____

✏ **EXERCISE 10.8** **Sentence Combining Options**

Use any method to combine the following sentences into one sentence.

1. The award-winning documentary was on television last night. My husband produced the documentary.

   _____

2. Elvis Presley died in 1977. His music is still popular today.

   _____

3. Uncle John loved to fish. He also loved to play golf and river raft.

   _____

4. Jesse walked slowly down the aisle of the church. He looked so serious.

   _____

5. Kim knows the trails well. She is capable of leading the scout troop.

   _____

6. The magazine article was about assisted suicide. The article upset many people.

   _____

7. Steve Prefontaine is a legend in Eugene, Oregon. He lived in Eugene. He was a world-class runner.

   _____

8. The wooden fence collapsed. It collapsed during a storm. There were heavy winds.

   _____

9. My aunt is an excellent cook. She volunteered to teach me to cook.

   _____

10. Music soothes my soul. Music always puts me in a good mood. I love music.

    _____

11. The coffee was too strong. The coffee had a mint flavor. Mary brewed the coffee.

    _____

12. Camcorders are dropping in price. Camcorders are used by many parents to document family events.

    _____

Select any word for this chapter's word list (pages 317–318) as the topic of two sentences. Write two simple sentences that use this word. Then try combining your two sentences using the techniques presented on page 353.

Two sentences: _____

_____

Technique 1: _____

Technique 2: _____

Technique 3: _____

Technique 4: _____

Technique 5: _____

Technique 6: _____

Technique 7: _____

Technique 8: _____

Other: _____

✎   EXERCISE 10.9 **Chapter Study Sheet**

In the right-hand column, write a definition for the term on the left, and respond to any prompts that appear. Then cover up the right-hand column and practice reciting.

Frequently Misspelled Words	**Three reasons that words are frequently misspelled:**
Frequently Confused Words	**Two reasons that words may be confused:**
Homonym	
Appositive	
Relative Pronoun	
Relative Pronoun Clause	

**Two Kinds of
Dependent Clause**

Fragment

Restrictive Clause

Nonrestrictive Clause

✏️ **CHAPTER REVIEW**

Match the word parts on the left with the definitions on the right.

_____ 1. *mono, uni*   a. three

_____ 2. *photo*   b. many

_____ 3. *oct, octo, octa*   c. two

_____ 4. *aqua, hydro*   d. man

_____ 5. *astro*   e. light

_____ 6. *tri*   f. earth

_____ 7. *poly, multi*   g. five

_____ 8. *geo*   h. books

_____ 9. *bi*   i. feeling, suffering

_____ 10. *chrono*   j. one

_____ 11. *penta*   k. one who studies

_____ 12. *graph*   l. eight

_____ 13. *quandr, quart*   m. written record of

_____ 14. *meter*   n. stars

_____ 15. *path, pathos*   o. four

_____ 16. *biblio*   p. fear

_____ 17. *anthro*   q. to measure

_____ 18. *phobia*   r. water

_____ 19. *ology*   s. study of

_____ 20. *ologist*   t. far

_____ 21. *sophos*   u. wise

_____ 22. *tele*   v. time

Match the words on the left with the definitions on the right.

———— 1.   *compliment*   a. ethically right

———— 2.   *complement*   b. a group or body of individuals

———— 3.   *counsel, advise*   c. to avoid or evade

———— 4.   *council*   d. lack of feelings or emotions

———— 5.   *affect*   e. flattering remarks or praise

———— 6.   *principal*   f. primary, most important; dean of a school

———— 7.   *principle*   g. an emotional attitude or spirit

———— 8.   *apathy*   h. something that completes or balances with

———— 9.   *empathy*   i. illegal

———— 10. *sympathy*   j. to give advice

———— 11. *personnel*   k. capacity to experience someone's feelings

———— 12. *advice*   l. an appearance or participation

———— 13. *moral*   m. to refer to indirectly

———— 14. *morale*   n. a rule or a theory

———— 15. *elude*   o. ability to understand or relate to someone's situation or feelings

———— 16. *allude*   p. to bring out or to evoke

———— 17. *elicit*   q. people employed in a business or organization

———— 18. *illicit*   r. gifts

———— 19. *presence*   s. to influence

———— 20. *presents*   t. a recommendation for a course of action

Proofreading

For each pair of words below, circle the word that is spelled correctly.

athelete	category	dilemna	alcohol
athlete	catagory	dilemma	alchohol

Febuary	disasterous	enterance	environment
February	disastrous	entrance	enviroment

restraunt	laboratory	mischievious	prescription
restaurant	laberatory	mischievous	perscription

mathamatics	optimistic	privelege	sophomore
mathematics	optomistic	privilege	sophmore

miscellanous	beauracracy	maintainence	questionnaire
miscellaneous	bureaucracy	maintenance	questionaire

surprize	arguement	conscienous	judgment
surprise	argument	conscientious	jugdement

archaologist	psycology	socialogy	gealogist
archaeologist	psychology	sociology	geologist

Circle the word parts below that are prefixes.

tri	sext	geo	poly	trans	inter

gamy	mono	tect	sept	cept	quadr

uni	ize	hexa	morph	hydro	bi

Circle the word parts below that are roots.

meter	ship	graph	penta	mune	spect

pathos	phobia	philos	ology	naut	ence

ment	gram	tetra	seismo	therma	astro

Complete each sentence by circling the correct word inside the parentheses.

1. The First Aid (Counsel, Council) gives parents free (advice, advise) for home emergencies.

2. The (principal, principle) was (conscious, conscience) right after the accident.

3. The (emigrants, immigrants) each had (personal, personnel) stories of hardships to tell.

4. The speaker (eluded, alluded) to the (presents, presence) of strange spirits in the room.

5. I can (consul, console) you, but I cannot (council, consul, counsel) you on your legal rights.

6. Everyone (accepted, excepted) the (complementary, complimentary) (presents, presence).

7. His mother's words became a (principle, principal) factor in the boost of his (moral, morale).

8. You have (eluded, alluded) my advances, and that has (affected, effected) my self-esteem.

9. The teacher gives (personnel, personal) (complements, compliments) to her students.

10. I made a (conscious, conscience) decision not to give her my (advice, advise).

11. The student body (counsel, council) took the lawyer's (advise, advice) to refrain from making (personnel, personal) attacks on the newspaper editor.

12. Altitude (effects, affects) people with high blood pressure; the (affects, effects) can be dangerous.

13. The stage (presents, presence) of the (principal, principle) actor overpowers the other actors.

14. You seem to be a very (conscious, conscientious) worker who lives by a strong set of (personal, personnel) (principals, principles).

15. This beautiful turquoise necklace will (compliment, complement) your stunning black dress and will result in (complements, compliments) from your admirers.

16. The new academic (counselor, councilor) can (advice, advise) you about graduation.

17. All of the visual (effects, affects) (accept, except) those used for the lightning storm were incredible.

18. The (principal, principle) told my son that his (presents, presence) in the classroom was causing disruptions.

Sentence Writing

For each sentence below, use the relative pronoun that is given and at least one word from the word lists on pages 317–318. Write a complex sentence.

1. who

_____

2. whom

_____

3. which

_____

4. that

_____

5. whose

_____

Use any of the techniques presented to combine the information below into one sentence.

1. The stock had tripled in value. The stock was given to me by my parents. It tripled in value in less than five years.

_____

_____

2. Carrie can translate the Spanish song for us. She can also translate this Spanish recipe. Carrie speaks Spanish fluently.

_____

_____

3. Triplicate copies of the agreement are needed. The agreement is a rental agreement. The agreement was signed this morning.

_____

_____

JOURNAL WRITING ASSIGNMENT

Topic: Self-Evaluation

Evaluate the progress you believe you made this term in the areas of spelling, grammar, sentence writing, and understanding the construction and function of words. Include in your evaluation specific examples that you feel demonstrate your progress. Your self-evaluation should also include any attitude changes you have noticed toward the area of spelling, grammar, or language skills in general.

PARAGRAPH WRITING ASSIGNMENT

Topic: Refinement

You have acquired many new skills throughout this course. You will now have the opportunity to apply the skills you have learned to improve a previous writing. Select any one of your journal writing entries. Consider the journal writing entry as a rough first draft. Complete the following steps:

1. Reread the entry. Consider ways this writing can be revised, reworded, reordered, or expanded to demonstrate a higher level of writing.

2. Use your ideas to write a second draft. Save both the first and the second draft.

3. Look at the kinds of sentences used in your second draft. Consider ways to combine the sentences for greater variety. Consider your choice of words; use a dictionary or an electronic spell checker with a thesaurus to find more expressive or concise wording.

4. Rewrite the information one more time. This time your work should show sentence variety and your ability to combine sentences correctly.

5. Turn in all the drafts with your final version.

ELEVEN

The Essentials of Paragraph Writing

The topics in this chapter include the following:

- Introduction to the parts of a paragraph:
    the topic and the topic sentence
    supporting details in the body of the paragraph
    the concluding sentence
- Introduction to the concepts of narrowing the topic
- Introduction to the concepts of developing the body of the paragraph
- Writing formulas for seven kinds of paragraphs:
    the narrative paragraph
    the definition paragraph
    the descriptive paragraph
    the examples paragraph
    the process paragraph
    the explanatory paragraph
    the comparison/contrast paragraph

Defining the Paragraph

A **paragraph** is a series of sentences that develop *one* main idea about a specific topic. After reading a well-developed paragraph, the reader should be able to identify the topic (the subject) of the paragraph and state the main point made by the writer.

The main point of the paragraph is often stated in a **topic sentence,** which can also be called a **main idea sentence** or **controlling sentence.** The remaining sentences in the paragraph support or develop the main idea more clearly by providing additional information or explanation through the use of **supporting details.** The supporting sentences appear in **the body** of the paragraph. A **concluding sentence** may be used to summarize the paragraph.

Key Terms

Paragraph	A series of sentences that develop one main idea about a specific topic.
Topic	The subject of the paragraph that answers the question "What is this paragraph about?"
Topic Sentence	The sentence in a paragraph that states the main idea and answers the question "What is the writer saying about the subject?"
Main Idea Sentence	Another term used for *topic sentence.*
Controlling Sentence	Another term used for *topic sentence.* This term reminds the reader (and the writer) that all the other sentences in the paragraph must fit under this "umbrella" or main idea sentence.
Supporting Details	Facts, examples, explanations, definitions, and any other kind of details that develop or support the main idea.
Body of the Paragraph	A term used for all the supporting sentences that develop the main idea.
Concluding Sentence	The last sentence in a paragraph, which restates the main idea or summarizes the main idea of the paragraph.

Narrowing the Topic

One of the first steps necessary for writing a paragraph is to select the topic and then *narrow the topic.* If your topic (or subject) is too broad or too general, you will have too many different points to make; you will move outside the boundaries of a paragraph and into an essay. Remember that a paragraph develops *one* main idea and one specific topic.

For example, if you decide to write a paragraph about computers, you will need to narrow the topic to a specific aspect about computers. Do you want to discuss the steps for selecting an appropriate computer to purchase? Do you want to compare two different computer platforms, such as Apple and IBM? Do you want to give examples of ways that computers have altered your home environment? If you do not take the time to think carefully about *what you want to say* about computers, you will quickly become frustrated by the amount of information that you need to present.

One way to narrow the topic is to make a **visual map** that places the topic in the center of the chart. Then take some time to **brainstorm** a variety of as-

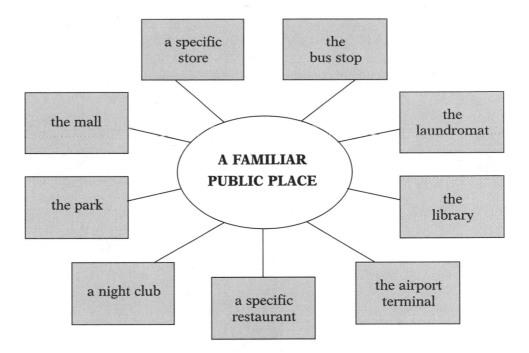

pects or subtopics that could be developed. Each new idea branches out from the center of the visual map. After you have completed your brainstorming, se-lect *one* of the branches to be your narrowed topic to write about in your para-graph. An example is done below for an assignment in which you are asked to describe a familiar public place.

Writing a Strong Topic Sentence

In many paragraphs, the first sentence of the paragraph is the topic sentence. Although the topic sentence does not have to appear in this location, placing the topic sentence at the beginning of the paragraph helps both you and the reader stay focused on the main idea that is to be developed. When a topic sen-tence is well-written, the body of the paragraph is easier to develop in a logical manner and the ideas are more likely to flow together smoothly. Therefore, spending ample time on developing a strong topic sentence is a writing habit you will want to develop.

Writing a strong topic sentence is essential for three reasons:

1. The topic sentence clearly identifies the narrowed topic or the subject of your paragraph.
2. The topic sentence provides the reader with a sense of your direction, pur-pose, or point of view. The reader should be able to predict what the para-graph will discuss.
3. The topic sentence serves as an "umbrella sentence" under which all other sentences must fit or belong. This sentence limits the kind of information that belongs in the paragraph to develop or support your main idea.

As an example, assume that you are enrolled in a communication class. An assignment is given for you to observe and record ways that individuals react to praise. After one week of observing, your assignment is to write a paragraph that presents your findings. In order to write this paragraph, you first need to identify the topic (ways individuals react to praise) and then write a strong topic sentence that will control your paragraph. To do this, you may want to make a visual mapping of your observations. Your mapping may look like this:

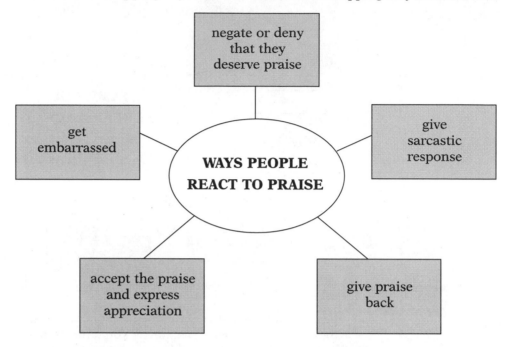

The following are a few possible attempts at writing a strong topic sentence. Which sentence do you feel clearly defines the narrowed topic, provides the reader with a sense of direction, purpose, or point of view, and serves as an "umbrella sentence" to control the content of the paragraph?

1. Many people don't know how to accept praise for their work.

2. People often get embarrassed when someone praises them for their work or accomplishments.

3. People may react to praise for their work or their accomplishments in five different ways.

4. Praise is often given when someone performs well or does something note-worthy.

5. The two best ways to respond to praise are accept the praise or give the person a compliment in return.

Sentence three is the strongest topic sentence. First, the topic has been narrowed; the reader knows that the paragraph will discuss ways that people react to praise for their work or their accomplishments. Second, the reader can predict that five different reactions will be discussed. Third, the writer (and the reader) know that all the supporting sentences will be related to the five kinds of reactions to praise; any other information or chain of thoughts does not belong in this paragraph.

Developing the Body of the Paragraph

The body of the paragraph consists of additional sentences that will support, explain, strengthen, or "prove" the main idea that was presented in the topic sentence. The type of paragraph being written will dictate to some degree the methods used to develop the body of the paragraph. For example, the body will be developed differently for narrative, definition, descriptive, examples, process, explanatory, or comparison/contrast paragraphs. Refer to the specific methods or "formulas" on the following pages for each type of paragraph.

Even though the "formula" for developing the body of different kinds of paragraphs will vary, the body of all well-developed paragraphs will have three common elements: **adequate details, unity,** and **coherence.** *Adequate details* simply means that enough *different* details have been provided to develop the main idea for the reader. A paragraph that is "padded" by using different words or phrases to repeat the same information or a paragraph loaded with "wordiness" and a limited number of different details is an underdeveloped paragraph. A paragraph can also have too many details and be overdeveloped. In such a case, the writer needs to combine some of the details or delete the weakest details in order to have a more manageable paragraph.

Unity means that all the supporting sentences in the paragraph are related to the main idea. Each sentence serves an important purpose to develop the main idea. A lack of unity occurs when a writer "sidetracks" or wanders away from the main idea by presenting unrelated information.

Coherence means that the ideas and the sentences flow together smoothly in a logical, organized manner. Developing coherence in the body of a paragraph requires the following writing skills:

1. Knowing how to organize information *chronologically* (in a time sequence), *spatially* (top to bottom, left to right, foreground to background, etc.), and *in order of importance or frequency* (most important to least important, or vice versa);

2. Knowing how to use sentence variety and how to combine sentences (simple, compound, and complex sentences); and

3. Knowing how to connect ideas and sentences by using *transition words (first, second, next, then, for example, also, in addition, on the other hand, however, yet,* etc.). Many transition words are conjunctive adverbs. Refer to Chapter 5, pages 138–139 for a list of conjunctive adverbs that often function as transition words.

Writing a Concluding Sentence

A concluding sentence signals the reader that you have presented all the ideas that you want to present and the paragraph is finished. There are four basic ways to develop the concluding sentence:

1. Use different words, but simply restate the main idea of the paragraph. This statement should "echo" or basically say the same thing as the main idea sentence.

2. Echo the topic sentence but also include key words from the supporting sentences.

3. Draw a logical conclusion based on the supporting details that have been presented.

4. End the paragraph by posing a thought-provoking question that is related to the main idea. Although this fourth method is used less frequently, it can be employed effectively in some paragraphs. If you recall the visual map on "Ways People React to Praise," that paragraph could use this concluding

sentence: "Using these five different reactions to praise, how would you react if I gave you praise right now in front of other class members?"

The Basic Paragraph

The following basic paragraph structure is the foundation for the writing formulas that will be presented for the narrative, definition, descriptive, examples, process, explanatory, and comparison/contrast paragraphs. This basic paragraph structure will help you organize and develop your ideas more quickly and effectively.

TOPIC SENTENCE

BODY (3–7 supporting sentences)

Use: Sufficient details

   Unity

   Coherence

CONCLUDING SENTENCE

A Few More General Writing Suggestions

1. Do *not* assume that you will produce a "perfect paragraph" on the first writing. Writing should occur in at least three writing stages: rough draft, editing and revising, and final writing. Often you may want to complete a writing task too quickly and as a one-step process. Plan from the start to create a rough draft with all your initial ideas. Then, plan to re-read; add or delete words, phrases, or ideas; change sentence patterns; substitute different words; and refine. Finally, plan to rewrite the paragraph and check for mechanical errors (spelling, punctuation, and grammar). Sometimes the writing process will involve more than these three steps. Be willing to accept that the writing process is seldom a one-step process.

2. Check your topic sentence. Ask yourself these questions: Is the narrowed topic clear? Does it give the reader a sense of my direction, purpose, or point of view? Does it work as a controlling or an umbrella sentence for all the other sentences?

3. Check for adequate details, unity, and coherence by asking yourself these questions: Did I give the reader enough, too much, or too little information to support my main idea? Are all the sentences in the paragraph directly related to the main idea? Do the ideas and the sentences flow together smoothly? Did I use transition words to connect ideas? Did I combine sentences effectively?

4. Avoid "weak sentence beginnings." All of the following sentence beginnings are weak. The sentences can be reworded to avoid using the "empty words" *there, here,* and *it.*

   There is a way to turn trash into money.

   There are five kinds of reactions to receiving praise.

   Here is my story about surviving an earthquake.

   Here are four steps to follow to file a lawsuit in a small claims court.

   It may lead to serious health consequences.

5. Avoid unnecessary introductory statements such as the following:

   I would like to tell you about . . .

   This story is about . . .

   I hope to explain how to . . .

6. Replace common, "boring," overused, or nondescriptive words with more descriptive, vivid, or sophisticated words. You can use a dictionary or a thesaurus to locate other words to consider using. The level of vocabulary in your work will affect the level of sophistication and impact. Strive to find words that clearly, concisely, and accurately express your ideas and feelings.

7. When possible, type your work on a computer or word processor. Your work, in most cases, will be much easier to read. Use the spell checker and check all of your work for spelling errors. In the era of computer technology, there are fewer reasons to turn in work with spelling errors. Hand-held spell checkers can also be used to selectively check the spelling of individual words.

8. Be willing to share your work with others and ask for feedback. The main purpose of writing is to communicate. Find readers to evaluate your writing. Discuss how effectively you were able to communicate. Ask for feedback: *Are my ideas clear to you? What was not clear? What did you like about this? How could I improve this further?*

Using "Formulas"

The following models or formulas serve as guides for writing different kinds of paragraphs. Pay close attention to the specific kind of information that should appear in the topic sentence. Then notice the recommendations given for ways to organize the supporting sentences and the details. Finally, use any of the methods already discussed for writing one concluding sentence.

Following each formula, you will find a beginning list of possible topics to select and narrow for a paragraph. After your paragraph has been written, ask a friend or a classmate to use the form at the end of this chapter to evaluate your paragraph and give you feedback on the effectiveness of your paragraph. You may want to use this feedback to revise your paragraph.

A Narrative Formula

A **narrative** paragraph tells a story. A narrative is often a personal story, so the pronoun *I* (**first person pronoun**) may be used throughout the story. If you decide to tell a story about someone else, you will be writing in **third person** (*he, she*); in the case of writing in third person, avoid referring to yourself as a subject of a sentence. Since a narrative tells about something that has already taken place, the verbs need to be in **past tense**. A final and important point about narratives is that narratives must have a purpose or make a special point. Reading about your daily commute to school or to work is uninteresting unless something special or unusual happened to you on a specific day as you commuted to school or to work. The narrative formula looks like this:

The Narrative Paragraph

Topic Sentence:	Specifically name the topic (the story) and state the significance, meaning, emotion, or point of view you want the story to develop.
Body:	Organize the sentences chronologically or in a natural time sequence. Tell what happened first, second, next, etc. in the same order that the events took place. Write all the sentences in past tense.
Concluding Sentence:	Use one of the four methods discussed on page 369.

Topics for a Narrative

1. Tell about a childhood experience that you will never forget because it was so exciting, scary, funny, humiliating, sentimental, enriching, motivational, etc.

2. Tell a short family story that has been passed down through the generations.

3. Tell a story about the significance of a specific situation that was a part of a process of change (a moving day, an interview, getting hired or fired, becoming engaged, ending a relationship, graduating, taking a test for a driver's license, etc.).

4. Tell a story about the first time you rollerbladed; skied; drove a car; flew in an airplane; saw the ocean, snow, or a volcano; got a speeding ticket; went on a date; remember telling a lie; performed in a concert; played in a competition; etc.).

5. Tell a story about your (most unusual, most memorable, best, worst) date.

6. Tell a story about the best prank, trick, or surprise that you pulled on someone.

7. Tell a story about your best accomplishment, award received, or victory.

8. Tell a story about a time you learned a valuable lesson, made a major decision, felt grateful, or felt proud.

The Definition Formula

A **definition** paragraph is one type of paragraph that is used frequently in college testing. The purpose of a definition paragraph is to show that you clearly understand a specific term. A definition paragraph often begins with a simple definition of the term. The supporting sentences expand this definition by including a larger category the term belongs in, other synonyms (words that have the same or similar meanings), examples, and negation (telling what it is not). For example, if you were asked to define *tolerance*, you might define it as the practice of recognizing and respecting the opinions, practices, and behaviors of others. Reference might be made to a larger classification or category by stating that it is an attitude a person takes toward other people. Your supporting sentences might use the words acceptance or nondiscrimination, and you might give examples of acts of tolerance. For negation, you might state that it does not mean you agree with, support, or practice those same opinions, beliefs, or behaviors. The supporting sentences can include a larger category, synonyms, examples, or negation, but all of these methods for expanding a definition do not need to be used in one definition paragraph.

The Definition Paragraph

Topic Sentence:	Name the term and give a basic definition. Use words such as *is defined as* or *means*.
Body:	Expand the definition by using one or more of the following methods: stating the larger category, using synonyms, giving examples, or telling what it is not (negation). Organize the supporting sentences in an order that allows the information to flow together smoothly.
Concluding Sentence:	Use one of the four methods discussed on page 369.

Topics for a Definition Paragraph

1. Define any word that refers to an emotion (jubilation, anticipation, anxiety, fear, love, anger, hatred, prejudice, commitment, pride, exasperation, inspiration.)

2. Define success, fame, wealth, or failure.

3. Define one type of personality (introvert, extrovert, aggressive, passive, Type A, perfectionist, egotist, masochist, charismatic).

4. Define a slang word or expression that is currently used.

5. Define a specific kind of person (feminist, sexist, racist, environmentalist, conservative, liberal, activist).

6. Define friendship, parenthood, marriage, divorce, death.

7. Define wisdom, knowledge, common sense, intuition, spirituality.

8. Define a specific term from any of your textbooks.

The Descriptive Formula

A **descriptive** paragraph is used to describe a person, a place, or an object so precisely that the reader "sees" the item clearly in his or her imagination. Vivid, well-organized details that refer to one or more of the five senses (seeing, hearing, smelling, touching, and tasting) are required. The supporting sentences with the vivid details should be organized *spatially*, the order in which they appear in space. A reader will have difficulty "seeing" a room if you describe different parts of it in a random order. A room can be seen, as if looking through a camera or through your eyes, if you describe it from left to right or from top to bottom. The writing topics below focus on writing strong descriptions; however, it is important to note that descriptive writing is also used in many of the other kinds of paragraphs.

The Descriptive Paragraph

Topic Sentence:	Specifically name the person, place, or thing that you wish to describe. Include a word that shows the feeling, mood, image, or point of view that you want to convey.
Body:	Use colorful, vivid, highly descriptive words. Try to include sensory images (how something looks, smells, sounds, feels, or tastes). Organize the supporting details spatially by describing the details from left to right, right to left, top to bottom, bottom to top, near to far, or far to near.
Concluding Sentence:	Use one of the four methods discussed on page 369.

Topics for a Descriptive Paragraph

1. Describe a favorite room at home, at school, or in a familiar building.
2. Describe a special place that makes you feel serene, content, secure, or reflective.
3. Describe a place that is chaotic, busy, crowded, or disorganized.
4. Describe a person whom you admire or see as a role model.
5. Describe your most unique, unusual, strange, or eccentric relative, friend, or acquaintance.
6. Describe a photograph or a picture from a magazine or a newspaper.
7. Describe a favorite possession, gadget, appliance, or tool.
8. Describe the ugliest, gaudiest, most tasteless, most bizarre, or most useless item you have ever seen.

The Examples Formula

In an **examples** paragraph, several carefully selected examples are given to support or clarify a specific statement or concept. Since many examples may be possible, the writer needs to select the examples that best develop the topic sentence. The individual examples are arranged in the order of importance by giving the most important, most familiar, or most powerful example first and ending with the least important, least familiar, or least powerful, or by reversing the order, starting with the least important and ending with the most important. Deciding which order has the greatest impact is up to the writer. Transition words (such as *for example, for instance, another example is,* or *to illustrate*) are frequently used to identify the individual examples in the supporting sentences.

The Examples Paragraph

Topic Sentence:	State the narrowed topic as a general statement or concept that needs further explanation.
Body:	Select three or more examples that support the topic sentence. More than one sentence may be used to explain each example. Sequence these examples in the order of importance. Use transition words to move from one example to another.
Concluding Sentence:	Use one of the four methods discussed on page 369.

Topics for an Examples Paragraph

Write a general statement that can be supported by examples. You may use one of the following or use the following as "springboards" for your own statement.

1. Single parents need to learn to "wear many hats."
2. Time-management skills are used on a daily basis by many professionals.
3. By people using a little more common sense, many accidents in the home could be prevented.
4. Some of the traditions I teach my children are the same traditions my parents taught me.
5. Several techniques can be used by students to reduce or eliminate test anxiety.

6. Teenagers in our town have many options for weekend recreation.
7. Several American holidays celebrate important events in American history.
8. Although publicity is often given to athletes who are poor role models, many athletes contribute in positive ways to their communities.
9. Students in my classes create some incredible excuses for not having homework done.
10. Some of the best commercials on television air during the Super Bowl.
11. Commercialism has altered the meaning of American holidays.
12. Many car owners could cut car repair costs by taking better care of their cars.

The Process Formula

The **process** paragraph gives steps to follow to do or make something, or the process paragraph explains how something works or how something happens. The topic sentence often uses the word *steps* or *stages* and states the number of steps or stages that are used. For example, a writer might state, "There are four steps required to varnish a hardwood floor." However, remember that beginning a sentence with *there are* results in a weak sentence. Reword the sentence by rearranging the order of the words; for example, the topic sentence could read, "Four steps are used to varnish a hardwood floor" or "A hardwood floor can be varnished by using four basic steps." The supporting sentences are arranged in chronological order to show the correct time sequence. Each new step should be clearly identified with transition words such as *first*, *second*, *the next step*, and *the final step*.

The Process Paragraph

Topic Sentence: State the specific process and the number of steps that are required to reach the outcome or the final product. Avoid beginning the sentence with the words *There are*.

Body: Present the steps in chronological order. More than one sentence may be used to explain each step. Use transition words to clearly identify each step.

Concluding Sentence: Use one of the four methods discussed on page 369.

Topics for a Process Paragraph

1. Explain how to give up a bad habit (procrastinating, overeating, biting nails, cursing, drinking, losing your temper, sloppiness, etc.).
2. Explain the steps to use to make an important decision.
3. Explain how to perform a specific work-related or home-related task.
4. Explain the steps to repair something (a hole in a wall, a torn screen door, etc.).
5. Explain the steps to use for job hunting.
6. Explain the steps to use to organize personal records in order to prepare tax returns.
7. Explain the steps to use to create a personal budget.
8. Explain how to log onto the Internet.

9. Explain how an election was won by a specific politician.

10. Explain how to organize information to study for a test.

11. Explain the steps to use to perform CPR.

12. Create your own question based on information learned in one of your classes. For example, "Explain the stages in Piaget's theory of child development" or "Explain the stages in Kübler-Ross's theory about facing death."

The Explanatory Formula

The **explanatory** paragraph explains why something happened by giving three or more reasons. The explanatory paragraph is frequently used on college tests to assess whether or not you understand *why* something happened as it did. Similar to the process paragraph, the topic sentence in an explanatory paragraph should clearly state how many reasons will be presented. (Remember to reword the topic sentence if the original sentence begins with *There are*.) One or two sentences are used for *each* of the reasons. If two sentences are used for each reason, the first sentence introduces the reader to the reason, and the second sentence adds more detail about the first reason. Each time a new reason is introduced, a transition word (such as *the second reason, another reason, the last reason*) should be used.

The Explanatory Paragraph

Topic Sentence:	State the event and the number of reasons for the event to have occurred as it did.
Body:	Present each reason in the order of importance. More than one sentence may be used to explain *each* reason or to give important related details. Use a transition word to introduce each new reason.
Concluding Sentence:	Use one of the four methods discussed on page 369.

Topics for an Explanatory Paragraph

1. Select an event from one of your textbooks. Write a sentence that begins with "Explain why. . . ." Write an answer. Example: "Explain why, in economical terms, the southern plantation owners opposed the abolition of slavery."

2. Explain why voters accepted or rejected a specific ballot measure.

3. Explain why you support or oppose a specific point of view on a controversial issue (television censorship, abortion, gun control, human cloning, smoking in nightclubs).

4. Read a short newspaper article. Explain why a specific event occurred as it did.

5. Explain why some employers do not want their employees to form a union.

6. Explain why regular class attendance is important to you.

7. Explain why your college charges students special fees in addition to tuition.

8. Explain why teenagers join gangs, smoking is hazardous to your health, public concern about the content of rap music has increased, a public image has earned a specific reputation, some people don't register to vote, etc.

The Comparison/ Contrast Formula

The **comparison** or **contrast** paragraph is used to discuss or explain the similarities or the differences between two or more items. *Compare* usually means to show the similarities; *contrast* always means to show the differences. A paragraph should be limited to comparing or contrasting, not both. Since most comparison or contrast assignments involve showing likenesses or differences between two items, the formula presented here is based on two items.

Prior to writing a comparison or a contrast paragraph, you should organize the information in the form of a chart. In the chart below, the first item is referred to as **A**; the second item is **B**. Begin by identifying the qualities or characteristics that you want to discuss about each item. Then, fill in the grid with the details for **A** and **B**. In a comparison or contrast paragraph, avoid writing about a characteristic that applies to only **A** or **B**; information on a specific quality or characteristic must exist for both **A** and **B** in order for it to be mentioned in the paragraph.

What qualities or characteristics could be used in the left column to *contrast* the use of a home answering machine and an answering service?

Qualities/ Characteristics	A = home answering machine	B = answering service
1.		
2.		
3.		

In the above chart, there are many possible qualities or characteristics that could be used. Cost, maintenance, privacy, length of message, ability to ask questions, and accuracy of messages are qualities or characteristics that could be used to contrast the two phone messaging systems.

After your chart has been developed, decide which of two different methods you prefer to use to organize the supporting details. The **block** approach is used when all the qualities or characteristics of **A** are discussed first; then, after a short transition such as *on the other hand* or *in contrast,* all the qualities of **B** are discussed. The **point-by-point** approach is used when one quality or characteristic at a time is discussed for both **A** and **B**. Then the second quality is discussed for **A** and then for **B**. This step-by-step process is used until all the qualities or characteristics have been discussed. The two methods look like this:

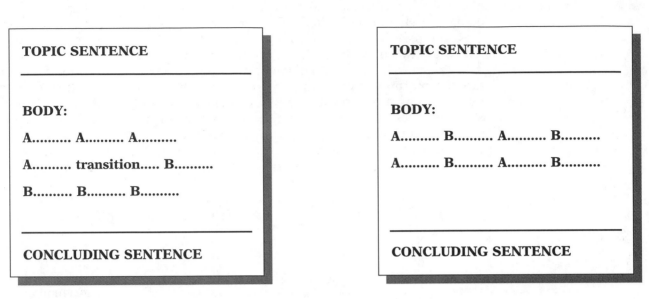

Both methods have their advantages. The block method is used most effectively when the paragraph is short and the qualities or characteristics being compared or contrasted are not very complex. With the block method, the reader gets a clear image of **A** and then is presented with **B** and how it compares to or differs from **A.** The point-by-point method is used most effectively when there are numerous details and the details are more complex. The reader is able to follow the comparison or the contrast more accurately when one characteristic or quality is discussed for both **A** and **B** before a new characteristic or quality is presented.

To see the different impact that the block and the point-by-point methods have, try writing your comparison or contrast paragraph using each of the methods. Then decide which method more clearly communicates your ideas and leaves the stronger impression on the mind of the reader.

The Comparison or Contrast Paragraph

Topic Sentence:	Clearly identify both subjects (**A** and **B**) and let the reader know if you will compare or contrast the two. (*Answering machines and answering services differ in three major ways.*)
Body:	Create a grid to show the qualities or characteristics that can be discussed for both **A** and **B**. Decide which of the approaches you want to use to organize the supporting sentences: the **block** approach or the **step-by-step** approach. Use the transition words to help the reader move back and forth between **A** and **B**.
Concluding Sentence:	Use one of the four methods discussed on page 369.

Topics for a Comparison or Contrast Paragraph

1. Compare or contrast two different philosophies, approaches, concepts, or topics learned in one of your classes.
2. Compare or contrast two family members, friends, or teachers.
3. Compare or contrast two different talk shows on television.
4. Compare or contrast two different basketball players (or football players, race car drivers, volleyball players, tennis players, comedians, actors, musicians, singers).
5. Compare or contrast how you were as a teenager (or child) to how you are now.
6. Compare or contrast two jobs you have worked.
7. Compare or contrast a single friend and a married friend.
8. Compare or contrast living in two different settings.
9. Compare or contrast two movies, television programs, or books.
10. Compare or contrast two kinds of cars (computers, rifles, garden fertilizers, etc.).

Peer Feedback

The **Feedback Form** on the next page can be used to evaluate your work or to have a peer comment on or evaluate your work. This Feedback Form can be used for any of the paragraphs you have written. When you evaluate a paragraph, refer to the previous directions stating the elements that should be used in the topic sentence, the body, and the concluding sentence for each type of paragraph.

The Feedback Form is designed to do exactly what the title indicates: to give you feedback. Carefully read the feedback and then decide whether you want to use the feedback to revise your paragraph before writing the final version.

Feedback Form

Writer's Name: _____   Today's Date: _____

Type of paragraph: _____   Evaluated by: _____

THE TOPIC SENTENCE

Is the topic narrowed?

Is the direction, purpose, or point of view clear?

Did the writer use the suggestions given in the formula for this paragraph style?

THE BODY

Are there adequate details to support the main idea?

Is there unity? Do all sentences belong under the topic sentence?

Is there coherence? Are supporting sentences logically organized?

Did the writer use the suggestions given in the formula for this paragraph style?

THE CONCLUDING SENTENCE

Does the concluding sentence work well for this paragraph?

WRITING MECHANICS

Did the writer avoid weak sentence beginnings and unnecessary introductory statements?

Did you notice any spelling or grammar errors?

Is there sufficient sentence variety (simple, compound, and complex)?

GENERAL

What did you like about this paragraph?

How could the paragraph be improved?

APPENDICES

Appendix A: Writing Help On Line

The Internet can be accessed for a wide variety of writing techniques and advice. Web sites can help you with grammar, punctuation, sentence writing, common writing errors, writing styles, generation of ideas or themes for paragraphs and essays, plus online tutoring and editing! Schools, colleges and universities are rapidly going online with their writing centers and writing resources. The following guidelines can help you access Internet resources.

1. If you do not have a specific web site address, you will be conducting an Internet search. There are a variety of search engines available to help you search the Internet and access the World Wide Web (www). You may get different results using different search engines, so consider trying more than one search engine if you don't immediately find the information desired.

   Find the line, usually a box, in which you will type the subject you wish to search for on the Internet. If the subject is more than one word, place quotation marks before and after the words; this keeps the search focused on the combination of words that makes up your subject. Click on "search," "Go find," or a similar direction that begins the search. The search engines do not use spell checkers, so check the accuracy of the spelling of all words.

   The following subjects will take you to interesting web sites for writing:

   "Writing Centers"   "Resources for Writers"   "Online Writing Tutors"

   Grammar   Punctuation   Essays

2. If you have the specific web site address, you will be able to go directly to the site. Once you are on the Internet, find the box that asks for the location. The box usually looks like this:

   location:

   Inside this box, type the web site address. The address must be exact. Every letter, space, period, and other keyboard symbols must be correct or the address cannot be located. Check your addresses, your typing and your spelling carefully. After you have typed the address, press enter. You will be taken to the site.

   Note: Web site addresses change. If you go to a web site and the information is not there, the web site may have moved without leaving a forwarding address, or the web site may have been discontinued.

3. The National Writing Centers Association has an interesting web site to explore. This is the address to type in the "location box":

   http://departments.colgate.edu/diw/NWCA.html

   Most web pages have links to other web pages. When you see a topic on a web page that is in colored print, when the cursor is moved to that colored print, the cursor becomes a pointing finger. That means that those words are a link to another web page. Double click on the words and you will be taken to a new web page or web site. Once you are on the new web page, you may find additional links to explore. Whenever you want to return to the previous screen or screens, use the BACK button that will appear on the web page.

Following is the most current web site home page of The National Writing Centers Association.

4. The following websites are excellent resources for you to explore:

http://cctc.commnet.edu/HP/pages/darling/grammar.htm

http://ansernet.rcls.org/deskref/drwrite.htm

http://longman.awl.com/englishpages/basic_wkbk_write.htm

http://www.edunet.com/english/grammar/subidx.html#alphabet

http://owl.english.purdue.edu/writers/

http://www.lynchburg.edu/public/writcntr/guide/index.htm

http://osf1.gmu.edu/~wcenter/handouts.html

http://www.wisc.edu/writing/Handbook/

http://www.leisurecity.com/library/lc000643.htm

http://www.english.upen.edu/~jlynch/grammar.html

http://www.urich.edu/~writing/wweb.html

http://www.uottawa.ca/academic/arts/writcent/hypergrammar/paragrph.html

When you click on each of the boxes, you will be given a list of additional resources or links to other web pages.

When you click on "Resources for Writers," you will find other links. Some of those links include:

- Handouts
- Grammar Hotline Directory
- Online Tutoring
- Strunk and White's Elements of Style
- Webster's Dictionary
- OneLook Dictionaries
- Roget's Thesaurus
- Paradigm Online Writing Assistant
- Resources of Writers
- Guide to Grammar and Writing

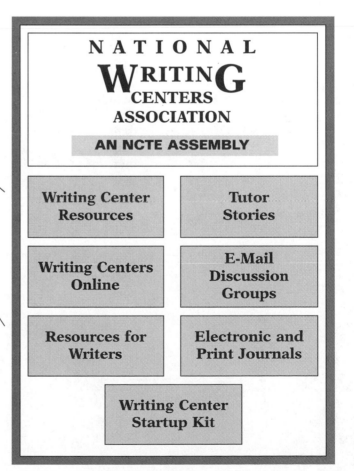

NATIONAL WRITING CENTERS ASSOCIATION

AN NCTE ASSEMBLY

Writing Center Resources

Tutor Stories

Writing Centers Online

E-Mail Discussion Groups

Resources for Writers

Electronic and Print Journals

Writing Center Startup Kit

Appendix B: Chapter Word Lists

Chapter 1 Word Lists

Basic Words

act
blend
boss
brass
brisk
brunch
brush
buzz
catch
cent
check
clamp
class
cloth
clutch
craft
crash
cross
dress
drift
duck
duct
dusk
dust
fact
fill
flesh
fresh
frost
fund
graph
hunt
inch
itch
lock
match
pack
patch
plant
pluck
quest
quick
ranch

rich
risk
rust
script
shift
sketch
slept
spell
sprint
squint
squish
stack
staff
stamp
stick
stitch
strand
stress
stretch
strict
strong
swift
switch
text
than
thank
then
thick
think
thrash
trunk
trust
when
which
wish

Expanded List

checkered
crossing
freshest
freshly
funded
inched
inching

locker
mismatched
quickest
quickly
rancher
ranching
recently
rechecking
refreshing
refunding
rematching
requested
requesting
restamped
restricted
rusted
rusty
stressfully
strictest
strictly
swiftest
swiftly
uncrossed
unlocked
unrestricted
unstamped
unstressed
unstretched

Prefixes

mis
re
un

Suffixes

ed
er
est
ful
ing
ly
y

Chapter 2 Word Lists

Basic List

absent	rest	dictions
address	saddle	disinfecting
band	sample	distraction
bandit	sandwich	distrusted
basket	scramble	indecent
brittle	sect	infected
campus	sent	injecting
canyon	simple	objecting
chicken	skill	objections
chuckle	spend	recently
common	sprinkle	reinject
connect	straddle	rejected
conquest	stumble	rejection
consent	subject	retraction
contact	sudden	subjected
contest	tact	subtracting
contract	tend	suddenly
convict	tennis	uncommon
crumble	tent	undetected
dent	test	uninfected
dribble	traffic	
fend	trumpet	**Prefixes**
gentle	twinkle	ab
handle	twist	ad
happen	vent	con
hassle		de
humble		dis
infant	**Expanded List**	in
infect	addiction	ob
insect	conducted	sub
insult	conquests	
kidnap	constricted	
list	contested	**Suffixes**
mangle	contracting	es
meddle	contracts	ion
mess	convicted	s
middle	conviction	
miss	deduction	
object	defection	**Roots**
picnic	defrosting	dict
print	dejected	fect
problem	detected	ject
rabbit	detecting	tect
	detesting	tract
	detracted	vict

Chapter 3 Word Lists

Basic List

bag	box	dim
brag	bug	drag
big	chip	drip
	cram	flag

flat
fit
fog
hit
hop
hot
hum
mad
map
mix
net
pit
plan
plug
quit
quiz
rob
rot
run
sad
scrap
scrub
ship
shop
skim
skin
slip
spit
spot
stun
swim
tax
tan
thin
trim
trip
wax
wit
whip

Expanded List
admission
admitting
combat
combatting

commit
commitment
compass
compassion
compel
compelling
compress
consisting
constantly
contender
decompression
deferment
destruction
dispelling
distantly
flatten
flattening
fundable
instantly
intention
percent
perfect
permission
permit
permitted
persist
persisted
predict
predictions
prefer
preferable
prefix
preplanned
present
presenter
pretend
product
profiting
project
projection
propel
propelled
protect
protection
protract

resisted
resubmitting
rotten
sadden
shipment
spendable
stretchable
stunningly
submission
swimmable
taxable
thinkable
transact
transaction
transfer
transit
transmission
transmit
transmitting
transplant
uncommitted
unpresentable
unprotected
unrefundable
untaxable

Prefixes
com
per
pre
pro
trans

Suffixes
able
en
ment

Roots
fer
mit
pel
sist
stant

Chapter 4 Word Lists

Basic List
base
baste
blaze
brake

brave
bribe
broke
change
chase

chime
chose
cute
drive
face

fame
flame
frame
fuse
grace
grate
grime
hate
home
late
male
mute
paste
phone
place
pride
quake
quite
safe
scale
shade
shake
shame
shine
spice
spire
spoke
state
stripe
taste
theme
trace
tribe
use
waste
zone

Short and Long Vowel Patterns

biting
bitten
caped
capped
coded
coping
copping
cuter
cutter
cutting
dimly
diner
dinner
filed
filled
finely

fuses
fusses
gaping
gapping
grimness
grimy
griped
gripped
hatless
hidden
hiding
hoped
hoping
hopping
manly
mated
matted
panes
panned
pasted
pastes
pasts
piles
pills
pining
pinning
planed
planned
ridden
ripen
ripped
robbed
robed
scraping
scrapping
shining
shinning
shiny
sliding
slimmer
slimy
spitting
striped
stripped
vanes
whiner
wining
winner
winning

Expanded List

bandage
basement
basting
bravely

bribery
broken
brokerage
changing
commotion
completeness
completion
computer
conceded
confusion
conspiring
consumer
cuteness
deciding
dimness
disputable
excluding
faceless
factual
factually
famous
flatness
gentleness
graceful
gracefully
grateful
homeless
hopelessness
indisputably
infamous
lateness
madness
message
mutual
mutually
perspiring
placement
precisely
precision
predisposed
producer
promotion
promotions
receding
reducing
reframing
refusal
reinstatement
remoteness
replaceable
replacement
reproducing
reputable
requirement
resuming

revision
sadness
shaky
shamefully
shameless
skinless
spiteful
spotless
stately
swiftness
tasteless
thankless
thickness
traceless
transfusion
translating
tribal

unexchangeable
ungrateful
uninspired
untraceable
unusually
usage
useless
uselessly
usual

Prefixes
ex

Suffixes
age
less

ness
ous
ual

Roots
cede
cide
cise
clude
duce
mote
plete
pute
quire
sume
vise

Chapter 5 Word Lists

Basic List
alley
beacon
bleach
braid
brain
bread
break
breath
breeze
cheap
chimney
claim
clean
coach
deaf
deal
dealt
each
eager
eagle
ease
faith
feather
feel
follow
freeze
grease
great
greet
grow
heavy
hoax

honey
instead
issue
jealous
keep
lay
leader
lease
meadow
measles
money
oath
owe
paid
paint
pay
peach
play
please
poultry
queasy
raise
reach
read
ready
reason
rescue
scream
sneeze
soul
speak
speech
sprain

spray
spread
steady
steak
sweat
teach
though
thread
threat
throw
valley
weather

Homonyms
beach
beat
beech
beet
board
bored
brake
break
coarse
course
dear
deer
die
doe
dough
dye
flea
flee
gait

gate
grate
great
heal
heel
lie
loan
lone
lye
made
maid
mail
main
male
mane
meat
meet
pain
pair
pane
pare
peak
pear
peek
praise
prays
preys
real
reel
road
rode
rowed
sole
soul
straight
strait
waist
wait
waive
waste
wave
way
weak
week
weigh
weight

Expanded List
accessible
admissible
alleys
bleachers
braids
breathlessly
breezy

capable
changeable
chimneys
cleans
combustible
compressible
curable
deafening
destructible
displeasing
distractible
easement
easy
ejected
elate
elections
emission
emit
emitting
evict
exchangeable
expelling
faithfully
faiths
forcible
freezer
freezers
greaseless
greasy
hoaxes
horribly
impairment
impeachment
impelling
imperfect
imperfections
impermissible
implant
impress
impression
imprint
incurable
indestructible
issuing
laying
lovable
notably
oaths
owing
payable
paying
payment
peaches
perfectible
permissible

played
players
possibly
predictable
preferable
reaches
readable
reducible
repaired
repaying
replaceable
reprintable
reproducible
rescues
rescuing
resistible
retraceable
sensible
solely
soulful
speeches
speechless
spendable
sprayed
sprayer
sprays
stretchable
sweaters
teaches
terribly
threatening
transmissible
transmittable
unbreakable
uneasy
unpredictable
unprepared
unreachable
unreasonable
unspeakable
unteachable
untraceable
visible
visibly
weightlessness

Prefixes
e
im

Suffixes
ible

Chapter 6 Word Lists

Basic List

achieve	piece	chief
alto	pity	conceit
ancient	potato	conceive
banjo	proof	conscience
beauty	radio	deceit
beef	reef	deceive
belief	relief	deficient
body	rodeo	deity
brief	roof	efficient
bronco	safe	eight
buffalo	scarf	either
calf	seize	feign
cameo	self	field
cargo	shelf	foreign
ceiling	shield	freight
cello	silo	friend
chef	solo	glacier
chief	soprano	grief
clef	spoof	grieve
copy	stereo	height
crazy	study	leisure
cry	surf	neighbor
dry	tattoo	neither
duty	their	niece
echo	they	patience
either	thief	patient
envy	tidy	perceive
friend	tiny	piece
fry	tomato	priest
glory	trophy	proficient
golf	try	protein
grey	tuxedo	receipt
grief	ugly	receive
gulf	veto	reign
half	volcano	reins
hero	wharf	relief
holy	wife	relieve
hoof	wolf	science
knife	yield	seize
lady	zero	shield
lazy	zoo	shriek
leaf		siege
leisure	*ie/ei* **Words**	sieve
life	achieve	sleigh
loaf	ancient	species
mango	anxiety	their
many	beige	thief
mosquito	belief	transient
neighbor	believe	veil
niece	brief	vein
piano	caffeine	view
	ceiling	weigh

weight
weird
wield
yield

Homonyms
drier
dryer
flier
flyer
gray
grey
peace
piece
their
theirs
there
there's
they're

Expanded Words
active
actively
anxieties
attractive
beautiful
bodily
compassion
composure
computation
conceivable
conceiving
conception
conceptually
conducive
confessed
confessing
congressional
contained
containment
copiable
copier
copies
copying
cried

deceiving
dictate
dictating
dictation
displeasure
duties
elation
clcctions
elective
envious
faithfully
friendliness
frying
glorious
gloriously
greeters
holiest
impatiently
impressive
increasingly
inspiration
inspirational
laziness
lecture
leisurely
objectively
obtained
passionately
perceptual
pertaining
pities
plantations
playfulness
pleasure
preconceived
preconceptions
pressure
procedures
productively
progress
progressive
progressively
protective
receiver
reception

receptions
refried
reputation
resistible
restrictive
retainers
scripture
secluded
seduced
seizures
selection
separation
sequestered
studies
studying
tenure
texture
transgression
trophies
trying
ugliness
unbelievable
unfriendly
unintentionally
unobtainable
unpleasing
unyielding
vetoing

Prefixes
se

Suffixes
ate
ive
ure

Roots
ceive
cept
fess
gress
lect
tain

Chapter 7 Word Lists

Basic Words
after
altar
alter
anger

arm
art
article
average
bar

bargain
barn
berth
birch
bird

birth
blur
blurt
border
burden
burglar
burn
burp
burst
calendar
caller
cancer
car
card
carp
carpet
cart
center
char
charge
chart
chirp
church
circle
circus
collar
cord
cork
corn
dark
dart
desert
dessert
dirt
dollar
dork
dorm
eager
earn
enter
ever
every
exert
far
farce
farm
fern
fir
first
flirt
flour
flower
for
force
forest

fork
form
forth
fur
furl
furnish
general
girl
gorge
govern
grammar
harass
hard
hark
harm
harp
harsh
harvest
heard
herb
herd
hurl
hurry
hurt
jar
larch
lard
lark
lord
lurch
lurk
mar
marble
march
mare
mark
market
marsh
marvel
master
mercy
merge
miner
minor
modern
more
morning
mourning
mystery
nerve
norm
normal
north
nurse
parch

park
part
perch
person
porch
pork
port
purge
purple
purse
pursue
salary
scar
scare
scarf
scorch
score
scorn
serve
share
shark
sharp
shirt
shore
short
skirt
slur
slurp
smart
smirk
snarl
snort
sort
spar
spark
sparkle
sparse
sport
spur
spurt
squirm
squirt
star
starch
stark
start
startle
starve
stationary
stationery
stern
stir
stork
storm
summary

surf
surgery
surprise
swirl
sword
sworn
tar
target
term
third
thirst
thorn
thunder
torch
torn
tornado
turn
under
urn
verb
verse
virtue
water
whisper
wonder
yard

Homonyms
altar
alter
berth
birth
caller
collar
earn
fir
flour
flower
fur
heard
herd
miner
minor
morning
mourning
stationary
stationery
urn

Expanded Words
adversary
alarmist
alteration
artist
artistic

averted
basic
blurry
cancerous
classic
clearances
competence
competent
concurrence
concurrent
conferences
conferencing
confidence
confident
darkening
darkest
defector
dependence
dependent
deportment
dictator
difference
different
dirtiest
distorted
distortionist
ejector
excellence
excellent
existence
existent
exports
expressionist
government
grievances
harshest
heroic
humorist
importance
important
independent
informally
insistence
intelligence
marketing
marriage
marriages
motorist
music
mysteriously
nervousness
novelist
observance
observant
occasion

occlude
occult
occur
occurrence
occurring
operator
perfectionist
permanence
permanent
persistence
persistent
pleasantly
portable
predictor
preference
purist
pursuing
racist
realistic
reference
referencing
reforestation
residence
resident
reversible
reverted
salaried
scarcely
sector
shortest
smartest
starvation
stormiest
subversive
summaries
supportive
surgeries
tolerance
tolerant
tornadoes
torturous
transportation
virtuous
wonderful
worrying

Prefixes
oc

Suffixes
ance
ant
ence
ent

ic	**Roots**	tort
ist	cur	verse
or	port	vert

Chapter 8 Word Lists

Basic Words

about	cloud	foil
annoy	coil	foist
assault	coin	fool
astronaut	construe	fought
audience	cook	found
audit	cool	four
auditorium	couch	fraud
authentic	cough	gauze
author	could	gawk
autumn	count	gloom
avenue	country	glue
awe	couple	goose
awful	courage	grew
awl	court	groin
awning	cousin	groom
bawl	coy	groove
because	craw	grouch
blew	crawl	ground
bloom	crew	group
blue	crouch	haul
boil	curfew	haunt
book	daughter	hawk
boom	dawn	hoist
boost	destroy	hook
booth	dew	hound
bought	doom	house
bounce	doubt	jaw
bound	draw	join
boy	drawl	joy
boycott	drawn	knew
brawl	drew	launch
brawn	drool	laundry
brew	droop	law
broil	drought	lawn
brook	due	loin
broom	enough	look
brought	exhaust	loon
cartoon	faucet	lounge
cause	fault	maneuver
caution	fawn	moist
chew	few	moon
choice	flaunt	moose
clause	flaw	mount
claw	flew	mouth
	flue	mushroom

nephew
new
noise
noodle
nook
noon
noose
noun
nourish
oil
ought
ounce
out
pause
paw
pawn
ploy
point
poise
poison
poodle
pool
pouch
pound
pout
prawn
proof
raccoon
raw
revenue
room
roost
round
route
routine
sauce
saw
school
scour
scout
scrawl
sewer
shawl
shook
should
shout
sirloin
slew
snout
soothe
sought
sound
soup
source
south

souvenir
spawn
spoil
spool
spoon
spouse
sprawl
sprout
squaw
squawk
stew
stool
stout
straw
strew
sue
tabloid
thought
thousand
threw
toil
took
tooth
touch
tour
toy
trauma
troop
trouble
trouser
trout
true
turmoil
turquoise
tycoon
typhoon
vault
voice
void
vowel
wound
yawn
yew
youth

Homonyms

blew
blue
clause
claws
dew
do
due
flew
flu

flue
for
fore
forth
foul
four
fourth
fowl
hall
haul
hour
knew
new
our
pause
paws
taught
threw
through
to
too
tot
troop
troupe
two
wood
would

Confusables

choice
choose
chose
loose
lose
loss
lost
thorough
though
thought
through

Expanded Words

aboard
abound
about
accord
account
accountant
across
activities
actualize
acute
addict
address
ado

adrift
affect
afford
aggravate
aggress
announce
annoy
annoying
application
apply
applying
appoint
area
arrange
array
asset
assist
assistant
atrophy
attendance
attire
attract
auditor
authorities
authorization
await
away
because
become
befit
before
befriend
behave
belittle
belonging
below
berate
berating
betray
bewitching
brotherhood
capitalism
capitalize
civilize
cloudiness
compensation
compensatory
composite
conceptualize
countries
courageous
courtship
criterion
criticism
criticize

curfew
dealership
definite
diary
dispense
disturbance
disturbances
disturbed
disturbing
disturbingly
enact
encase
enforce
enforcing
engulf
enlarge
enlighten
enlist
enraged
enrich
entail
entrust
expensive
fellowship
feudalism
formalities
formalization
formalize
friendship
friendships
fuel
genius
giant
graphite
gravity
heroism
hoofs
hooves
idea
imposition
indispensable
inexpensively
infinity
innately
joyous
launches
lenient
likelihood
linear
livelihood
manhood
mania
mannerisms
medium
membership

national
nationalism
nationalities
nationality
nationalize
native
nativity
natural
naturalist
naturalize
naturally
nature
neighborhood
noisy
pancreas
parenthood
partnership
pension
pensions
pensive
period
perturbed
perturbing
pewter
piano
productivity
professionalism
proofs
propensity
quiet
racism
realism
reality
realize
receivership
reinforcements
relationship
sanitation
sanity
scarcity
science
shouldering
sisterhood
sociable
social
socialism
socialistic
socialite
socialization
socialize
socializing
socially
stadium
subduing
suicide

suspension
terrorism
theory
tourism
township
unsociable
verbalize
violin
voiceless
voucher
womanhood

Prefixes

a
be
en

Suffixes

hood
ism
ite
ize
ship

Roots

nate
pense
soci
turb

Chapter 9 Word Lists

Basic Words

answer
balk
blight
bought
bright
brought
campaign
castle
chalk
climb
column
comb
condemn
corps
debt
exhibit
fasten
fight
flight
fought
gnarl
gnaw
heir
honest
honor
hour
hustle
knead
kneel
knight
knit
knot
knuckle
light
limb
listen
might
mortgage

muscle
night
often
plight
plumber
reign
rhyme
rhythm
right
rough
rustle
salmon
scene
sight
sign
slight
sought
stalk
subtle
talk
tight
walk
wrap
wrestle
wright
wring
wrinkle
write
written
wrong
wrought

Homonyms

air
cite
core
corps
heir
hour

knead
knight
knot
need
night
not
our
rain
rap
reign
rein
right
rights
ring
rites
rot
scene
seen
sight
site
wrap
wright
wring
write
wrought

Expanded Words

answering
assignments
babyish
collapse
collate
collect
collide
columnist
commotion
communal
commune
communicable

communication
Communist
communities
consignment
cordial
demote
demoted
designation
designers
dishonorable
disrespectful
emote
emotionally
excitement
exhibitionist
exhibitor
facial
fastener
fastening
financially
foolish
foolishly
forbid
forget
forgive
format
honestly
honorable
immune
immunities
immunization
impartiality
indebtedness
inspect
inspectors
insurmountable
interact

interactive
intercept
interceptions
interchange
interchangeable
interfacing
interjection
intermittent
international
internet
interracial
intersections
introduce
introduction
introspect
introspection
introvert
knitted
knots
listener
motives
obscenity
partial
plumbers
promote
promoters
promoting
promotional
prospect
prospector
racial
reassignment
redesigning
remote
remotely
resignations
respect

respectfully
rhyming
roughest
scenic
selfish
signaling
signature
surcharge
surface
surmise
surpassing
surpluses
surreal
surrealist
surrounding
ticklish
wrappable
wrestling
wrongfully

Prefixes
col
for
inter
intro
sur

Suffixes
ial
ish

Roots
mote
mune
spect

Chapter 10 Word Lists

Basic Words
acknowledge
advise
affect
alcohol
alphabet
amateur
anxious
argument
athlete
bureaucracy
category
chocolate

compliment
conscientious
counsel
dilemma
disastrous
education
elicit
elude
emigrate
entrance
environment
except
fatigue

February
government
guarantee
judgment
laboratory
maintenance
mathematics
miscellaneous
mischievous
moral
optimistic
personnel
prejudice

prescription
presence
principal
privilege
questionnaire
restaurant
schedule
sophomore
surprise
syllable
technique
vacuum

Homonyms

complement
complementary
complimentary
compliment
council
councilor
counsel
counselor
presence
present's
presents
principal
principle

Confusables

accept
advice
advise
affect
allude
conscience
conscientious
conscious
console
consul
council
counsel
effect
elicit
elude
emigrant
emigrate
except
illicit
immigrant
immigrate
moral
morale
personal
personnel

Prefixes

bi
hepta
hexa
mono
multi
oct (octa, octo)
penta
poly
quadr (quad, quart)
sept (sep)
sex (sext)
tetra
tri
uni

Words with Prefixes

monogamy
monogram
monologue
monomial
monoplane
monopod
monorail
monotone
unicorn
uniform
unify
unilateral
unisex
unison
unity
universe
biweekly
bimonthly
bicycle
bifocals
bilateral
bilingual
binomial
bipartisan
biplane
bipod
bipolar
bisect
biracial
triad
triangle
triarchy
tricycle
trilateral
trilogy
trimester
trinomial
triple

triplex
triplicate
tripod
quadrangle
quadruple
quadruplet
quartet
tetragon
tetrapod
pentagon
pentathlon
hexagon
hexagram
hexapod
sextant
sextuplet
heptagon
heptahedron
septet
septuple
September
octagon
octave
octet
octopod
octopus
octuple
October
multiethnic
multimedia
multiped
multiple
multiply
multitude
polyandry
polychrome
polygamist
polygamy
polyglot
polygon
polygraph
polygyny
polynomial

Roots

anthro (anthropo)
aqua
astro
audi
biblio
bio
chrono (chronos)
gene (gen)
geo
graph (graphy)

gram
hydro
meter
morph (morphe)
naut
path (pathos)
philos (phile)
phobia
photo
psyche (psych)
ology
ologist
seismo
sophos (sopho)
tele
therma

Words with New Roots
anthropologist
anthropology
apathy
aquanaut
archaeology
astrology
astronaut
astronomy
audiology
audiometer
bibliography
biography
chronological
chronology
corporal
criminology
ecology
empathy
genealogy
geography
geologist
geology
gerontology

graphology
gynecology
heliocentric
hydroelectric
hydrology
hydrophobia
meteorology
methodology
microbiology
morphograph
morphology
mythology
parapsychology
pathology
philanthropy
philanthropist
philosopher
philosophy
photograph
physiology
polygamy
polygraph
psychologist
psychology
seismograph
sociology
sophomore
sympathy
telecommunication
telegram
telegraph
theology
thermometer
thermotherapy
volcanology
zoology

Expanded Words
acknowledgment
advisor
affectionate

alphabetically
amateurish
argumentative
astrological
athletically
bibliophile
bicyclist
biographical
categories
chronologically
compliments
congenial
educationally
effectively
geographic
geological
geothermal
governmental
graphics
hydroplaning
immorality
judgmental
laboratories
multiplication
philanthropist
philosophical
principality
psychics
sympathizing
telecommunication
telephoning
television
trilogies
uniformity
unifying
universally
vacuuming

Appendix C: Answer Keys for Numbered Exercises

Chapter 1

Beginning with the Basics

Practice	Blend	Digraph	Rule
1. staff	st		*F, L, S, Z* Rule
2. stamp	st, mp		
3. act	ct		
4. brass	br		*F, L, S, Z* Rule
5. fact	ct		
6. ranch		ch	
7. patch		tch	*Tch* Rule
8. than		th	
9. clamp	cl, mp		
10. craft	cr, ft		
11. match		tch	*Tch* Rule
12. graph	gr	ph	
13. catch		tch	*Tch* Rule
14. check		ch	*CK* Rule
15. quest	st		*Qu* Rule
16. text	xt		
17. stress	str		*F, L, S, Z* Rule
18. when		wh	
19. slept	sl, pt		
20. fresh	fr	sh	
21. cent	nt		
22. stretch	str	tch	*Tch* Rule
23. sketch	sk	tch	*Tch* Rule
24. then		th	
25. flesh	fl	sh	
26. quick			*Qu* Rule, *Ck* Rule
27. think	nk	th	
28. switch	sw	tch	*Tch* Rule
29. fill			*F, L, S, Z* Rule
30. script	scr, pt		
31. which		wh, ch	
32. thick		th	*CK* Rule
33. inch		ch	
34. swift	sw, ft		
35. strict	str, ct		
36. brisk	br, sk		

Practice	Blend	Digraph	Rule
37. itch		tch	*Tch* Rule
38. rich		ch	
39. cross	cr		*F, L, S, Z* Rule
40. strong	str, ng		
41. boss			*F, L, S, Z* Rule
42. lock			*Ck* Rule
43. cloth	cl	th	
44. rust	st		
45. duct	ct		
46. brunch	br	ch	
47. buzz			*F, L, S, Z* Rule
48. trunk	tr, nk		
49. dusk	sk		
50. fund	nd		

Exercise 1.1

1. stamp, stomp, stump   staff, stiff, stuff   clamp, clump   bass, boss   patch, pitch   quack, quick   lack, lick, lock, luck   flash, flesh   string, strong, strung   than, then, thin   fend, fond, fund   thick

2. thick   silk   pack, patch   stretch   brunch   ink, inch   ick, itch   rick, rich   sketch   lock   think   match   check   trunk   catch   ranch, rank

3. a. then   b. then   c. than   d. than   e. than   f. then   g. then

Exercise 1.2

Short *a:*	1. fact than	2. catch brass	3. staff stamp/craft	4. stamp graph
Short *e:*	1. check quest	2. text stress	3. fresh flesh	4. stretch then
Short *i:*	1. think switch	2. text strict	3. swift brisk	4. which fill
Short *o:*	1. strong cross	2. boss lock	3. strong cloth	4. cross cloth
Short *u:*	1. rust duct	2. buzz brunch	3. fund trunk	4. dusk fund

Five sentences: Answers will vary.

Example: My (boss) wants to be (rich.)

Exercise 1.3

1. requested requesting **2.** unstamped restamped **3.** rancher ranching

4. mismatched rematching **5.** checkered rechecking **6.** stressfully unstressed

7. refreshing freshest **8.** quickest quickly **9.** inched inching

10. swiftly swiftest **11.** strictly unrestricted **12.** crossing uncrossed

13. unlocked locker **14.** rusted rusty **15.** refunding funded

Exercise 1.4

Answers will vary.

Exercise 1.5

Answers will vary.

Example for the top: He (requested) an (unstamped) postcard.

Example for the bottom: James (thanked) me for the (frosted) cake.

Exercise 1.6

staff	act	brass	fact
match	check		stretch
quick		switch	fill
		itch	cloth
buzz	dusk	strand	blend
wish		clutch	trust
	brush	stack	squint

Exercise 1.7

1. <u>man</u> <u>yelled</u>
2. <u>smell</u> <u>filled</u>
3. <u>trunk</u> <u>hit</u>
4. <u>glass</u> <u>shattered</u>
5. <u>blender</u> <u>arrived</u>
6. <u>stress</u> <u>leads</u>
7. <u>well</u> <u>attracts</u>
8. <u>fist</u> <u>left</u>
9. <u>funds</u> <u>provided</u>
10. <u>cramp</u> <u>lasted</u>
11. <u>buzzer</u> <u>sounded</u>
12. <u>men</u> <u>squinted</u>
13. <u>plot</u> <u>lost</u>
14. <u>stuffing</u> <u>stuck</u>
15. <u>crust</u> <u>crumbled</u>

Exercise 1.8

Answers will vary.

Exercise 1.9

Use the information in the instructional boxes in the chapter to complete these definitions.

Chapter 2

Multi-Syllable Words

Practice	C/C	CLE	ES or S Suffix
1. trum′ pet	x		trumpets
2. ban′ dit	x		bandits

Practice	C/C	CLE	*ES* or *S* Suffix
3. rab′ bit	x		rabbits
4. can′ yon	x		canyons
5. traf′ fic	x		
6. hap′ pen	x		happens
7. bas′ ket	x		baskets
8. chick′ en	*(ck* can't be divided)		chickens
9. cam′ pus	x		campuses
10. ten′ nis	x		
11. pic′ nic	x		picnics
12. kid′ nap	x		kidnaps
13. in′ fant	x		infants
14. prob′ lem	x		problems
15. sud′ den	x		
16. sand′ wich	x		sandwiches
17. com′ mon	x		commons
18. ad′ dress, ad dress′	x		addresses
19. ab′ sent	x		
20. in′ sult	x		insults
21. in fect′	x		infects
22. in′ sect	x		insects
23. con′ test, con test′	x		contests
24. con nect′	x		connects
25. con′ vict, con vict′	x		convicts
26. con sent′	x		consents
27. con quest′	x		conquests
28. con′ tact	x		contacts
29. con′ tract, con tract′	x		contracts
30. ob′ ject, ob ject′	x		objects
31. sub′ ject, sub ject′	x		subjects
32. scram′ ble		x	scrambles
33. twin′ kle		x	twinkles
34. brit′ tle		x	
35. sprin′ kle		x	sprinkles
36. chuck′ le	*(ck* can't be divided)		chuckles
37. strad′ dle		x	straddles
38. sad′ dle		x	saddles
39. sam′ ple		x	samples
40. crum′ ble		x	crumbles
41. stum′ ble		x	stumbles
42. gen′ tle		x	
43. sim′ ple		x	
44. hum′ ble		x	humbles
45. med′ dle		x	meddles
46. mid′ dle		x	middles
47. has′ sle		x	hassles
48. man′ gle		x	mangles
49. drib′ ble		x	dribbles
50. han′ dle		x	handles

Exercise 2.1

1. can' yən   hap' pen   fran' tic   prob' ləm
   sud' den   in' fənt   com' mən   ab' sent
   cən nect'   con sent'   con' quest   con' tract or con tract'
2. sult   fect   sect
3. test   nect   vict   tact
   tract   text   sent   quest
4. brittle   straddle   saddle   meddle   middle   hassle   dribble

Exercise 2.2
(Answers may vary from the ones given below.)

1. chicken basket   2. traffic campus   3. infant problem   4. trumpet address
5. contest tennis   6. connect canyon   7. common infect   8. insult sudden
9. consent contract   10. subject brittle   11. object meddle   12. handle saddle
13. gentle twinkle   14. contact sample   15. middle crumble

The following words should be circled.

trumpet	traffic	—	problem
—	sandwich	address	convict
twinkle	sprinkle	sample	—
—	—	hassle	handle

Answers will vary for the sentences.

Example sentences: The trumpet is stored in a black, leather case. The hassle between the two neighbors ended in court.

Exercise 2.3

1. infected   defection   2. objections   rejected
3. conviction   convicted   4. distraction   contracting
5. addiction   dictions   6. undetected   detecting
7. reinject   dejected   8. uninfected   disinfecting
9. retraction   subtracting   10. subjected   objecting
11. suddenly   12. uncommon   13. detesting   14. indecently
15. deduction   16. distrusted   17. contested   18. conquests
19. recently   20. constricted   21. conducted   22. defrosting

Exercise 2.4

Answers will vary.

Exercise 2.5

Answers will vary.

Example sentences: (top) Her (addiction) caused the family a lot of pain.

(bottom) Seeing a child with this much musical talent is (uncommon.)

Exercise 2.6

1. con′ vict	N	con vict′	V
2. ad′ dress	N	ad dress′	V
3. in′ sult	N	in sult′	V
4. con′ test	N	con test′	V
5. con′ tract	N	con tract′	V
6. ob′ ject	N	ob ject′	V
7. sub′ ject	N	sub ject′	V

What pattern do you see when the first syllable is the accented syllable? <u>The word is a noun.</u>

What pattern do you see when the second syllable is the accented syllable? <u>The word is a verb.</u>

1. V **2.** N **3.** V **4.** N **5.** N **6.** V (infinitive)

7. V **8.** N **9.** N **10.** V **11.** N **12.** V (infinitive)

13. V (infinitive) **14.** N

picnic	N V	consent	N V
sandwich	N V	twinkle	N V
sprinkle	N V	chuckle	N V
saddle	N V	meddle	V
hassle	N V	dribble	N V
handle	N V	miss	N V
band	N V	dent	N V
list	N V	tend	V
twist	N V	print	N V
test	N V	skill	N
plant	N V	blend	N V
stick	N V	wish	N V
duck	N V	thank	V
inch	N V	sketch	N V
flesh	N	match	N V
graph	N V	trumpet	N V

Sentence writing: Answers will vary.

Exercise 2.7

1. <u>driver</u> <u>hassled</u>   **2.** <u>twist</u> <u>landed</u>   **3.** <u>objections</u> <u>resulted</u>

4. <u>I</u> <u>defrosted</u>   **5.** <u>connection</u> <u>is</u>   **6.** <u>level</u> <u>was</u>

7. <u>retraction</u> <u>appeared</u>   **8.** <u>cowboy</u> <u>straddled</u>   **9.** <u>workers</u> <u>consented</u>

10. <u>We</u> <u>vented</u>   **11.** <u>problem</u> <u>seems</u>   **12.** <u>manager</u> <u>conducts</u>

13. <u>We</u> <u>misspelled</u>   **14.** <u>stitching</u> <u>is</u>   **15.** <u>teenagers</u> <u>inched</u>
16. <u>You</u> <u>seem</u>   **17.** <u>flag</u> <u>fell</u>   **18.** <u>section</u> <u>was</u>
19. <u>mechanic</u> <u>twisted</u>   **20.** <u>We</u> <u>try</u>

Exercise 2.8

Answers will vary. Examples: (P) The lawyers objected to the television cameras in the courtroom.
(PR) The lawyers object to the television cameras in the courtroom.
(F) The lawyers will object to the television cameras in the courtroom.

Answers will vary for subjects, verbs, and verb tenses. Example: The infant rests comfortably in the new crib.

Exercise 2.9

Use the information in the instructional boxes in the chapter to complete these definitions.

Chapter 3

Beginning with the Basics

Base + *ed*	Sound of *ed*	One More Suffix
1. bagged	d	bagging, bagger, baggy
2. bragged	d	bragging, bragger
3. X	X	bigger, biggest
4. boxed	t	boxing, boxes, boxer
5. bugged	d	bugging, buggy
6. chipped	t	chipping, chipper
7. crammed	d	cramming, crammer
8. dimmed	d	dimming, dimmer, dimmest
9. dragged	d	dragging, dragger
10. dripped	t	dripping, drippcr, drippy
11. flagged	d	flagging, flagger
12. X	X	flatter, flattest
13. X	X	fitting, fitter, fittest
14. fogged	d	fogging, fogger, foggy
15. X	X	hitting, hitter
16. hopped	t	hopping, hopper
17. X	X	hotter, hottest
18. hummed	d	humming, hummer
19. X	X	madder, maddest
20. mapped	t	mapping, mapper
21. mixed	t	mixing, mixer, mixes
22. netted	ed	netting
23. pitted	ed	pitting, pitty
24. planned	d	planning, planner
25. plugged	d	plugging

Base + *ed*	Sound of *ed*	One More Suffix
26. X	X	quitting, quitter
27. quizzed	d	quizzing, quizzer, quizzes
28. robbed	d	robbing, robber
29. rotted	ed	rotting
30. X	X	running, runner, runny
31. X	X	sadder, saddest
32. scrapped	t	scrapping, scrappy
33. scrubbed	d	scrubbing, scrubber
34. shipped	t	shipping, shipper
35. shopped	t	shopping, shopper
36. skimmed	d	skimming, skimmer
37. skinned	d	skinning, skinner, skinny
38. slipped	t	slipping, slipper
39. X	X	spitting, spitter
40. spotted	ed	spotting, spotter, spotty
41. stunned	d	stunning
42. X	X	swimming, swimmer
43. taxed	t	taxing, taxes, taxer
44. tanned	d	tanning, tanner, tannest
45. thinned	d	thinning, thinner, thinnest
46. trimmed	d	trimming, trimmer
47. tripped	t	tripping, tripper
48. waxed	t	waxing, waxes, waxy
49. X	X	witty
50. whipped	t	whipping, whipper

Exercise 3.1

madly	Not doubled because the suffix is not a vowel suffix.
maddest	Doubled because this is a one-syllable CVC word with a vowel suffix added.
quizzing	(Same as above.)
softer	Not doubled because this is not a CVC word.
crammed	Doubled because this is a one-syllable CVC word with a vowel suffix added.
waxed	Not doubled because the consonant *x* is never doubled.
witty	Doubled because this is a one-syllable CVC word with a vowel suffix added.
happened	Not doubled because the primary accent for the word is not on the last CVC.
unbefitting	Doubled because the CVC syllable is accented and a vowel suffix is added.
submitting	(Same as above.)
untaxable	Not doubled because the consonant *x* is never doubled.

Exercise 3.2

1. <u>motorist</u> flagged *or* flags   **2.** <u>Aunt Jeannie</u> trimmed *or* trims

3. <u>We</u> swimming   **4.** <u>Jimmy</u> chipped

5. <u>teacher</u> quizzed *or* quizzes   **6.** <u>windows</u> fogged *or* fog

7. <u>doctor</u> scrubbed *or* scrubs   **8.** <u>boys</u> hitting

9. <u>manager</u> planned *or* plans **10.** <u>stock market</u> netted, nets

11. <u>dog</u> dragged **12.** <u>She</u> thinning

13. <u>He</u> tripped, trips **14.** <u>bully</u> bragged, brags

15. <u>I</u> quitting **16.** <u>restaurant</u> dimmed, dims

17. <u>Grandma</u> hummed, hums **18.** <u>child</u> plugging

Exercise 3.3

1. protection **20.** unpresentable
2. permission **21.** projection
3. flattening **22.** stunningly
4. projections **23.** commitment
5. predictions **24.** profiting
6. resisted **25.** decompression
7. permitted **26.** compelling
8. transaction **27.** constantly
9. compassion **28.** destruction
10. preferable **29.** persisted
11. uncommitted **30.** dispelling
12. instantly **31.** contender
13. transmission **32.** transmitting
14. combatting **33.** unrefundable
15. untaxable **34.** preplanned
16. deferment **35.** resubmitting
17. intention **36.** presenter
18. admitting **37.** admission
19. unprotected **38.** submission

Exercise 3.4

Answers will vary.

Exercise 3.5

Answers will vary.

Exercise 3.6

bag	N V	chip	N V	cram	V		
for	P	around	P	hum	N V		
map	N V	by	P	mix	N V		
plug	N V	scrap	N V	until	P		
shop	N V	slip	N V	down	N V P		
quiz	N V	trim	N V	wit	N		
drag	N V	rot	N V	near	P		
transplant	N V	admit	V	project	N V		

compress	N V	between	P	combat	N V
defer	V	present	N V	prefix	N
percent	N	transfer	V	perfect	N V

Sentence writing: Answers will vary.

Example: trim (noun) The trim (on the tree) was perfect.
(verb) We trim the rose bushes (in the front yard) every February.

Exercise 3.7

1. <u>fees</u> (for the merchandise) <u>are</u>
2. <u>groups</u> <u>want</u> [to protect] (from the inferior products)
3. <u>station</u> <u>is</u> [to place] (about the upcoming concert)
4. <u>transmission</u> <u>was removed</u> (from the first car) (in the third row) (of the dealership lot)
5. [to reach] <u>you</u> <u>will need</u> [to go] (up the hill), (past the barn), (beyond the railroad tracks)
6. <u>Raymond</u> <u>received</u> [to be able] [to do] (with Joe)
7. <u>puppy</u> (along with two kittens) <u>slipped</u> (through the side door) (of the church)
8. (Without a doubt) <u>transplant</u> <u>added</u> (to my father's life)
9. (According to the newspaper) <u>protesters</u> <u>stood</u> (outside the construction site) (for six hours)
10. <u>salmon</u> <u>swim</u> (against the current) (in an effort) [to spawn]
11. <u>lumber</u> (under the back porch) <u>started</u> [to rot] [to attract] termites
12. <u>connection</u> (between the two crimes) <u>was discovered</u> (by a young detective)
13. <u>company</u> <u>decided</u> [to submit] [to request] (for expansion)
14. <u>Melinda</u> <u>keeps</u> (inside the glove compartment) (of her father's car)
15. <u>You</u> <u>can stop</u> (over your shoulder) (for Amy)
16. <u>We</u> <u>were told</u> [to quit] (to Australia) (on our short-wave radio)
17. <u>judge</u> <u>objected</u> (to the constant outbursts) (in her courtroom)
18. (At the scene) (of the crime) <u>bodies</u> <u>were burned</u> (beyond recognition)

Exercise 3.8

Answers will vary.
(top) Examples: (about two men)   (about noon)   (about school)   (about the river)
(bottom) Examples: 1. They prefer to walk (through the woods) to get to church.
2. The radio operators are transmitting messages (from Alaska).

Exercise 3.9

Use the information in the instructional boxes in this chapter to complete the definitions.

Chapter 4

Beginning with the Basics

Word + *ed*	Sound of *ed*	Base Word + *ing*
1. based	d	basing
2. basted	ed	basting

Word + *ed*	Sound of *ed*	Base Word + *ing*
3. blazed	d	blazing
4. braked	t	braking
5. braved	d	braving
6. chanced	t	chancing
7. changed	d	changing
8. faced	t	facing
9. X	X	X
10. flamed	d	flaming
11. framed	d	framing
12. graced	t	gracing
13. grated	ed	grating
14. hated	ed	hating
15. X	X	X
16. X	X	X
17. pasted	ed	pasting
18. placed	t	placing
19. quaked	t	quaking
20. X	X	X
21. scaled	d	scaling
22. shaded	ed	shading
23. X	X	shaking
24. shamed	d	shaming
25. stated	ed	stating
26. tasted	ed	tasting
27. traced	t	tracing
28. wasted	ed	wasting
29. bribed	d	bribing
30. chimed	d	chiming
31. X	X	driving
32. X	X	X
33. prided	ed	priding
34. X	X	X
35. shined (*also* shone)	d	shining
36. X	X	X
37. spiced	t	spicing
38. striped	t	striping
39. X	X	X
40. X	X	X
41. X	X	X
42. X	X	homing
43. phoned	d	phoning
44. X	X	X
45. zoned	d	zoning
46. X	X	X
47. X	X	X
48. fused	d	fusing
49. muted	ed	muting
50. used	d	using

Exercise 4.1

Final *E* Dropping Rule: When a word ends in *e*, drop the *e* if you are adding a suffix that begins with a vowel.

Soft *C* and *G* Rule: When a word ends in *ce* or *ge*, drop the *e* only if the suffix begins with *e*, *i*, or *y*. If the suffix begins with another letter, you must keep the *e*.

These vowel suffixes should be circled:

able	en	es
ion ing	ed er	est
y	age	ous ual

Word combining:

basement	basting
bravely	changing
famous	graceful
grateful	cuteness
shameless	placement
tribal	stately
usage	broken

Read without errors:

grīped	grĭpped	dīner	dĭnner
hōping	hŏpping	shĭnning	shīning
pīning	pĭnning	pănned	pānes
rōbed	rŏbbed	găpping	gāping
căpped	cāped	cūter	cŭtter
māted	mătted	plāned	plănned
strīped	strĭpped	wĭnning	whīning
cŏpping	cōping	whīner	wĭnner
fĭlled	fīled	scrāping	scrăpping

Mark the vowels:

bĭtten	cōded	dĭmly	bīting	rĭdden
shīny	slīding	vānes	hĭdden	finely
hīding	mănly	slĭmmer	pāsted	slīmy
grĭmness	rĭpped	grīmy	rīpen	spiteful
fŭsses	hătless	spĭtting	fūses	păsts
cŭtting	pāstes	hōped	pīles	pĭlls

Exercise 4.2

    N   N
1. place (on the side) (of the car) [to paint] stripe

    N   V
2. shame [to waste]

    N   V
3. chance [to drive] (to the coast) (in my truck)

    N   N
4. trace (of the village) (after the devastating quake)

    V   N
5. taste spice (in the chicken casserole)

       N   V

6. chance [to state/change]

         V   N

7. [to phone] home

8. in quite brave attempt [to save] (Note: *Quite* is an adverb, and *brave* is an adjective.)

         N

9. theme (of the play) (about hate crimes) (in America) (Note: *Hate* is used as an adjective.)

       V   N

10. chose frame (for her gift)

     V   N

11. use paste (for Italian sauces)

              N

12. flame (on the blaze) (by careless campers) (Note: *Flame* is used as an adjective.)

      N   N

13. shade (for the lamp) (with the yellow base)

      V   V

14. broke spoke (to her ex-roommate)

      N   N

15. face (of pride) (at my college graduation)

      V   N

16. shake [to remove] grime

         N   N

17. (of the tribe) [to make] change (in the treaty)

                                  N

18. (With a cute little smile) (on her face) grace (before dinner) (Note: *Cute* is an adjective.)

Exercise 4.3

1. infamous	**19.** completion
2. precisely	**20.** shamefully
3. reputable	**21.** untraceable
4. unusually	**22.** gracefully
5. ungrateful	**23.** hopelessness
6. uninspired	**24.** perspiring
7. promotions	**25.** replaceable
8. bribery	**26.** mutually
9. commotion	**27.** excluding
10. reframing	**28.** undisputably
11. uselessly	**29.** producer
12. requirement	**30.** reproducing
13. factually	**31.** replacement
14. confusion	**32.** shaky
15. reinstatement	**33.** transfusion
16. conspiring	**34.** refusal
17. brokerage	**35.** unexchangeable
18. translating	**36.** predisposed

Exercise 4.4

Answers will vary.

Exercise 4.5

Answers will vary. Example sentences follow:

(top) I really (hate) to (grate) onions.

(middle) My sister (ripped) her presents open without waiting for the guests.

(bottom) The police charged him with six counts of (bribery.)

Exercise 4.6

base	N V	baste	V	brake	N V
bribe	N V	change	N V	face	N V
fame	N	frame	N V	fuse	N V
grace	N V	grate	N V	hate	N V
home	N V	male	N	phone	N V
place	N V	pride	N V	safe	N
scale	N V	shade	N V	shake	N V
shame	N V	shine	N V	spice	N V
spoke	N V	stripe	N V	taste	N V
theme	N	use	N V	waste	N V

Sentence writing: Answers will vary.

Exercise 4.7

SS–V	**1.** <u>workers</u> <u>Coast Guard</u> <u>dragged</u> (for the sunken car)
S–V	**2.** <u>predictions</u> <u>are</u>
S–V	**3.** (For your own protection) <u>you</u> <u>need</u> (in mutual funds) (in municipal bonds)
S–VV	**4.** <u>logs</u> (by the riverbed) <u>rotted</u> <u>started</u> (down the swollen river)
S–V	**5.** <u>plan</u> <u>was</u> (with a going-away party)
S–V	**6.** <u>Both</u> (of the women) (on the city council) <u>voted</u>
SS–V	**7.** <u>fishermen</u> <u>plants</u> <u>were</u> <u>profiting</u> (from the longer fishing season)
S–V	**8.** <u>girls</u> <u>spent</u> (in the mall)
SS–V	**9.** <u>hole</u> <u>docks</u> <u>are</u> (to the public)
S–VV	**10.** <u>part</u> (of the desert) <u>heats up</u> <u>becomes</u> (in the summer)
SS–VV	**11.** <u>permit</u> <u>card</u> <u>were found</u> <u>turned in</u> (to the camp ranger)
S–V	**12.** <u>transaction</u> (at the bank) <u>was processed</u> (within five minutes)
S–VV	**13.** <u>cement</u> <u>was mixed</u> <u>poured</u> (for the patio) (on Saturday)
S–VV	**14.** (During the race) <u>runner</u> <u>skinned</u> <u>pulled</u>
SS–VV	**15.** <u>toddler</u> <u>brother</u> <u>threw</u> <u>tossed</u> (out of the cart)
S–V	**16.** <u>Protecting</u> (in the forests) <u>is</u> (of the non-profit organization)
SS–V	**17.** <u>commitment</u> <u>dedication</u> (to the cause) <u>inspires</u>
S–VV	**18.** <u>fog</u> <u>rolled in</u> (from the ocean) <u>shut down</u>
S–VV	**19.** <u>fighter</u> <u>quit</u> <u>started</u>
S–V	**20.** <u>Running</u> <u>requires</u> (of hard training)

Exercise 4.8

Answers will vary.

The following "patterns" can be used in these sentences.

<u>Wasting</u> <u>occurs</u>...............

(Gerund) (verb) (Finish the thought.)

_____ <u>are wasting</u>...............

(Any subject) (Verb phrase with a helping verb: am, is, are, was, were) (Finish the thought)

(Bottom of page 106)

Answers will vary. Example sentences are shown below. Do not use these in your work.

1. The confusion led to a great misunderstanding.
2. Bob and Billy swam to the raft in the middle of the lake.
3. Bribing officials will land you in jail.
4. The amateur and his golf instructor drive the green and chip into the hole.

Exercise 4.9

Use the information in the instructional boxes in the chapter to complete these definitions.

Chapter 5

Beginning with the Basics

Word	Vowel Digraph	With Any Suffix (Answers will vary.)
1. braid	ai	braided, braiding, braids
2. brain	ai	brains, brainy, brainless
3. claim	ai	claimed, claims, claiming
4. faith	ai	faithful, faithless, faiths
5. paid	ai	x
6. paint	ai	painted, painting, painter, paints
7. raise	ai	raised, raising, raises
8. sprain	ai	sprained, spraining, sprains
9. lay	ay	laying, lays, layer (*not* layed)
10. pay	ay	paying, payment, pays, payer, payable (*not* payed)
11. play	ay	playing, played, playful, player
12. spray	ay	spraying, sprayed, sprayer
13. breeze	ee	breezes, breezy, breezeless
14. feel	ee	feeling, feels (*not* feeled)
15. freeze	ee	freezing, freezes, freezer, freezable (*not* freezed)
16. greet	ee	greeting, greeted, greets, greeter
17. keep	ee	keeping, keeper, keeps (*not* keeped)
18. sneeze	ee	sneezing, sneezed, sneezes
19. speech	ee	speeches, speechless
20. bleach	ea	bleaching, bleached, bleaches
21. cheap	ea	cheaper, cheapest, cheapness, cheapy

Word	Vowel Digraph	With Any Suffix (Answers will vary.)
22. clean	ea	cleaned, cleaning, cleans, cleaner, cleanest
23. deal	ea	dealing, dealer, deals (*not* dealed)
24. each	ea	x
25. ease	ea	eased, easing, easy, easement, eases
26. grease	ea	greasing, greased, greases, greasy
27. lease	ea	leased, leasing, leases
28. peach	ea	peaches, peachy
29. please	ea	pleased, pleasing, pleases, pleaser
30. reach	ea	reaching, reached, reaches, reachable
31. scream	ea	screaming, screamed, screams, screamer
32. speak	ea	speaking, speaker, speakable (*not* speaked)
33. teach	ea	teaching, teacher, teachable (*not* teached)
34. alley	ey	alleys
35. chimney	ey	chimneys
36. honey	ey	honeys, honeyed, honeying
37. money	ey	moneys, moneyed
38. valley	ey	valleys
39. coach	oa	coaches, coaching, coached, coachable
40. hoax	oa	hoaxes, hoaxing, hoaxed, hoaxer
41. oath	oa	oathes
42. poultry	ou	x
43. though	ou	x
44. soul	ou	souls, soulful, soulless
45. follow	ow	follows, following, followed, follower
46. grow	ow	grows, growing, grower (*not* growed)
47. owe	ow	owes, owing, owed
48. throw	ow	throws, throwing, thrower, throwable
49. issue	ue	issues, issuing, issued
50. rescue	ue	rescues, rescuing, rescued, rescuer, rescuable

Exercise 5.1

1.
feel	reach	speak	speech
sneeze	bleach	ease	scream
deal	clean	lease	breeze

2. *ES* Rule: Use *es* with words that end in *s, x, z, sh,* or *ch.*

braids	faiths	sprays	speeches
cleans	peaches	reaches	teaches
alleys	hoaxes	rescues	oaths

3. Final *E* Dropping Rule: When a word ends in final *e,* drop the *e* when you add a vowel suffix.

owing	breezy
freezer	easy
issuing	easement

4. Vowel + *Y* Rule: When a word ends in a vowel + *y,* add the suffix without making any spelling changes.

paying	played
sprayed	player

laying	payment
chimneys	sprayer

5. lay laid   pay paid

feel felt   freeze froze

deal dealt   speak spoke

grow grew   throw threw

keep kept   teach taught

6. alley   chimney   honey

money   valley   poultry

follow   issue   rescue

Exercise 5.2

1. The <u>jockey</u> **rode** the prize-winning racehorse (to **gate**) three.
2. <u>Using</u> tact <u>is</u> one **way** [to avoid] making **waves** (at the meeting).
3. **Praise** <u>is given</u> [to teach] a dog [to **heel**].
4. A short **break** <u>will be given</u> (between the two **main** keynote speakers).
5. <u>Hundreds</u> (of refugees) <u>tried</u> [to **flee**] (across the border) (during the **peak**) (of the war).
6. The **beat** (of the music) <u>could be heard</u> all (along the **beach**).
7. Several <u>sailors</u> **die** each year trying [to maneuver] (through the **strait**).
8. The **break** (in your fibula) <u>will take</u> (about ten **weeks**) [to **heal**].
9. The <u>president</u> (of the **board**) <u>has reached</u> the **peak** (of his career).
10. A **straight course** <u>is</u> the quickest way (to your destination).
11. The old movie **reel** <u>was</u> a **waste** (of my money).
12. The <u>reporter</u> <u>wanted</u> a **peek** (at the executive officer's bank **loan** files).
13. The **lone** <u>survivor</u> <u>had lost</u> a **great** deal (of **weight**).
14. That **great** <u>writer</u> <u>was</u> a **dear** friend (of my sister).
15. Our <u>manager</u> <u>decided</u> [to **waive**] the deposit (for room and **board**).
16. Your <u>decision</u> [to invest] (in the televised **course**) <u>carried</u> a lot (of **weight**).
17. (On our farm,) <u>we</u> never **waste** the nuts (from the **beech** trees).
18. The <u>climbers</u> <u>vowed</u> [to **meet**] (on the top) (of the mountain **peak**).
19. <u>Competing</u> (in the upcoming track **meet**) <u>is</u> one way [to **break**] the record.
20. The <u>customers</u> <u>had</u> [to wait] an hour (for the **main course**).
21. Unfortunately, many <u>people</u> <u>waste</u> the **heel** (of the bread).
22. <u>They</u> **bored** a tunnel (in an attempt) [to **flee**] (from the guards).
23. The aluminum **die** <u>is</u> too **weak** and <u>will break</u>.
24. The <u>tailor</u> **made** the **waist** (on the tuxedo) too small.
25. The stained glass window **pane** <u>is</u> very **dear** (to me).
26. (In the soap opera) last **week,** <u>Karen</u> <u>loved</u> Brian (with all her heart and **soul**).
27. <u>Marsha</u> <u>used</u> the dull **paring** knife [to peel] the **beets.**
28. The **pair** (of sea gulls) <u>landed</u> (on the iron **gate**).
29. <u>Roberto</u> **weighs** the significance (of being) the **sole** heir (of the estate).
30. The packaging <u>plant</u> <u>waits</u> (for the troller) [to bring in] fresh **sole** and salmon.
31. The **board** <u>ordered</u> all managers [to **pare**] their budgets (by twenty percent).
32. <u>Cindy</u> <u>wants</u> [to **break**] her unlucky streak (by using) her new fishing **reel.**
33. The **course** (of the night) <u>changed</u> (with one roll) (of the **die**).
34. The new <u>collar</u> <u>causes</u> **fleas** [to **die**] (within a few hours).

35. Willy's **weight** and the <u>size</u> (of his **waist**) <u>were</u> the source (of many jokes).
36. <u>You</u> <u>will need</u> [to **wait**] (for the fifty-pound **weights**).
37. The **lone** <u>coyote</u> <u>is preying</u> (on the farmer's chickens) and <u>ruining</u> the garden.
38. The **sole** <u>survivor</u> <u>gave</u> a lot (of **praise**) (to the Coast Guard rescue crew).

Exercise 5.3

1. faithfully	21. repaying
2. freezers	22. speechless
3. bleachers	23. impeachment
4. displeasing	24. unreachable
5. unteachable	25. deafening
6. unreasonable	26. threatening
7. unbreakable	27. breathlessly
8. sweaters	28. indestructible
9. weightlessness	29. payable
10. greaseless	30. soulful
11. breezy	31. repaired
12. unprepared	32. incurable
13. impermissible	33. untraceable
14. reproducible	34. expelling
15. emitting	35. rescuing
16. impression	36. impelling
17. emission	37. impermissible
18. unpredictable	38. imperfections
19. greasy	39. uneasy
20. unspeakable	40. solely

Exercise 5.4

1. beacon	ēā	15. weather	ĕ
2. thread	ĕ	16. eager	ĕā
3. eagle	ĕā	17. steak	ā
4. deaf	ĕ	18. feather	ĕ
5. deal	ĕā	19. dealt	ĕ
6. read	ĕā *or* ĕ	20. steady	ĕ
7. leader	ĕā	21. jealous	ĕ
8. bread	ĕ	22. break	ā
9. great	ā	23. spread	ĕ
10. instead	ĕ	24. breath	ĕ
11. heavy	ĕ	25. measles	ĕā
12. reason	ĕā	26. meadow	ĕ
13. queasy	ĕā	27. ready	ĕ
14. threat	ĕ	28. sweat	ĕ

Exercise 5.5

Answers will vary.

Exercise 5.6

braid	N V	claim	N V	paint	N V
raise	N V	pay	N V	spray	N V
freeze	N V	greet	V	ease	N V
scream	N V	teach	V	money	N
coach	N V	hoax	N V	poultry	N
follow	V	issue	N V	rescue	N V
waive	V	road	N	beat	N V
praise	N V	weigh	V	lie	N V
emit	V	resist	V	cure	N V
sweat	N V	breath	N	break	N V
reason	N V	threat	N	spread	N V

Choose any five words above that can work as nouns and as verbs.

Example: braid 1. The braid hung down her back, and it reached her waist. (Braid is used as a noun, and it is in a compound sentence with a coordinating conjunction.) 2. Mom braided my sister's hair; then, she braided my hair into two braids. (Braid is used as a verb in a compound sentence with a semicolon and a conjunctive adverb.)

Exercise 5.7

S   1. The fishing reel was old and rusty.

S   2. The rescue workers worked (through the night) and finally located the sunken boat.

C   3. The trees were sprayed, for they were infested (with insects).

C   4. The brakes were frayed; consequently, the driver lost control (on a steep hill).

C   5. Your lease will expire (at the end) (of the month); you will need [to negotiate] a new contract.

C   6. The evidence was presented (by her lawyer), but it was too weak [to win] the case.

S   7. The chimneys were cleaned and repaired (after the tropical storm).

S   8. (After a long wait), the singer finally greeted the audience.

S   9. An outbreak (of measles) spread (throughout the young population).

C   10. Ali was solely responsible (for the success) (of the paper); he deserved the recognition.

C   11. The loan application was completed, and an interview (with the bank) was scheduled.

S   12. We can begin the process now or wait for another week.

Notice the punctuation that has been added to each sentence. A reminder is in parentheses at the end of each sentence.

C   1. The plane landed safely, and no one (on board) or (on the ground) was injured. (comma)

C   2. Mentors taught students techniques (for studying) (for tests); as a result, the students showed improvements (in test scores). (semicolon and a comma)

C   3. The windows were boarded up; unfortunately, the winds ripped (off the boards). (semicolon and a comma)

S   4. The course taught students [to give] speeches and [to be] comfortable (in front) (of an audience).

C   5. The horse's mane was brushed (for the judging), and his hoofs were polished. (comma)

C   6. The food (at the diner) was greasy, but the prices were very reasonable. (comma)

S   **7.** The <u>road</u> (to success) <u>involves</u> hard work and undying commitment.

S   **8.** The <u>child</u> <u>screamed</u> (at the top) (of her lungs) (for her mother's attention).

S   **9.** <u>Care</u> <u>must be given</u> (for proper handling and cooking) (of chicken).

C **10.** The <u>peaches</u> <u>are</u> ripe, and <u>it</u> <u>is</u> time [to pick] them and [to pack] them (for the stores). (comma)

C **11.** The <u>money</u> (from the lottery) <u>will be taxed</u>; however, the final <u>earnings</u> <u>will</u> still <u>be</u> well over eight hundred thousand dollars. (semicolon and a comma)

C **12.** The <u>pair</u> <u>did</u> not <u>want</u> [to travel] overseas, nor <u>did</u> <u>they</u> <u>want</u> [to leave] their home state. (comma)

S **13.** <u>We</u> <u>strolled</u> (through the narrow alleys and cobblestone streets).

C **14.** Patty's physical <u>impairments</u> <u>do</u> not <u>slow</u> her down; in fact, few <u>people</u> <u>can keep up</u> (with her level) (of energy). (semicolon and comma)

C **15.** The <u>nurse</u> <u>felt</u> queasy; then, <u>she</u> <u>fainted</u> (in the operating room). (semicolon and comma)

Exercise 5.8

Sentences 1–10: Answers will vary.

Sentences 1–13. Answers will vary. A few model sentences are: 1. My study break was really needed, for my back was getting too sore. (This is a compound sentence with the coordinating conjunction "for", break is the subject of the first independent clause, and the sentence is in past tense.) 2. Faith and determination helped me get through the hard times. (Faith and determination are the two subjects in this simple sentence.)

Exercise 5.9

Use the information in the instructional boxes in the chapter to complete these definitions.

Chapter 6

Beginning with the Basics

Word	Sound
1. beauty	y = ĕ
2. body	y = ĕ
3. copy	y = ĕ
4. crazy	y = ĕ
5. duty	y = ĕ
6. envy	y = ĕ
7. glory	y = ĕ
8. holy	y = ĕ
9. lady	y = ĕ
10. lazy	y = ĕ
11. many	y = ĕ
12. pity	y = ĕ
13. study	y = ĕ
14. tidy	y = ĕ
15. tiny	y = ĕ
16. trophy	y = ĕ
17. ugly	y = ĕ

Word	Sound
18. grey	ey = ā
19. they	ey = ā
20. cry	y = ī
21. dry	y = ī
22. fry	y = ī
23. try	y = ī
24. echo	o = ō
25. hero	o = ō
26. piano	o = ō
27. potato	o = ō
28. radio	o = ō
29. stereo	o = ō
30. tomato	o = ō
31. veto	o = ō
32. achieve	ie = ē
33. ancient	ie = ə
34. belief	ie = ē
35. brief	ie = ē
36. ceiling	ei = ē
37. chief	ie = ē
38. either	ei = ē *or* ī
39. friend	ie = ĕ
40. grief	ie = ē
41. leisure	ei = ē
42. niece	ie = ē
43. neighbor	ei = ā
44. piece	ie = ē
45. relief	ie = ē
46. seize	ei = ē
47. shield	ie = ē
48. their	ei = ā
49. thief	ie = ē
50. yield	ie = ē

Exercise 6.1

1. cry   dry   fry   try
2. (any six words): beauty, body, copy, crazy, duty, envy, glory, holy, lady, lazy, many, pity, study, tidy, tiny, trophy, ugly
3. pianos, radios, stereos
4. echoes, heroes, potatoes, tomatoes, vetoes
5. No answer is needed.
6. Homonyms are words that sound the same, but they have different spellings and different meanings.

   a. piece   **a.** there   **a.** theirs
   b. peace   **b.** their   **b.** There's
   c. peace   **c.** They're   **c.** theirs
   d. piece   **d.** There   **d.** There's

e. piece　　**e.** There
f. peace　　**f.** their
　　　　　　　g. their
　　　　　　　h. there

7. Consonant + *Y* Rule: When a word ends in a consonant plus a *y*, change the *y* to an *i* before you add the suffix, unless the suffix begins with *i*.

   Y to *I* + *ES* Rule: Change the *y* to *i* and add *es* (not *s*).

beautiful	bodily
copier	copying
copies	duties
envious	glorious
holiest	laziness
studies	studying
pities	trophies
ugliness	cried
frying	trying

8. Use *ie* when you hear a long *e,* except after *c.*

   Use *ei* if you do not hear a long *e.*

   Use *ei* if the vowel sound you hear is *a.*

   Use *ei* right after the letter *c.*

   Use *ie* right after the letter *c* when the letter *c* sounds like *sh.*

   Use *ie* when you hear both vowels and when each vowel is in a separate syllable.

veil	reign	achieve	conceit
receive	grief	ancient	weight
science	piece	siege	shield
neighbor	anxiety	priest	brief
friend	view	patient	patience
species	efficient	weird	leisure
protein	caffeine	neither	conscience

Exercise 6.2

S　**1.** **Their** <u>belief</u> <u>honors</u> all men and all living creatures.

S　**2.** The family <u>members</u> **<u>grieve</u>** the loss (of **their** last grandparent).

S　**3.** Some **<u>relief</u>** (in the turmoil) <u>will come</u> (with the new **peace** agreements).

C　**4.** <u>It's</u> hard [to **believe**], but <u>they</u> finally <u>fixed</u> the **dryer** (at the lumber mill).

C　**5.** The union <u>leaders</u> <u>will</u> **<u>relieve</u>** him (of his duties); however, **<u>they're</u>** not <u>revoking</u> his membership.

S　**6.** **There** <u>were</u> <u>signs</u> (of anger and **grief**) (on the faces) (of the homeless).

S　**7.** **<u>They're</u>** <u>trying</u> [to **piece**] together the complicated jigsaw puzzle.

C　**8.** **Their** <u>clothes</u> <u>are</u> drier, for <u>they</u> finally <u>repaired</u> the dryer.

C　**9.** Our <u>product</u> <u>is</u> good, but **<u>theirs</u>** <u>is</u> more effective [to **relieve**] back pains.

C　**10.** **There's** a <u>crack</u> (in the kitchen ceiling), so <u>we</u> <u>accepted</u> **their** offer (of a lower sale price).

These words can work as verbs:

copy		envy		pity	study
tidy	cry	dry	fry	try	echo
		veto	achieve		believe
			seize	shield	yield

Exercise 6.2 sentences: Answers will vary. A few example sentences are: 1. Present tense verb phrase: The investment **is yielding** a nine percent return. 2. Compound sentence with a coordinating conjunction and the verb in past tense: We copied the report, and we distributed it to every office. 3. The word "fry" in a simple sentence in simple present tense with a singular subject: The chef fries our hamburgers on an electric grill.

Exercise 6.3

1. displeasure
2. objectively
3. unpleasing
4. actively
5. productively
6. containment
7. perceptual
8. deceiving
9. transgression
10. selection
11. seduced
12. refried
13. anxieties
14. seizures
15. vetoing
16. impatiently
17. gloriously
18. friendliness
19. conceiving
20. protective
21. impressive
22. progressively
23. conducive
24. passionately
25. preconceptions
26. receiver
27. conceivable
28. secluded
29. sequestered
30. unyielding
31. unbelievable
32. reception
33. leisurely
34. copiable
35. procedures
36. separation

Exercise 6.4

zeroes	buffaloes	mosquitoes	banjos
solos	cellos	volcanoes	altos
sopranos	cameos	cargoes	silos
echoes	pianos	mangoes/mangos	tuxedos/tuxedoes
lives	leaves	safes	
proofs	thieves	calves	
elves	chefs	chiefs	
roofs/rooves	wolves	hoofs/hooves	
shelves	selves	clefs	
loaves	beefs/beeves	halves	
knives	gulfs	briefs	
beliefs	surfs	golfs	
wives	dwarves/dwarfs	reefs	
spoofs	scarves/scarfs	wharves/wharfs	

Word List Expansion
Answers will vary. Check each part of the words you create. You should be able to identify the root or the base word, plus any prefixes or suffixes you added to the roots or bases.

Exercise 6.5

Answers will vary.

Exercise 6.6

beauty	N A	crazy	N A	holy	A		
lazy	A	tidy	V A	trophy	N A		
ugly	A	grey	N V A	cry	N V		
potato	N A	tomato	N A	ancient	A		
brief	N V A	chief	N A	piece	N V		
seize	V	shriek	N V	wield	V		
view	N V A	conscience	N	beige	N A		
eight	N A	freight	N A	feign	V		
reign	N V	protein	N A	vein	N V		

Sentences will vary. Each sentence should have a noun from above as the subject of a compound sentence.

Example: The <u>freight</u> will arrive by train at midnight.

Sentences will vary. Each sentence should have a verb from the above list. You should also have one prepositional phrase and two adjectives in each sentence.

Example: The aging king <u>reigned</u> over his tiny kingdom for fifty years.

Sentences will vary. Each sentence must have one adjective from above that is used in the Adjective Pattern 1 (right before the noun).

Example: The <u>beige</u> couch was delivered on Saturday.

Sentences will vary. Each sentence will have an adjective from the list above. The adjective will be in Adjective Pattern 2, which means it will appear after a linking verb. The adjective will refer back to the subject of the sentence.

Example: The ancient book is <u>holy.</u>

Exercise 6.7

1. This body cream costs twelve dollars per jar.
2. The relief pitcher stepped onto the muddy field, and the hometown crowd cheered loudly.
3. Our new, little kitten is playful and mischievous.
4. After a leisurely walk, the retired couple sat down on the park bench and reminisced.
5. My youngest nephew is loud, conceited, and rude.
6. The piano bar features local artists and superb, inexpensive food.
7. The best radio station in our little town went off the air at midnight.
8. Betty is my study partner; she is intelligent and enthusiastic.
9. The lighted trophy case held football trophies and twelve game balls.
10. Your computations were correct; you received a high score on the physics exam.
11. The active ingredients are listed on the blue part of the label.

12. The recluse lives in a (beautiful) (log-cabin) home in the (remote) area of the (northern) region.

13. (Our) (new) (stereo) system is (beautiful.)

14. Mrs. Jacobson is the (friendliest) teacher and the (best) teacher in (our) (entire) school.

15. Uncle Ben was (active,) (sharp,) and (healthy;) (his) life was (productive) and (rewarding.)

16. The jars of (pickled) beets were placed inside a (pressure) cooker.

17. The (main) speaker at the (fund-raising) event was (inspirational) and (dedicated.)

18. A (stale) loaf of (wheat) bread lay on the (kitchen) counter for (three) weeks.

Exercise 6.8

Answers will vary. The example shows how the sentence was expanded by adding one prepositional phrase and at least two adjectives: 1. The Caribbean cruise ship headed out to sea (for the third time) this month.

Answers will vary. The example sentences use the adjectives first in the Adjective Pattern 1 position and then in the Adjective Pattern 2 position: **useful** 1. The cookbook was a very useful gift. 2. The cookbook will be useful.
loyal 1. My most *loyal* friend is my dog. 2. Mary has always been very *loyal*.

-er and *-est*

crazy	crazier	craziest	lazy	lazier	laziest
tiny	tinier	tiniest	ugly	uglier	ugliest
thick	thicker	thickest	quick	quicker	quickest
thin	thinner	thinnest	foggy	foggier	foggiest
bossy	bossier	bossiest	gentle	gentler	gentlest
big	bigger	biggest	flat	flatter	flattest
hot	hotter	hottest	mad	madder	maddest
tan	tanner	tannest	brave	braver	bravest
late	later	latest	safe	safer	safest
cute	cuter	cutest	cheap	cheaper	cheapest
clean	cleaner	cleanest	great	greater	greatest

Sentences will vary. Example sentences are: I wanted a thick piece of wood. I bought a thicker piece of wood. You will need to cut the thickest piece of wood.

Chapter 7

Multi-Syllable Words with R-Controls

Word	With *ing*	With Any Suffix (Answers will vary.)
1. article	X	articles
2. bargain	bargaining	bargains, bargained, bargainer
3. carpet	carpeting	carpets, carpeted

Word	With *ing*	With Any Suffix (Answers will vary.)
4. harvest	harvesting	harvests, harvested, harvester
5. marble	marbling	marbled, marbles
6. market	marketing	marketed, markets, marketable
7. marvel	marveling	marveled, marvelous, marvels
8. sparkle	sparkling	sparkled, sparkler, sparkles
9. startle	startling	startled, startles
10. target	targeting	targeted, targets
11. summary	X	summaries
12. salary	X	salaries, salaried
13. harass	harassing	harassment, harassed
14. burglar	X	burglary, burglaries, burglars
15. calendar	calendaring	calendars, calendared
16. grammar	X	X
17. dollar	X	dollars
18. alter	altering	alters, altered
19. anger	angering	angers, angered
20. average	averaging	averages, averaged
21. cancer	X	cancers, cancerous
22. center	centering	centers, centered
23. desert	deserting	deserted, deserts, deserter
24. dessert	X	desserts
25. eager	X	eagerness, eagerly
26. general	X	generals
27. govern	governing	governed, government
28. master	mastering	mastered, masterful, masters
29. mercy	X	merciful, merciless
30. merge	merging	merges, merged, merger
31. modern	X	X
32. mystery	X	mysteries, mysterious
33. person	X	persons, personable
34. thunder	thundering	thundered, thunderous
35. whisper	whispering	whispered, whispers
36. wonder	wondering	wondered, wonderful, wonderous
37. circus	X	circuses
38. virtue	X	virtues, virtuous, virtual
39. border	bordering	bordered, borders
40. forest	foresting	forested, forests, forestation
41. gorge	gorging	gorged, gorgeous
42. morning	X	mornings
43. normal	X	normally
44. tornado	X	tornadoes
45. burden	burdening	burdened
46. furnish	furnishing	furnished, furnishes
47. hurry	hurrying	hurried, hurries
48. pursue	pursuing	pursued, pursuer
49. surgery	X	surgeries
50. surprise	surprising	surprises, surprised

Exercise 7.1

1. Second CVC Doubling Rule: Double the last consonant in a multi-syllable CVC word when the CVC is accented and when you add a vowel suffix.

   Answers will vary. Any ten of the following words will be correct.

carpet	market	marvel	target	burglar
cancer	grammar	dollar	alter	anger
person	center	eager	wonder	master
border	thunder	whisper		circus
	normal	burden		

2. *-LE* Syllable Rule: The *-le* syllable usually has one more consonant before the *-le*.

article	marble	sparkle	startle

3. summary   salary   burglar   calendar   grammar   dollar

4. color   motor   work   world   worry   rumor
   doctor   armor   parlor   memory   humor

5. toward   embarrass   scarce   marry   carry

6. Consonant + *Y* Rule: When a word ends with a consonant and a *y*, change the *y* to *i* before you add any suffix, unless the suffix begins with *i*.

   summary = summaries
   salary = salaries
   mercy = mercies
   mystery = mysteries
   hurry = hurries
   surgery = surgeries

7. harasses   circuses   tornadoes

8. average   cancer   center   general   mercy
   merge   circus   gorge   surgery

Exercise 7.2

The correct homonym is in bold print.

1. (Many) people cut (Douglas) **fir** (at (Christmas) time).

2. The (animal's) **fur** was (smooth) and (soft.)

3. (Metal) **urns** are used to store ashes.

4. You will need to **earn** (your) keep (by doing) chores.

5. The couple awaited the **birth** (of (their) (first) child).

6. The **berth** (on the submarine) is (narrow) and (uncomfortable.)

7. The caterer placed a (delicate) **flower** (on the top) (of the cake).

8. (My) (neighbor's) son is (allergic) (to (white) **flour**).

9. The (flea) **collar** irritated the (dog's) neck.

10. The family is (in **mourning**) (for a (full) year).

11. The (**morning**) sun poured in (through the (stained-glass) windows).

12. (After kneeling) (at the **altar**), the (solemn) man asked (for forgiveness).

13. The architects can **alter** the blueprints to make a (larger) (master) bedroom.

14. He was a **minor** (in possession), so he must appear (in court).

15. The **stationery** comes (with paper and (matching) envelopes).

16. The (third) hurricane (of the season) is (**stationary**) (over the Bahamas).

17. Everyone (in the park) **heard** the (young) child scream.

18. The **herd** (of (wild) elephants) stampeded (through the (tropical) jungle).

1. deserting	**2.** targeting *or* centering	**3.** averaging	**4.** bargaining
5. carpeting	**6.** Harassing	**7.** marketing	**8.** harvesting
9. sparkling	**10.** startling		

1. Mastering	**2.** merging	**3.** whispering	**4.** bordering
5. hurrying	**6.** pursuing	**7.** surprising	**8.** furnishing
9. governing	**10.** wondering		

Exercise 7.3

1. distortionist	**20.** reversible
2. reverted	**21.** independent
3. conferencing	**22.** torturous
4. marriage	**23.** occurrence
5. reference	**24.** pleasantly
6. transportation	**25.** supportive
7. deportment	**26.** occurring
8. distorted	**27.** exports
9. portable	**28.** informally
10. blurry	**29.** nervousness
11. starvation	**30.** darkening
12. marketing	**31.** summaries
13. salaried	**32.** alteration
14. cancerous	**33.** government
15. mysteriously	**34.** virtuous
16. reforestation	**35.** wonderful
17. tornadoes	**36.** pursuing
18. surgeries	**37.** worrying
19. scarcely	**38.** persistent

Exercise 7.4

Answers will vary.

Exercise 7.5

Answers will vary. Check carefully that you have written a compound sentence and that you have included two words with AR or OR.

Example: The average salary increase is 4 percent; however, I was given a ten percent raise.

BOTTOM: Answers will vary. Check carefully that each sentence has two words from the ER, IR, UR word list and that you have at least one prepositional phrase and one adjective. These sentences do not need to be compound sentences.

Example: Everyone hurried to get away (from the destructive tornado). (Two words with r-controls: hurried and tornado; adjective: destructive; the prepositional phrase is marked)

(Top) Homonym sentences: Answers will vary.

(Bottom) Answers will vary. Three sentences must have the adjectives placed before the nouns they modify (Adjective Pattern 1). Three sentences must have the adjectives placed after a linking verb.

Example (Adjective Pattern 1): The marble statue was placed in the rose garden.

(Adjective Pattern 2): The barbed wire was sharp.

Exercise 7.6

independent	N A	humorist	N	modern	A
wonder	N V	mysterious	A	mystery	N A
occur	V	sector	N	department	N A
sparse	A	stormy	A	harmful	A
exert	V	squirming	V A	darkness	N
starving	V A	editor	N	marble	N A
calendar	N V	furnished	V A	basic	A
supportive	A	repellent	N	reference	N

Sentences with nouns will vary. Example: The calendar was useless; it was for 1994.

Sentences with verbs will vary. Example: The tired, impatient children were squirming throughout the entire movie.

Sentences with adjectives will vary. Example: The furnished apartment will be available September 1.

Sentences with adjectives will vary. Example: Melissa's parents were supportive.

Exercise 7.7

1. The (well-known) promoter (of (boxing) champions) met the press and expressed (his) opinion.

2. The morning seemed (normal,) but then (strange) events started [to happen] (at the mansion).

3. There were (three) transmitters damaged (by the tornado); consequently, the community had (no) electricity.

4. You were (smart) [to swerve] and were (lucky) [to miss] hitting the deer (in the road).

5. The (surprised) motorist was angered (by the (careless) littering) (by the driver) (in front) (of him).

6. The novelist is a perfectionist; her work is recognized (throughout the (literary) circles).

7. (Lisa's) parents were (supportive) (of her decision) [to marry]; however, (Jimmy's) parents objected (to the decision).

8. (My) brother is exploring opportunities (in the (import) and (export) business).

9. The (transportation) department announced a change (in collecting) (road) fees.

10. The stationery is (wonderful;) I will use it (for (my) (thank-you) notes).

11. All (of the residents) gave the manager an (excellent) recommendation.

12. The differences (in (our) opinions) resulted (in (many) disagreements); we are no longer friends.

13. I was the (innocent) target (of (his) anger), but I refused [to quit] or [to pursue] (other) avenues.

14. The composer and the sculptor promoted the (cultural) event and received praise (for (their) work).

15. The surf pounded the shores (of Miami Beach); (all) swimmers were asked [to leave] the water.

16. The (top) berth broke; there were (no) (extra) berths (on the train).

17. The reporter expressed the importance (of independence and freedom) (for (his) country).

18. Observance (of the (Martin Luther King) holiday) occurs (in (most) (state) and (government) offices).

This exercise is the same as the previous exercise except there may be run-on sentence errors or comma splice errors. Check your answers carefully to be sure you corrected any of the grammatical errors.

1. (Run-on)

The existence (of UFO's) is debated; however, I believe (in (their) existence).

2. (Correct)

The (harshest) winter (on record) (for flooding) occurred (during the year) (of 1996).

3. (Correct)

The governor whispered (to (his) assistant) and scribbled a (short) message (on the notepad).

4. (Correct)

(One) swimmer could not escape the (swirling) waters (of the (rapid) river).

5. (Run-on)

He is a master (of deception); (his) performances sell out (in (every) city).

6. (Correct)

The golfers and the gallery left the course [to seek] shelter (from the (lightning) storm).

7. (Correct)

(One) predictor (of (college) success) is (regular) attendance (in classes).

8. (Comma splice)

Food <u>was</u> (scarce;) <u>starvation</u> and <u>diseases</u> <u>were killing</u> (entire) populations.

9. (Run-on)

(Marble) <u>tiles</u> <u>were laid</u> (in the hallways); (plush) <u>carpeting</u> <u>was laid</u> (in (every) room).

10. (Run-on)

Fortunately, the <u>wind</u> (in the gorge) <u>died down</u>, but <u>motor homes</u> still <u>could</u> not <u>get</u> (through the canyon).

11. (Correct)

The <u>summary</u> <u>disclosed</u> the importance (of the merger) (of the (two) (largest) companies).

12. (Correct)

(Security) <u>clearances</u> <u>were given</u> (for us) [to attend] the (press) conference (at the Capitol).

13. (Run-on)

<u>You</u> <u>will need</u> [to use] (wheat) flour; (white) flour <u>does</u> not <u>work</u> (in (this) recipe).

14. (Comma splice)

(All) <u>references</u> <u>must be typed</u> (in (alphabetical) order); (handwritten) <u>work</u> <u>will</u> not <u>be accepted.</u>

15. (Correct)

(In a spurt) (of creativity), the <u>artist</u> <u>altered</u> (his) painting (by using) an (air-brush) technique.

16. (Run-on)

(Many) <u>grievances</u> <u>were filed</u>; the <u>miners</u> <u>protested</u> the (working) conditions.

17. (Correct)

The (cancer) <u>center</u> <u>was awarded</u> a (private) grant [to research] cancer (in children).

18. (Comma splice)

<u>She</u> <u>is</u> (wonderful;) <u>she</u> never <u>wastes</u> time worrying (about (little) things) (in life).

19. (Run-on)

The <u>editor</u> (of the newspaper) <u>displayed</u> (our) poster (on (his) wall); <u>it</u> <u>became</u> a (conversation) piece.

20. (Correct)

(Upon (my) (supervisor's) insistence), <u>I</u> <u>applied</u> (for the job) and <u>was hired.</u>

Exercise 7.8

Sentence combining: Answers will vary.

Sentence expansion: Answers will vary.

Exercise 7.9

Use the information in the instructional boxes in the chapter to complete these definitions.

Chapter 8

Words with Vowel Diphthongs

Word	Diphthong and Sound
1. tycoon	oo = oo
2. author	au = ŏ
3. trouser	ou = ŏw
4. tabloid	oi = oi
5. raccoon	oo = oo
6. source	ou = or
7. avenue	ue = oo
8. turmoil	oi = oi
9. poison	oi = oi
10. construe	ue = oo
11. astronaut	au = ŏ
12. curfew	ew = ŭ
13. ounce	ou = ŏw
14. doubt	ou = ŏw
15. trauma	au = ŏ
16. boycott	oy = oy
17. nephew	ew = ŭ
18. autumn	au = ŏ
19. souvenir	ou = oo
20. courage	ou = er
21. vowel	ow = ŏw
22. typhoon	oo = oo
23. because	au = ŏ
24. audience	au = ŏ (i—e = two different syllables)
25. laundry	au = ŏ
26. revenue	ue = oo
27. caution	au = ŏ
28. exhaust	au = ŏ
29. audit	au = ŏ
30. faucet	au = ŏ
31. turquoise	oi = oi

Word	Diphthong and Sound
32. routine	ou = oo
33. assault	au = ŏ
34. daughter	au = ŏ
35. thousand	ou = ŏw
36. enough	ou = ŭ
37. sewer	ew = oo
38. news	ew = oo
39. annoy	oy = oy
40. maneuver	eu = oo
41. could	ou = oo
42. count	ou = ŏw
43. country	ou = ŭ
44. authentic	au = ŏ
45. auditorium	au = ŏ
46. nourish	ou = er
47. sirloin	oi = oi
48. destroy	oy = oy
49. cartoon	oo = oo
50. cousin	ou = ŭ

ty/coon	au/thor	trou/ser	tab/loid
rac/coon	tur/moil	av/e/nue	cur/few
poi/son	con/strue	trau/ma	a/stro/naut
boy/cott	neph/ew	au/tumn	sou/ve/nir
ty/phoon	vow/el	be/cause	au/di/ence
laun/dry	rev/e/nue	cau/tion	as/sault
au/dit	fau/cet	tur/quoise	thou/sand
ma/neu/ver	coun/try	au/then/tic	au/di/to/ri/um
car/toon	sir/loin	cou/sin	nour/ish

Exercise 8.1

1. source   ounce   doubt   news   could   count
2. doubt   autumn   exhaust   could
3. author   trouser   turmoil   curfew   turquoise   daughter   sewer   maneuver   auditorium   sirloin   cartoon
4. source   ounce   courage   audience   faucet
5. nephew   typhoon
6. **a.** is   **b.** covers   **c.** shows

Exercise 8.2

1. audience   astronaut
2. turmoil
3. courage   tycoon
4. tabloids   construe

5. source author's

6. doubt curfew

7. Typhoons autumn

8. nephew's trauma

9. souvenir raccoon

10. avenue boycott

1. audit revenue

2. destroy faucet

3. turquoise country

4. caution exhaust

5. could sewer

6. cousin maneuver

7. assault news

8. daughter enough

9. authentic auditorium

10. thousand sirloin

Sentences with adjectives in Adjective Pattern 1: Answers will vary.

Sentences with adjectives in Adjective Pattern 2: Answers will vary.

Past Tense of Verbs:

1. shot   2. stood   3. taught   4. caught   5. saw   6. wound

7. blew   8. knew   9. slew   10. threw   11. fought   12. brought

13. sought   14. bought

Exercise 8.3

1. feudalism   20. assistant
2. sanitation   21. berating
3. attendance   22. naturalize
4. application   23. applying
5. bewitching   24. imposition
6. productivity   25. propensity
7. mannerisms   26. infinity
8. conceptualize   27. belonging
9. friendships   28. reinforcements
10. enforcing   29. professionalism
11. formalization   30. authorization
12. authorities   31. formalities
13. activities   32. scarcity
14. disturbance   33. perturbed
15. innately   34. naturally
16. nationality   35. socializing
17. unsociable   36. compensation
18. indispensable   37. pensions
19. accountant   38. enraged

Exercise 8.4

Check the spelling of the words dictated to you by your partner.

Exercise 8.5

Homonym sentences: Answers will vary.
Sentences with confusables: Answers will vary.
Seven coordinating conjunctions: for, and, nor, but, or, yet, so
Compound sentences: Answers will vary.

Exercise 8.6

1. when I filed the request for a hearing
2. Because Lynn is going on vacation,
3. Since the order was turned in on time,
4. until you finish your research project.
5. Although Becky is old enough to drive,
6. As soon as I receive the refund,
7. where you put your briefcase
8. before I shower and dress.
9. If you boil the shrimp too long,
10. While you were out of the office,
11. Though the boycott lasted only one day,
12. unless you ask us for an extension.
13. because her work is the best in the industry.
14. unless I bring them each a souvenir.
15. after I did eight loads of laundry.
16. Whether the astronaut leaves the spaceship or not,
17. Since I have the flu,
18. Although the trauma center has an excellent reputation,
19. Once I spent the whole day at the county fair,
20. because the cat was ruining too many pieces of furniture

Subjects and Verbs:
1. I can remember   I filed
2. Lynn is going   I volunteered
3. order was turned in   books will be
4. You can get   you finish
5. Billy is   he has
6. I receive   I will apply
7. I do know   you put
8. I drink   I shower   dress
9. you boil   it will be   lose
10. you were   reporters came
11. boycott lasted   effects were
12. book   will be due   you ask

13. <u>cartoonist</u> <u>is</u>   <u>work</u> <u>is</u>
14. <u>children</u> <u>will be</u>   <u>I</u> <u>bring</u>
15. <u>I</u> <u>was</u>   <u>I</u> <u>did</u>
16. <u>astronaut</u> <u>leaves</u>   <u>mission</u> <u>is</u>
17. <u>I</u> <u>have</u>   <u>I</u> <u>have</u>
18. <u>center</u> <u>has</u>   <u>it</u> <u>finds</u>
19. <u>I</u> <u>spent</u>   <u>I</u> <u>had</u>
20. <u>claws</u> <u>were removed</u>   <u>cat</u> <u>was ruining</u>

Exercise 8.7

S   1. There <u>was</u> so much <u>turmoil</u> during the discount sale.

C   2. Four <u>raccoons</u> <u>entered</u> our campground; (unfortunately,) <u>they</u> <u>ate</u> all of our food.

CX   3. I <u>will buy</u> the lounge chair this week (since) the <u>voucher</u> <u>expires</u> in seven days.

CX   4. The financial <u>planner</u> <u>decided</u> to sell the stock (because) <u>it</u> <u>was dropping</u> in value.

C   5. The <u>dessert</u> <u>is loaded</u> with calories, (for) <u>it</u> <u>consists</u> of four kinds of chocolate.

C   6. The <u>sirloin</u> <u>was</u> tough and burned, (but) the <u>boys</u> <u>ate</u> it anyway.

S   7. The <u>revenue</u> from this project <u>will reduce</u> the amount of company debt.

C   8. The country <u>singers</u> <u>were</u> fantastic, (but) the opening comedy <u>act</u> <u>was</u> disappointing.

CX   9. (Although) <u>autumn</u> <u>is</u> beautiful with all the colored leaves, my favorite <u>season</u> <u>is</u> spring.

C   10. Not many <u>people</u> <u>wanted</u> to live there, (for) the sewage <u>plant</u> really <u>stank.</u>

CX   11. Not many <u>people</u> <u>wanted</u> to live there (because) the sewage <u>plant</u> really <u>stank.</u>

S   12. The <u>cook</u> <u>took</u> the spoons off the hooks and <u>washed</u> them thoroughly.

S   13. The <u>dew</u> <u>covered</u> the ground and <u>felt</u> cool on our bare feet.

C   14. The mail <u>route</u> <u>goes</u> around the lake; (however,) many <u>days</u> the roads <u>are closed.</u>

CX   15. Mom <u>brought</u> the tourists to our house (when) the <u>storm</u> <u>closed</u> the airport.

Pay special attention to the punctuation that has been added to these sentences. If punctuation was needed, a reminder is shown in parentheses at the end of the sentence.

C   16. The <u>price</u> of the computer <u>is</u> $2,000; however, <u>you</u> <u>can get</u> a student discount. (semi-colon and a comma)

C   17. The <u>proof</u> <u>may exist</u>, but <u>I</u> <u>have</u> not yet <u>seen</u> it. (comma)

CX   18. If your <u>spouse</u> <u>is interested</u>, <u>you</u> <u>can sign up</u> for these dance lessons. (comma)

CX   19. Wherever <u>Arthur</u> <u>goes</u>, <u>she</u> always <u>follows.</u> (comma)

CX   20. The <u>school</u> <u>launched</u> a new fund-raising drive because the <u>band</u> <u>needed</u> uniforms.

CX   21. When the <u>parade</u> <u>is</u> in progress, the <u>avenues</u> <u>will be closed.</u> (comma)

C   22. <u>Rusty</u> <u>was</u> a loyal dog, and <u>I</u> <u>was</u> his proud owner. (comma)

CX   23. Although <u>curfew</u> <u>is</u> at midnight, many <u>teenagers</u> <u>are</u> still out on the streets. (comma)

S   **24.** Throughout the neighborhood, <u>flags</u> <u>were flying</u> and <u>flapping</u> in the wind.

S   **25.** The true <u>stories</u> <u>will</u> not <u>be found</u> in the tabloids.

CX   **26.** An <u>ounce</u> of gold <u>was taken</u> from the river when <u>we</u> <u>panned</u> for gold.

CX   **27.** When <u>Herman</u> <u>was</u> in the Army, <u>maneuvers</u> in Panama <u>lasted</u> two weeks. (comma)

C   **28.** The <u>instructor</u> <u>taught</u> us the rules; as a result, <u>we</u> all <u>passed</u> the test. (semicolon and a comma)

S   **29.** A thousand young <u>fans</u> <u>stomped</u> their feet and <u>yelled</u> throughout the entire concert.

CX   **30.** Since <u>Halloween</u> <u>is</u> on Tuesday, most Halloween <u>parties</u> <u>will be held</u> on Saturday. (comma)

C   **31.** The <u>investors</u> <u>were elated</u>, for the <u>stock market</u> <u>was</u> at an all-time high. (comma)

S   **32.** <u>Mushrooms</u> in salads <u>taste</u> good and <u>are</u> good for you.

CX   **33.** When the <u>tot</u> <u>bounced</u> the basketball, his <u>parents</u> <u>grabbed</u> the video camera. (comma)

C   **34.** Raw <u>tuna</u> <u>was served</u>; however, <u>I</u> <u>refrained</u> from trying it. (semicolon and a comma)

CX   **35.** Until the <u>torch</u> <u>is lit</u>, the <u>Olympics</u> <u>have</u> not officially <u>started.</u> (comma)

Exercise 8.8

Sentence writing with subordinate conjunctions: Answers will vary.

Sentence combining: Answers will vary. See the examples on page 266.

Sentences with specific directions: Answers will vary.

Exercise 8.9

Use the information in the instructional boxes in the chapter to complete these definitions.

Chapter 9

Beginning with the Basics

Word	Silent	Add Any Suffix (Answers will vary.)
1. answer	w	answering, answered, answers
2. campaign	g	campaigning, campaigned, campaigner
3. castle	t	castles
4. climb	b	climbs, climber, climbing, climbed
5. column	n	columnist, columns
6. comb	b	combing, combed, combs
7. condemn	n	condemns, condemnation, condemned
8. corps	ps	X
9. debt	b	debts, debtor
10. exhibit	h	exhibiting, exhibitor, exhibits
11. fasten	t	fastening, fastener, fastened
12. gnarl	g	gnarled, gnarls, gnarling
13. gnaw	g	gnawing, gnawed, gnaws
14. heir	h	heirs, heiress
15. honest	h	honestly, honesty

Word	Silent	Add Any Suffix (Answers will vary.)
16. honor	h	honorable, honors, honored
17. hour	h	hourly, hours
18. hustle	t	hustler, hustling
19. knead	k	kneaded, kneading, kneads
20. kneel	k	kneeling, kneels (*not* kneeled)
21. knight	k	knights, knighthood, knighted
22. knit	k	knitting, knits, knitted
23. knot	k	knotting, knotted, knots
24. knuckle	k	knuckles, knuckling
25. light	gh	lights, lightable, lightly, lightness
26. limb	b	limbs, limber
27. listen	t	listens, listening, listened, listener
28. mortgage	t	mortgages, mortgaged, mortgaging
29. muscle	c	muscles
30. often	t	X
31. plumber	b	plumbers
32. reign	g	reigns, reigned, reigning
33. rhyme	h	rhyming, rhymed, rhymes
34. rhythm	h	rhythms, rhythmic
35. rough	gh	roughly, roughness, roughed
36. rustle	t	rustlers, rustled, rustling
37. salmon	l	X
38. scene	c	scenic, scenes
39. sign	g	signing, signal, signed, signs
40. sight	gh	sighting, sights, sighted
41. subtle	b	subtleness, subtlety, subtly
42. walk	l	walking, walked, walker
43. wrap	w	wrapped, wrapping, wraps, wrapper
44. wrestle	w, t	wrestler, wrestled, wrestling
45. wring	w	wringing, wringer (*not* wringed)
46. wrinkle	w	wrinkled, wrinkling
47. write	w	writing, writer (*not* writed *or* writen)
48. written	w	X
49. wrong	w	wrongful, wrongfully, wrongs
50. wrought	w, gh	X

Exercise 9.1

1. castle   hustle   knuckle   muscle   subtle   wrestle   wrinkle

2. /CLE Syllable Rule: The consonant *le* usually has one more consonant with it. If you don't hear the consonant, use the consonant at the end of the previous syllable.

   cas/tle   hus/tle   knuck/le   mus/cle   sub/tle   wres/tle   wrin/kle

3. First CVC Doubling Rule: When a one-syllable word ends in CVC, double the last consonant when you add a vowel suffix.

   knit   knot   wrap

4. Second CVC Doubling Rule: When a multi-syllable word ends in CVC, double the last consonant if the CVC syllable is the accented syllable and if you add a vowel suffix.

answer	exhibit	fasten
honor	listen	often
plumber	salmon	written

5. honorable   answering

    exhibitor   fastener

    knitted   knots

    plumbers   wrappable

6.

castle ā	climb ī	comb ō	condemn ə
debt ē	fasten ā	hustle ŭ	knead ĕ
knight ī	knot ō	limb ī	reign ā
rhyme ī	rhythm ī	rustle ŭ	salmon ə
scene ĕ	sign ī	sight ī	subtle ŭ
wrap ā	wrinkle ī	write ī	written ī

7. r-controls: ar, er, ir, or, ur

    answer   corps   gnarl

    honor   mortgage   plumber

Exercise 9.2

1. heir reigns	**2.** corps right	**3.** sighting not
4. sites right	**5.** wrought rot	**6.** rap ring
7. scene sight	**8.** seen rings	**9.** knight reign
10. raining site	**11.** need core	**12.** needs site
13. sighted knot	**14.** rites rings	**15.** our ring hour
16. not ring	**17.** knight's not right	**18.** rites site
19. wrapped our	**20.** ring rites	

Exercise 9.3

1. indebtedness	**13.** international
2. fastening	**14.** impartiality
3. dishonorable	**15.** interfacing
4. surrealist	**16.** communicable
5. rhyming	**17.** interchangeable
6. scenic	**18.** financially
7. signaling	**19.** designation
8. wrestling	**20.** consignment
9. immunization	**21.** exhibitionist
10. insurmountable	**22.** honestly
11. surrounding	**23.** interactive
12. interjection	**24.** listener

25. roughest	**33.** interracial
26. signature	**34.** intermittent
27. foolishly	**35.** surpassing
28. wrongfully	**36.** communication
29. surpluses	**37.** intersections
30. excitement	**38.** columnist
31. introspection	**39.** obscenity
32. interceptions	**40.** communities

Exercise 9.4

1. redesigning	**2.** assignments	**3.** resignations	**4.** designer
5. reassignment	**6.** promotional	**7.** promoting	**8.** commotion
9. promoters	**10.** remotely	**11.** emotionally	**12.** motives
13. demoted	**14.** immunities	**15.** Communist	**16.** communal
17. prospector	**18.** respectfully	**19.** inspectors	**20.** disrespectful

Exercise 9.5

Answers will vary for the first twenty sentences.

Past Tenses	**Past Tenses**
answered	campaigned
climbed	condemned
exhibited	fastened
gnarled	gnawed
honored	hustled
knelt	knitted *or* knit
mortgaged	rhymed
roughed	wrinkled
wrapped	wrung
wrestled	wrote

Answers will vary for the ten complex sentences in past tense. Example: When the hikers climbed out of the canyon, the rescue crews cheered.

Exercise 9.6

answer	N V	blight	N V
campaign	N V A	combing	N V
flight	N V A	soon	ADV
gnarl	N V	gnawing	N V A
honorable	A	hourly	A ADV
lightness	N	limber	V A
reign	N V	rhythm	N A
salmon	N A	scenic	A
signal	N V A	least	A ADV

wring	V	wrong	N V A ADV
cite	V	sight	N V
babyish	A	collide	V
design	N V A	emotionally	ADV
fastening	N V	forgiveness	N
inspector	N	quite	ADV
very	ADV	now	ADV
introvert	N V	remotely	ADV
selfishly	ADV	wrongfully	ADV
surcharge	N	signature	N A
seldom	ADV	partially	ADV
respect	N V	never	ADV
tomorrow	N ADV	subtle	A
rightfully	ADV	foolish	A

1. A   **2.** ADV   **3.** A   **4.** N   **5.** V   **6.** N
7. ADV   **8.** N   **9.** ADV   **10.** V   **11.** ADV   **12.** ADV
13. ADV   **14.** N   **15.** ADV

Exercise 9.7

1. Our summer vacation (to Europe) <u>was</u> thoroughly <u>enjoyed</u> (by the entire family).
   N = Our, summer; ADV = thoroughly; N = entire

2. The landing site <u>is</u> most frequently <u>visited</u> (by tourists) (during the summer months).
   N = landing; ADV = most frequently; N = tourists; N = summer

3. Communication skills <u>can be</u> extremely difficult (for introverted individuals) [to develop].
   N = Communication; ADV = extremely; N = difficult; ADV = introverted

4. The <u>directions</u> <u>said</u> [to turn] right (at the intersection) and then [to go] three blocks.
   N = directions; ADV = right; N = intersection; ADV = then; N = three

5. <u>All</u> (of the salmon runs) <u>are recorded</u> annually and <u>examined</u> extensively (by conservationists).
   N = salmon; ADV = annually; ADV = extensively; N = conservationists

6. There <u>was</u> quite an <u>increase</u> (in the mortgage payment) (for our new home).
   ADV = quite; ADV = an; N = increase; N = mortgage; N = our

7. All passengers <u>are required</u> [to fasten] their seat belts properly.
   N = All passengers; N = their; ADV = properly

8. The screaming child <u>was</u> clearly not <u>interested</u> (in listening) (to her mother).
   N = screaming; ADV = clearly; ADV = not; N = listening; N = her

9. All complaints <u>will be handled</u> much more promptly (under this new system).
   N = All complaints; ADV = much; ADV = more; ADV = promptly; N = this new

10. My youngest sister <u>is</u> the most jealous person (in our family).
    N = My youngest; ADV = most; N = jealous; N = our

Exercise 9.8

Answers will vary for changing fragments into complete sentences. Examples: 1. The mailroom clerk was tightly wrapping the boxes for shipping. 2. The columnist for the local newspaper plans to retire in December.

RO	**1.**	yesterday; the sponsors
RO	**2.**	outage; she lost
O	**3.**	
CS	**4.**	King Henry III; he
O	**5.**	
CS	**6.**	hair; consequently,
O	**7.**	
O	**8.**	
O	**9.**	
O	**10.**	
RO	**11.**	back; they
RO	**12.**	citation; it
O	**13.**	
O	**14.**	
O	**15.**	
CS	**16.**	weeks; all
RO	**17.**	made; I don't
O	**18.**	

Exercise 9.9

Use the information in the instructional boxes in the chapter to complete these definitions.

Chapter 10

Exercise 10.1

1. Answers will vary. Any six of the following words are correct.

advise	affect	anxious	athlete	counsel	elude	entrance	except
fatigue	judgment	moral	presence	schedule	surprise	technique	vacuum

2. Answers will vary. Any six of the following words are correct.

acknowledge	alcohol	alphabet	amateur	argument	chocolate	
compliment	dilemma	disastrous	elicit	emigrate	government	guarantee
maintenance	mischievous	personnel	prejudice	prescription	principal	
privilege	questionnaire	restaurant	sophomore	syllable		

3. Answers will vary. Any six of the following words are correct.

bureaucracy	conscientious	category	education	environment
February	mathematics	optimistic		

4. laboratory   miscellaneous

5. emigrate   guarantee   February
technique   disastrous   dilemma
maintenance   sophomore   restaurant
entrance   category   amateur

6. **a.** ad-vise   **b.** com-ply-ment   **c.** e-duce-ate-ion   **d.** e-lude
e. ex-cept   **f.** govern-ment   **g.** pre-script-ion

7. anxious   conscientious   disastrous   miscellaneous   mischievous

8. argument   compliment   environment   government

9. education   prescription

10. Answers will vary. Any eight of the following words are correct.
acknowledge   bureaucracy   elicit   except   judgment   maintenance
miscellaneous   prejudice   presence   principal

Exercise 10.2

1. council
2. counselor
3. counsel
4. principal
5. complimentary
6. presence
7. presents
8. compliment
9. principal
10. principal
11. principle
12. presence
13. complement
14. counsel
15. counselor, council
16. compliment
17. present's
18. complement
19. principal
20. counselors, principal

Exercise 10.3

1. acknowledgment
2. affectionate
3. amateurish
4. athletically
5. educationally
6. judgmental
7. vacuuming
8. uniformity
9. universally
10. trilogies
11. astrological
12. chronologically
13. geographic
14. television
15. philosophical
16. philanthropist
17. telecommunication
18. geothermal
19. congenial
20. compliments
21. advisor *or* adviser
22. alphabetically
23. argumentative
24. categories
25. governmental
26. laboratories
27. principality
28. unifying
29. bicyclist
30. multiplication
31. biographical
32. psychics
33. graphics
34. telephoning
35. hydroplaning
36. geological
37. sympathizing
38. bibliophile
39. effectively
40. immorality

Exercise 10.4

1. God, theologian
2. stars, astrologist
3. weather, meteorologist
4. environment, ecologist
5. living physical forms, physiologist
6. small life forms, microbiologist
7. supernatural bodies or spirits, parapsychologist
8. crime, criminologist
9. animals, zoologist
10. women's medicine, gynecologist
11. ancient life, archaeologist
12. aging or elderly, gerontologist
13. skin, dermatologist

1. The sun is the center.
2. related to the body
3. many marriage partners

1. apathy = without feelings   2. sympathy = feelings with or like someone's   3. empathy = same feelings in you

Note the differences: Apathy occurs when someone simply does not care about something. Sympathy means you can *understand* and relate to someone's feelings because you have had similar feelings. Empathy means you are *capable of experiencing* the same feelings or situations.

4. polygraph   5. photograph   6. seismograph   7. telegraph
8. phil = love   anthropo = man (mankind)   Process of loving or showing love for people
Consult a dictionary for the exact meaning.
philanthropist

Exercise 10.5

V 1.	A 2.	V 3.	N 4.	N 5.	V 6.
V 7.	N 8.	V 9.	A 10.	N 11.	A 12.
A 13.	V 14.	N 15.	A 16.	V 17.	A 18.

Answers will vary for the sentence writing.

Exercise 10.6

1. The compliment was paid to Joe by the young lady whose office was next to his.

2. All the vehicles that have bad brakes were removed from service.

3. The young boy who has already been in several plays will play the leading role of Romeo.

4. The vase that you broke was a valuable antique.

5. The chief mechanic who was trained in Germany is capable of repairing any foreign model.

6. The famous writer who lives in San Francisco has ten books on the best-seller list.

7. Joan, who is my very best friend, writes to me at least once a week.

8. The tiger, which is the team's mascot, leads the cheers at the games.

9. Guitars that are not played very often lose their pitch and need to be retuned.

10. The octopus, which usually has eight legs, lost one leg during an underwater battle.

11. <u>Stephen King</u> <u>is</u> one author whom many <u>people</u> <u>admire.</u>

12. <u>We</u> <u>parked</u> the car in the lot which <u>is</u> close to the campus bookstore.

13. <u>I</u> <u>wonder</u> whose <u>name</u> <u>will appear</u> on the top of the list.

14. <u>We</u> <u>can meet</u> at the park where there <u>is</u> a rose <u>garden.</u>

15. <u>Mr. Chee.</u> who <u>is</u> my landlord, <u>lives</u> in the penthouse.

16. <u>All</u> of the new buildings <u>have</u> windows which <u>cannot</u> <u>be opened.</u>

17. <u>People</u> who <u>are</u> optimistic <u>tend</u> to have happier lives.

18. The <u>knowledge</u> that <u>you</u> <u>learn</u> in school often <u>helps</u> you later in life.

19. The <u>answer</u> that <u>was given</u> in class <u>was</u> incorrect.

20. <u>It</u> <u>was</u> very apparent that <u>he</u> <u>wanted</u> the job.

If no commas are given in the following answers, then no commas are needed.

1. that *or* which	**2.** , which . . . tape,	**3.** , whose . . . wise,	**4.** who
5. , who . . . conscious,	**6.** that *or* which	**7.** that *or* which	
8. , which . . . athletes,	**9.** , which	**10.** that *or* which	
11. whom	**12.** , where . . . docked,	**13.** who	
14. who	**15.** that *or* which	**16.** that *or* which	
17. , whom . . . good,	**18.** who	**19.** , which . . . dollars,	
20. that *or* which			

Exercise 10.7

A **complex sentence** is a sentence that has at least one dependent clause and one independent clause.

Note: The dependent clauses in italics below should be boxed on your paper. Also, any punctuation added below should appear in your work.

that	**1.** *that you ordered*
which	**2.** *, which has only thirteen letters,*
where	**3.** *where they could see the entrance to the bank*
though	**4.** *Though everyone was to sing in unison,*
who	**5.** *, who is an excellent tennis player,*
if	**6.** *if you take time to listen to your inner voice*
who	**7.** *who was to receive the award*
when	**8.** *When the monorail begins operating on Monday,*
whose	**9.** *whose research on delayed memories is being widely debated*
when	**10.** *when the photographs are developed*
whom	**11.** *whom I chose to research*
who	**12.** *who was originally named Aristocles*
when	**13.** *when meteor showers will appear in our hemisphere*
which	**14.** *, which is the study of aging,*
as	**15.** *As the baby boomers age,*

Fragments: Answers will vary.

Exercise 10.8

Answers will vary.

Exercise 10.9

Use the information in the instructional boxes in this chapter to complete these definitions.

Appendix D: Summary Charts

Word Parts

Ch.	Prefixes			Roots			Suffixes		
1	mis-	re-	un-				-ed	-er	-est
							-ful	-ing	-ly -y
2	ab-	ad-	con-	dict	fect	ject	-es	-ion	-s
	de-	dis-	in-	tect	tract	vict			
	ob-	sub-							
3	com-	per-	pre-	fer	mit	pel	-able	-en	-ment
	pro-	trans-		sist	stant				
4	ex-			cede	cide	cise	-age	-less	-ness
				clude	duce	mote	-ous	-ual	
				plete	pute	quire			
				sume	vise				
5	e-	im-					-ible		
6	se-			ceive	cept	fess	-ate	-ive	-ure
				gress	lect	tain			
7	oc-			cur	port	tort	-ance	-ant	-ence
				verse	vert		-ent	-ic	-ist
							-or		
8	a-	be-	en-	nate	pense		-hood	-ism	
				soci	turb		-ite	-ize	
							-ship		
9	col-	for-	inter-	mote	mune	spect	-ial	-ish	
	intro-	sur-							
10	bi-	hepta-		anthro, anthropo					
	hexa-	mono-		aqua	astro				
	multi-	oct-, octa-, octo-		audi	biblio				
	penta-	poly-		bio	chrono, chronos				
	quadr-, quad-, quart-			gene, gen	geo				
	sept-, sep-	sex-, sext-		graph, graphy					
	tetra-	tri-		gram	hydro				
	uni-			meter	morph, morphe				
				naut	path, pathos				
				philos, phil					
				phobia	photo				
				psyche, psych					
				ology	ologist				
				seismo	sophos, sopho				
				tele	therma				

Prefixes		Roots		Suffixes
a	se	anthro, anthrop	mote	able
ab	sept, sep	aqua	mune	age
ac	sex, sext	archae	nate	ance
ad	sub	astro	naut	ant
af	sur	audi, audio	ologist	ate
ag	tetra	biblio	ology	ed
an	trans	bio	path, pathos	en
ap	tri	cede	pathy	ence
as	un	ceive	pel	ent
at	uni	cept	pense	er
be		chrono, chronos	philos, phile	es
bi		cide	phobia	est
col		cise	photo	ful
com		clude	physio	hood
con		corpor	plete	ial
de		cur	port	ible
dis		dermat	psych, psyche	ic
e		dict	pute	ing
en		duce	quire	ion
ex		eco	seismo	ish
for		fect	sist	ism
hepta		fer	soci	ist
hexa		fess	sophos	ite
im		gamy	sopho	ive
in		gene, gen	spect	ize
inter		genea	stant	less
intro		geo	sume	ly
mis		geront	tain	ment
mono		gram	tect	ness
multi		graph	tele	or
ob		graphy	theo	ous
oc		gress	therma	s
oct, octa, octo		gynec	tort	ship
penta		helio	tract	ual
per		hydro	turb	ure
poly		ject	verse	y
pre		lect	vert	
pro		meter	vict	
quadr, quad,		micro	vise	
quart		mit		
re		morph		
		morphe		

Common Verbs, Adverbs, and Prepositions

Verbs	Prepositions		Adverbs	
Linking Verbs:	about	in spite of	almost	sometimes
am	above	like	already	soon
is	according to	near	also	still
are	across	next	back	then
was	after	of	better	there
were	against	on	down	today
look	ahead of	off	early	tomorrow
sound	along	onto	even	too
smell	among	out of	ever	up
taste	around	outside	far	very
feel	at	over	here	yesterday
seem	before	past	home	
appear	behind	since	how	
	below	through	late	Plus most
Helping Verbs:	beneath	throughout	later	words with
am	beside	till	least	an -*ly* suffix:
are	between	to	less	
be	beyond	toward	more	quickly
been	by	under	most	softly
being	despite	until	much	honestly
can	down	unto	never	loudly
could	during	underneath	now	slightly
did	except	up	often	frequently
do	for	upon	quite	carefully
does	from	with	rather	brightly
had	in	within	really	casually
has	inside	without	seldom	formally
have	into		so	
is				
may				
might				
must				
shall				
should				
was				
were				
will				
would				

Appendix E: Quiz Forms A and B

Quiz # _____   Name _____

Form A   Date _____

Dictation

1. _____   14. _____

2. _____   15. _____

3. _____   16. _____

4. _____   17. _____

5. _____   18. _____

6. _____   19. _____

7. _____   20. _____

8. _____   21. _____

9. _____   22. _____

10. _____   23. _____

11. _____   24. _____

12. _____   25. _____

13. _____

Sentences

1. _____

2. _____

3. _____

4. _____

5. _____

6. _____

7. _____

8. _____

Quiz # _____   Name _____

Form A   Date _____

Dictation

1. _____   14. _____
2. _____   15. _____
3. _____   16. _____
4. _____   17. _____
5. _____   18. _____
6. _____   19. _____
7. _____   20. _____
8. _____   21. _____
9. _____   22. _____
10. _____   23. _____
11. _____   24. _____
12. _____   25. _____
13. _____

Sentences

1. _____
2. _____
3. _____
4. _____
5. _____
6. _____
7. _____
8. _____

Quiz # _____   Name _____

Form A   Date _____

Dictation

1. _____   14. _____
2. _____   15. _____
3. _____   16. _____
4. _____   17. _____
5. _____   18. _____
6. _____   19. _____
7. _____   20. _____
8. _____   21. _____
9. _____   22. _____
10. _____   23. _____
11. _____   24. _____
12. _____   25. _____
13. _____

Sentences

1. _____
2. _____
3. _____
4. _____
5. _____
6. _____
7. _____
8. _____

Quiz # _____   Name _____

Form A   Date _____

Dictation

1. _____   14. _____
2. _____   15. _____
3. _____   16. _____
4. _____   17. _____
5. _____   18. _____
6. _____   19. _____
7. _____   20. _____
8. _____   21. _____
9. _____   22. _____
10. _____   23. _____
11. _____   24. _____
12. _____   25. _____
13. _____

Sentences

1. _____
2. _____
3. _____
4. _____
5. _____
6. _____
7. _____
8. _____

Quiz # _____   Name _____

Form A   Date _____

Dictation

1. _____   14. _____

2. _____   15. _____

3. _____   16. _____

4. _____   17. _____

5. _____   18. _____

6. _____   19. _____

7. _____   20. _____

8. _____   21. _____

9. _____   22. _____

10. _____   23. _____

11. _____   24. _____

12. _____   25. _____

13. _____

Sentences

1. _____

2. _____

3. _____

4. _____

5. _____

6. _____

7. _____

8. _____

Quiz # _____   Name _____

Form B   Date _____

Dictation

1. _____
2. _____
3. _____
4. _____
5. _____
6. _____
7. _____
8. _____
9. _____
10. _____
11. _____
12. _____
13. _____
14. _____
15. _____
16. _____
17. _____
18. _____
19. _____
20. _____
21. _____
22. _____
23. _____
24. _____
25. _____
26. _____
27. _____
28. _____
29. _____
30. _____
31. _____
32. _____
33. _____
34. _____
35. _____
36. _____
37. _____
38. _____
39. _____
40. _____

Quiz # _____   Name _____

Form B   Date _____

Dictation

1. _____   21. _____

2. _____   22. _____

3. _____   23. _____

4. _____   24. _____

5. _____   25. _____

6. _____   26. _____

7. _____   27. _____

8. _____   28. _____

9. _____   29. _____

10. _____   30. _____

11. _____   31. _____

12. _____   32. _____

13. _____   33. _____

14. _____   34. _____

15. _____   35. _____

16. _____   36. _____

17. _____   37. _____

18. _____   38. _____

19. _____   39. _____

20. _____   40. _____

Quiz # _____   Name _____

Form B   Date _____

Dictation

1. _____	21. _____
2. _____	22. _____
3. _____	23. _____
4. _____	24. _____
5. _____	25. _____
6. _____	26. _____
7. _____	27. _____
8. _____	28. _____
9. _____	29. _____
10. _____	30. _____
11. _____	31. _____
12. _____	32. _____
13. _____	33. _____
14. _____	34. _____
15. _____	35. _____
16. _____	36. _____
17. _____	37. _____
18. _____	38. _____
19. _____	39. _____
20. _____	40. _____

Quiz # _____   Name _____

Form B   Date _____

Dictation

1. _____   21. _____
2. _____   22. _____
3. _____   23. _____
4. _____   24. _____
5. _____   25. _____
6. _____   26. _____
7. _____   27. _____
8. _____   28. _____
9. _____   29. _____
10. _____   30. _____
11. _____   31. _____
12. _____   32. _____
13. _____   33. _____
14. _____   34. _____
15. _____   35. _____
16. _____   36. _____
17. _____   37. _____
18. _____   38. _____
19. _____   39. _____
20. _____   40. _____

Index